LEGO®

CiTY
UNDERCOVER

INTRODUCTION

THANK YOU FOR PURCHASING PRIMA'S OFFICIAL GAME GUIDE TO *LEGO CITY UNDERCOVER*. THIS GUIDE HAS EVERYTHING YOU NEED TO CLEAN UP THE STREETS OF LEGO CITY AND FIND EVERY HIDDEN GOODY IN THE GAME!

HOW TO USE THIS GUIDE

LET'S SEE WHAT EACH CHAPTER OF THIS CRIME-FIGHTING GUIDE HAS IN STORE FOR YOU.

★ PAGE 4

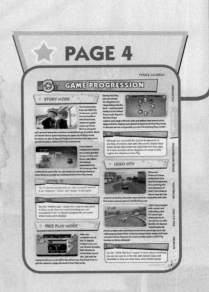

★ PAGE 15

★ PAGE 34

★ PAGE 222

PAGE 430

POLICE ACADEMY

LEGO City Undercover features many familiar controls and elements from past LEGO games, but there are some new tricks to learn, too. This chapter brings you up to speed with the latest controls and details how you progress through the main Story mode and what you can do with the snazzy Wii U GamePad.

CHARACTERS AND VEHICLES

LEGO City is loaded with 400 different characters and vehicles for you to unlock, and this chapter reveals how to find them all. There's quite a lot to know about character abilities, too, so review this chapter for a full overview.

WALKTHROUGH

LEGO City Undercover is the biggest and most ambitious LEGO game to date, with a massive city to explore and 15 Special Assignments to conquer. This huge adventure can seem a little intimidating, but never fear: just follow our step-by-step walkthrough, and you'll never become stuck or lost while playing through Story mode. Secrets are showcased, puzzle solutions are provided, and labeled maps reveal the locations of every hidden goody in the 15 Special Assignments. And if you've beaten Story mode and are simply replaying the levels in search of collectibles, you'll appreciate our quick-reference checklists and colorful Free Play sidebars, which provide all the info you need to track down every hidden goody in the missions.

LEGO CITY TOUR

Story mode is massive, but the adventure doesn't end there. *LEGO City Undercover* sets you free in a gigantic city, with over 20 unique districts for you to explore. This sprawling metropolis is filled with car thieves to bust, mischievous aliens to capture, lost pigs to rescue, and of course, hundreds upon hundreds of collectibles. It's enough to overwhelm just about anybody, but don't worry: our "LEGO City Tour" chapter has you covered with labeled maps of every district, plus plenty of checklists and images to help you track down all of LEGO City's best-kept secrets!

CHECKLISTS

In case we haven't made it clear, there's a ton of cool things to discover in this game. Whenever you have a question on finding a specific item, simply flip to the back of the book to find pages of quick-reference checklists. Use these handy lists to track your spoils by marking off super-special goodies you've found.

LEGO CITY'S FINEST

Rex Fury has devilish plans for LEGO City, but the fine men and women sworn to serve and protect aren't about to let him succeed. Let's meet the main characters of *LEGO City Undercover*!

CHASE MCCAIN

Officer Chase McCain is a brilliant detective, and the only person to ever successfully apprehend the nefarious Rex Fury. Unfairly banished to Brick County for a teeny-weeny little mistake he made, Chase has been summoned back to LEGO City because Rex Fury has escaped. This could spell disaster for someone very dear to Chase...Oh, and for the rest of LEGO City, too!

NATALIA KOWALSKI

An old acquaintance of Chase McCain, Natalia helped convict Rex Fury during his trial a few years ago. Now that Rex is on the loose again, Natalia is in grave danger. Chase will do everything he can to keep Natalia safe...but will that be enough?

FRANK HONEY

Newly promoted to an officer position, Frank Honey is the most well-meaning blockhead you could ever hope to meet. Wherever he goes, disaster follows—but despite all odds, he actually does manage to help Chase from time to time.

CHIEF MARION DUNBY

Keenly intelligent, a master of deduction, and scrupulously fair—none of these words apply to LEGO City's police chief, Marion Dunby. Angry and petty, Dunby has never seen eye-to-eye with Chase—which is surprising, considering everyone in LEGO City is about the same height. Chief Dunby believes Rex Fury simply fled LEGO City after escaping prison and refuses to assist Chase's investigation. Will his stubborn blindness spell LEGO City's downfall?

MAYOR GLEESON

Chase McCain's old chief is now the mayor of LEGO City. Intelligent, caring, and fair, Mayor Gleeson respects Chase and has gone over Chief Dunby's head to bring McCain back into the fold. She's certain that Rex Fury is behind the city's latest crime wave and knows that LEGO City will soon be lost without Chase's help.

REX FURY

Scourge of LEGO City, Rex Fury was the mind and muscle behind a rash of crimes that plagued the city several years ago. He was eventually brought to justice by supercop Chase McCain, and after a powerful testimony presented by Natalia Kowalski, Rex was quickly sentenced and locked up in Albatross Island Prison. But now Rex has escaped, and crime is on the rise again. Can Rex Fury avoid apprehension as his goons wreak havoc across LEGO City? Not if Chase McCain has anything to say about it!

POLICE ACADEMY

Only the finest can serve in the LEGO City Police Department, and you'll be ready for the streets after you read through this chapter. Even if you're familiar with LEGO games, you may find yourself surprised by some of the changes in *LEGO City Undercover*—not the least of which is the addition of the Wii U GamePad!

ONE MAN, ENDLESS POSSIBILITIES

IN *LEGO CITY UNDERCOVER*, YOU PLAY AS SUPERCOP CHASE MCCAIN—MASTER OF DISGUISE. CHASE CAN IMPERSONATE ANYONE AND CAN EVEN ASSUME THEIR UNIQUE ABILITIES. IN FACT, YOU NEVER ACTUALLY PLAY AS ANYONE *BUT* CHASE. WHETHER YOU'RE PLAYING STORY MODE, GOING BACK INTO MISSIONS FOR FREE PLAY, OR EXPLORING THE SPRAWLING METROPOLIS OF LEGO CITY, YOU'LL ALWAYS BE IN CONTROL OF MCCAIN. SO DON'T LET THE LIPSTICK AND FEATHERED HAIR FOOL YOU—THAT'S NOT INTREPID REPORTER NATALIA KOWALSKI SLAPPING THE CUFFS ON CROOKS, BUT LEGO CITY'S GREATEST DETECTIVE IN DISGUISE!

TIP

Check the "Characters and Vehicles" section to learn more about how to switch disguises, and the different skills and abilities Chase gains when going incognito.

GAME PROGRESSION

STORY MODE

The moment you boot up *LEGO City Undercover*, you're thrown headfirst into Story mode, where you guide supercop Chase McCain along his epic quest to bring the notorious criminal Rex Fury to justice. Much of Chase's time is spent exploring the open city in Story mode, but there are also 15 Special Assignment missions that play out in specific locations within LEGO City and beyond.

Every Special Assignment mission has several goodies for you to find, and these collectibles are tracked separately from the many goodies scattered the open city. You can replay Special Assignments as many times as you like by revisiting them in Free Play mode.

NOTE

The 15 Special Assignments are also commonly referred to as "missions," "levels," and "stages" in this guide.

TIP

See the "Walkthrough" chapter for a step-by-step guide to Story mode. Here we reveal everything you can accomplish in the 15 Special Assignments, no matter which mode you're playing!

FREE PLAY MODE

After you complete one of the 15 Special Assignments, you can choose to replay that mission as many times as you like. Just look for replay level icons on the Wii U GamePad map. Tap these icons to get the option to replay the level in Free Play mode.

During Free Play, you can choose the disguises that Chase brings into the level—and you aren't limited to the default Story mode disguises. This lets Chase

explore each stage with new skills and abilities that weren't at his disposal before. Replay each Special Assignment in Free Play mode to discover secrets and goodies you don't find during Story mode!

TIP

Although you can revisit the Special Assignments at any time, it's best to wait until after you've beaten Story mode. By the time Chase has solved the Rex Fury case, he'll have unlocked all the disguises he needs to fully explore the missions in Free Play.

LEGO CITY

Whenever Chase isn't deep undercover on a Special Assignment, he's exploring the vast openness of LEGO City. Chase is free to tour the city as much as he likes, but some areas won't be accessible until after he's made some progress in the Rex Fury case.

LEGO City is loaded with secrets and collectibles, and it's easy to get distracted by all the city has to offer. But like the Special Assignments, it's best to progress through Story mode before you begin your city-wide treasure hunt: Once Chase has beaten Story mode, he'll have unlocked all the disguises he needs to fully explore LEGO City, leaving no stone unturned.

TIP

See the "LEGO City Tour" chapter to learn about everything you can see and do in the city, with labeled maps and checklists to help you track down every hidden goody!

INTRODUCTION

POLICE ACADEMY

CHARACTERS AND VEHICLES

WALKTHROUGH

LEGO CITY TOUR

CHECKLISTS

COMMON COLLECTIBLES

⭐ LEGO STUDS

LEGO studs are scattered throughout the city and are often rewarded for smashing and building objects. Collect every stud you see to pad Chase's bankroll, then visit the LEGO City Police Station in Cherry Tree Hills to spend studs and unlock characters, vehicles, and red bricks you've collected. Collect lots of studs during each Special Assignment mission, and you'll become a LEGO City Hero—this earns you a gold brick! Your current stud total is shown at the top-left corner of your screen.

- **Silver studs** are common and worth 10 studs.
- **Gold studs** are common and worth 100 studs.
- **Blue studs** are uncommon and worth 1,000 studs.
- **Purple studs** are rare and worth 10,000 studs.

TIP

Follow trails of LEGO studs—they often lead to important areas or secrets!

⭐ BRICKS

Smash LEGO objects to discover bricks. These special items are similar to studs, but instead of spending them to purchase goodies at the Police Station, Chase uses bricks to construct giant superbuilds throughout LEGO City. Your current brick total is shown at the top-right corner of your screen.

NOTE

Your brick multiplier is also shown in the top-right corner of your screen. Destroy lots of LEGO objects as quickly as you can to increase your brick multiplier and score more bricks for each LEGO object you smash. Try speeding around the city in a vehicle and smashing LEGO objects to quickly boost your brick multiplier!

Superbricks

Superbricks are larger and worth more than regular bricks. Some superbricks require special skills to discover, but many can be collected simply by exploring the city and smashing stuff.

- **Small** (square) **superbricks** are worth 1,000 bricks.
- **Large** (rectangular) **superbricks** are worth a whopping 10,000 bricks.

Gold Bricks

You receive gold bricks whenever Chase accomplishes something significant. For example, Chase earns a gold brick each time he completes a Special Assignment in Story mode.

INTRODUCTION

POLICE ACADEMY

CHARACTERS AND VEHICLES

WALKTHROUGH

LEGO CITY TOUR

CHECKLISTS

There are 450 gold bricks to gather in all, and you can collect them in the following ways:

- Beat a Special Assignment mission in Story mode.
- Collect all four police shield pieces in a Special Assignment mission.
- Fill a Special Assignment mission's LEGO City Hero meter by collecting lots of studs during the mission.
- Earn gold bricks by accomplishing special feats in LEGO City (e.g., constructing superbuilds, activating train stations, etc.).

Red Bricks

Red bricks are the rarest collectibles in *LEGO City Undercover*—there are only 40 to find in the game. One red brick is hidden in every Special Assignment mission, and there are 25 more to discover in LEGO City itself.

Each red brick grants a special power. Once you collect a red brick, visit the LEGO City Police Station in Cherry Tree Hills and spend studs to unlock it. After that, you can turn the red brick's power on and off at any time through the Pause menu.

⭐ TOKENS

Keep an eye out for character and vehicle tokens. Collect these small, spinning disks to unlock new disguises and vehicles for purchase at the LEGO City Police Station!

Simply visit the Police Station and spend studs to purchase the character and vehicle tokens you've found. There are four tokens to find in every Special Assignment level, and many more are scattered across LEGO City. As a bonus, every character and vehicle token you collect in LEGO City also earns you a gold brick!

CHASE'S MOVES

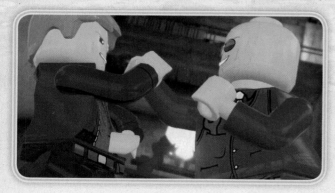

As the greatest detective LEGO City has ever known, Chase McCain can bust out all sorts of special moves that you'll want to understand. The following sections reveal the moves that are always available to Chase, regardless of his current disguise. For details on Chase's many disguise-related abilities, flip ahead to the "Characters and Vehicles" chapter.

★ BASIC MOVES

On Foot

In *LEGO City Undercover*, Chase spends a lot of time with his feet on the ground (or perhaps on a tightrope!). These controls are easy to master, although some actions aren't available to Chase until you unlock them over the course of Story mode (as noted in the following tables).

CONTROLS (ON FOOT)

CONTROLS	ACTIONS	NOTES
Ⓛ (Left stick)	Move	Apply light pressure to walk; use full pressure to run.
Ⓡ (Right stick)	Look around	A good way to spot nearby goodies.
Ⓧ	Enter vehicle/counter enemy/Disguise Wheel (hold)	Countering enemies requires Story mode progression.
Ⓨ	Attack/throw enemy/ build bricks (hold)/ aim (hold)	Throwing enemies requires Story mode progression.
Ⓐ	Interact/grab enemy	Grabbing enemies requires Story mode progression.
Ⓑ	Jump/perform free run moves	Free run moves require Story mode progression.
ⓏⓁ or ⓏⓇ	Change disguise	Requires Story mode progression.
Ⓛ	Police whistle	Requires Story mode progression.
Ⓡ	Take photograph	Requires Story mode progression.

TIP

Blowing your whistle in traffic is a great way to stop an oncoming car so you can safely commandeer it. That's one of the perks of being a cop!

On Wheels or in a Boat

Criminals are a pesky lot, often inclined to run from the police rather than surrender. You'll need to make use of cars, trucks, motorcycles, and boats throughout your adventures in LEGO City.

CONTROLS (LAND AND WATER VEHICLES)

CONTROLS	ACTIONS	NOTES
Ⓛ (Left stick)	Steer (press for horn or siren)	Traffic moves out of your way when you turn on sirens.
Ⓡ (Right stick)	Look around	A good way to spot nearby goodies.
ⓏⓇ or Ⓐ	Accelerate	Oh yeah, hit the gas!
ⓏⓁ or Ⓑ	Brake	Oh no, hit the brakes!!!
Ⓛ	Horn/siren	Traffic moves out of your way when you turn on sirens.
Ⓡ	Hold to take photograph	Requires Story mode progression.
Ⓧ	Exit vehicle/enter new vehicle	You can leap out of one vehicle and into another when you're close by!
Ⓨ	Turbo boost	Only some vehicles have turbos—look for sporty cars and emergency vehicles.
Shake the Wii U GamePad	Jump	A good way to right yourself if your vehicle has been knocked over.

NOTE

Check out the next chapter, "Characters and Vehicles," to learn how to unlock every character and vehicle in the game.

In the Air

Helicopters are unlocked shortly after you beat Special Assignment 9: "Hot Property." These airborne vehicles can help you quickly travel across LEGO City. Use helipads to call in helicopters, then hop into the pilot's seat and take to the sky!

CONTROLS (AIRCRAFT)

CONTROLS	ACTION
Ⓛ (Left stick)	Move
Ⓡ (Right stick)	Look around
ⓏⓇ or Ⓐ	Increase height
ⓏⓁ or Ⓑ	Decrease height
Ⓡ	Horn or siren
Ⓧ	Exit helicopter

INTRODUCTION

POLICE ACADEMY

CHARACTERS AND VEHICLES

WALKTHROUGH

LEGO CITY TOUR

CHECKLISTS

NOTE

You can only exit a helicopter at a helipad or crash mat or by flying low and leaping into another vehicle. See the "LEGO City Tour" chapter to discover the locations of every helipad and crash mat in the city.

⭐ FIGHTING

Criminals are a violent bunch, and most won't go down without a fight. Fortunately, Chase McCain is a master of hand-to-hand combat!

Most enemies can be defeated just by hitting them a few times. Rapidly tap Ⓨ to throw combos with Chase's fists or with whatever weapon he has equipped with his current disguise.

After Chase completes Special Assignment 4: "Kung Fool," he learns several new fighting techniques. One of the most useful is the enemy counter.

Simply stand in front of enemies and wait for them to begin their attack. An Ⓧ icon will appear over the enemy's head—quickly press Ⓧ to counter their attack with an unexpected move!

Some enemies are stronger than others and will shrug off Chase's regular attacks and counters. To best these burly brutes, rapidly tap Ⓐ to

grab and overpower them. Chase will then lift the enemy over his head. Either tap Ⓨ to throw the goon, or hold Ⓨ to aim and then release Ⓨ to throw the goon into another enemy.

Slapping on the Handcuffs

After knocking a criminal to the ground, Chase has just seconds to slap on the handcuffs and bring them to justice. Get close and press Ⓐ to

slap on the cuffs. Handcuffing enemies is important when facing a large number of goons—don't dally, or those groggy goons will recover and rejoin the fight!

⭐ SMASHING STUFF

To catch a criminal, sometimes you have to think and act like one. Don't be shy about smashing every object Chase encounters—most will give off studs or bricks, both of which are crucial in his quest to stop Rex Fury.

⭐ BUILDING STUFF

Glowing piles of bouncing LEGO bricks can be built into useful objects. Hold Ⓨ while standing near bouncing bricks, and see what Chase can build. You're often rewarded with studs when he completes the object.

⭐ FREE RUN MOVES

After Chase completes the first Special Assignment mission, he gains the ability to perform several special free run moves. These flashy actions allow Chase to reach areas he otherwise couldn't by performing a variety of slick acrobatic maneuvers. Whenever you see blue and white LEGO objects, you know that you can perform free run moves. Let's review the many different free run moves available to Chase.

NOTE

Sometimes you need to complete the blue and white patterns of free run objects by blasting them with the robber disguise's color gun. If you see a blank white LEGO object, chances are you need to blast it with blue coloring to activate it. See the next chapter for details on disguise-related abilities.

Vault

As Chase races around LEGO City, he'll occasionally encounter low barriers with a blue and white pattern on top. Press Ⓑ to smoothly vault these minor obstacles.

Climb

Using his free run skills, Chase can climb several different objects. These include blue and white LEGO walls, LEGO patches, and drainpipes. Climb these objects whenever you see them to find higher ground or cross long gaps that you can't jump.

Wall-Jump

Chase sometimes encounters parallel walls with blue and white LEGO arrows running up them. Make Chase jump between such walls by rapidly pressing Ⓑ to help him bounce up to higher ground.

Catapult Pads

These special blue and white springboards will launch Chase through the air when he steps on them, helping him clear long distances. You can't control Chase's path of flight, so just sit back and enjoy the ride!

Wall Runways

Wall runways look similar to catapult pads, and they also launch Chase the moment he steps on them. But instead of sending him soaring through the air, wall runways make Chase deftly sprint along the nearby wall, helping him cross wide gaps he couldn't have jumped.

Slippery Slopes

Chase can sprint up long slopes, so long as they sport a surface of blue and white LEGOs. Rapidly tap Ⓑ to make Chase run up such slopes, and look for flat areas where he can catch his breath.

Hang and Shimmy

Chase commonly encounters handholds from which he can hang. Once he's hanging from a handhold, Chase can move right or left to shimmy across or simply jump to the next ledge or handhold. Some handholds are too stubby for Chase to shimmy across.

Tiptoe

Chase must occasionally traverse narrow blue beams or tightropes in order to cross long, treacherous gaps. It's best to slowly walk onto these objects, letting Chase find his footing before hurrying him across.

Tightrope Slide

In many places around LEGO City, angled tightropes stretch between tall buildings. Jump onto a tightrope's higher end to make Chase quickly slide down. Wahoo!

LEGO CITY LANDMARKS

Now that we've covered Chase's moves, let's take a peek at some of the more noteworthy objects you'll encounter as you explore LEGO City. Note that this is just a quick glance at the city's more important landmarks—flip ahead to the "LEGO City Tour" chapter for a more in-depth look at everything the city has to offer.

SUPERBUILDS

Large LEGO pads signify spots where Chase can construct something really big and important. Spend bricks to construct these superbuilds, and help restore LEGO City to its former glory.

NOTE

You earn a gold brick each time you construct a superbuild in LEGO City (nice!), but not when you build them inside Special Assignments (aw!).

TIP

Short on bricks? Never fear! Whenever you discover a superbuild, rest assured that there are plenty of superbricks nearby. Simply smash and interact with nearby objects in search of superbricks, or fire up Data Scan mode on the Wii U GamePad and scan your surroundings for them (more on this ahead).

HELIPADS AND CALL-IN POINTS

02-038 Once you build helipads and vehicle call-in points, you can use them to instantly order any of your unlocked vehicles for special delivery, totally free of charge. Note that Chase must progress a ways into Story mode before he can unlock vehicle call-in points and helipads.

NOTE

While you can pilot boats and other seacraft you find docked around LEGO City, you cannot call in for them. Only land vehicles and aircraft can be ordered at these special sites.

TRAINS AND FERRIES

Activate train stations and ferries to unlock fast-travel options around LEGO City. Using trains and ferries is completely free, and as a special bonus, you earn a gold brick each time you activate a new train station or ferry route!

INTRODUCTION

POLICE ACADEMY

CHARACTERS AND VEHICLES

WALKTHROUGH

LEGO CITY TOUR

CHECKLISTS

⭐ DISGUISE BOOTHS

Though Chase can utilize hundreds of disguises, he can only carry one disguise with him per disguise category. Whenever you want to choose different disguises for each category (Police Officer, Robber, etc.), simply visit a disguise booth. You'll find these booths all over the city—there's even one at the LEGO City Police Station in Cherry Tree Hills! Pop into a disguise booth, then choose which disguises you wish to use.

NOTE

Disguise booths must be built before you can use them. You earn a gold brick each time you build a new disguise booth.

All disguises that belong to a particular disguise category bestow similar advantages to Chase—the difference is purely cosmetic. For instance, all Police Officer disguises allow Chase to use the grapple gun, while all Robber disguises let him use the crowbar and stethoscope. See the next chapter for more info on disguise categories and their unique abilities.

USING THE WII U GAMEPAD

An exciting new addition to the LEGO experience is the Wii U GamePad. This second screen provides useful information vital to stopping Rex Fury's terrible crime wave!

⭐ CHECKING THE MAP

LEGO City is vast, but the detailed map on your Wii U GamePad helps you keep your bearings. The city features several zones— the name of your current zone is shown at the top of the map, along with the zone's major collectibles. Tap the small "i" icon near the zone's name to call up a more detailed list of collectibles for that zone.

TIP

The GamePad map can be zoomed in twice for added detail.

NOTE

Keep in mind that you might need to progress through Story mode before you can access certain areas.

MAP ICONS

 Your location and the direction you're facing

 Your objective

 Replay level (Free Play mode)

 Vehicle call-in point

 Helipad

 Crash mat

 Scan spot

 Superbuild

 Character token

 Vehicle token

 Disguise booth

 Train station

 Ferry station

 Gang activity

 Vehicle robbers

 ATM

 Vehicle robbery

 Special boulder

 Silver statue

 Alien crate

 Astronaut flag

 Flower bed

 Pig rescue

 Cat rescue

 BBQ fire

 Coffee break station

 Drill thrill

 Free run challenge

 Time trial

 Super Star

 ? Block

 Warp Pipe

NOTE

See the "LEGO City Tour" chapter for full disclosure on everything you can see and do in the city.

INTRODUCTION

POLICE ACADEMY

CHARACTERS AND VEHICLES

WALKTHROUGH

LEGO CITY TOUR

CHECKLISTS

⭐ SETTING GPS ROUTES

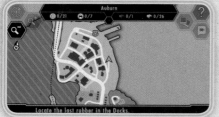

Tap and hold anywhere on the GamePad map screen to create a waypoint. A trail of green studs then appears that guides you toward your destination. When no waypoint is set, the game defaults to directing you toward the next Story mode objective.

⭐ RECEIVING CALLS

Chase isn't alone out there on the street—friends and acquaintances commonly contact him with important information. Press the video call icon whenever it flashes on the Wii U GamePad to answer a call and hear what Chase's allies have to say.

⭐ DATA SCAN MODE

At various points, Chase will need to scan his surroundings for a clues. When prompted, press the Data Scan button, hold up the Wii U GamePad in front of you, then slowly look around. At this point, you are acting as Chase, and everything you see on the Wii U GamePad is what Chase is seeing in his environment. Onscreen arrows indicate the direction you must look to track down the clue.

TIP

You can activate Data Scan mode anywhere in LEGO City. By scanning the city with the Wii U GamePad, you can detect nearby goodies, such as superbricks. Once located, these items will appear on your map, and an onscreen marker will guide you toward them. Data Scan mode is an essential tool in your quest to find every last item in LEGO City!

NOTE

Data Scan mode can be upgraded by collecting and activating various red bricks. Flip to the checklists at the back of this book for a quick list of every red brick, what they do, and where they can be found.

⭐ CRIMINAL SCAN MODE

At several points during Story mode, Chase must use his communicator to scan the area for criminal activity. You can do this only while standing in a criminal scan spot. From there, press Ⓐ to fire up Criminal Scan mode.

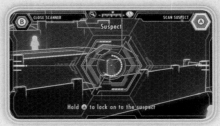

While using Criminal Scan mode, hold the Wii U GamePad in front of you, just as you would during a data scan. This time, however, you're searching for nearby crooks! Slowly look around, centering the GamePad on characters in the vicinity. Hold Ⓐ to target suspects and advance the plot.

⭐ AUDIO SCAN MODE

Whenever Chase discovers special audio scan spots, you can use the Wii U GamePad to eavesdrop on nearby conversations. This  is useful at several points during Story mode.

 Hold the Wii U GamePad up to the screen, then center the GamePad on a nearby noise disturbance. Hold Ⓐ to unscramble the conversation of the conspiring crooks. You might need to eavesdrop on a few conversations before you detect the suspects Chase is after.

TIP

Always unscramble vital conversations by holding Ⓐ. If you aren't prompted to unscramble the conversation, then it doesn't pertain to your mission!

⭐ SNAPPING PHOTOS

After you've progressed through Story mode a bit, you'll unlock the ability to take pictures with the Wii U GamePad. Simply press and hold Ⓡ to snap a photo of whatever's onscreen. Use this feature at any time to collect and store memories of your favorite moments and locations as you enjoy your time in LEGO City.

CHARACTERS AND VEHICLES

THERE ARE HUNDREDS OF CHARACTERS AND VEHICLES TO UNLOCK IN *LEGO CITY UNDERCOVER*, AND COLLECTING THEM ALL IS A HUGE UNDERTAKING. FORTUNATELY, THIS ESSENTIAL CHAPTER FULLY EXPOSES EVERY CHARACTER AND VEHICLE IN THE GAME, REVEALING HOW AND WHERE TO FIND THEM AND THE UNIQUE ABILITIES THAT EACH CHARACTER DISGUISE BESTOWS.

UNLOCKING CHARACTERS

There are 290 character disguises to find in *LEGO City Undercover*, and unlocking them all would be impossible for the average civilian. But for Chase McCain, this is just another day at the office!

You can unlock character disguises in the following ways:

- By completing Story mode missions. (Chase must find new disguises as he progresses through Story mode.)
- By finding character tokens hidden in Special Assignments. (Two character tokens are hidden in each level.)
- By searching LEGO City for character tokens. (The city is filled with character tokens.)

STORY MODE DISGUISES

Disguises unlocked through the course of Story mode are available right away for use. These disguises are vital in Chase's quest to end Rex Fury's crime wave.

These are the Story mode disguises that Chase unlocks while working the Rex Fury case:

- Chase McCain (Civilian)
- Chase McCain (Police)
- Chase McCain (Robber)
- Chase McCain (Miner)
- Chase McCain (Astronaut)
- Chase McCain (Farmer)
- Chase McCain (Fireman)
- Chase McCain (Construction)

CHARACTER TOKENS

All other disguises are unlocked by collecting special goodies called *character tokens*. However, these disguises are not immediately available for use.

Instead, after Chase collects a character token, he must visit the LEGO City Police Station and spend his hard-earned

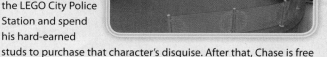

studs to purchase that character's disguise. After that, Chase is free to place the character disguise in his Disguise Wheel.

INTRODUCTION

POLICE ACADEMY

CHARACTERS AND VEHICLES

WALKTHROUGH

LEGO CITY TOUR

CHECKLISTS

THE DISGUISE WHEEL

Chase McCain is a master of disguise, and as such, he can change his identity with ease. All of Chase's disguises are stored in his Disguise Wheel—press and hold Ⓧ to bring up the Disguise Wheel at any time. Here you will see the disguises that Chase is carrying for each of the eight disguise categories (Civilian, Police Officer, Robber, etc.). Use Ⓛ to pick a disguise, then release Ⓧ to close the Disguise Wheel.

TIP

You can also quickly cycle through Chase's disguises by pressing ㉄ or ㉡.

★ CHANGING DISGUISES

Though Chase can unlock a multitude of disguises, he can only carry one disguise with him per disguise category (Civilian, Police Officer, Robber, etc.). To wear different disguises that you've purchased, direct Chase to a disguise booth—you can find one in most city zones, and there's one inside the LEGO City Police Station. Disguise booths let you pick the disguises that Chase will carry for each disguise category.

NOTE

You're also prompted to pick Chase's disguises whenever you choose to replay levels in Free Play.

DISGUISE CATEGORIES

Each of the 290 character disguises in *LEGO City Undercover* belongs to one of the following eight disguise categories:

- Police Officers
- Criminals & Robbers
- Miners
- Astronauts
- Farmers
- Firefighters
- Construction Workers
- Civilians/Specials

★ UNDERSTANDING DISGUISES

All character disguises that fall into the same disguise category possess the same special abilities. For example, all police officer disguises have the grapple gun, while all miner disguises can smash boulders and handle dynamite. The following sections reveal the unique abilities that each disguise category provides.

NOTE

Rex Fury disguises are the unique exceptions. Regardless of the disguise category, any character disguise named Rex Fury can rip apart superstrength objects that have big orange handles. Only Rex Fury disguises can interact with superstrength objects, making them very valuable.

⭐ POLICE

Number of Disguises: 35

Anyone trying to make a difference and keep LEGO City safe falls into the Police category. Not only does this include the boys (and girls!) in blue, but also forest rangers, private detectives, and security guards.

Abilities

Grapple Gun: Used in specific locations to pull down objects or to quickly ascend to higher areas.

Detective Scan: Available at blue detective scan spots. Chase uses his communicator to follow footprints and uncover clues.

Data Scan: Available anytime. Hold up the Wii U GamePad and look around to discover hidden goodies in the vicinity.

Criminal Scan: Available at yellow criminal scan spots. Hold up the Wii U GamePad and scan the area for crooks.

Audio Scan: Available at green audio scan spots. Hold up the Wii U GamePad and scan the area for conversations that Chase can eavesdrop on.

⭐ CRIMINALS & ROBBERS

Number of Disguises: 50

Anyone who threatens the safety or the property of LEGO City's citizens is considered a criminal. And, boy, does this city have a lot of crooks!

Abilities

Crowbar: For some reason, citizens of LEGO City tend to lock their doors. Thanks to the handy crowbar, criminals have no problem prying them open. Used at locations with the crowbar symbol.

Stethoscope: No safe is, uh, safe with a criminal around. They can use their stethoscope to crack open any strongbox that sports the stethoscope symbol.

Color Gun: This handy sidearm fires gobs of colored energy, useful for a variety of purposes. Find and use color swappers to change the color of the color gun's energy.

 NOTE

The color gun isn't available until you unlock it during Story mode.

⭐ MINERS

Number of Disguises: 8

You don't just go undercover in LEGO City—you go underground. Miners love laying waste to objects that are too tough for others to deal with.

Abilities

Pickax: Rock-hard boulders are no match for the miner's mighty pickax. Try jumping and attacking to slam the ground and smash whole piles of boulders!

Dynamite: When you need to blow something up, the miner can put dynamite into special barrels for a big boom. Silver objects are prime targets—look around for some dynamite, which is often located in red vending machines called *dynamite dispensers*.

⭐ ASTRONAUTS

Number of Disguises: 17

Space may be the final frontier, but these brave men and women will have to settle for exploring LEGO City!

Abilities

Teleport: Astronauts can use transport pads to teleport over long distances.

Beam-in Support: By inputting a simple color sequence, astronauts can activate space crates that beam in useful materials.

Jetpack Jump: Astronauts can boost around with their jetpacks, traveling higher and farther than normal jumps would take them. Activate jetpack symbols, then boost through the rings to travel even farther!

Raise the Flag: Throughout LEGO City, there are places where only an astronaut dare tread. By raising a flag at these towering heights, Chase can lay claim to part of the city—and earn a gold brick in the process!

NOTE

Astronauts won't sport jetpacks until you unlock this ability during Story mode.

INTRODUCTION · POLICE ACADEMY · CHARACTERS AND VEHICLES · WALKTHROUGH · LEGO CITY TOUR · CHECKLISTS

⭐ FARMERS

Number of Disguises: 11

When city life becomes a little too hectic, there's always a place for Chase down on the farm.

Abilities

Chicken-Glide: Farmers have a special relationship with chickens. They always carry one around and can use their fowl friends to glide short distances, helping them clear gaps. Activate chicken symbols, then glide through the rings to soar much farther than normal!

Watering Can: With the aid of their trusty watering can, farmers can grow plants and vines anywhere they see a watering can symbol. Climb tall plants and vines to reach new areas.

⭐ FIREFIGHTERS

Number of Disguises: 10

Any fire in LEGO City has met its match!

Abilities

Extinguisher: Firefighters can easily douse any LEGO blaze with their trusty fire extinguishers. In addition, use extinguishers to fill objects with water, such as swimming pools.

Fire Axe: Any door that's covered with wooden boards can be easily chopped open with the razor-sharp fire axe.

⭐ CONSTRUCTION WORKERS

Number of Disguises: 14

LEGO City is an ever-expanding metropolis, and construction workers are the ones who keep the city going.

Abilities

Pneumatic Drill: This powerful tool is ideal for drilling through loose, shaky pavement.

Hammer: Construction workers use their trusty hammers to knock some sense into fuse boxes on the fritz.

Coffee Break: As a union worker, it's important to exercise your right to a break every now and then. Look for special coffee break stations around LEGO City, and use a construction worker disguise to take a breather!

⭐ CIVILIANS & SPECIALS

Special 1 Disguises: 47 **Special 2 Disguises: 39**
Service Disguises: 33 **Residents Disguises: 34**

There are lots of interesting people (and aliens!) wandering the streets of LEGO City. While these zany characters aren't especially helpful for completing missions or attaining collectibles, you can have lots of fun running around with them!

Abilities

None! Civilians and special characters have no specific abilities. Chase can only use his basic skills (covered in the previous chapter, "Police Academy") while decked out in a civilian or special disguise.

CHARACTER LIST

Now that we've gone over the disguise categories, let's check out all of the different character disguises that can be unlocked and worn by Chase in *LEGO City Undercover*.

POLICE

CHASE MCCAIN (POLICE)

Location: Police Station

How to Get: Story mode progression

CHASE UNDERCOVER

Location: Police Station

How to Get: Story mode progression

CHASE SUIT

Location: Special Assignment 7: "Scrapyard Scrap"

How to Get: ack the safe inside the trailer

BEA HECKERSON

Location: Fort Meadows

How to Get: Smash three yellow hay bales around Farmer Hayes's fields, then build their bricks into scarecrows.

BLUBS

Location: Paradise Sands

How to Get: Hidden in a silver rock under the grotto.

BRICKETT

Location: Bluebell National Park

How to Get: Complete the zone's free run.

BUTCH PATTERSON

Location: Cherry Tree Hills

How to Get: Inside the police booth near the ferry.

CACEY

Location: Downtown

How to Get: Near the top of the bank.

CHUCK MORRISON

Location: N/A

How to Get: Complete all "Vehicle Robbers Arrested" in LEGO City

CLUTCH

Location: Pagoda

How to Get: Inside the pigeon coop on the roof of Hank's garage.

DAMUMBO

Location: Auburn Bay Bridge

How to Get: Above the drainpipe at the top of the bridge.

DETECTIVE

Location: Cherry Tree Hills

How to Get: Use the scan spot near the large billboard by the radio tower.

DOORLOCK HOMES

Location: Kings Court

How to Get: Paint four phone boxes red to unlock this token.

DR. WHATSIT

Location: Kings Court

How to Get: Paint the LEGO brick statue to reveal this character token.

DUKE HUCKLEBERRY

Location: Bluebell National Park

How to Get: Build the stunt ramp superbuild.

ELLIE PHILLIPS

Location: Lady Liberty Island

How to Get: Break into the information hut.

FRANK HONEY

Location: Heritage Bridge

How to Get: Appears after you construct the model citizen superbuild.

FRANK POOLSIDE

Location: Paradise Sands

How to Get: Complete the zone's free run.

HORACE CONE

Location: Kings Court

How to Get: Near the train station.

LAGNEY

Location: Pagoda

How to Get: On the north side of the canal.

MARION DUNBY

Location: N/A

How to Get: Complete all "Gangs Arrested" in LEGO City

MAYOR GLEESON

Location: Kings Court

How to Get: Get Bullet Bill to follow you to the cage. Once he blows up the cage, you can grab the token.

OFFICER PARK

Location: Uptown

How to Get: On an awning outside the Herbert Hotel.

PAT PATTERSON

Location: Bright Lights Plaza

How to Get: Paint the "L" of the "Hotel" sign yellow.

PRISON GUARD

Location: Albatross Island

How to Get: Build the disguise booth.

QUENTIN SPENCER

Location: Pagoda

How to Get: To the left once you're on the TV store rooftop.

RANGER BARBER

Location: Bluebell National Park

How to Get: Build the disguise booth.

RANGER LEWIS

Location: Bluebell National Park

How to Get: Pry open the skylight atop Sheriff Huckleberry's police station, then drop inside.

INTRODUCTION

POLICE ACADEMY

CHARACTERS AND VEHICLES

WALKTHROUGH

LEGO CITY TOUR

CHECKLISTS

RODNEY BAXTER

Location: Paradise Sands

How to Get: On top of an awning at a hotel in the bazaar.

SECURITY GUARD

Location: Cherry Tree Hills

How to Get: Inside the police booth behind the police station.

STUDSKI

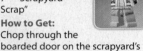

Location: Special Assignment 7—"Scrapyard Scrap"

How to Get: Chop through the boarded door on the scrapyard's right side (Free Play).

SECURITY SUPERVISOR

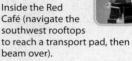

Location: Lady Liberty Island

How to Get: Build the disguise booth.

SHAKY HARRY

Location: Cherry Tree Hills

How to Get: Inside the Red Café (navigate the southwest rooftops to reach a transport pad, then beam over).

TED BAXTER

Location: Heritage Bridge

How to Get: Atop the west tower of the bridge.

TRAFFIC COP

Location: Downtown

How to Get: Paint the three silver traffic post tops near the back yellow.

⭐ CRIMINALS & ROBBERS

CHASE MCCAIN (ROBBER)

Location: Special Assignment 2: "Trouble in Stir"

How to Get: Progress through Story mode.

BANDIT

Location: N/A

How to Get: Complete all "ATMs Smashed" in LEGO City

BEEFY BAKER

Location: Albatross Island

How to Get: Hidden in a pallet near the prison offices.

BLUE WHITTAKER

Location: Special Assignment 2: "Trouble in Stir"

How to Get: Fix the elevator fuse box and climb up to the fourth floor. Find dynamite in the kitchen and blast open the storage area. (Free Play)

BUCKY BUTLER

Location: Uptown

How to Get: Paint the knight statues outside the museum.

CARLO CONE

Location: Crescent Park

How to Get: Paint the balloons on the gazebo the correct colors.

CARLO JEROME

Location: Fresco

How to Get: Build the ice cream statue by rolling the three metal scoops onto the bowl outside Pappalardo's.

CHAN CHUANG

Location: Pagoda

How to Get: Build the Bob-omb and then throw it at the locked cage.

CHAO HUI

Location: Pagoda

How to Get: Paint the silver lanterns red.

CLOWN ROBBER LOU

Location: Cherry Tree Hills

How to Get: Atop the LEGO City Bank. Navigate the southeast rooftops to reach.

CLOWN ROBBER MAX

Location: Auburn

How to Get: Pry open the metal door at the base of one of the docks' north cranes.

CLOWN ROBBER WES

Location: LEGO City Airport

How to Get: Paint the flowers the correct colors.

DOUGY DUNGAREES

Location: Fort Meadows

How to Get: Inside the cabin with the crowbar door.

EDDIE JOJO

Location: Bright Lights Plaza

How to Get: Earned after painting the three ice cream dispensers pink.

FENG

Location: Pagoda

How to Get: Paint the lampposts around the big pagoda yellow.

FORREST BLACKWELL CASUAL

Location: Special Assignment 14: "Breaking and Reentering"

How to Get: Use Rex Fury to rip apart the super-strength crate on the roof (Free Play).

FORREST BLACKWELL SUIT

Location: Special Assignment 10: "Smash 'n' Grab"

How to Get: Use Rex Fury to rip apart the boards in the lounge's right foreground corner, then fix the fuse box (Free Play).

FORREST BLACKWELL TUXEDO

Location: Fresco

How to Get: Behind a block only Rex Fury can destroy, in the corner room of a building along the west edge of Fresco.

FU

Location: Pagoda

How to Get: On top of the south Arch of Tranquility.

GANGSTER

Location: Fresco

How to Get: In between Pappalardo's and Little Venice.

GRUBBY GRUBSTER

Location: Cherry Tree Hills

How to Get: Scale the police station's exterior stairs and pry open the exterior jail cell.

HAI CHEN

Location: Pagoda

How to Get: Near the big dragon statues on the east side of Pagoda.

HOT TUB HARRY

Location: Albatross Island

How to Get: Use the transporter pad under the guard tower, then use the super jetpack rings to get across to the correct tower.

HOT TUB MCCREEDY

Location: Auburn

How to Get: Paint five buoys red in the water by the beach.

JAMES CURRY

Location: Bright Lights Plaza

How to Get: On the ceiling of the lower level of the shopping mall.

JIMMY GROSSMAN

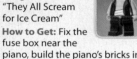

Location: Special Assignment 11: "They All Scream for Ice Cream"

How to Get: Fix the fuse box near the piano, build the piano's bricks into a catapult pad, and launch up to the token.

LI

Location: Pagoda

How to Get: Atop the north Arch of Tranquility. (Free Play)

LUCKY PETE

Location: Fresco

How to Get: Behind a locked door on the roof of the garage on the docks.

MAXIMILIAN JARVIK

Location: Crescent Park

How to Get: Teleport onto the top of the gazebo.

MIKEY SPOILERS

Location: Fresco

How to Get: At the north end of the canal.

MOE DELUCA

Location: Special Assignment 10: "Smash 'n' Grab"

How to Get: Fix the fuse box on the first ledge, pry open the door, and then pull the lever.

OLD QUIANG

Location: N/A

How to Get: Complete all "Vehicle Robberies Completed" in LEGO City

PAULIE BLINDFOLDS

Location: Fresco

How to Get: On a sunroof at the highest point of south apartments A.

PRISONER

Location: Special Assignment 2: "Trouble in Stir"

How to Get: Smash a desk, then follow footprints to discover the token hidden in the warden's desk.

REX FURY

Location: Special Assignment 15: "Fly Me to the Moon"

How to Get: During the final descent, after falling past the spinning energy beams and exiting the rocket, pass through the first stud ring you see.

REX FURY BARE CHEST

Location: Bluebell National Park

How to Get: Use Rex Fury to rip open the super-strength handle crate near the north train tunnel.

SALVATORE CALZONE

Location: Fresco

How to Get: Behind a boarded up door on the roof of south apartments A.

SENTINEL CHANNARD

Location: Fresco

How to Get: Grapple up to the balcony on the south apartments.

SENTINEL DECKER

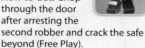

Location: Special Assignment 14: "Breaking and Reentering"

How to Get: Cross the tightrope on the roof's left side to reach a transporter pad. Beam into a small room and smash the sand castle.

SHUI XUE

Location: Pagoda

How to Get: Ring the bells at the three red pagodas.

SNAKES SQUEALER

Location: Special Assignment 1: "Some Assaults"

How to Get: Chop through the door after arresting the second robber and crack the safe beyond (Free Play).

SPIKEY DON

Location: Special Assignment 3: "Miner Altercation"

How to Get: Repair the mobile drill's fuse box, then pry open the manhole cover.

TIM WELCH

Location: Fresco

How to Get: Hidden in a rock near the helipad behind Blackwell's (vault the fence to reach). (Free Play)

TONY ONE-TIME

Location: Fresco

How to Get: Inside a fenced area past the greenhouse.

SENTINEL CHANNARD

VERNE

Location: Albatross Island

How to Get: On a guard tower, up the stairs from the helicopter superbuild.

VINNIE CLOWN

Location: Festival Square

How to Get: Inside the clock tower.

VINNIE PAPPALARDO

Location: Special Assignment 11: "They All Scream for Ice Cream"

How to Get: Automatically received when you rescue Vinnie from the freezer and rebuild him.

VINNIE TRACKSUIT

Location: Fresco

How to Get: After completing the ice cream statue puzzle, paint the ice cream to unlock this token.

VITUS TINKLEMAN

Location: Blackwell Bridge

How to Get: Found under the bridge use uphill run to get to him

WARDEN STONEWALL

Location: Albatross Island

How to Get: Complete the zone's free run event.

⭐ MINERS

CHASE McCAIN (MINER)

Location: Special Assignment 3: "Miner Altercation"

How to Get: Progress through Story mode.

BARNEY GREENSCHIST

Location: N/A

How to Get: Complete all "Boulders Destroyed" in LEGO City

BEN MOSELEY

Location: Bluebell National Park

How to Get: Use a fish to lure the bear away from the large campsite, then build and color the two tents to match their interior blankets.

BILL DERBY

Location: Bluebell National Park

How to Get: Astronaut-boost onto the small shack west of the Bluebell Mine.

MINE FOREMAN

Location: N/A

How to Get: Complete all "Silver Statues Destroyed" in LEGO City

OTTO HORNFELS

Location: Crescent Park

How to Get: Floating near the shark poster inside the tunnel.

STINKY FLETCHER

Location: Fort Meadows

How to Get: Paint three hay bales yellow around the farm and fields.

TODD GREYWACKE

Location: Bluebell National Park

How to Get: Astronaut-boost up near the alien space crate.

⭐ ASTRONAUTS

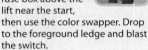

CHASE McCAIN (ASTRONAUT)

Location: Apollo Island

How to Get: Progress through Story mode.

BEN SHARPLES

Location: Special Assignment 15: "Fly Me to the Moon"

How to Get: Fix the fuse box above the lift near the start, then use the color swapper. Drop to the foreground ledge and blast the switch.

BRANTFORD CUBBERY

Location: Apollo Island

How to Get: Build the disguise booth

BUD HAWKINS

Location: Apollo Island

How to Get: Complete the zone's free run event.

CAL WAINWRIGHT

Location: Kings Court

How to Get: Behind the boarded up door on the docks.

CLASSIC ALIEN

Location: Apollo Island

How to Get: Directly above the transporter pad when you teleport into the research bunker.

DREW CALHOUN

Location: Kings Court

How to Get: Floating above a sign at the docks.

DUTCH DANISH

Location: Apollo Island

How to Get: Complete the "Spinning Shuttle Program" superbuild.

FORREST BLACKWELL

Location: Apollo Island

How to Get: Use Rex Fury to rip open the barrier and get underneath the water tower.

HENRIK KOWALSKI

Location: Auburn

How to Get: Navigate the south-central buildings, using the southeast access point; leap to the water towers and use a jetpack jump to reach the hovering token.

JENNY RATHBONE

Location: Apollo Island

How to Get: On the roof of the runway garage.

JONLAN REGNIX

Location: Apollo Island

How to Get: Super-jetpack hover from the roof of the garage to the tightrope above the rusty pipes. Slide down the tightrope.

REX FURY

Location: N/A

How to Get: Complete all "Districts Conquered" in LEGO City

DREW CALHOUN (cont.)

SPACE ALIEN

Location: N/A

How to Get: Complete all "Aliens Caught" in LEGO City

SPACEMAN

Location: Apollo Island

How to Get: Build the Space Shuttle superbuild.

SPACE SCIENTIST

Location: Special Assignment 6: "Astronaughty"

How to Get: Smash the remaining "planet" after making the solar system diorama fall.

SPACE VILLAIN

Location: Special Assignment 6: "Astronaughty"

How to Get: Use Rex Fury to rip apart the strength crate in the lobby. (Free Play)

⭐ FARMERS

CHASE McCAIN (FARMER)

Location: Fort Meadows

How to Get: Progress through Story mode.

FARMER BALES

Location: Kings Court

How to Get: Behind the Rex statue on the roof of city hall.

FARM WORKER BILL

Location: Fort Meadows

How to Get: Jetpack jump onto a cabin's roof, then cross a tightrope to reach the token in the nearby tree.

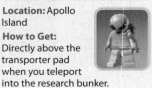

FARM WORKER BOB

Location: Fort Meadows

How to Get: Water a planter near the sawmill, then climb the sunflower to reach the token on its roof.

JETHRO HAYES

Location: N/A

How to Get: Complete all "Pigs Returned" in LEGO City

PATTY HAYES

Location: Crescent Park

How to Get: Behind the boarded up door inside the tree house.

ROOSTER

Location: Fort Meadows

How to Get: Jetpack jump up and climb the blue and white LEGO patch on the wall under the elevated train tracks.

SQUIRREL MCTAVISH

Location: N/A

How to Get: Complete all "Flowers Watered" in LEGO City

TROUBLEMAKER PHIL

Location: Cherry Tree Hills

How to Get: Paint the three white trees near the southeast road green.

TROUBLEMAKER TIM

Location: Lady Liberty Island

How to Get: Turn the four silver trees brown to make this token appear.

TROUBLEMAKER TOM

Location: Paradise Sands

How to Get: Paint the three palm tress brown.

FIREFIGHTERS

CHASE MCCAIN (FIREMAN)

Location: Special Assignment 9: "Hot Property"

How to Get: Progress through Story mode.

BRAD HOGGLE

Location: Grand Canal

How to Get: Behind a boarded up door on the canal walkway.

BUDDY WEINGARTNER

Location: Fort Meadows

How to Get: Inside the cabin with the boarded door.

CHARLOTTE HANNON

Location: Special Assignment 9: "Hot Property"

How to Get: Run on either of the treadmills inside the station.

CORNELIUS BURNS

Location: N/A

How to Get: Complete all "Cat Rescued" in LEGO City

FOREST FIREMAN

Location: N/A

How to Get: Complete all "BBQ Fires Extinguished" in LEGO City

JESSIE WEINGARTNER

Location: Bluebell National Park

How to Get: Douse five small campfires around the park.

OLIVER DUFFY

Location: Pagoda

How to Get: Fill the three empty fountains with water.

RAMON LOPEZ-DELGADO

Location: Special Assignment 9: "Hot Property"

How to Get: Douse the barrel fire that the firemen are gathered around.

RYAN MCLAUGHLIN

Location: Bright Lights Plaza

How to Get: Build the five watercoolers around Bright Lights Plaza to unlock.

CONSTRUCTION WORKERS

CHASE MCCAIN (WORKER)

Location: Special Assignment 12: "High Steal"

How to Get: Progress through Story mode.

ALBERT SPINDLEROUTER

Location: N/A

How to Get: Complete all "Coffee Breaks Completed" in LEGO City

BOBBY HAMMER

Location: Auburn

How to Get: Navigate the south buildings, starting from the flower pot; the token is on a high crate at the end of the run.

CONSTRUCTION FOREMAN

Location: Special Assignment 12: "High Steal"

How to Get: Use the astronaut's jetpack jump to reach the small room above the ladder you must pull down with the grapple gun. Smash the blue cabinet.

DOCKS CRANE DRIVER

Location: Auburn

How to Get: Climb the docks' eastern crane; the token is at the top.

DOCKS FOREMAN

Location: Auburn

How to Get: Beat the zone's free run event.

GARAGE WORKER

Location: Auburn

How to Get: Smash four objects around the beach and build their bricks into palm trees and other objects.

HARBOR WORKER

Location: Auburn

How to Get: Build the disguise booth.

LANCE LINBERGER

Location: Auburn

How to Get: Navigate the south-central buildings, using the chimney updrafts to reach the hovering token.

MAINTENANCE WORKER

Location: Cherry Tree Hills

How to Get: Build the disguise booth.

MILES REBAR

Location: Pagoda

How to Get: On a ledge above the stores on the east end of Pagoda.

PATRICK WENHAM

Location: Special Assignment 12: "High Steal"

How to Get: Fix the fuse box near the right gate, use the color swapper, blast the nearby wall and climb it, smash the junk on the ledge.

ROD STANCHION

Location: N/A

How to Get: Complete all "Drill Thrills Completed" in LEGO City

TOW TRUCK DRIVER

Location: Auburn

How to Get: Complete the timed stud run around the crates at the North Docks.

⭐ CIVILIANS: SPECIAL 1

BASEBALL PLAYER

Location: Cherry Tree Hills

How to Get: Beat the zone's free run event.

CAVEMAN

Location: Special Assignment 8: "The Colossal Fossil Hustle"

How to Get: Use Rex Fury to rip apart the super-strength crate on the right, then build the Dry Bones exhibit. (Free Play)

CHEERLEADER

Location: Bright Lights Plaza

How to Get: Beat the zone's free run event.

CIRCUS CLOWN

Location: Festival Square

How to Get: Paint the balloons red and yellow to unlock this token.

COWBOY

Location: Uptown

How to Get: Beat the zone's free run event.

DEEP SEA DIVER

Location: Festival Square

How to Get: Build the Deep Sea Spin superbuild.

DEMOLITION DUMMY

Location: Lady Liberty Island

How to Get: Hovering in the walkway underneath the Statue of Lady Liberty.

DISCO DUDE

Location: Bright Lights Plaza

How to Get: Over the disco ball on top of the giant Disco Dude statue.

ELF

Location: Bluebell National Park

How to Get: Smash three LEGO trees around the park and build three birdhouses from their bricks.

EXPLORER

Location: Lady Liberty Island

How to Get: Build the four sets of binoculars to reveal this token.

FISHERMAN

Location: Crescent Park

How to Get: Use the fishing rod on the pier. The fish you catch drops the token.

FORESTMAN

Location: Bluebell National Park

How to Get: Build the Bluebell Tree superbuild, then climb up to the tree house.

GORILLA SUIT GUY

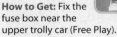

Location: Festival Square

How to Get: Paint the three basketball backboards red, then win nine games of hoops.

HULA DANCER

Location: Paradise Sands

How to Get: Paint the four flowers the correct colors.

KARATE MASTER

Location: Special Assignment 4: "Kung Fool"

How to Get: Use a torch to light the large lantern on the ground in the courtyard's left foreground corner.

LIFEGUARD

Location: Crescent Park

How to Get: Go to the pier and paint the three life preservers red.

MAGICIAN

Location: Bright Lights Plaza

How to Get: Above the transporter pad inside the west side shops' gym.

MARACA MAN

Location: Paradise Sands

How to Get: Build the three jukeboxes to unlock.

MIME

Location: Downtown

How to Get: On a ledge along the side of the bank.

MUMMY

Location: Special Assignment 8: "The Colossal Fossil Hustle"

How to Get: Fix the fuse box near the upper trolly car (Free Play).

NINJA

Location: Downtown

How to Get: Beat the zone's free run event.

NURSE

Location: Crescent Park

How to Get: Create matching sets of flowers on the bridge with the color gun.

PHARAOH

Location: Uptown

How to Get: Paint the pharaoh statue outside the museum.

PILOT

Location: LEGO City Airport

How to Get: Build the Stunt Ramp superbuild.

POP STAR

Location: N/A

How to Get: Find all five Super Stars hidden in LEGO City.

RACE CAR DRIVER

Location: Auburn

How to Get: Build the Stunt Ramp superbuild.

RAPPER

Location: Cherry Tree Hills

How to Get: Above the rooftop DJ stage (navigate the northeast rooftops to reach).

RINGMASTER

Location: Downtown

How to Get: Super build the Ferris wheel, then drive a car through the center of it.

ROBOT

Location: Festival Square

How to Get: At the very top of the mega building.

SAMURAI WARRIOR

Location: Bluebell National Park

How to Get: Ring the three gongs along the trail east of Barry Smith's Kung-Fu Dojo.

SKATER

Location: Crescent Park

How to Get: Beat the zone's free run.

SKIER

Location: Heritage Bridge

How to Get: Beat the zone's free run.

SNOWBOARDER

Location: Bluebell National Park

How to Get: Paint three road signs yellow around the main road that runs through the park.

SPACE ALIEN
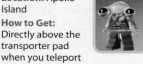
Location: Apollo Island

How to Get: Directly above the transporter pad when you teleport into the research bunker.

SPACEMAN

Location: Apollo Island

How to Get: Build the Space Shuttle superbuild.

SPACE VILLAIN
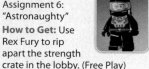
Location: Special Assignment 6: "Astronaughty"

How to Get: Use Rex Fury to rip apart the strength crate in the lobby. (Free Play)

SPARTAN WARRIOR

Location: Bright Lights Plaza

How to Get: Drive a car off the ramp near the Atlas statue so that you drive through the globe.

SUMO WRESTLER

Location: Festival Square

How to Get: Jump five times inside the bouncy castle to make this token appear.

SUPER WRESTLER

Location: N/A

How to Get: Find all five ? Blocks hidden around LEGO City.

SURFER

Location: Paradise Sands

How to Get: Rip the door off the super sand castle after building it.

TENNIS PLAYER
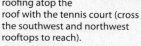
Location: Cherry Tree Hills

How to Get: Drill one of the two patches of shaky roofing atop the roof with the tennis court (cross the southwest and northwest rooftops to reach).

TRAFFIC COP

Location: Downtown

How to Get: Paint the three silver traffic post tops near the back yellow.

TRIBAL CHIEF

Location: Festival Square

How to Get: Inside the bookstore.

TRIBAL HUNTER

Location: Albatross Island

How to Get: Find three pallets spread across the beach; smash each one and build sand castles from their broken blocks.

VAMPIRE

Location: Fort Meadows

How to Get: Beat the zone's free run event.

WEIGHT LIFTER

Location: Festival Square

How to Get: Show you're a strong man by ringing the three bells in the carnival games.

ZOMBIE

Location: Bright Lights Plaza

How to Get: At the top of the mall.

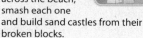
CIVILIANS: SPECIAL 2

ARTIST

Location: Downtown

How to Get: Color the artist statue's painting.

BANDIT

Location: N/A

How to Get: Complete all "ATMs Smashed" in LEGO City

BOXER

Location: Albatross Island

How to Get: Paint the three silver punching bags yellow.

BUTCHER

Location: Albatross Island

How to Get: On the way toward the prison, hug the fenced wall and move around to the other side.

CAVE WOMAN
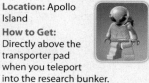
Location: Fort Meadows

How to Get: Smash a rock inside the spiderweb cave.

CLASSIC ALIEN

Location: Apollo Island

How to Get: Directly above the transporter pad when you teleport into the research bunker.

CLOCKWORK ROBOT

Location: Bright Lights Plaza

How to Get: On the stage next to the giant toy statue of the west side shops.

CRAZY SCIENTIST

Location: Paradise Sands

How to Get: Super build the Orion's Rockets, then hop on and ride the roller coaster.

DETECTIVE

Location: Cherry Tree Hills

How to Get: Use the scan spot near the large billboard by the radio tower.

FITNESS INSTRUCTOR

Location: Auburn Bay Bridge

How to Get: Beat the zone's free run event.

GANGSTER

Location: Fresco

How to Get: In between Pappalardo's and Little Venice.

GLADIATOR
Location: Uptown

How to Get: Build the three fishing rods along the docks.

GRADUATE

Location: Kings Court

How to Get: Inside an office on the west side of Kings Court.

HAZMAT GUY

Location: Auburn

How to Get: Build the Auburn chimney atop the north-central buildings, then use the chimney's updraft to reach the hovering token.

HIGHLAND BATTLER

Location: Fort Meadows

How to Get: Paint three wheelbarrows blue around the zone.

HOCKEY PLAYER

Location: Lady Liberty Island

How to Get: Beat the zone's free run event.

ICE FISHERMAN

Location: Paradise Sands

How to Get: Build the Stunt Ramp superbuild.

ICE SKATER

Location: Cherry Tree Hills

How to Get: Appears near the wishing fountain after you complete the superbuild.

INTERGALACTIC GIRL

Location: Special Assignment 5: "Dirty Work"

How to Get: Use the transporter pad in the water near the start (Free Play).

LIZARD MAN

Location: Bright Lights Plaza

How to Get: Collect after building the LEGO sets in the LEGO Store.

LUMBERJACK

Location: Fort Meadows

How to Get: Inside the lumberjack's log cabin (must construct the superbuild first).

MECHANIC

Location: Auburn

How to Get: Build the Sky Glide superbuild atop the water tower near the south buildings, then use the updraft to reach the hovering token.

MINOTAUR

Location: Downtown

How to Get: Paint the bull statue gold.

THE MONSTER

Location: Fort Meadows

How to Get: Climb to the top of the castle, chop through the boarded door, build the catapult pad, and launch to the flagpole.

MUSKETEER

Location: Crescent Park

How to Get: Build the three sand castles along the beach.

PUNK ROCKER

Location: Pagoda

How to Get: Super build and then ride the Frightful Freefall.

ROMAN SOLDIER

Location: Uptown

How to Get: Hidden on a ledge of a building that borders the airport.

ROYAL GUARD

Location: Kings Court

How to Get: Above a statue near Blackwell Tower.

SAILOR

Location: Crescent Park

How to Get: Paint the fancy house's three ship wheels orange.

SKATER GIRL

Location: LEGO City Airport

How to Get: Beat the zone's free run event.

SLEEPYHEAD

Location: Cherry Tree Hills

How to Get: Appears on the front steps of the Hillside House superbuild (you must construct the superbuild first).

SNOWBOARDER GUY

Location: Fresco

How to Get: Climb the drainpipe at the far end of the south apartments B.

SOCCER PLAYER

Location: Fresco

How to Get: Rip the ball free from the soccer player statue to reveal this token.

STREET SKATER

Location: Kings Court

How to Get: Beat the zone's free run event.

SURFER GIRL

Location: Paradise Sands

How to Get: Paint the three silver surfboards yellow.

SURGEON

Location: Festival Square

How to Get: Grapple gun up above the front door of the hospital.

VIKING

Location: Paradise Sands

How to Get: Hop on the Viking ride.

WEREWOLF

Location: Cherry Tree Hills

How to Get: Smash three LEGO trees and build three doghouses out of their bricks.

ZOOKEEPER

Location: Crescent Park

How to Get: Build the three birdhouses in the park.

⭐ CIVILIANS: SERVICE

AIR HOST

Location: LEGO City Airport

How to Get: Behind a locked door on the roof of the airport's north wing.

AIR HOSTESS

Location: LEGO City Airport

How to Get: Hovering in the air underneath the freeway.

AIRLINE ATTENDANT 1

Location: LEGO City Airport

How to Get: Build the disguise booth.

AIRLINE ATTENDANT 2

Location: LEGO City Airport

How to Get: In an office at the airport's north wing. Drill through the ceiling to get inside.

AIRLINE PILOT

Location: LEGO City Airport

How to Get: Build the LCX Control Tower, then climb to the top and use the grapple point to reach this token.

ANCHOR MAN

Location: Cherry Tree Hills

How to Get: Atop the radio tower (chicken-glide from the lookout point, then activate the updraft fan).

BANK MANAGER

Location: Special Assignment 5: "Dirty Work"

How to Get: Activate the space crate in the bank lobby, beam up to the balcony, color the statue brown and blue, then enter the room on the right. (Free Play)

BUS DRIVER

Location: Uptown

How to Get: Build the disguise booth.

CAPTAIN BLUFFBEARD

Location: Paradise Sands

How to Get: Build Bluffbeard's Lighthouse, then break into the front door to find the token at the top.

CHAT SHOW HOST

Location: Apollo Island

How to Get: Build the Stunt Ramp superbuild.

CHEF

Location: Crescent Park

How to Get: Drive a car off the ramp and launch over the giant coffee cup near the fancy house.

CLEANER

Location: LEGO City Airport

How to Get: Paint the three bins red, green, and yellow.

COASTGUARD

Location: Paradise Sands

How to Get: Build the disguise booth.

DOCTOR JONES

Location: Festival Square

How to Get: On top of the theater awning.

DOCTOR SMITH

Location: Festival Square

How to Get: Build the disguise booth.

DOORMAN

Location: Paradise Sands

How to Get: On an awning in the bazaar.

GARBAGE MAN

Location: Apollo Island

How to Get: Paint the four silver troughs yellow.

GAS STATION MANAGER

Location: Fort Meadows

How to Get: Build the disguise booth.

JANITOR

Location: Uptown

How to Get: Build the four bubble gum machines around uptown.

MAIL MAN

Location: Cherry Tree Hills

How to Get: Paint three mailboxes red around Cherry Tree Hills.

NEWS READER

Location: Pagoda

How to Get: Build the four bonsai trees to unlock this token.

PAPARAZZO

Location: Bright Lights Plaza

How to Get: Build the disguise booth.

PARAMEDIC

Location: Crescent Park

How to Get: Paint the four silver posts in the tunnel yellow.

PIZZA DELIVERY BOY

Location: LEGO City Airport

How to Get: Paint the silver phones orange to unlock this token.

PRESS PHOTOGRAPHER

Location: Albatross Island

How to Get: Hidden inside a boulder next to the small lagoon at the beach.

RADIO DJ

Location: Apollo Island

How to Get: Build the three mini-satellites spread around the island.

SUBMARINE CAPTAIN

Location: Special Assignment 13: "Disruptive Behavior"

How to Get: After jetpack jumping to the base's right side, inch around the thin ledge.

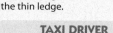

TAXI DRIVER

Location: Cherry Tree Hills

How to Get: Bounce off the train station's patio tables to reach its roof, then beam over to the archway with the token.

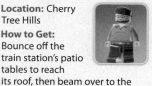

TRAIN DRIVER BILL

Location: Cherry Tree Hills

How to Get: Pry open the train station's second-floor door, then crack the safe inside the station.

TRAIN DRIVER BOB

Location: Fort Meadows

How to Get: Inside the train station's waiting booth (must construct the train station superbuild first).

TV REPORTER

Location: Cherry Tree Hills

How to Get: Build four satellite dishes on the roofs of the zone's northwest mansions.

WAITRESS

Location: Crescent Park

How to Get: Build the disguise booth.

WEATHER GIRL

Location: Downtown

How to Get: Next to the astronaut flag symbol atop the glass tower.

⭐ CIVILIANS: RESIDENTS

CHASE MCCAIN (CIVILIAN)

Location: N/A

How to Get: Available right from the start of Story mode.

ALEXANDRA GREENWOOD

Location: LEGO City Airport

How to Get: Behind a fence at the far south end of the airport.

ALLIE JAESCHKE

Location: Auburn

How to Get: Climb the building near Professor Kowalski's lab, then jump up the three chimneys to reach the hovering token.

INTRODUCTION

POLICE ACADEMY

CHARACTERS AND VEHICLES

WALKTHROUGH

LEGO CITY TOUR

CHECKLISTS

BARRY SMITH

Location: Special Assignment 4: "Kung Fool"

How to Get: Smash the cabinets on the dojo balcony's right side to find a small idol. Place the idol on the stand downstairs. (Free Play)

BEACH DUDE

Location: Paradise Sands

How to Get: Build the three sand small sand castles on the beach.

BECKY BALLANTINE

Location: Paradise Sands

How to Get: On a hotel awning at the bazaar.

BRYONY MUSKA

Location: Fresco

How to Get: In the sunroom on the roof of the north apartments.

CHRIS PARRY

Location: Auburn

How to Get: Pull down the ladder near the south buildings, pry open the skylight, drop inside, and open the safe.

CHRIS WYATT

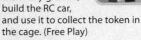

Location: Bright Lights Plaza

How to Get: Along the R&J sign near the top of the shopping mall.

CONRAD PETERS

Location: Special Assignment 1: "Some Assaults"

How to Get: Drill the shaky ground, build the RC car, and use it to collect the token in the cage. (Free Play)

DAVE SOMETHING

Location: Cherry Tree Hills

How to Get: Grapple up to the transport pad atop the security building's entry steps, then beam over to the token.

DEBORAH GRAHAM

Location: Auburn

How to Get: Navigate the north-central buildings, cross the blue balance beam, circle around the right side of the building, and search for the hidden token behind an Octan gas tank.

DISGUISED NATALIA

Location: Pagoda

How to Get: Beat the zone's free run event.

GEORGE FARTARBENSONBURY

Location: Cherry Tree Hills

How to Get: Paint two pieces of furniture red inside the shop with the revolving doors near the Red Café.

HENRIK KOWALSKI

Location: Special Assignment 13: "Disruptive Behavior"

How to Get: Fix the fuse box behind one of the Rex Fury super-strength crates near the submarine (Free Play).

HUGH HUNTER

Location: Downtown

How to Get: Build the disguise booth.

JO CHALKLEY

Location: Downtown

How to Get: Behind the Y building, in a little nook by a decorative cannon.

KARATE CHAMP

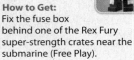

Location: Bluebell National Park

How to Get: Grapple and pull the two radar dishes atop Sheriff Huckleberry's police station.

KARATE GUY

Location: Bluebell National Park

How to Get: Appears over the Serenity Bridge after you construct the superbuild.

KEVIN JACOBS

Location: Uptown

How to Get: In the back of the arcade.

LOUIE MITCHELL

Location: Auburn

How to Get: Hidden in a nook beneath the final leg of the free run course. Smash a blue barrel, build a trampoline, then bounce up and shimmy along the overhead LEGO patch to reach.

LOUISE ANDREW

Location: Cherry Tree Hills

How to Get: Inside the southeast train tunnel.

LUKE CASHMORE

Location: Bright Lights Plaza

How to Get: Inside the room with the locked door, at the top of Ellie's apartment.

MIKE NORTHEAST

Location: Uptown

How to Get: On a thin ledge around the back side of the Museum of Natural History's east tower.

NATALIA KOWALSKI

Location: Festival Square

How to Get: Behind the boarded up door on the hospital rooftop.

ROSS WILDING

Location: Special Assignment 3: "Miner Altercation"

How to Get: Use the grapple gun to flip over the floating pallet near the mission's start.

RUDOLPH PIANOLA

Location: Paradise Sands

How to Get: There are three flamingos around the hotel; paint them pink.

SAM PENN

Location: Bluebell National Park

How to Get: Climb to the top of the metal bridge east of the dam.

SAMSON CROW

Location: Auburn

How to Get: Paint the bananas yellow on the pallets along the east road near the docks.

SARAH HORNER

Location: Auburn

How to Get: Atop the large cargo ship at the northeast docks.

STEPHEN RHODES

Location: Auburn

How to Get: Inside the gas station near Hank's Garage.

STREET RACER

Location: Cherry Tree Hills

How to Get: Build five bubble gum dispensers around the train station and waterfront (smash brown crates to find their bricks).

TROUSERLESS BARRY

Location: Bluebell National Park

How to Get: Behind Barry Smith's Kung-Fu Dojo. Trick the Piranha Plant into burning away the spiderweb.

VIOLET DE BURGH

Location: Auburn

How to Get: Paint three crates of cherries red around Auburn.

UNLOCKING VEHICLES

Vehicles are unlocked much like character disguises. While you gain a few vehicles over the course of Story mode, most you must earn by collecting the many vehicle tokens scattered across LEGO City and hidden in the 15 Special Assignments. Each Special Assignment has two vehicle tokens for Chase to track down.

Like character tokens, Chase must visit the LEGO City Police Station and spend his hard-earned studs to purchase vehicles whose tokens he's collected. Also, like character disguises, every vehicle belongs to a specific category. However, the only noteworthy difference between the vehicle categories is that most emergency vehicles have sirens that cause traffic to move out of your way. In addition, some vehicles have turbos, while others don't.

ORDERING VEHICLES

Of course, if you're less picky, you can make Chase hop into any vehicle he sees. Get close and press Ⓧ to make him hop in, and off you go! He'll kick out the driver and be on his way. Hey, it's all in the name of justice!

Ordering vehicles couldn't be easier. After you purchase one, simply visit any vehicle call-in point and order it up for immediate delivery. Note that you can only order helicopters at helipads.

NOTE

You must progress through Story mode before you can use vehicle call-in points and helipads.

Though Chase can captain boats docked around LEGO City, he's unable to purchase them for on-demand delivery.

TIP

Press Ⓛ to blow Chase's police whistle and stop a moving vehicle. This makes commandeering the vehicle a little easier.

NOTE

Chase is so daring, he won't hesitate to leap from one moving vehicle into another. Simply steer close to another vehicle, and press Ⓧ when the icon appears to make the switch. Chase can even leap from a helicopter into a land vehicle or boat!

INTRODUCTION

POLICE ACADEMY

CHARACTERS AND VEHICLES

WALKTHROUGH

LEGO CITY TOUR

CHECKLISTS

VEHICLES LIST

⭐ AIRCRAFT

CAMEL

Location: LEGO City Airport

How to Get: Construct the Helipad superbuild.

CHOPPER

Location: Albatross Island

How to Get: Construct the Helipad superbuild.

CLOUD

Location: Special Assignment 14: "Breaking and Reentering"

How to Get: Smash the chair on the right side of the small room near the playground.

HERA

Location: Auburn

How to Get: Construct the Helipad superbuild.

JUPITER

Location: Special Assignment 13: "Disruptive Behavior"

How to Get: Use Rex Fury to rip apart the super-strength crate in the base's final area (Free Play).

RESPONDER

Location: Cherry Tree Hills

How to Get: Construct the Helipad superbuild.

REX'S TEMPEST

Location: Special Assignment 15: "Fly Me to the Moon"

How to Get: Smash the remains of the T-Rex during the final battle against Rex Fury.

SKYBRINGER

Location: Bluebell National Park

How to Get: Construct the Helipad superbuild.

SWOOPER

Location: N/A

How to Get: Gained automatically when helipads become unlocked.

UFO

Location: Apollo Island

How to Get: Construct the Helipad superbuild.

⭐ BIKES

BUZZER

Location: Special Assignment 10: "Smash 'n' Grab"

How to Get: Grow and climb the vines, jump to the thin ledge, chop through a door, and beam into a small background room with the token.

GROUNDHOG

Location: LEGO City Airport

How to Get: Super build the Loop de Loop, then drive up it.

HAIRDRYER

Location: Special Assignment 4: "Kung Fool"

How to Get: Beam up to the dojo's balcony, drop to the lower foreground balcony, smash the cabinet to find dynamite, and blast the silver wall downstairs. (Free Play)

REDEEMER

Location: Lady Liberty Island

How to Get: Beat the time trial.

REVOLVER

Location: Cherry Tree Hills

How to Get: Construct the Emergency Crash Mat superbuild.

REX'S BRUTE

Location: Special Assignment 13: "Disruptive Behavior"

How to Get: Drill through the shaky floor in the base's final area.

SEGWAY

Location: Special Assignment 2: "Trouble in Stir"

How to Get: Break into the workshop with the fire axe, smash the background cabinet, crack the wall safe, blast the silver sink with dynamite, and ride the water geyser (Free Play).

SWEETIE

Location: Paradise Sands

How to Get: Super build the Loop de Loop on the beach, then drive up it.

VOR

Location: LEGO City Airport

How to Get: Beat the time trial.

WASH WAGON

Location: Apollo Island

How to Get: Build the Loop de Loop on the runway, then drive up it.

⭐ COMPACTS

ACESO

Location: Special Assignment 11: "They All Scream for Ice Cream"

How to Get: Smash the cabinet atop the parlor stairs, build the bricks into an ice cream ball, roll over the red switch to the left, use the transporter to reach the overhead lights.

ANCESTOR

Location: Special Assignment 8: "The Colossal Fossil Hustle"

How to Get: After building the plane, climb the pirate ship's ladder and jump over to its cannon. Blast the background wall.

ARBALEST

Location: Kings Court

How to Get: Beat the Vehicle Robber Arrested event.

CABRAKAN

Location: Compact

How to Get: Construct the Ferry superbuild.

CRATER

Location: Fresco

How to Get: Construct the Call-in Point superbuild.

DOWNFORCE

Location: Kings Court

How to Get: Beat the Vehicle Robbery Completed event.

EARWIG

Location: Downtown

How to Get: Construct the Call-in Point superbuild.

FLARE

Location: Uptown

How to Get: Beat the Vehicle Robber Arrested event.

GRASSMAN

Location: Cherry Tree Hills

How to Get: Beat the Vehicle Robber Arrested event.

HESTIA

Location: Uptown

How to Get: Construct the Call-in Point superbuild.

JALOPY

Location: Special Assignment 7: "Scrapyard Scrap"

How to Get: Drill the shaky ground on the scrapyard's right side, place the gear onto the catapult, pull the lever, then beam over and collect the token. (Free Play)

PUMPKIN

Location: Cherry Tree Hills

How to Get: Construct the Ferry superbuild (accomplished during Story mode).

REX'S GALICAN

Location: Crosstown Tunnel

How to Get: Along the north walkway, behind a door only Rex Fury can rip open.

SCHMOOZER

Location: Special Assignment 7: "Scrapyard Scrap"

How to Get: Drill the shaky ground near the start, then ride up the water geyser (Free Play).

SEVILA

Location: Kings Court

How to Get: Construct the Ferry superbuild.

SMALLISIMO

Location: Uptown

How to Get: Beat the Vehicle Robbery Completed event.

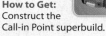

SQUEAKY

Location: Fresco

How to Get: Construct the Call-in Point superbuild.

TALOS

Location: Paradise Sands

How to Get: Construct the Swimming Pool superbuild (accomplished in Story mode).

⭐ EMERGENCY

BASTION

Location: Special Assignment 1: "Some Assaults"

How to Get: Use the transporter near the start to reach a color swapper. Blast the switch and then repair the fuse box (Free Play).

CHASER

Location: Bright Lights Plaza

How to Get: Construct the Call-in Point superbuild.

DOUSER

Location: Festival Square

How to Get: Construct the Call-in Point superbuild.

EXTENDER

Location: Special Assignment 9: "Hot Property"

How to Get: Use Rex Fury to rip apart the super-strength crate in the garage beyond the gate. (Free Play)

FIRE TRACKER

Location: Special Assignment 9: "Hot Property"

How to Get: Use Rex Fury to rip apart the super-strength crate in the burning building. Carry the lever handle over to the garages and pull the lever, then enter the vehicle. (Free Play)

HERO

Location: Bluebell National Park

How to Get: Beat the Vehicle Robber Arrested event.

IMPRISONER

Location: Cherry Tree Hills

How to Get: Construct the Call-in Point superbuild.

INFERNO

Location: Festival Square

How to Get: Beat the Vehicle Robber Arrested event.

M.O.V.

Location: LEGO City Airport

How to Get: Construct the Call-in Point superbuild.

PANACEA

Location: Festival Square

How to Get: Beat the Vehicle Robbery Completed event.

PATROLLO

Location: Downtown

How to Get: Construct the Call-in Point superbuild.

RINO

Location: Special Assignment 2: "Trouble in Stir"

How to Get: Break into the workshop with the fire axe, build the RC car, use it to open the background cage, collect the valve wheel, and use it to open the furnace doors (Free Play).

SQUADDIE

Location: N/A

How to Get: Gained automatically when Call-in Points become unlocked.

TRACKER

Location: Bluebell National Park

How to Get: Beat the time trial.

T.R.E.V.

Location: Crescent Park

How to Get: Beat the Vehicle Robbery Completed event.

TROOPER

Location: Fort Meadows

How to Get: Construct the Call-in Point superbuild (accomplished in Story mode).

VIGILANT

Location: Bluebell National Park

How to Get: Construct the Call-in Point superbuild.

 ★ **HEAVY**

BROADCASTER

Location: Special Assignment 1: "Some Assaults"

How to Get: Obtain dynamite from the space crate, destroy the silver skylight, and drop through (Free Play).

CHAN'S IRONBACK

Location: Bluebell National Park

How to Get: Beat the time trial.

COCOON

Location: Apollo Island

How to Get: Beat the time trial.

GALLEON

Location: Paradise Sands

How to Get: Beat the time trial.

GARRANO

Location: Special Assignment 6: "Astronaughty"

How to Get: Fix the fuse box on the hangar's high walkways, climb the wall, and cross the handholds (Free Play).

GOTLAND

Location: Special Assignment 5: "Dirty Work"

How to Get: Swim into the background cage before crossing the toxic waste.

IRONBACK

Location: Special Assignment 11: "They All Scream for Ice Cream"

How to Get: Water the planter in Vinnie's office.

L.E.R.V.

Location: Special Assignment 6: "Astronaughty"

How to Get: Drill the shaky ground in the hangar (Free Play).

MUNCHER

Location: Fresco

How to Get: Beat the time trial.

OLDSTER

Location: Bluebell National Park

How to Get: Beat the time trial.

REX'S RIOT

Location: Auburn

How to Get: Beat the Vehicle Robbery Completed event.

RUGGED

Location: LEGO City Airport

How to Get: Beat the Vehicle Robbery Completed event.

SQUADMOBILE

Location: Fresco

How to Get: Beat the time trial.

TORSION

Location: Fort Meadows

How to Get: Construct the Call-in Point superbuild.

TRANSTER

Location: Fresco

How to Get: Beat the Vehicle Robber Arrested event.

WANDERER

Location: Apollo Island

How to Get: Construct the Call-in Point superbuild.

 ★ **PERFORMANCE**

ATHENA

Location: Paradise Sands

How to Get: Beat the Vehicle Robbery Completed event.

BEARER

Location: Downtown

How to Get: Beat the Vehicle Robbery Completed event.

CETAN

Location: Bright Lights Plaza

How to Get: Beat the Vehicle Robbery Completed event.

CHAN'S DRAKONAS

Location: Pagoda

How to Get: Beat the Vehicle Robbery Completed event.

DRAKONAS

Location: Downtown

How to Get: Beat the time trial.

DULLAHAN

Location: Special Assignment 14: "Breaking and Reentering"

How to Get: Pry open the sewer cover on the grounds' left side.

ENBERG

Location: Auburn

How to Get: Beat the Vehicle Robbery Completed event.

FALCHION GT

Location: Fresco

How to Get: Beat the Vehicle Robbery Completed event.

GERSEMI

Location: Bright Lights Plaza

How to Get: Beat the Vehicle Robber Arrested event.

LANTOS

Location: Cherry Tree Hills

How to Get: Beat the time trial.

LUSCA

Location: Paradise Sands

How to Get: Beat the Vehicle Robber Arrested event.

NARYM

Location: Downtown

How to Get: Beat the Vehicle Robber Arrested event.

ROAR

Location: Special Assignment 4: "Kung Fool"

How to Get: Smash the courtyard's boulders, then drill the shaky ground beneath them (Free Play).

SCOUT

Location: Special Assignment 10: "Smash 'n' Grab"

How to Get: Pry open the wall panel on the right side of Blackwell's lounge.

SILVERSMITH

Location: Special Assignment 8: "The Colossal Fossil Hustle"

How to Get: Fix the fuse box near the totem pole exhibit, beam down to the brontosaurus exhibit, climb the tail, grapple up to the pterodactyl, and pull the lever (Free Play).

SPHINX

Location: Auburn

How to Get: Beat the Vehicle Robber Arrested event.

TIGERELLA

Location: Pagoda

How to Get: Beat the Vehicle Robber Arrested event.

VALKYRIE

Location: Cherry Tree Hills

How to Get: Beat the Vehicle Robbery Completed event.

WRATH

Location: Auburn Bay Bridge

How to Get: Beat the time trial.

> ⭐ **WORKER**

ARMADILLO

Location: Fort Meadows

How to Get: Beat the time trial.

ATLAS

Location: Apollo Island

How to Get: Beat the time trial.

BRAWN

Location: Auburn

How to Get: Beat the time trial.

BRISTLER

Location: Kings Court

How to Get: Construct the Call-in Point superbuild.

DRAGGER

Location: Auburn

How to Get: Construct the Call-in Point superbuild.

DUMPER

Location: Special Assignment 3: "Miner Altercation"

How to Get: Astronaut boost over the electrified rails, fix the fuse box, use the color swapper, backtrack out and climb the nearby ledge, blast the switch, and ride the elevator (Free Play).

EPONA

Location: Paradise Sands

How to Get: Construct the Call-in Point superbuild.

FOUNDATION

Location: Special Assignment 12: "High Steal"

How to Get: Use the small cement mixer in the right foreground corner to blast down some bricks, then build an elevator platform and ride up to the token.

HAZARD

Location: Uptown

How to Get: Construct the Call-in Point superbuild.

INDULGA

Location: Pagoda

How to Get: Construct the Call-in Point superbuild.

KOWALSKI'S SHIFTER

Location: Kings Court

How to Get: Construct the Emergency Crash Mat superbuild.

PAYLOAD

Location: Special Assignment 15: "Fly Me to the Moon"

How to Get: Use Rex Fury to rip apart the strength crate in the rocket's loading bay (Free Play).

PROTECTOR

Location: LEGO City Airport

How to Get: Construct the Call-in Point superbuild.

RELOCATOR

Location: Special Assignment 5: "Dirty Work"

How to Get: Drill the shaky ground in the final sewer area (Free Play).

ROLLER

Location: Special Assignment 12: "High Steal"

How to Get: ·Smash the debris in the corner before sliding down the tube in the mission's second area.

SHIFTER

Location: LEGO City Airport

How to Get: Beat the Vehicle Robber Arrested event.

SLICKER

Location: Fort Meadows

How to Get: Construct the Emergency Crash Mat superbuild.

STEADFAST

Location: Special Assignment 3: "Miner Altercation"

How to Get: Astronaut boost on top of the elevator and get the box of bricks. Place it on the green pad and build the gears (Free Play).

TAXI CAB

Location: Kings Court

How to Get: Beat the time trial.

TRASHER

Location: Auburn

How to Get: Construct the Call-in Point superbuild.

> **NOTE**
>
> While Chase can pilot just about any boat or ship he sees, there are no call-in points by the water, and thus no sea vessels to unlock in *LEGO City Undercover*.

WALKTHROUGH

CHAPTER 1: NEW FACES AND OLD ENEMIES

IT'S BEEN YEARS SINCE SUPERCOP CHASE MCCAIN HAS SET FOOT IN LEGO CITY, AND THE TEEMING METROPOLIS HASN'T FARED WELL DURING HIS ABSENCE. STEPPING OFF THE FERRY, MCCAIN FINDS NONE OTHER THAN MAYOR GLEESON AWAITING HIM AT THE PIER. THE MAYOR HAS BAD NEWS: THE NOTORIOUS CRIMINAL REX FURY HAS ESCAPED PRISON, AND LEGO CITY HAS FALLEN UNDER THE GRIP OF A TERRIBLE CRIME WAVE! THE MAYOR ASKS CHASE TO HURRY TO THE POLICE STATION AND GET TO WORK ON APPREHENDING REX FURY.

CITY EXPLORATION

 ## OBJECTIVE: GET IN THE POLICE CAR

LEGO City Undercover is quite different from other LEGO games you've enjoyed in the past. Rather than simply playing through one level after the next, you must explore LEGO City in search of important clues that advance the plot. Fortunately, you don't have to explore this huge city on foot—approach the police car that Mayor Gleeson has left for you, and press Ⓧ to hop in.

NOTE

Important objectives, like the police car, are often marked with special onscreen indicators to help you find them.

 ## OBJECTIVE: GO TO THE POLICE STATION

Now that you've found some wheels, drive to the LEGO City police station. Simply follow the trail of green LEGO studs on the road; they'll lead you straight to your destination. Use ⓏⓇ to accelerate, Ⓩ Ⓛ or Ⓑ to brake and reverse, and hold Ⓨ to kick on the turbos!

The police station isn't far—just keep following those green studs. Park inside the glowing objective beacon when you arrive.

NOTE

Police vehicles and sports cars are usually turbocharged, but other vehicles may not have turbos.

INTRODUCTION

POLICE ACADEMY

CHARACTERS AND VEHICLES

WALKTHROUGH

LEGO CITY TOUR

CHECKLISTS

LEGO CITY POLICE STATION

⭐ OBJECTIVE: REPAIR THE MAIN COMPUTER

Chase meets a goofy cop named Frank Honey just outside the police station. Approach Frank after you enter the building—he's highlighted by a green objective marker.

While trying to fix the station's main "compuper," Frank accidentally blows it up. What a goof! Stand near the remains of the computer and hold Ⓐ to build the bouncing LEGO bricks, repairing the damage. Build all three piles of LEGO bricks to fully repair the computer.

After repairing the main computer, follow Frank to the nearby elevator on the right. Police Chief Dunby steps out of the elevator as you approach, and he's in an awful mood. He doesn't seem to like Chase very much, but Mayor Gleeson has insisted that Chase lead the Rex Fury case, so the chief's hands are tied.

⭐ OBJECTIVE: EXPLORE THE BASEMENT

After your awkward chat with Chief Dunby, Frank gives you the grand tour of the station's basement. Follow him downstairs, then smash three gray boxes to discover more LEGO bricks. Hold Ⓐ to build these into a locker, then open the locker to discover the Chase McCain (Police Officer) disguise!

Now that you've found a new disguise, you can change your appearance at any time by holding Ⓧ to open the Disguise Wheel and selecting the outfit you wish to wear. Do this now and change into the Chase McCain (Police Officer) outfit.

TIP

Quickly change disguises by pressing ⓏⓁ or ⓏⓇ to cycle through them.

Follow Frank back upstairs. He stops near a police shield icon. Stand on this icon. Now that you've changed into your police officer disguise, press Ⓐ to gain access to the requisitions desk. Step up to the desk to speak with Ellie Phillips, who hands you a newfangled police communicator.

OBJECTIVE: ACTIVATE THE POLICE COMMUNICATOR

Take the elevator back up to the station's lobby and approach the main computer. Stand before the computer and press Ⓐ to sync up your communicator. Now your Wii U GamePad will show you a handy map of your surroundings!

OBJECTIVE: WAKE THE CHIEF

Police Chief Dunby has fallen asleep at his desk, and it's up to Chase to wake him. Follow Frank upstairs and, when prompted, answer an incoming call on your GamePad by touching the flashing video call icon. The caller is Ellie from requisitions, and she tells you how to use the communicator to search for clues!

Go left to discover Chief Dunby's office. The door is locked, and you need to find a key to get inside. Stand on the nearby glowing scan spot, then press Ⓐ to put your communicator into Detective Scan mode. Shine the communicator's blue light on the ground to discover a hidden trail of footprints!

The footprints lead to a small cupboard on the right. Press Ⓐ to open the cupboard and find the key to the chief's office. Nice work!

NOTE

You must follow the footprints all the way to the cupboard to discover the key.

Press Ⓐ to pick up the key, then carry it over to the left. Press Ⓐ to insert it into the lock near the chief's door, then press Ⓐ again to turn the key and open the door.

Now you just need to wake the chief! Smash the file cabinet near the window to uncover some LEGO bricks, then build these into a stereo. Chase cranks up the volume and wakes the chief, who angrily orders everyone into the briefing room.

OBJECTIVE: ATTEND THE BRIEFING

Chief Dunby orders everyone into the briefing room, then recounts the story of Rex Fury's historic capture—and recent escape. The briefing is cut short when a video feed shows robbers pulling off a heist at LEGO City Bank. All right, time to fight some crime!

INTRODUCTION

POLICE ACADEMY

CHARACTERS AND VEHICLES

WALKTHROUGH

LEGO CITY TOUR

CHECKLISTS

CITY EXPLORATION

⭐ OBJECTIVE: GO TO CHERRY TREE BANK

Now that you're armed with your police communicator, your GamePad shows you a handy map of LEGO City whenever you're exploring outdoors. On the GamePad is a police shield icon that shows the location of your next objective—the bank that's being robbed. Press and hold the police shield icon to set a waypoint, and a navigation route will lead you straight there. Hop into the nearby Squaddie and follow those green studs to reach the bank!

Chase arrives just in time to witness a bunch of clowns fleeing the bank with big bags of cash. Looks like you got here just in time!

⭐ OBJECTIVE: ARREST THE GETAWAY DRIVER

You've gotta catch those clowns! Pursue their getaway van through the city, following the green studs to help you track it down. Press and hold Ⓨ to use turbos and catch up to the van. Ram into the van four times to destroy it.

The getaway driver flees on foot after you destroy his van. Press Ⓧ to exit your vehicle and pursue him on foot. Chase is a faster runner than the getaway driver, and it won't be long before you catch him. Just keep running until you get close, then press Ⓐ when prompted to knock down the driver.

Nice work! Quickly press Ⓐ again to slap on the handcuffs and arrest the robber. Chase then receives a call on his communicator after arresting the getaway driver. Answer it to receive your next objective.

⭐ OBJECTIVE: LOOK FOR A ROBBER AT THE RED CAFE

A suspicious clown has been spotted at the Red Cafe—he could be one of the bank robbers! Press Ⓛ to blow your police whistle and stop a passing vehicle; then press Ⓧ to commandeer the vehicle. Being a police officer has its advantages!

Follow the green studs to reach the Red Cafe. When you arrive, exit your vehicle and step into the small objective beacon. A trail of studs appears, guiding you up the nearby stairs. Follow the studs to the upstairs patio.

Ellie calls and informs Chase that she has upgraded his communicator with a new tool. Approach the nearby scan spot and press Ⓐ to activate your new Criminal Scan mode. Hold your Wii U GamePad up to your TV screen to begin searching for hidden suspects!

When you discover a suspect, keep him centered on your scanner until you establish a lock. No crook can hide from Chase McCain!

⭐ OBJECTIVE: ENTER THE GARDEN AND ARREST THE ROBBER

The suspect is hiding inside a shed in the garden across the street. Enter the garden by climbing the LEGO vines that the gardener grows.

Run to the right and stand on the action symbol in front of the shed. Press Ⓐ to open the shed—the robber then flees to higher ground.

Pick up the crate of junk inside the shed and carry it to the left. Place the crate on the green LEGO mat to empty its contents and discover some LEGO bricks.

You know what to do! Build those bricks to create a useful object—in this case, a large mushroom. Jump on the mushroom, then jump again and hold Ⓑ to bounce off the mushroom, soaring up to the garden's upper level.

The robber flees to an even higher level. You've got to catch him! Approach the nearby scan spot and use your communicator to discover a trail of footprints, just as you did back at the police station.

The footprints lead to a suspicious pile of leaves. Press Ⓐ to search through them and discover a valve wheel.

Pick up the valve wheel and place it on the nearby water pump. The pump starts working, but the water won't spray because the hose is being blocked!

Unblocking the Hose

Follow the hose to discover the first object that's blocking the water flow—a large rock. Smash the rock to remove this first obstacle.

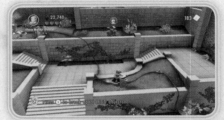

Continue to follow the hose and smash a trash can that's also causing a blockage. Almost there!

The next object that's blocking the hose is a lawn chair. Smash this as well.

Keep following the hose to discover a green Dumpster that's causing the final blockage. Destroy this last obstacle to fully restore the water flow and make some LEGO vines grow. Climb those vines and hurry after that crook!

The robber flees as soon as Chase approaches. Hurry after him and press Ⓐ when you get close to trip him, just as you did to the getaway driver.

Quickly press Ⓐ again to cuff the robber. Way to go!

⭐ OBJECTIVE: LOCATE THE LAST ROBBER

The third and final clown crook has been spotted near the docks. Press L to blow your whistle and stop a passing vehicle, then hop in and follow the green studs to reach the docks. Park inside the glowing objective beacon, and Chase will spy a nearby scan spot.

Jump up the crates to reach the scan spot. Use Criminal Scan mode again to search the docks for the hiding robber.

The communicator reveals that the robber is hiding aboard a large cargo ship. However, the pier's gate is closed—approach the gate to speak with a friendly dockworker who needs help opening the gate.

The dockworker drives his forklift over to a nearby building. Follow him and then jump onto the forklift, which will lift you to the building's roof. Smash the clutter on the roof to unblock a door, then go inside.

Pull the lever inside the building to open the pier's gate. Well, that was easy!

Boarding the Cargo Ship

Now you just need to get onto that cargo ship. Another dockworker will help you—after you help him first by retrieving his lost sandwich.

Go to the nearby scan spot and use your communicator to follow a seagull's waddling footprints. Sure enough, the footprints lead to the thieving seagull.

Pick up the sandwich and bring it back to the dockworker.

Hand the worker his "sammich," and he'll order the crane operator to lower a lift. Chase steps onto the lift and is quickly hoisted onto the cargo ship.

Open the doors on the cargo ship to discover the hiding robber. Pursue the crooked clown through the ship, then jump into the water and chase him up some stairs. Keep at it until you finally manage to apprehend the thief. Case closed!

INTRODUCTION

POLICE ACADEMY

CHARACTERS AND VEHICLES

WALKTHROUGH

LEGO CITY TOUR

CHECKLISTS

CHAPTER 2: BLAST FROM THE PAST

IT'S HIS VERY FIRST DAY BACK IN LEGO CITY, AND CHASE MCCAIN HAS ALREADY MANAGED TO APPREHEND A TRIO OF BANK ROBBERS. THIS HASN'T BROUGHT OUR HERO ANY CLOSER TO REX FURY, BUT IT HAS PROVEN THAT CHASE HASN'T LOST HIS CRIME-FIGHTING SKILLS! BUT BEFORE CHASE CAN PUT THOSE SKILLS TO GOOD USE AGAIN, HE GETS A CALL FROM CHIEF DUNBY, WHO ORDERS CHASE TO ORGANIZE A ROADBLOCK.

CITY EXPLORATION

⭐ OBJECTIVE: GO TO THE ROADBLOCK

Commandeer a vehicle and follow the green studs to reach the nearby Auburn Bay Bridge. Chase arrives just in time to organize a roadblock—and to see his former sweetheart, Natalia, speed by in a sports car!

⭐ OBJECTIVE: BUILD A CALL-IN POINT

After an emotional chat with Natalia, Chase receives new orders. Head down the hill to reach a gas station, and move into the objective beacon to advance the plot.

After you repair all four pumps, the owner gladly hands Chase a rare superbrick. These special goodies give you many more bricks than you'd receive just by smashing up random LEGO objects and are vital when you need lots of bricks to build something—like the nearby call-in point!

The gas station's owner needs help: His station's pumps have all broken! Fix all four of the broken pumps by approaching them and holding Ⓐ to build their bouncing LEGO bricks.

Collect the superbrick, then use the nearby scan spot to follow some footprints over to a bin that contains another superbrick. This should give you plenty of bricks to build the call-in point (you need 8,000 bricks).

INTRODUCTION

POLICE ACADEMY

CHARACTERS AND VEHICLES

WALKTHROUGH

LEGO CITY TOUR

CHECKLISTS

TIP

Run around and smash objects if you need more bricks.

Move onto the large superbuild pad near the gas station—this is where you can build the call-in point. Press Ⓐ to spend 8,000 bricks and build the call-in point. Now you can use this station to request any of the vehicles that you've unlocked!

NOTE

Large structures built from bricks, such as call-in points, are known as superbuilds. Each time you assemble a superbuild in LEGO City, you earn a gold brick! There are many other ways of earning gold bricks in LEGO City—see the "LEGO City Tour" chapter for complete details on the city's many secrets and collectibles.

Completing superbuilds often unlocks vehicle or character tokens. Building this call-in point has earned you the Trooper vehicle token. The next time you visit the police station, you'll be able to purchase the Trooper vehicle!

Now that you've built the call-in point, use it to request a new vehicle. Right now, the only one you can call for is the Squaddie. Use your GamePad to select the Squaddie, and it will be instantly delivered to the call-in point. Cool!

⭐ OBJECTIVE: GET THE GRAPPLE GUN

You receive new orders after your Squaddie arrives: Robbers have barricaded themselves atop some tall buildings, but you need a special tool to reach them. Hop into the Squaddie and motor off to Sheriff Huckleberry's office. It's a bit of a drive, so don't hesitate to use those turbos!

Sheriff Huckleberry runs a smaller police station on the outskirts of town. He hands Chase a shiny new grapple gun, which is sure to come in handy!

⭐ OBJECTIVE: GO TO JENNY'S BURGER BAR

Armed with the grapple gun, Chase is ready to go after those robbers. Return to your Squaddie and head to Jenny's Burger Bar—the robbers are hiding on a nearby rooftop.

Next, grapple the ladder above the drive-through and then move backward to pull it down. Now you can climb even higher!

The burger-shaped roof of Jenny's Burger Bar makes a perfect spot to scan for the robbers. Exit your vehicle and use your newfound grapple gun to climb to the Burger Bar's roof. Simply press Ⓐ to latch on to the grapple point above the drive-through and zip upward.

Stand on the scan spot you find atop Jenny's Burger Bar, and use your GamePad to scan the two tall buildings across the street. Keep searching until you locate the robbers atop the building on the right.

⭐ OBJECTIVE: GET TO THE LEGO CITY TV BUILDING

You've found the robbers—now you just need to apprehend them. Drop from the Burger Bar and cross the street, then use the left building's grapple point to begin your ascent.

Use the grapple gun three times to climb up to an objective beacon. Step into the beacon to begin your rooftop pursuit.

INTRODUCTION

POLICE ACADEMY

CHARACTERS AND VEHICLES

WALKTHROUGH

LEGO CITY TOUR

CHECKLISTS

SPECIAL ASSIGNMENT 1: SOME ASSAULTS

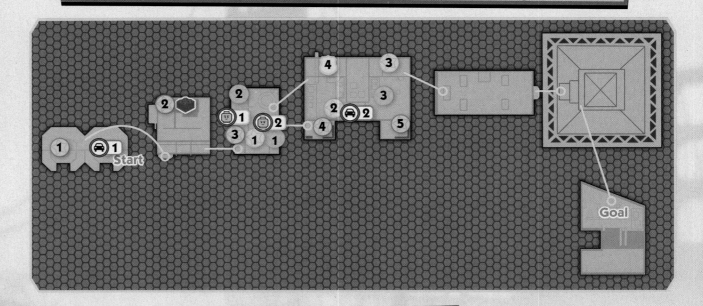

STAGE COLLECTIBLES: "SOME ASSAULTS"

MAP ICON(S)	TYPE	MODE	NOTES	GOT IT?
1	"Bastion" vehicle token	Free Play	Use the transporter near the start to reach a color swapper. Blast the switch and then repair the fuse box.	1
1 to 5	Police Shield Piece 1	Free Play	Find and water five planters around the rooftops. Some can only be reached during Free Play.	2
	Red Brick—Fast Build	Free Play	Astronaut boost up to a higher roof, build three solar panels to power a fan, float up to the brick.	3
1 to 3	Police Shield Piece 2	Story	Build three antennas around the rooftops.	4
1 to 3	Police Shield Piece 3	Free Play	Fix three satellite dishes around the rooftops as the Construction Worker.	5
1	"Snakes Squealer" character token	Free Play	Chop through the door after arresting the second robber and crack the safe beyond.	6
2	"Conrad Peters" character token	Free Play	Drill the shaky ground, build the RC car, and use it to collect the token in the cage.	7
4	Police Shield Piece 4	Story	Earned automatically when you arrest the third robber.	8
2	"Broadcaster" vehicle token	Free Play	Obtain dynamite from the space crate, destroy the silver skylight, and drop through.	9

LEGO CITY HERO STUD REQUIREMENT:

90,000

NOTE

Special Assignments serve as the missions in *LEGO City Undercover*. They have their own maps, and all of the collectibles you find during these missions are considered separate from the ones you find in the city. Like other LEGO games, you're shown a breakdown of your accomplishments after you complete each Special Assignment mission. After you beat a Special Assignment, you can revisit it in Free Play simply by returning to its starting point in the city. Revisit Special Assignments in Free Play to discover all of their hidden goodies!

⭐ OBJECTIVE: REACH THE OTHER BUILDING

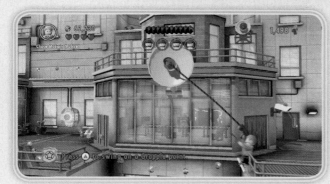

Your grapple gun's about to get a workout in this Special Assignment. Latch on to the first two overhead grapple points and swing across two wide gaps on your way across the balcony. Jump at the end of each swing to ensure you clear the gaps.

FREE PLAY
VEHICLE TOKEN 1: BASTION

During Free Play, swing across the first gap and then toggle to the astronaut disguise. Use a transporter pad to beam up to a higher rooftop you couldn't otherwise reach.

Switch to the robber disguise and pry open a door after transporting. Use the color swapper in the small room beyond to fill your color gun with green energy.

Travel back through the transporters and blast the red switch on the background wall with green energy. This opens two nearby doors.

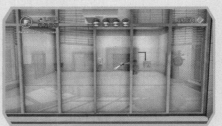

Enter the door on the right and repair the fuse box in the small room beyond. This opens the elevator, exposing a vehicle token!

INTRODUCTION

POLICE ACADEMY

CHARACTERS AND VEHICLES

WALKTHROUGH

LEGO CITY TOUR

CHECKLISTS

FREE PLAY
POLICE SHIELD PIECE 1

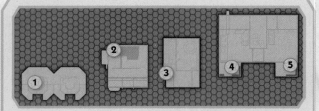

Find and water five planters around the rooftops to score a shield piece. The first one is hidden in the room

to the left of the transporter pad, which you can open only during Free Play. See the previous "Vehicle Token 1: Bastion" Free Play sidebar for details on how to open this room. Check the maps to see where all five planters are found.

Use another grapple point to zip up to the balcony, then jump onto the thin white and blue ledge to the right. Chase automatically performs a wall hug when he stands on thin ledges like this. Inch over to the next balcony on the right.

Snare the next grapple point, then move backward to pull down an overhead object. The object smashes into LEGO bricks; build them into a trampoline, then bounce up to the next balcony.

Smash the highest balcony's patio furniture, then build the bricks into a special object called a catapult pad. Run onto the catapult pad, and it will send you flying over to the neighboring building. Wahoo!

⭐ OBJECTIVE: ARREST THE FIRST ROBBER

The robbers flee when Chase lands on their building. You've got to catch them! Climb the nearby blue drainpipe to begin your pursuit.

Chase gets a chance to show off his acrobatic skills during his rooftop pursuit. Run to the right, and press Ⓑ each time you near a vent that's covered with blue and white LEGOs. Chase will either vault the vent or slide underneath it, without skipping a beat!

FREE PLAY
RED BRICK: FAST BUILD

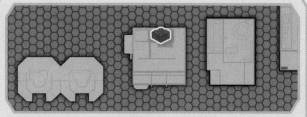

Jump up the blue and white handholds beyond the balance beam to reach a higher balcony. Chase catches up to the first robber here.

Press Ⓧ to toss him to the ground, then quickly press Ⓐ to arrest him while he's down.

During Free Play, toggle to the astronaut disguise and jump onto the blue and white LEGO vents, rather than vaulting them. Then boost up to the rooftop.

Smash three air conditioners on the rooftop, then build their bricks into three solar panels. This powers a nearby generator, which starts up a floor fan.

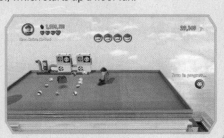

Jump into the fan's updraft, and it will blow you up to a higher roof, where this stage's red brick sits.

POLICE SHIELD PIECE 2

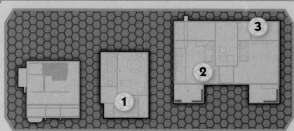

After arresting the first robber, smash a nearby pink cart to discover some bricks that you can assemble into an antenna. Find and build two more antennas around the rooftops to earn a shield piece! Check the maps to see where the antennas are located.

FREE PLAY
POLICE SHIELD PIECE 3

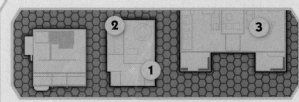

Run straight across the blue balance beam that follows. If you keep falling, try slowly stepping onto the beam first, then start running after Chase finds his balance.

After arresting the first robber, jump the railing to the right and land on a lower rooftop below. Switch to the construction worker disguise and fix a fuse box down here to activate a satellite dish. Find and repair two more satellites around the rooftops to score a shield piece! Check the maps to see where the satellites stand.

INTRODUCTION

POLICE ACADEMY

CHARACTERS AND VEHICLES

WALKTHROUGH

LEGO CITY TOUR

CHECKLISTS

FREE PLAY
CHARACTER TOKEN 1: SNAKES SQUEALER

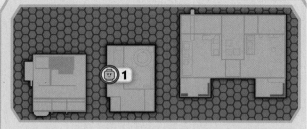

Chop through the boarded door on the rooftop where you find the first robber, then crack the safe in the small room beyond to discover this stage's first character token.

⭐ OBJECTIVE: ARREST THE SECOND ROBBER

After arresting the first robber, climb the nearby blue and white wall to reach the rooftop. Run to the right and jump onto a tightrope, and you'll slide over to the next building.

FREE PLAY
CHARACTER TOKEN 2: CONRAD PETERS

Before sliding down the tightrope, toggle to the construction worker and drill the shaky ground on the roof above the blue and white climbable wall. This uncorks a water geyser that boosts you up onto the nearby water tower.

Pull the water tower's lever to make some bricks spill out onto the roof. Drop and build these into an RC car.

Jump onto the nearby cage and stand on the action symbol. Press Ⓐ to take control of the RC car, then drive it into the cage's small opening. Use the RC car to collect the character token inside the cage.

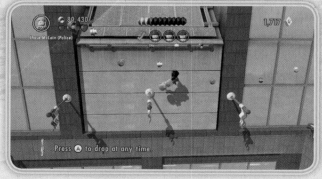

Chase must swing from a series of blue and white flagpoles to advance. Just keep swinging and leaping between the flagpoles until you reach the far balcony. Grab the handhold on the balcony's edge, then jump up to solid ground.

Next, climb some vines to reach a small balcony. Climb the nearby blue and white drainpipe to reach the building's roof.

Run to the left to locate a wall runway. These are similar to catapult pads, except they make Chase perform a wall-run instead of simply thrusting him through the air. Step onto the wall runway, and watch as Chase deftly sprints across the wall of the building!

The second robber makes his stand on the roof beyond the wall runway. Throw him to the ground as you did before, then slap on the cuffs to bring him to justice.

⭐ ARREST THE THIRD ROBBER

You're doing great! Run toward the background and jump between the blue and white walls to wall-jump up to a higher roof.

All right, you've already caught the third robber! These guys must be getting tired from running. Make the arrest, then begin your pursuit of the robber leader.

POLICE SHIELD PIECE 4

Arresting the third robber earns you this stage's final shield piece. Easy enough!

FREE PLAY
VEHICLE TOKEN 2: BROADCASTER

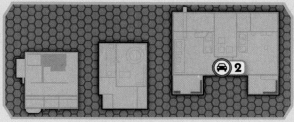

After busting the third robber, slide under the vent to the left and open the space crate to beam in some dynamite.

Carry the dynamite over to the right. Instead of skipping across the thin poles, drop to the lower roof to discover a silver skylight. Blast this to bits with the dynamite, then drop through the hole.

You land in a small office, where a vehicle token sits. Score!

INTRODUCTION

POLICE ACADEMY

CHARACTERS AND VEHICLES

WALKTHROUGH

LEGO CITY TOUR

CHECKLISTS

⭐ ARREST THE ROBBER LEADER

After arresting the third robber, notice a pair of thin poles to the right. Chase can hop across poles like these with ease! Just jump onto the first pole, then jump again to land on the second. Make one last leap to reach the far roof.

Vault the blue and white vent beyond the thin poles, and you'll land near the robber leader. The crook isn't about to be caught so easily, though, and quickly slides down a tightrope. Hurry after him!

The tightrope leads to a building with a steep, sloped roof. Just keep pressing the Jump button to run up the roof without slipping. Take a breather on one of the flat areas if you like.

Jump up the handholds that stick out from the next building. You soon catch up to the robber leader, but he flees yet again by hoisting himself up in a lift. Use your grapple gun again to zip upward and continue this epic pursuit!

Use a catapult pad to soar over to a foreground building. At last, Chase catches up to the robber leader, who misjudged his jump and is clinging desperately to the roof's edge. Chase takes the opportunity to question the crook before reaching down to save his life.

Slide down the roof's other side to catch up to the robber leader. Again, the crook flees—but not before he destroys the balance beam he used to reach the next building. Fortunately, a news helicopter flies up between the buildings. Latch on to the chopper's grapple point and swing across!

NOTE

Congratulations, you've beaten your first Special Assignment! Free Play for this mission is now unlocked, meaning you can revisit the mission at any time and play through it again with Chase's advanced skills and abilities. After you've beaten all of Story mode, return to Special Assignments and seek out their hidden Free Play goodies! Simply scan the GamePad map for replay level icons, then travel to each one to revisit the missions.

You've unlocked free running! Keep an eye out for blue and white LEGO objects in the city, and perform free run moves to access new areas.

INTRODUCTION

POLICE ACADEMY

CHARACTERS AND VEHICLES

WALKTHROUGH

LEGO CITY TOUR

CHECKLISTS

CHAPTER 3: GO DIRECTLY TO JAIL

AT LAST, CHASE MCCAIN HAS UNCOVERED A LEAD IN THE REX FURY CASE. THE GANG OF ROBBERS THAT CHASE RECENTLY BUSTED HAD BEEN WORKING FOR REX, AND ALTHOUGH THEY DON'T KNOW WHERE TO FIND FURY, THEY'VE POINTED CHASE IN THE DIRECTION OF ALBATROSS PRISON. REX WAS IMPRISONED AT ALBATROSS FOR YEARS, AND THE ROBBERS BELIEVE THAT AN INMATE NAMED BLUE MAY KNOW MORE ABOUT FURY'S WHEREABOUTS.

CITY EXPLORATION

⭐ OBJECTIVE: FIND A WAY TO ALBATROSS PRISON ISLAND

Albatross Prison is built on an island, and getting there won't be easy. Chase wishes to keep his investigation private from Chief Dunby, so he must find a covert means of reaching the island.

Commandeer a vehicle and drive to the police station. Don't enter the building; instead, sneak around the back and smash a blue and white Dumpster to discover some LEGO bricks. Use these to add a blue and white bar to the nearby fence so that you may vault it and reach the pier behind the station.

Chase chats with a ship captain on the pier and learns that the ferry to Albatross Island has sunk. Guess you'll just have to build a new one!

Building a ferry will cost 15,000 bricks! Fortunately, Ellie updates your communicator with an all-new data scan function. Now you can use the communicator to search for nearby collectibles—including superbricks!

Tap the data scan icon on your GamePad to fire up Data Scan mode. Hold your Wii U GamePad up to the TV screen afterward, then look around for items of interest. There are four attainable superbricks in your vicinity. Focus on one to lock it in, and an icon will appear on the GamePad map, revealing its location. A handy marker will also appear on your TV screen to help you track it down. Nice!

Superbrick 1

This superbrick is an easy grab—just climb up the nearby police booth and collect it.

Superbrick 2

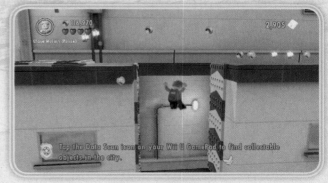

Run toward the police station and jump between the blue and white walls to reach the upper ledge.

Use a wall runway to dash over to a handhold, then climb the blue and white LEGO patch on the side of the police station to reach the superbrick floating atop the "Police" sign.

Superbrick 3

Smash the small blue drum near the elevated train track's steel supports. Build the remaining bricks into a handhold, then climb up.

Jump and grab the overhead LEGO patch above the handholds, then shimmy over to the roof of the nearby garage.

Run to the left, across the garage's roof, and slide under the blue steel tower to reach the superbrick.

Superbrick 4

After collecting the third superbrick, slide back out from the tower and climb up the ladder to reach the tower's top. A large superbrick floats just above the tower. Score!

Building the Ferry

You should now have enough superbricks to build the ferry. Run to the superbuild near the pier and press Ⓐ to spend 15,000 bricks and build the ferry. This one simple act scores you two gold bricks—one for completing the superbuild and another for activating one of LEGO City's three ferry routes!

After building the ferry, use the nearby ticket machine to travel to Albatross Prison Island. Use your GamePad to confirm your destination and set sail.

INTRODUCTION

POLICE ACADEMY

CHARACTERS AND VEHICLES

WALKTHROUGH

LEGO CITY TOUR

CHECKLISTS

⭐ OBJECTIVE: TALK TO BLUE IN THE PRISON YARD

You've reached Albatross Prison. Now you just need to track down Blue. Begin your infiltration of the prison by smashing the brown crate near the guard tower to discover a box of LEGO bricks.

Carry the box to the nearby green pad, then set it down. Build the LEGO bricks to add a bar to the top of the fence, then vault over.

Exit the building and pass through the gate. Turn left and smash a Dumpster to discover some LEGO bricks. Build them into a blue and white wall.

Jump between the blue and white walls to climb to a steep slope. Tap Ⓑ to sprint up the slope without slipping backward.

Smash another brown crate on the fence's other side to discover a scan spot. Use Detective Scan to follow a trail of footprints over to a pile of debris. Search the debris to discover a key.

Jump onto the thin ledge above the slope, then inch your way around. Look for a bar running along the top of the fence, and vault it.

Collect the key, then backtrack a bit and use it to open the nearby door. Use the control panel inside the building to open the gate.

Use the grapple gun to zip up to a grapple point beyond the fence. Slide beneath the blue and white LEGOs to reach a superbrick, then slide back under and head to the right, around the rampart.

Use the grapple gun again to zip to the top of the guard tower at the rampart's end. Leap to the nearby pole, then slide down to at last reach the prison yard.

Closed Court

Use the yard's exercise equipment if you like, then approach the pair of inmates near the basketball court. They agree to let Chase into the court, but only if he first retrieves a basketball that some bullies stole.

Run toward the background wall and climb up to a thin ledge. Drop from the ledge to land on the other side of the fence.

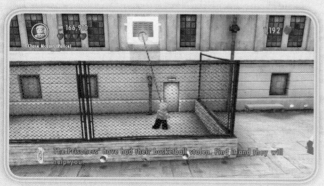

Use the grapple gun to pull down an air conditioner, which shatters into LEGO bricks. Build these into a catapult pad, then use the pad to soar over to the right. Drop into a lower area and confront the bullies who stole the basketball.

The bullies aren't interested in sharing their ball, so you'll have to "persuade" them. Throw them around and slap handcuffs on them while they're down. Subdue all of the bullies and then claim the basketball.

Hurry back to the two inmates by the basketball court. Hand them the ball, and they'll open the court's gate. Run over to the inmate in the blue hat—that's got to be Blue!

Blue isn't sure how Rex Fury managed to escape the prison, but he agrees to help Chase find out. Blue tells Chase to get some gear from his cell; then he'll call him on his communicator with more information.

OBJECTIVE: ENTER THE PRISON CELL BLOCK

Speaking with Blue turned out to be very beneficial. Now you just need to raid Blue's cell and find the gear he mentioned. Leave the basketball court and move to the nearby objective beacon to enter the prison and begin your search for clues.

INTRODUCTION

POLICE ACADEMY

CHARACTERS AND VEHICLES

WALKTHROUGH

LEGO CITY TOUR

CHECKLISTS

 SPECIAL ASSIGNMENT 2: TROUBLE IN STIR

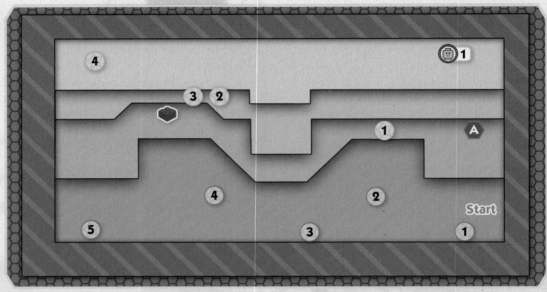

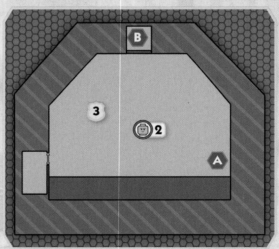

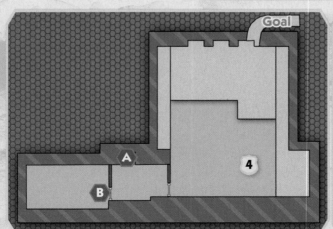

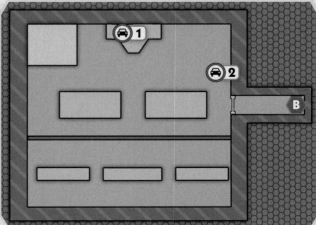

STAGE COLLECTIBLES: "TROUBLE IN STIR"

MAP ICON(S)	TYPE	MODE	NOTES	GOT IT?
1 to 5	Police Shield Piece 1	Free Play	Douse five barrel fires around the prison's ground floor.	1
⬢	Red Brick	Story	After climbing up to the second floor, pry open a cell and then smash through its left wall.	2
1 to 4	Police Shield Piece 2	Free Play	Destroy four piles of contraband inside the prison cells. Free Play skills are needed to reach some of them.	3
👤1	"Blue Whittaker" character token	Free Play	Fix the elevator fuse box and climb up to the fourth floor. Find dynamite in the kitchen and blast open the storage area.	4
3	Police Shield Piece 3	Story	Ride the mechanical bull inside the warden's office.	5
👤2	"Prisoner" character token	Story	Smash the desk on the right, then follow the footprints to discover the token in the warden's desk.	6
🚗1	"Rino" vehicle token	Free Play	Break into the workshop with the fire axe, build the RC car, use it to open the background cage, collect the valve wheel, and open the furnace doors.	7
🚗2	"Segway" vehicle token	Free Play	Break into the workshop with the fire axe, smash the background cabinet, crack the wall safe, blast the silver sink with dynamite, and ride the water geyser.	8
4	Police Shield Piece 4	Story	Use the bench press in Rex's cell, then smash the nearby furniture and build a drum set. Play the drums.	9

LEGO CITY HERO STUD REQUIREMENT: 63,000

⭐ OBJECTIVE: SUBDUE THE INMATES

Chase arrives just in time to witness Albatross's inmates going berserk in the cell block. You've got to subdue those prisoners!

Run around the cell block's ground floor and beat up six escaped prisoners. Slap handcuffs on each inmate to subdue them.

Happy to have order restored, the prison guard gladly unlocks Blue's cell, granting Chase access to a locker. Enter the cell and open the locker to discover the Chase McCain (Robber) outfit!

FREE PLAY
POLICE SHIELD PIECE 1

Use the fireman disguise's extinguisher to douse five barrel fires around the prison's ground floor, and you'll rescue a sizzling shield piece!

INTRODUCTION

POLICE ACADEMY

CHARACTERS AND VEHICLES

WALKTHROUGH

LEGO CITY TOUR

CHECKLISTS

⭐ OBJECTIVE: ENTER THE WARDEN'S OFFICE

Now that you've found the robber disguise, you can explore much more of the prison. Run to the left and look for a cell with a crowbar symbol in front of it. Switch to the Chase McCain (Robber) outfit, then stand on the crowbar symbol and rapidly press Ⓐ to pry open the cell's door.

Nice work! Now smash the crate inside the cell to discover some LEGO bricks. Build these into a climbable wall, then head up to the prison's second floor.

RED BRICK: STUDS X2

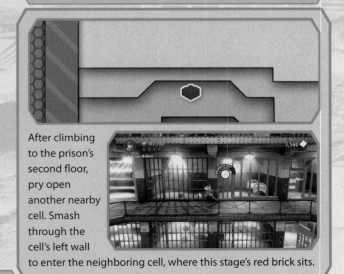

After climbing to the prison's second floor, pry open another nearby cell. Smash through the cell's left wall to enter the neighboring cell, where this stage's red brick sits.

On the second floor, go right and smash a cart to discover a scan spot. Press Ⓩⓛ to toggle back to the Chase McCain (Police Officer) outfit so you may use Detective Scan mode. Follow the trail of footprints to a nearby cabinet, inside which you discover a key.

Use the key to unlock the nearby cell. Enter and smash the cell's right wall to reach the neighboring cell. Exit the cell and carefully cross the blue balance beam to reach the second floor's right side.

TIP

Walk slowly onto balance beams at first, then sprint across after Chase finds his balance.

FREE PLAY
POLICE SHIELD PIECE 2

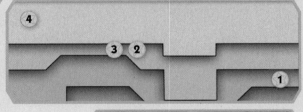

Chop through the boarded door beyond the balance beam to enter a cell. Smash through the cell's left wall to enter the neighboring cell, then destroy a pile of contraband in the corner. Find and destroy four contraband piles in these prison cells to receive a shield piece! The maps show where each contraband pile is located—you'll need to visit the fourth floor to reach some of them.

Run to the right to discover another crowbar symbol near a cell. Press ZR to change back into the robber disguise, then pry open the cell with the crowbar. Enter and stand on the stethoscope symbol near the safe. Press Ⓐ to begin cracking the safe. When the dial's red light turns green, press Ⓐ again to open the safe.

Good job! Collect the key card you discover inside the safe, then backtrack to the second floor's left side. Insert the key card into the far-left machine to open the nearby cell. Use the control panel inside the cell to shut off the neighboring cell's electric fence.

Enter the neighboring cell that was previously blocked by the electric fence, then change into the police officer outfit. Now you can use Chase's grapple gun to zip up to the third floor!

FREE PLAY
CHARACTER TOKEN 1: BLUE WHITTAKER

Go right after climbing up to the third floor, then use the construction worker disguise to fix the fuse box. This opens the nearby elevator. Climb the chain to reach the fourth floor.

Go right and smash up the kitchen until you discover a scan spot. Follow the footprints to the oven, inside which you discover some dynamite.

Use the dynamite to blast the silver bars to the right. Now you can collect the character token in the storage area beyond!

INTRODUCTION

POLICE ACADEMY

CHARACTERS AND VEHICLES

WALKTHROUGH

LEGO CITY TOUR

CHECKLISTS

Look out! Deactivating the electric fence has also shut off all of the cells' magnetic locks, freeing the rest of the inmates. Subdue them as you explore the third floor, and use the robber outfit's crowbar again to pry open another cell.

Smash three walls to pass through the third floor's cells and reach its right side. Smash the red cabinet near the door to the warden's office, then build the remaining LEGO bricks into a control panel. Activate the panel to open the warden's office.

⭐ OBJECTIVE: SEARCH THE WARDEN'S OFFICE FOR CLUES

The warden strolls into the bathroom just as Chase slips into his office. Change into the police officer outfit and use the grapple gun to yank down the overhead chandelier. Build the chandelier's bricks to create a powerful lock that seals the warden in the bathroom. Now you can search his office unhindered!

CHARACTER TOKEN 2: PRISONER

Smash the desk on the right side of the warden's office to discover a scan spot. Trace the footprints to the warden's desk, then open the drawer and grab a character token!

POLICE SHIELD PIECE 3

Ride the mechanical bull inside the warden's office to rope up another shield piece. Simply press the appropriate buttons as they move past the indicator to avoid being bucked off.

Switch to the robber disguise and use the stethoscope to crack the safe near the bathroom door. Out pops the warden's prized record!

Pick up the record and place it onto the player on the right. Chase cranks up the volume, and the background speakers explode, revealing some bouncing LEGO bricks!

You know what to do! Build those bouncing bricks into a control panel, then use the panel to uncover a secret elevator behind the warden's portrait. Sneaky!

⭐ OBJECTIVE: INVESTIGATE REX'S CELL

Great work—you've discovered Rex Fury's private cell! Who says crime doesn't pay? Use the robber disguise's crowbar to pry open the cell door.

FREE PLAY
VEHICLE TOKEN 1: RINO

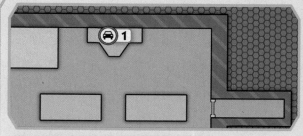

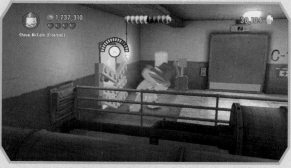

Before breaking into Rex's cell, chop through the boarded door on the left to enter the prison's workshop.

Smash the crate that sits atop one of the workshop's long tables to discover some bricks. Build these into an RC car.

Stand on the action symbol and take control of the RC car. Drive it through the small opening in the background cage and park it atop the red button to open the cage's door.

Enter the cage and collect a valve wheel. Place this onto the notch to the right, then turn the wheel to open the nearby doors, exposing a vehicle token! Extinguish the flames around the token before you try to grab it.

INTRODUCTION

POLICE ACADEMY

CHARACTERS AND VEHICLES

WALKTHROUGH

LEGO CITY TOUR

CHECKLISTS

FREE PLAY
VEHICLE TOKEN 2: SEGWAY

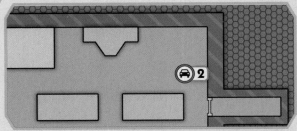

Inside the prison's workshop, smash a background cabinet to discover a wall safe. Crack this to obtain some dynamite.

Use the dynamite to destroy the silver sink on the right, and a jet of water will spout up. Jump into the water jet; it boosts you up to a hovering vehicle token!

Subdue the goons inside Rex's cell, then change into the police officer disguise and use the grapple gun to pull apart the hot tub. (Hot tub?!) Jump onto the red button inside the tub, and one of the three lights on the background wall will shut off. Intriguing!

Run to the foreground and use the punching bag. Rapidly tap Ⓐ to punch the bag until it explodes, exposing another button. Step on the button to shut off another light.

POLICE SHIELD PIECE 4

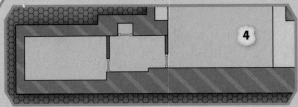

Use the bench press inside Rex's cell, then smash the nearby furniture to discover some LEGO bricks. Build these into a drum set, then play the drums to earn a rockin' shield piece!

The Last Button

Just one more button to find! Smash the cell's toilet to make a geyser gush upward. Jump into the geyser to reach a high ledge.

Shimmy across the LEGO patch on the ceiling to reach the opposite ledge, then smash some machinery to discover a scan spot. Use this to trace a trail of footprints toward a cabinet.

Open the cabinet, and LEGO bricks will tumble out. Build these into the final button, then step on it to shut off the last light. This opens a secret passage in the background wall.

So this is how Rex made his escape! Jump into the secret passage to see where it leads.

CITY EXPLORATION

INTRODUCTION

POLICE ACADEMY

CHARACTERS AND VEHICLES

WALKTHROUGH

LEGO CITY TOUR

CHECKLISTS

⭐ OBJECTIVE: GO TO CHERRY TREE STATION

The secret passage from Rex's cell lands Chase in hot water. Chief Dunby is waiting on the other side, furious over McCain's meddling. Fortunately, Chase has discovered a vital clue: a small hammer that Rex must have used to tunnel his way out of prison. A small etching on the hammer reveals that it came from the Bluebell Mine!

After your run-in with Dunby, you find yourself back at the pier near the police station. Run toward the station and vault the fence, then follow your objective marker to locate the nearby train station.

Use the ticket machine outside the station to choose a destination—in this case, the Bluebell Mine. Confirm the location on your communicator, and Chase will hop aboard the train after it arrives.

⭐ OBJECTIVE: ENTER THE MINE

It's not long before you're dropped off at the Bluebell Mine. Simply follow the objective marker to locate the mine's entrance. Unfortunately, the workers won't let any unauthorized personnel into the mine. You'll have to get rid of them!

Follow your objective marker to locate a nearby storage shed. Use the crowbar to break in, then crack the safe to discover a valve wheel.

Carry the valve wheel over to the nearby steam whistle. Place the valve wheel onto the whistle, then turn it to signal the workers that it's quittin' time. Enter the mine to begin searching for clues.

PRIMA OFFICIAL GAME GUIDE

SPECIAL ASSIGNMENT 3: MINER ALTERCATION

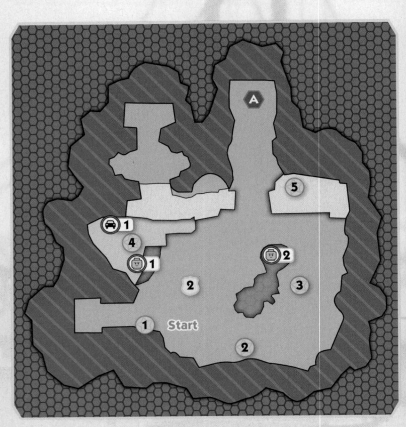

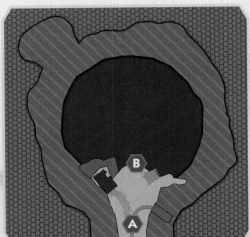

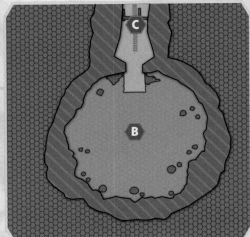

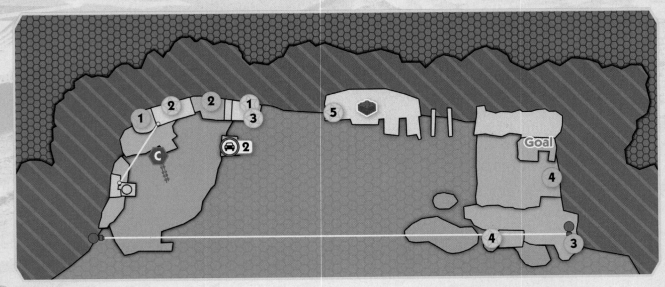

pr**i**magames.com

STAGE COLLECTIBLES: "MINER ALTERCATION"

MAP ICON(S)	TYPE	MODE	NOTES	GOT IT?
⊙1	"Ross Wilding" character token	Story	Use the grapple gun to flip over the floating pallet near the start.	1
⊙2	"Spikey Don" character token	Free Play	Repair the mobile drill's fuse box, then pry open the manhole cover.	2
⊙1	"Dumper" vehicle token	Free Play	Astronaut boost over the electrified rails, fix the fuse box, use the color swapper, backtrack out and climb the nearby ledge, blast the switch, and ride the elevator.	3
1 to 5	Police Shield Piece 1	Free Play	Douse five barrel fires around the entry cavern.	4
2	Police Shield Piece 2	Story	Use the pickax to smash the pile of boulders near the start.	5
⊙2	"Steadfast" vehicle token	Free Play	Astronaut boost on top of the elevator and get the box of bricks. Place it on the green pad and build the gears.	6
1 to 5	Police Shield Piece 3	Free Play	Destroy five gold ingots around the final mine cavern with the grapple gun or astronaut's laser.	7
1 to 4	Police Shield Piece 4	Story	Free four caged birds around the final cavern.	8
⬛	Red Brick— Unlimited Dynamite	Free Play	Chicken-glide from the final platform, then climb up to the brick.	9

LEGO CITY HERO STUD REQUIREMENT: 72,000

⭐ OBJECTIVE: FIND CLARENCE "STINKY" FLETCHER

You've infiltrated the Bluebell Mine; now you just need to locate an associate of Rex's named "Stinky." Unfortunately, some of Rex's goons have entered the mine as well, and they detonate explosives to trap you in the entry cavern. You'll need to find a way to destroy those boulders!

CHARACTER TOKEN 1: ROSS WILDING

Use the grapple gun to flip over a floating pallet on the entry cavern's left side. Jump onto the pallet and collect the character token!

INTRODUCTION

POLICE ACADEMY

CHARACTERS AND VEHICLES

WALKTHROUGH

LEGO CITY TOUR

CHECKLISTS

FREE PLAY
CHARACTER TOKEN 2: SPIKEY DON

During Free Play, toggle to the construction worker disguise and repair the fuse box on the side of the mobile drill near the cavern's center. This starts up the drill and causes the nearby pool to drain.

With the water gone, a manhole is exposed. Pry open the manhole to discover a character token!

FREE PLAY
VEHICLE TOKEN 1: DUMPER

Use the astronaut disguise's jet pack to boost over the electrified rails in the cavern's background. After you land, pull a lever to shut off the electricity so you can safely return later.

Repair the fuse box beyond the rails to power the nearby color swapper. Use this to fill the robber's color gun with green energy.

Backtrack across the rails and go left to locate a wall with a blue and white LEGO patch. Climb up to a ledge, then jump over to the other nearby ledge with the handhold. Blast the red switch on this ledge with green energy to activate the elevator below you.

Drop from the ledge and step onto the elevator. This lifts you up to a vehicle token. Nice!

FREE PLAY
POLICE SHIELD PIECE 1

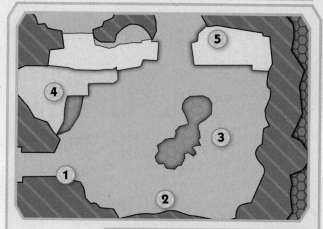

Douse five barrel fires around the first mine cavern with the fireman's extinguisher to score a shield piece! Check the maps to see where the five barrel fires are located.

Climb up the blue and white wall beyond the stairs, then use the grapple gun to swing over to the right.

Smash some blue and white equipment to discover some bricks, then build a catapult pad. Use the pad to soar over to a shed.

Break into the shed, then open the locker within to discover the Chase McCain (Miner) disguise. Nice!

Locating the Miner Disguise

Crowbar the background door to access a fenced-off area that contains a lever. Pull this to make a bunch of bricks fall down from above.

Build the bricks into a crate, then shove the crate all the way to the left along the checkered tiles. Now you can jump from the crate to reach the broken wooden stairs above!

Unblocking the Mine Tunnel

The miner disguise grants Chase the use of a powerful pickax. Swing the ax at the boulders outside the shed to destroy them and expose a hole in the fence. Slip through the hole and drop down to the cavern's ground level.

> **TIP**
>
> Jump and then attack with the pickax in midair. You'll slam the ground and destroy whole piles of boulders!

INTRODUCTION

POLICE ACADEMY

CHARACTERS AND VEHICLES

WALKTHROUGH

LEGO CITY TOUR

CHECKLISTS

Destroy more boulders on the ground level to discover a lever handle. Insert this into a nearby switch, then pull the lever to make more bricks fall from above.

POLICE SHIELD PIECE 2

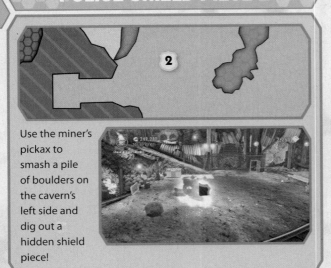

Use the miner's pickax to smash a pile of boulders on the cavern's left side and dig out a hidden shield piece!

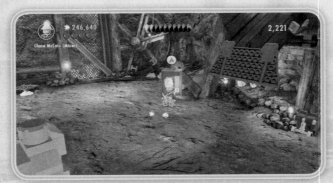

Build the bricks into a unique vending machine with a picture of dynamite on its front. Use the machine to obtain some dynamite, which Chase can pick up only while wearing his miner disguise.

Carry the dynamite over to a small barrel near a blocked mechanism. Place the dynamite in the barrel, then run away before it goes *boom*!

NOTE

Sparkling silver LEGO objects can be destroyed only by dynamite. Keep an eye out for them!

The dynamite destroys the silver obstruction and unblocks the mechanism. This causes a large crane to drop a pile of bricks near the mine cart track. Head over and build the bricks to repair the track.

Nice work! Now simply shove the mine cart, which is loaded with dynamite, along the track. It destroys the pile of boulders ahead, unblocking the mine tunnel. Unfortunately, it also frees a couple of enemy goons! Subdue the goons, then stroll into the mine tunnel to reach the next area.

One Long Drop

More thugs await in the next cavern. Beat them up, then use the nearby dispenser to obtain more dynamite. Place the dynamite in the small barrel near the silver outhouse.

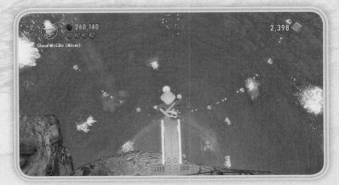

The outhouse erupts into a pile of bouncing bricks. Build these into a diving board, then step to the edge. Take a deep breath and then make a daring leap into the giant mine shaft!

Wahoo! The mine shaft is ridiculously deep, and Chase just keeps falling. Avoid obstacles and try to pass through the rings of studs as you plummet. You'll collect all the studs when you pass through the rings!

TIP

Press Ⓐ to slow down and Ⓑ to speed up as you fall.

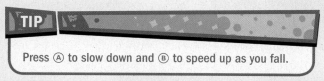

Eventually, Chase will deploy a parachute to slow his descent. (Now that's planning ahead!) Try passing through the last few stud rings before splashing down in the water, then climb a ladder to reach solid ground.

Use the pickax to smash through the pile of boulders that block the next mine tunnel, and head through to the next area. Stinky can't be far!

Cable Car Construction

To progress farther into the mine, you must build a cable car. This will cost you 22,000 bricks, but never fear—there are superbricks nearby!

Superbrick 1

The first superbrick is easy to find—just pry open the door of the red storage shed to the right. Head inside and claim it.

FREE PLAY
VEHICLE TOKEN 2: STEADFAST

After claiming the first superbrick, toggle to the astronaut disguise and boost onto the top of the elevator to the right. Collect the box of bricks you find up here, and carry them to the green pad below.

Place the box on the pad, then build the bricks to add a gear to the elevator mechanism. The elevator arrives, delivering a vehicle token to you.

Superbrick 2

Next, smash the boulders in front of the central mine cart to discover a scan spot. Follow the footprints to a pile of debris, then clear away the debris to discover some dynamite. This should come in handy!

Place the dynamite in the barrel next to the mine cart and then run!

INTRODUCTION

POLICE ACADEMY

CHARACTERS AND VEHICLES

WALKTHROUGH

LEGO CITY TOUR

CHECKLISTS

After the blast, build the remains of the mine cart into a crate, and shove the crate along the checkered floor. Jump from the crate to reach the ledge above.

Subdue the goons on the ledge, then smash the boulders on the left to discover the second superbrick.

Superbrick 3

Climb a pipe on the right to reach a higher ledge. Smash the crates up here to find more bricks, then build a catapult pad.

FREE PLAY
POLICE SHIELD PIECE 3

Before launching off the catapult pad, aim at the nearby gold ingot on the side of the cavern wall, and blast it with either the grapple gun or the astronaut's laser to wreck it. Find and destroy a total of five gold ingots around this cavern to receive a shiny shield piece! One of these ingots is located in an area that is accessible only during Free Play. Check the maps to see where to find all five ingots.

The catapult pad rockets you up to an even higher ledge. Use the grapple gun to pull down the bridge to the left.

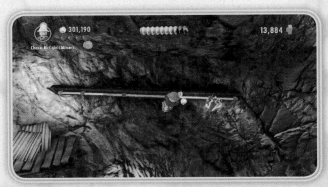

Before crossing the bridge, go right and jump onto a handhold. Shimmy to the right and collect a superbrick.

Superbrick 4

Now cross the bridge and smash a small blue drum to discover more bricks. Build these into a handhold, then jump up the handholds to climb even higher.

Smash through some boulders to reach a larger blue drum. Smash the drum to find more bricks, and build these into a balance beam. Cross the beam to discover a torch on the wall.

Quickly carry the torch back to the left, and use it to light the fuse on the ground. You've got to be quick—torches burn out after a short time.

TIP

Return to collect another torch if yours burns out.

The fuse detonates a bunch of dynamite above you, exposing a handhold. Jump up to reach a high ledge, then flip across the series of lantern poles to the right.

POLICE SHIELD PIECE 4

Before flipping across the lantern poles, jump onto the left ledge and use the crowbar to free a caged bird. Free four caged birds in this cavern to earn a shield piece! Check the maps to see where to find the four caged birds.

After flipping across the lantern poles, climb a ladder and then jump to a higher platform on the left. Climb across some blue and white LEGO patches, collecting a superbrick as you go.

Superbrick 5

The LEGO patch leads you to the cavern's highest platform. Climb a ladder and use a tightrope to slide down to a lower ledge, where a large superbrick sits. Score!

Superbrick 6

Slide down a chain to reach a lower ledge. Destroy the boulders here to discover another superbrick. You should have plenty of bricks by now!

Building the Cable Car

Drop to the ground level and run toward the foreground to find the LEGO pad where you can build the cable car. Spend 22,000 bricks to build the cable car, then step aboard to ride over to the cavern's far-right side.

The Search for Stinky

Meddlesome goons cause your cable car to crash en route to the cavern's right side. Those punks! Climb the blue and white LEGO patch on the wall, making your way up to the goons.

CAUTION

Beware the boulders that the goons drop! Wait for them to fall past before you start to climb.

Beat up the bad guys after you climb up to their ledge, then scale the background ramp to locate a shaft. Use the grapple gun to zip up the shaft.

Beware! A mechanical grinder will make short work of Chase if he falls into it. Wait for a red-hot boulder to fall into the grinder, then quickly climb the blue and white LEGO patch to scale the shaft.

Cross the conveyor belt and bust more thugs as you work your way upward. Smash a few crates here to discover some bricks and build a dynamite dispenser.

Use dynamite to destroy the nearby outhouse. Build the remaining bits into a catapult pad that delivers you to a higher ledge.

FREE PLAY
RED BRICK: UNLIMITED DYNAMITE

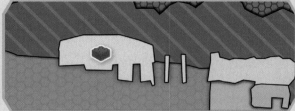

After launching off the catapult, toggle to the farmer disguise, then activate the nearby chicken symbol and glide through the rings to reach a distant platform on the left.

Beware the rolling boulders as you scale the sloping platform and ladders that follow— they've got dynamite strapped to them! Duck into background nooks to avoid the boulders as head up.

A red brick awaits you at the top of the platforms. Collect this worthy prize, then use the nearby transporter pad to beam back over to the ledge with the chicken symbol.

Run to the right and drop through a hole in the roof of the foreground shed to land near a safe. Crack the safe to discover a voice recorder left behind by none other than Clarence "Stinky" Fletcher! Discovering this tape recorder ends your mission in the mines.

INTRODUCTION

POLICE ACADEMY

CHARACTERS AND VEHICLES

WALKTHROUGH

LEGO CITY TOUR

CHECKLISTS

CHAPTER 4: WHEN THE GOING GETS TOUGH...

CHASE DIDN'T FIND CLARENCE "STINKY" FLETCHER INSIDE THE BLUEBELL MINE—ONLY A VOICE RECORDING THAT STINKY MADE. THE RECORDING REVEALS THAT STINKY WAS CAPTURED BY REX FURY'S GOONS, AND UPON LEAVING THE MINE, CHASE ENCOUNTERS NONE OTHER THAN REX FURY HIMSELF! UNFORTUNATELY, REX PROVES TOO STRONG FOR CHASE TO HANDLE, AND THE VILLAIN FLEES AFTER KNOCKING MCCAIN FOR A LOOP.

CITY EXPLORATION

OBJECTIVE: VISIT THE TEMPLE DOJO

If Chase is going to stand a chance against Rex Fury, he'll need to hone his fighting skills. Sheriff Huckleberry suggests that Chase learn kung fu and hands McCain a brochure for a nearby dojo.

Good idea! Hop into the nearby police vehicle and speed off.

Unfortunately, the bridge that leads to the temple is out. You'll need to construct a superbuild to repair it. A whopping 30,000 bricks are required to build the Serenity Bridge, so you'd better start searching for superbricks! Fire up Data Scan mode and use the GamePad to scan your surroundings in search of the following superbricks.

Large Superbrick 1

You can find several small superbricks by smashing piles of boulders near the campsite across the street, but large superbricks are far more valuable. The first large superbrick sits atop a rock formation near the campsite. To reach it, smash the pile of boulders near the cliff to discover some bricks that you can build into a large, rolling boulder.

Press Ⓧ to jump onto the boulder, then ride it over to the indicated spot near the rock formation. Now you can jump onto the rock formation!

Run around one side of the rock formation to claim a small superbrick. Next, slide down the rock formation to snag the large superbrick.

Large Superbrick 2

This superbrick is located in a nearby shack. Pry open the shack's door with the crowbar to enter and collect the superbrick.

Large Superbrick 3

This superbrick sits atop the same small shack. Smash the boulders near the shack to discover some bricks, then build the bricks into a trampoline. Bounce onto the shack's roof and collect the superbrick.

Large Superbrick 4

Cross the street and smash the objects around the patio of the restaurant near the waterfall. You'll discover small superbricks in some objects. The green bin near the blue Dumpster contains a large superbrick!

Building the Bridge

You should now have plenty of bricks. Follow your objective marker back to the superbuild and spend 30,000 bricks to construct the temple bridge. Great! Now sprint across and head up to the temple dojo.

SPECIAL ASSIGNMENT 4: KUNG FOOL

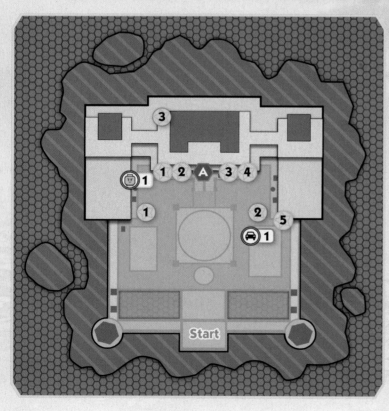

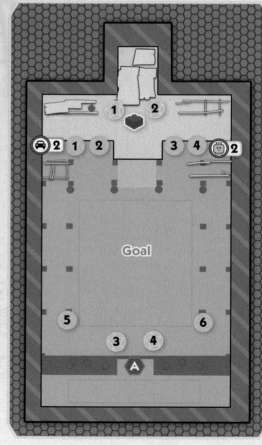

INTRODUCTION

POLICE ACADEMY

CHARACTERS AND VEHICLES

WALKTHROUGH

LEGO CITY TOUR

CHECKLISTS

STAGE COLLECTIBLES: "KUNG FOOL"

MAP ICON(S)	TYPE	MODE	NOTES	GOT IT?
1 to 3	Police Shield Piece 1	Story	Smash three lion statues around the courtyard, and build "hat stands" (training dummies) out of their bricks.	1
1 to 5	Police Shield Piece 2	Story	Shoot five red, hanging ornaments around the courtyard with the grapple gun.	2
1	"Roar" vehicle token	Free Play	Smash the courtyard's boulders, then drill the shaky ground beneath them.	3
1	"Karate Master" character token	Story	Use a torch to light the large lantern on the ground in the courtyard's left foreground corner.	4
1 to 6	Police Shield Piece 3	Free Play	Water six green planters around the dojo.	5
1 to 4	Police Shield Piece 4	Free Play	Beam up to the dojo's balcony, use the color swapper, then paint four statues around the dojo gold.	6
2	"Barry Smith" character token	Free Play	Smash the cabinets on the dojo balcony's right side to find an idol. Place the idol on the stand downstairs.	7
2	"Hairdryer" vehicle token	Free Play	Beam up to the dojo's balcony, drop to the lower foreground balcony, smash the cabinet to find dynamite, and blast the silver wall downstairs.	8
	Red Brick—Super Throw	Free Play	Spin the dojo balcony crates so that their symbols match up with the disguise portraits on the lower foreground balcony.	9

LEGO CITY HERO STUD REQUIREMENT: 42,800

⭐ OBJECTIVE: ENTER THE DOJO

You've reached the temple courtyard, but the dojo is locked tight. Looks like you'll need a key to get inside.

The key is in plain sight, held by the frozen hand of an ice sculpture. To claim the key, you must collect 40,000 bricks and build a dragon sculpture at the central superbuild pad. Lucky for you, there are several superbricks located around here!

Superbrick 1

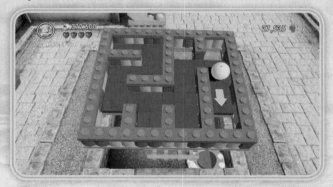

Play and win the simple maze game to the left of the superbuild. Tilt the Wii U GamePad to roll the ball over to the bottom-right corner. The ball falls on a button, causing a firework to rise from the ground nearby.

Collect the firework and place it onto one of the four drums around the superbuild. The firework blasts off and the drum explodes, revealing a superbrick!

Superbrick 2

Smash the lion statue near the ice sculpture to discover a scan spot. Follow the footprints to a pile of leaves, then sweep them away to discover another firework.

Again, place the firework into another drum to set it off and discover another superbrick. This firework flies off-course and strikes a gong, destroying it and exposing some dynamite.

POLICE SHIELD PIECE 1

Smash three more lion statues around the courtyard to discover LEGO bricks that you can build into "hat stands." (They're actually training dummies, but Chase doesn't realize this at first.) Build all three "hat stands" to score a shield piece! Check the map to see where these three special lion statues lie (one is up on the roof).

POLICE SHIELD PIECE 2

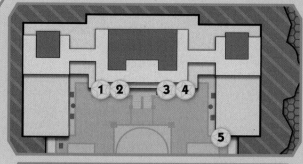

Shoot five red hanging ornaments around the courtyard to earn another shield piece. The ornaments are strung all around and are easy to miss, so hold Ⓨ to aim and fire at them. You can use the grapple gun to shoot them down.

FREE PLAY

VEHICLE TOKEN 1: ROAR

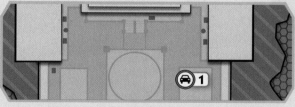

Smash the large pile of boulders on the courtyard's right side to uncover a patch of shaky ground. Switch to the construction worker and drill here to dig up a vehicle token!

Superbrick 3

Collect the dynamite after setting off the second firework, then carry it over to the blue-capped poles in the foreground. Use the dynamite to blast the tallest pole.

The dynamite knocks the tall pole down to size. Now you can jump up the poles to reach the courtyard's outer wall!

Pull down a ladder with the grappling gun, then climb to the dojo's roof. Run across the roof, smashing the ornaments near other ladders to lower them as well. This makes it easier to return to the roof if you fall.

> **TIP**
>
> Check the roof's back corners to discover valuable purple studs!

Smashing one of the roof's ornaments causes a paper lantern to rise like a hot-air balloon. Grapple the lantern after it rises, and you'll zip up to the balcony above.

Use the balcony's dragon-shaped furnace to ignite a torch. This should come in handy!

Collect the torch, then run to the right and light a pair of spinning fireworks. Light both spinners to raise a case that contains a proper firework.

Carry the firework down to the ground level and place it in another drum. The firework blasts off, leaving a superbrick behind.

CHARACTER TOKEN 1: KARATE MASTER

Use another torch to light the large paper lantern in the courtyard's left corner. The lantern floats away, leaving a character token behind!

Superbrick 4

Return to the dojo's rooftop balcony and collect another torch from the furnace. This time, run to the left and use the torch to light a pair of lanterns. This raises another case, delivering the final firework.

You know what to do! Bring that firework down to the last drum and set it off to score the final superbrick. Now you can build the dragon statue!

Claiming the Key

Spend 40,000 bricks to build the dragon in the center of the temple grounds. The dragon breathes out a burst of fire that melts the ice sculpture. Great work! Now you can collect the key.

You're all done here. Grab the key and use it to open the dojo's front door. Time to learn some kung fu!

⭐ OBJECTIVE: LEARN SELF-DEFENSE

Master Barry isn't around—you'll need to get his attention. Collect the mallet from the far altar and whack the nearby gong.

FREE PLAY
POLICE SHIELD PIECE 3

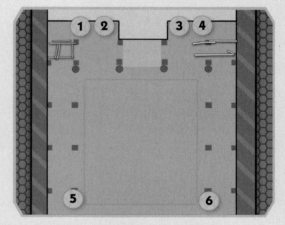

Before ringing the gong, water six blue planters around the dojo to receive a shield piece! Check the maps to see where the six planters sit.

INTRODUCTION

POLICE ACADEMY

CHARACTERS AND VEHICLES

WALKTHROUGH

LEGO CITY TOUR

CHECKLISTS

FREE PLAY
POLICE SHIELD PIECE 4

Use the transporter pad to beam up to the dojo's balcony. Smash a crate on the balcony's left side to discover some bricks that you can build into a trampoline.

Bounce off the trampoline to reach some high handholds. Flip from a flagpole to reach the background scaffolding, then climb a drainpipe.

The drainpipe leads to a color swapper. Use this to fill your color gun with gold energy.

Drop from the color swapper platform and blast the two background statues with the color gun to paint them both gold.

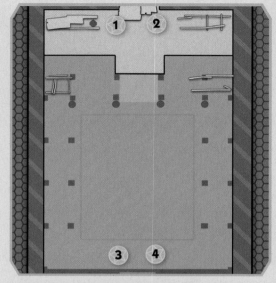

Drop to the dojo's main floor and run to the foreground to discover two more statues. Blast these as well to receive this stage's final shield piece!

FREE PLAY
CHARACTER TOKEN 2: BARRY SMITH

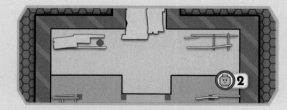

Beam back up to the dojo's balcony and smash the ornate cabinets on the right to discover a small idol.

Collect the idol and drop to the dojo's main floor. Place the idol on the indicated stand to open a secret nook that contains a character token.

FREE PLAY

VEHICLE TOKEN 2: HAIRDRYER

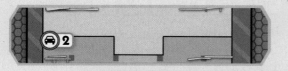

Return to the dojo's balcony and carefully drop off the foreground ledge to land on a lower balcony. Smash the red cabinet on the left to discover some dynamite.

Collect the dynamite and carry it down to the dojo's main floor. Use the dynamite to destroy the silver wall on the left. There's a vehicle token in the nook beyond!

FREE PLAY

RED BRICK: SUPER THROW

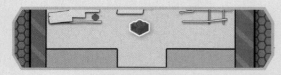

Beam up to the dojo's balcony one final time. Drop to the lower balcony in the foreground and notice the four portraits of Chase in various disguises. These are vital clues!

Jump up the handholds to return to the upper balcony. There are four large crates here. The sides of each crate are painted with different action symbols—one for each disguise. Turn the valve wheels to spin the crates so that the action symbols match the disguise portraits on the lower foreground ledge. After you properly align all four crates, a red brick appears on the balcony!

Barry proves too much for Chase to handle and instructs McCain to train against his students instead. Press Ⓨ to perform quick throws against three students to pass the first test.

Press Ⓧ to counter the second group of students' attacks. An Ⓧ icon appears above each student just before they strike, signaling that you can perform the counter.

During the third lesson, press Ⓐ to grab the students, then press Ⓨ to throw them. Hold Ⓨ to aim after grabbing a student, then release Ⓨ to throw the student into objects or other students!

Chase faces stronger students during the fourth lesson. These guys can't be taken down with quick throws, and they resist your attempts to grab them. Rapidly tap Ⓐ to overpower these stronger foes, then use Ⓨ to throw them.

In the fifth and final lesson, put all of your training to work and defeat a whole group of students. Use quick throws and counters to defeat the ones in white, and overpower the stronger students in brown by tapping Ⓐ, then throw them.

Barry is impressed at your newfound fighting abilities and hands you a commemorative belt. Great work! You've unlocked Chase's advanced combat skills.

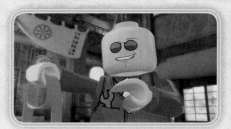

INTRODUCTION

POLICE ACADEMY

CHARACTERS AND VEHICLES

WALKTHROUGH

LEGO CITY TOUR

CHECKLISTS

CITY EXPLORATION

⭐ OBJECTIVE: RESCUE FRANK

As Chase strolls out of the temple dojo, self-confidence restored, he receives a call from Frank Honey. It seems that Frank has been kidnapped, along with LEGO City's brand-new police truck! Fortunately, Frank is able to tell Chase where to find him. Commandeer a vehicle and speed off to the rescue!

Put your newfound fighting skills to use as you battle the punks. Use normal quick throws against single enemies, and go for counters whenever possible. Be sure to slap on those handcuffs once you get the goons to the ground!

You find the police truck near the shore, and Frank is indeed trapped inside. Unfortunately, a bunch of angry goons aren't about to let you leave!

The shirtless bad guys are stronger and can be hard to take down. Press Ⓐ to grab and overpower them, then throw them with Ⓨ. Take that!

⭐ OBJECTIVE: RETURN THE TRUCK TO CHERRY TREE HILLS

To rescue Frank, defeat all of the goons, along with the reinforcements that arrive. Now you've just got to return the police truck to Cherry Tree Hills in time for Mayor Gleeson's big unveiling! You have only five minutes to reach your destination, so don't dally.

Unfortunately, those goons aren't about to let you get away so easily. They soon arrive in suped-up gang vehicles, intent on ramming you off the road. Do your best to stay on track as you hurry toward Cherry Tree Hills!

CHAPTER 5: UNDERCOVER

WHILE BATTLING THE EVIL GOONS WHO KIDNAPPED OFFICER FRANK HONEY, CHASE OVERHEAD ONE OF THEM USE THE NAME "CHAN." FRANK HAS HEARD OF THIS PERSON—HE'S A SUSPECTED GANG LEADER WHO'S RELATIVELY NEW TO LEGO CITY. CHASE BELIEVES THAT CHAN MUST HAVE SOME CONNECTION TO REX FURY, AND AFTER A BIT OF PRESSURE FROM MAYOR GLEESON, CHIEF DUNBY IS FINALLY FORCED TO GIVE MCCAIN HIS BLESSING TO GO UNDERCOVER AND INFILTRATE CHAN'S GANG.

INTRODUCTION

POLICE ACADEMY

CHARACTERS AND VEHICLES

WALKTHROUGH

LEGO CITY TOUR

CHECKLISTS

CITY EXPLORATION

⭐ OBJECTIVE: TRAVEL TO CHAN'S SCRAPYARD

Since you're going deep undercover, Ellie provides you with some new duds: the Chase McCain (Undercover) disguise! You retain all of Chase's police officer abilities (grapple gun, etc.) while wearing this new outfit, and as a bonus, enemies won't recognize you as a cop.

Hop into a vehicle and follow the green studs to locate a scrapyard owned by Chan. After you arrive, Ellie calls and informs you that she's updated your communicator with a new Audio Scan mode. Now you can listen in on distant conversations!

⭐ OBJECTIVE: EAVESDROP ON CHAN'S GANG

Time to try out your new toy. Cross the street and then climb a blue drainpipe to reach a nearby roof.

Carefully tiptoe across the tightrope to reach another building's roof.

The tightrope leads to a scan spot. Press Ⓐ to try out your new Audio Scan mode.

Cross a wooden footbridge and grapple up to a higher roof.

Hold the Wii U GamePad up to your TV screen and search for persons of interest, just like you did with Criminal Scan mode. Lock on to someone to listen to their conversation. Some won't pertain to Chan's gang, but one of them will!

OBJECTIVE: FIND BUCKY BUTLER

Ram into Bucky's vehicle four times to destroy it, then chase the thief on foot. Trip Bucky and then slap on the cuffs. Nice work! Now you can impersonate Bucky and infiltrate Chan's gang.

Your eavesdropping proves fruitful: A hopeful recruit named Bucky Butler is apparently late for a meeting with Chan's gang. If you can intercept and impersonate Bucky, you might be able to join the gang in his place!

Find some wheels and motor toward your next destination—the museum. Park and then move to the nearby scan spot to use Audio Scan mode again.

OBJECTIVE: GO TO CHAN'S LIMO COMPANY

Scan the museum until you overhear Bucky's conversation. The crook spots Chase when he exits the museum, then flees. Hurry after him!

Bucky was set to meet a contact at Chan's limo company, so that's where you need to go. Travel there, then speak with the old man who awaits you. The old man is named Old Quiang, and he gives you instructions to pick up the famous millionaire Forrest Blackwell, who awaits you at Blackwell Tower in King's Court.

OBJECTIVE: ARREST BUCKY BUTLER

OBJECTIVE: PICK UP FORREST BLACKWELL

Bucky hops into a car and speeds off. Chase commandeers a vehicle and hurries after Bucky in hot pursuit. Chase Bucky through the city, using turbos to catch up.

Now you're getting somewhere! Drive the limo to Blackwell Tower, and pick up Mr. Blackwell. The famous millionaire is swamped by paparazzi but manages to fight his way into the limo.

INTRODUCTION · POLICE ACADEMY · CHARACTERS AND VEHICLES · WALKTHROUGH · LEGO CITY TOUR · CHECKLISTS

OBJECTIVE: BRING MR. BLACKWELL TO GILLESPIE THEATER

TIP

The limo doesn't have any turbos, so get creative and make lots of sudden turns to give the paparazzi the slip! Mr. Blackwell won't mind.

Well done! Now you've just got to bring Mr. Blackwell to the Gillespie Theater. Unfortunately, the paparazzi don't give up easily and quickly pursue you. Mr. Blackwell despises the paparazzi, so you'll need to give them the slip before you can deliver him to the theater.

Pull up to the theater after losing the paparazzi, and drop off Mr. Blackwell. The millionaire is thankful for your efforts and tells you not to wait—he has arranged for other means of getting home.

OBJECTIVE: MEET CHAN NEAR THE SCRAPYARD

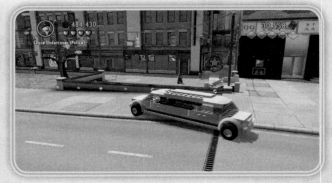

Old Quiang calls shortly after you drop off Mr. Blackwell, pleased with your work. He invites you to meet Master Chan in an alley near his scrapyard. This could be your big break! Hurry there without delay.

Exit your vehicle and enter the alley to meet with Chan. The sinister villain hints that he may have a job for you and hands you a list of instructions. Great, more errands to run!

OBJECTIVE: RETRIEVE THE CAR

Chan's note instructs you to steal a car from his rivals while they're busy having a party. Sounds fun! Speed over to Paradise Sands, where the party is going down.

The car is visible inside a garage, but a pair of bodyguards have it locked down tight. You'll need to create a distraction or two to get rid of the toughs.

Poolside Barbecue

Head to the pool behind the garage to find a chef in distress. His barbecue is broken, and he needs help repairing it. Smash the remains of the barbecue, along with the nearby patio furniture, to discover some bricks. Build these into a new barbecue for the chef.

The chef is thrilled to have his barbecue back—now he just needs something to cook on it. Run around the pool and find a box of chicken drumsticks beneath a blue and white striped stand. Pick up the drumsticks and carry them back to the chef.

Place the drumsticks on the green pad near the barbecue, then place the drumsticks on the grill. The aroma sends one of the bodyguards into a frenzy, causing him to leave his station. One more guard to go!

Party Tunes

Circle around the pool to find a DJ in despair. Use the bouncing bricks near the DJ to rebuild his broken turntable.

Nice work! Now you just need to find a record to spin. Approach the nearby magician, who has just made an innocent bystander vanish. Speak with the magician, and he'll pull a record out of his hat. Fair enough!

Place the record on the turntable, then start scratching. To scratch the record in time with the beat, simply press the appropriate direction on ✛ when the arrow icons pass through the circle. Keep it up until the party starts bumping!

The remaining bodyguard can't help but be moved by the rhythm, and leaves his post to join the party. Great job! Now you can break in and steal the car for Chan.

Grand Theft LEGO

With both bodyguards out of the picture, return to the front of the garage and use the crowbar to break in. Before you can steal Chan's wheels, a gang of costumed goons storms out of the building, intent on picking a fight!

INTRODUCTION

POLICE ACADEMY

CHARACTERS AND VEHICLES

WALKTHROUGH

LEGO CITY TOUR

CHECKLISTS

Beat up all of the thugs, then break into the garage and steal the car. Now you just need to make your escape!

Race through the city streets in your stolen vehicle, heading for Chan's scrapyard. The police don't know you're actually a cop and will try to stop you—don't let them! Use your turbos to stay ahead of the police as you motor toward the scrapyard.

OBJECTIVE: INVESTIGATE THE ALARM

Chan calls after you successfully deliver the car to his scrapyard. It seems an alarm has been triggered at Chan's limo company—better hurry over there and see what's up!

Sure enough, Chase spots a masked intruder rifling through Chan's cabinets. But before our hero can make an arrest, the intruder flees to the streets!

OBJECTIVE: PURSUE THE INTRUDER

You've got to catch the mysterious intruder! Chase the intruder around the building, and jump up the handholds on the vertical "limo" sign.

Hurry across the limo company's roof, vaulting an obstacle on your way to some scaffolding. Climb onto the scaffolding and pursue the intruder to the right.

Wall-jump to a higher stretch of scaffolding, then run back to the left. Flip across a flagpole and slide down a tightrope to reach another building.

After landing from the tightrope slide, climb a ladder and sprint up the wooden ramp on the left. (Don't climb the drainpipe around to the right.) Vault an obstacle, then make a daring leap over to the building on the left.

This is quite a chase! Run around the building's metal balcony, then climb another ladder. Scale a blue and white wall to reach the building's roof.

Cross the roof and vault the far wall to reach a catapult pad. Use the pad to bound over to another building.

After you land, use a wall runway to cross the wide gap to the right. The intruder then vanishes into a building, locking the door behind him. No fair!

You can't let the intruder get away! Climb up to the roof by jumping between the narrow walls near the door through which the intruder fled. Slide down a tightrope to reach the roof of another building.

At last, Chase manages to catch up to the intruder, who turns out to be...Natalia! She thought Chase was one of Chan's men and admits that she was trying to find out what might have happened to her father, who was recently kidnapped. Things just keep getting worse!

INTRODUCTION

POLICE ACADEMY

CHARACTERS AND VEHICLES

WALKTHROUGH

LEGO CITY TOUR

CHECKLISTS

CHAPTER 6: ALL IN THE FAMILY

NATALIA'S FATHER HAS BEEN KIDNAPPED AND WAS LAST SEEN ENTERING A LIMOUSINE—ONE OF CHAN'S, NO DOUBT. IN NATALIA'S RECENT BREAK-IN OF CHAN'S LIMO COMPANY, SHE FOUND EVIDENCE OF A LINK BETWEEN CHAN AND VINNIE PAPPALARDO—ONE OF LEGO CITY'S MOST NOTORIOUS CRIME BOSSES. SOUNDS LIKE IT'S TIME CHASE GOT IN GOOD WITH VINNIE'S GANG!

CITY EXPLORATION

⭐ OBJECTIVE: BORROW A PRISON TRANSFER TRUCK

Chase hopes to get on Vinnie's good side by rescuing his right-hand man, Moe DeLuca, from prison. To do this, Chase will need a prison transfer truck. Find a vehicle and follow the green studs to the police station's rear compound.

A mechanic named Chuck is expecting you but insists that you do him a few favors before he'll loan you the truck. Pick up the nearby crate and follow Chuck into the garage.

Place the crate on the green pad near Chuck to empty out its bricks. Build these into a motorcycle chassis.

Finding the Tires

Now you just need to find the tires! The first one isn't far. Crowbar into the police station's storage area, then smash the junk to the left to find some bricks. Build the bricks into a ladder, then climb up to the top shelf.

Smash everything on the top shelf as you make your way over to a superbrick. You'll discover the tire on the top shelf as you go.

Carry the tire back to Chuck and place it on his bike. One more to go!

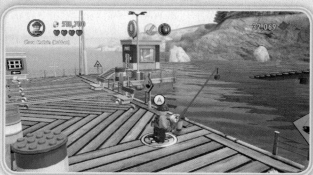

Run down to the nearby pier and look for a fishing pole. Use the pole, and you'll pull up another tire! Carry this back to Chuck to finish his bike.

Taking a Spin

Chuck is thrilled to have his bike built, but he wants you to try it out. Hop onto the bike and complete a simple circuit around Cherry Tree Hills.

Follow the green studs through each of the checkpoints. You'll add time to the clock each time you pass through a checkpoint. Keep it up until you reach the police station.

Return to Chuck to prove that his bike is in perfect working order. The mechanic happily lets you borrow the police transfer truck.

TIP

Use turbos to increase your speed down straights, and look for ramps that you can launch off!

NOTE

Nice work! You've unlocked vehicle time trials! Now you can participate in races around LEGO City for fun and profit.

⭐ OBJECTIVE: GO TO THE COURTHOUSE

You've got the prison transfer truck—now you just need to get to the courthouse. Follow the green studs to get there.

Chase's ruse works like a charm, and Vinnie's right-hand man, Moe DeLuca, is promptly stuffed inside of Chase's transfer truck. Hurry and drive off before anyone notices!

⭐ OBJECTIVE: LOSE THE POLICE

It doesn't take long for the cops to wise up and chase after you. Drive recklessly to give them the slip, taking sudden turns and using turbos as often as possible. After you lose the police, simply follow the green studs to Moe DeLuca's hideout.

Moe couldn't be happier at having his freedom restored, and he promises to be in touch. Way to go!

⭐ OBJECTIVE: MEET MOE AT THE AIRPORT

It's not long before you receive a call from Moe. A truck full of high-tech gizmos are on their way in from the airport, and Moe thinks that stealing these will put you in Vinnie's good graces. Arrange for a means of transportation and head for the airport.

Moe arrives right on time and has a surprise for you: a new car! Actually, it's his brother's car, but Moe doesn't care much about his brother. He gives you permission to smash up the car as much as you like while you attempt to stop the delivery truck, which soon passes by.

⭐ OBJECTIVE: STOP THE DELIVERY TRUCK

There's no time to lose! Hop into the car that Moe has provided and race after the delivery truck. You know the drill: ram the truck four times until its driver is forced to flee.

Chase's meeting with Vinnie Pappalardo goes well. The crime boss asks him to test out a brand-new weapon during a heist at the LEGO City Bank. Sounds like a good way to make a name for yourself with Vinnie!

Steal the delivery truck after ramming it off the road, then follow the green studs to find the Pappalardo plant. Park to deliver the truck and at last meet with LEGO City's most notorious crime lord.

You'll need to slip into the bank by way of its sewer entrance. Follow your objective marker to locate a sewer cover, then pry open the cover with the crowbar and head inside.

INTRODUCTION

POLICE ACADEMY

CHARACTERS AND VEHICLES

WALKTHROUGH

LEGO CITY TOUR

CHECKLISTS

SPECIAL ASSIGNMENT 5: DIRTY WORK

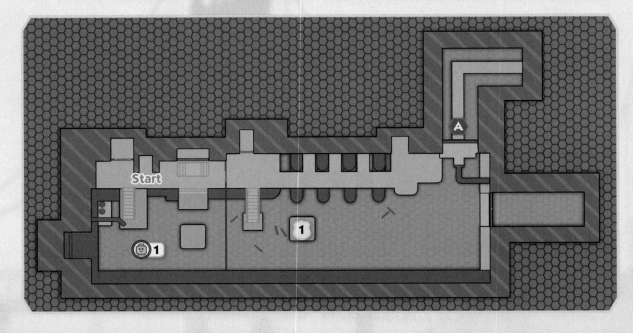

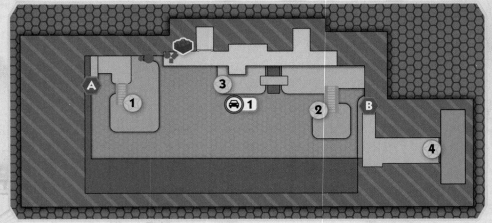

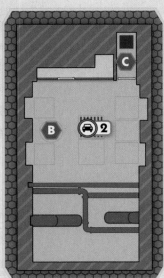

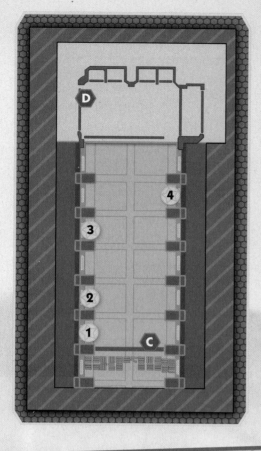

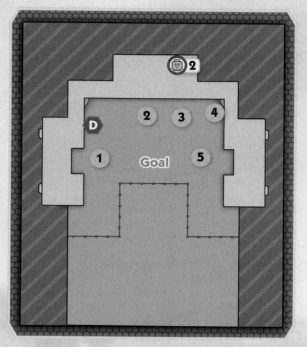

STAGE COLLECTIBLES: "DIRTY WORK"

MAP ICON(S)	TYPE	MODE	NOTES	GOT IT?
1	"Intergalactic Girl" character token	Free Play	Use the transporter pad in the water near the start.	1
1	Police Shield Piece 1	Free Play	Rip apart the super-strength crate in the water with Rex Fury, then complete the RC boat race.	2
1	"Gotland" vehicle token	Story	Swim into the background cage before crossing the toxic waste.	3
1 to 4	Police Shield Piece 2	Free Play	Rip apart the super-strength crate on the far right, then fill the color gun with yellow energy and blast the four rubber duckies around the sewer.	4
	Red Brick— Studs x4	Story	Pry open the door near the red color swapper.	5
2	Relocator	Free Play	Drill the shaky ground in the final sewer area.	6
1 to 4	Police Shield Piece 3	Story	Crack four wall safes around the vault.	7
1 to 5	Police Shield Piece 4	Story	Use the floor buffer to polish five stains around the bank lobby.	8
2	"Bank Manager" character token	Free Play	Activate the space crate in the bank lobby, beam up to the balcony, color the statue brown and blue, and enter the room on the right.	9

LEGO CITY HERO STUD REQUIREMENT:

58,000

INTRODUCTION

POLICE ACADEMY

CHARACTERS AND VEHICLES

WALKTHROUGH

LEGO CITY TOUR

CHECKLISTS

★ OBJECTIVE: GET THROUGH THE SEWER

Nice work! Now you just need to pass through the sewer and breach the bank. Smash the green and white drum to the starting point's left to discover a crowbar symbol. Pry open the nearby metal door to find a valve wheel.

Carry the valve wheel down the stairs and place it on the indicated panel. Turn the wheel to open a nearby hatch, inside which lies a key.

Jump into the water and collect the key. Carry the key upstairs and insert it into the keyhole near the fence on the right. Turn the key to open the fence's door.

FREE PLAY
CHARACTER TOKEN 1: INTERGALACTIC GIRL

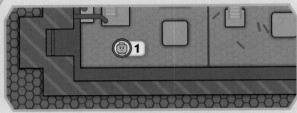

Use the transporter pad near the key hatch to beam up to a nook in the left wall. A platform then extends, and a floating character token appears. Leap from the platform and collect your prize!

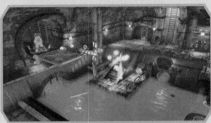

FREE PLAY
POLICE SHIELD PIECE 1

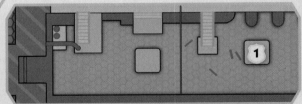

Use Rex Fury to rip apart the super-strength crate in the water beyond the locked fence. After destroying the crate, you'll discover an action symbol.

Stand on the action symbol and press Ⓐ to take control of the nearby RC boat. Race the boat through a series of checkpoints around the water. Reach the final checkpoint before time runs out, and a shield piece will be yours!

All Steamed Up

Note the red switch on the wall beyond the locked fence. You'll soon activate this with your color gun. For now, simply inch down the thin ledge that runs along the walkway to the right. It's the only way past those pesky steam vents!

Turn the valve beyond the steam vents to activate a nearby color swapper. Use this station to fill your color gun with green energy.

Return to the walkway with the steam vents and smash a pile of boulders with the pickax. Pull the lever you discover behind the boulders to shut off the vent to the left.

Pry into the cage that follows, then pull the lever inside the cage to shut off the next vent on the left. Pull another nearby lever to shut off the final vent on the far left. Now you can move through unhindered!

Green Means Go

Return to the red switch you noticed earlier. Hold Ⓨ to aim the color gun, and target the switch. Release Ⓨ to fire a gob of green energy at the switch.

Shooting the switch turns it from red to green and opens the nearby cage. Collect a box of LEGO bricks from within.

Carry the box of bricks over to the right, past the steam valves you've shut off. Place the bricks on the green LEGO pad near the blue and white wall, then build the bricks to restore the wall so you may climb up to a high handhold.

TIP

Find purple studs in this area by swimming near the foreground and by jumping up the thin ledges on the far right. During Free Play, you can also score a purple stud by climbing the blue pipe that runs around the steam vents. Simply douse the flame on the pipe with the fireman's extinguisher.

Shimmy to the right along the handhold, then drop onto a walkway. Pry open a door and head through to the next section of the sewer.

INTRODUCTION

POLICE ACADEMY

CHARACTERS AND VEHICLES

WALKTHROUGH

LEGO CITY TOUR

CHECKLISTS

⭐ OBJECTIVE: EXIT THE SEWER

You're getting there! Smash a barrel in the sewer's second section to discover a scan spot. Follow the footprints down to a panel, then search the panel to find some dynamite.

TIP

During Free Play, repair the fuse box near the scan spot to score a bunch of bonus studs!

Change into the miner outfit, then pick up the dynamite and place it in the small barrel near a large silver pipe. The explosion bursts the pipe, causing some bricks to spill out.

Build the bricks into an air mattress. Now you can safely explore the sewer's right side!

Jump onto the air mattress and swim to the right. Only the air mattress can safely ferry you across the toxic waste in the water.

VEHICLE TOKEN 1: GOTLAND

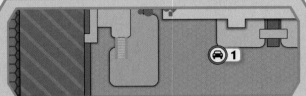

Just before you reach the toxic waste, hop off the air mattress and swim into the hole in the background gate to claim a vehicle token.

FREE PLAY
POLICE SHIELD PIECE 2

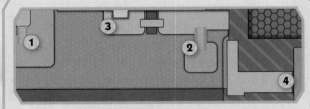

After swimming past the toxic waste and going upstairs, rip apart another super-strength crate with Rex Fury to discover a yellow color swapper.

Fill your color gun with yellow energy, then backtrack and blast two rubber duckies to paint them yellow. Find

two more duckies in this section of the sewer and paint them yellow as well to earn a shield piece! Check the maps to see where the four rubber duckies are located.

After swimming past the toxic waste, head upstairs and run to the left. Slide under some pipes and pry open a metal door to discover a valve wheel.

Carry the valve wheel over to the right and insert it into a panel. Turn the valve to make a water geyser gush up nearby.

Let the water geyser lift you up, then smash some boulders to discover a green switch. Looks like you need to find a red color swapper!

Continue to the left and obtain some dynamite from the dispenser. Use this to destroy the silver gate to the left, exposing a red color swapper.

RED BRICK: STUDS X4

This red brick is an easy grab—just pry open the door near the red color swapper and claim it!

You know what to do! Use the color swapper to change your color gun's ammo to red, then run back to the right and fire a gob of red energy at the green switch.

The green switch turns red, and a nearby platform lowers. Step onto the platform and jump onto a blue pipe. Climb the pipe to reach a ledge with a long ladder. The ladder leads up to the next area.

⭐ OBJECTIVE: SNEAK INTO THE BANK

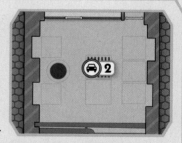

You're almost inside! Use the grapple gun to pull down a metal grate, exposing a ventilation shaft. That's your ticket into the bank!

FREE PLAY
VEHICLE TOKEN 2: RELOCATOR

In the sewer's final area, drill the shaky ground with the construction worker to break into a secret tunnel. Run into the foreground to collect a hidden vehicle token that's stashed down here.

INTRODUCTION

POLICE ACADEMY

CHARACTERS AND VEHICLES

WALKTHROUGH

LEGO CITY TOUR

CHECKLISTS

Smash the crates in the corner, then build the remaining bricks into another crate. Shove this one along the checkered floor until it lines up with the opening in the ventilation shaft.

Jump into the shaft, then collect some dynamite from its right side. Exit the shaft and use the dynamite to destroy some nearby silver piping.

Hey, there's another vent behind that piping! Pry it open and head inside.

⭐ OBJECTIVE: STEAL THE EMERALD

At last, you've snuck into the bank vault. Now you just need to disable the security system and steal the Bell Pepper Emerald for Vinnie. Begin by prying open a couple of wall safes and building the bricks that tumble out into a silver color swapper.

POLICE SHIELD PIECE 3

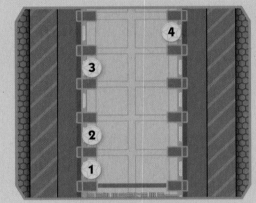

Crack four wall safes in the vault, and you'll snag a shield piece! Check the map for the three safes' locations (they're all near the security lasers).

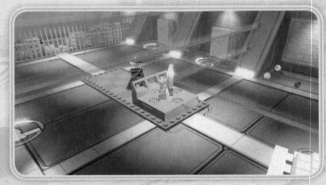

Fill your color gun with silver energy, then blast the nearby radar dish to paint it silver. Now shove the dish along the checkered track in the floor so that it redirects the lowest security laser, letting you slip past on the right.

Next, use the grapple gun to pull another radar dish along a checkered track. The dish will redirect the security laser into a crate, causing an explosion that shuts off the lasers.

Sift through the remains of the crate to discover a box of bricks. Bring these over to the pad on the right, then set them down and build a blue color swapper.

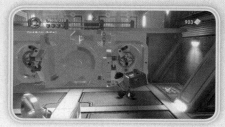

Fill your color gun with blue energy, and blast the white LEGO wall on the left. With the wall colored blue and white, you can now climb to the vault's upper level.

Safe Crackin'

On the vault's second floor, use a computer to open a nearby gated area, exposing a tall safe.

Use the stethoscope to crack a tall safe and discover a bunch of bricks. Build these into a green color swapper.

Fill your color gun with green energy, then aim and fire a gob at the red switch on the left. This raises more gates, exposing three control stations.

Collect the valve wheels that lie on the ground in front of each control station, and place the valves into the nearby slots. Turn each valve wheel to make the control station's central handle spin. Match the handles' colors with the colored dots on the outside of each control station. A green light blinks on above each station when you've successfully matched the handles with the dots.

The main safe opens after you successfully activate all three stations. Hurry down there and swipe that giant emerald!

Great Escape

You've stolen the Bell Pepper Emerald for Vinnie. Now you need to make yourself scarce! Climb back up the ladder to return to the vault's second floor, then beat up the security guards who have arrived. Hurry through the now-open left door to reach the lobby.

INTRODUCTION

POLICE ACADEMY

CHARACTERS AND VEHICLES

WALKTHROUGH

LEGO CITY TOUR

CHECKLISTS

⭐ OBJECTIVE: ESCAPE THE BANK

The bank's luxurious lobby is filled with security guards on high alert. Knock them all for a loop, and notice the central superbuild. You need 30,000 bricks to build the Relocator—your ticket out of here! As luck would have it, there just happens to be several superbricks hidden around the lobby.

POLICE SHIELD PIECE 4

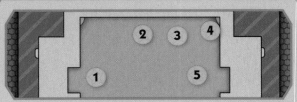

Hop onto the floor buffer in the lobby's left foreground corner, then drive around and look for five stains that need to be buffed out of the marble. Clean all five stains to score a shield piece!

Superbrick 1

Use the grapple gun to pull down a pair of paintings near the statue in the lobby's left background corner. Build the remains of the paintings into two signs: a blue "III" and a green "VII."

Run to the foreground and notice a trio of giant slots. Spin the valve wheels so that the blue slot comes up "III" and the green slot comes up "VII." Now simply spin the red slot to make it read "X."

Solving the slots puzzle scores you a key. Carry the key into the background and use it to unlock a door that leads behind the left tellers' counter. Head inside and collect the superbrick that sits out in the open.

Superbricks 2 and 3

Collect some dynamite from the dispenser behind the left tellers' counter. There's probably a good reason why this is here!

Carry the dynamite out of the back area and over to the lobby's right background statue. The explosion sends part of the statue rolling through the right half of the bank tellers' counter!

Pass through the hole you've created and crack open the two safes you can now reach. Each one contains a superbrick!

FREE PLAY

CHARACTER TOKEN 2: BANK MANAGER

Activate the space crate in the lobby's right foreground corner to make a transporter pad materialize nearby. Use the pad to beam up to the lobby's balcony.

Step off the transport pad and fill your color gun with brown energy at the nearby swapper. Run to the left and blast the chair of the statue to paint it brown.

The statue isn't quite finished yet. Keep going left to find another color swapper. This one isn't working. Fix the nearby fuse box to power it.

Now use the color swapper to fill your gun with blue energy. Return to the statue and blast its base to paint it blue.

With the statue's chair painted brown and its base blue, the nearby doors swing open. Enter the door on the right to snag this stage's final collectible—a character token!

Time to Relocate

You've found plenty of bricks, so go ahead and build the Relocator at the lobby's central superbuild pad. Chase makes his epic escape, smashing out of the bank in style!

NOTE

The scepter you find in the room on the left belongs on the Egyptian display stand downstairs near the transporter pad. Smash the other display stands around the lobby's main floor to discover a spear, and place this on the Roman display stand, which is also near the transporter pad. With both the spear and scepter placed, a shower of studs rains down around you!

INTRODUCTION

POLICE ACADEMY

CHARACTERS AND VEHICLES

WALKTHROUGH

LEGO CITY TOUR

CHECKLISTS

CITY EXPLORATION

⭐ OBJECTIVE: TAKE THE EMERALD TO VINNIE

Excellent work! You've stolen the Bell Pepper Emerald. Now you need to bring it to the drop-off point. Do your best to avoid the police on your way, and use the Relocator's turbos to smash through barricades.

Vinnie's contact awaits you beneath one of the city's bridges. Just keep following the green studs until you drive down a ramp and make the drop.

⭐ OBJECTIVE: GATHER EVIDENCE AGAINST CHAN'S MEN

Chase's success with Vinnie means he's finished working with Chan's gang. Chief Dunby therefore orders Chase to gather photographic evidence against Chan's men. Commandeer a vehicle and follow the green studs to a favorite hangout of Chan's.

Take the stairs outside the color swapper shop and climb up the handhold to reach a green switch. Blast this with red energy to shut off the nearby fans.

With the fans powered down, you can use a catapult pad to rocket over to the scan spot that overlooks the noodle restaurant. Now you're in a perfect spot to eavesdrop!

You soon reach your objective: a noodle restaurant that Chan enjoys. This is a perfect place to eavesdrop on his gang's activity. Break into a nearby building to access a red color swapper.

Chan's men soon arrive. Use Audio Scan mode to listen in on their conversation inside the noodle restaurant.

Pagoda Pics

Your eavesdropping proves fruitful. Chan's men are set to perform several crimes around a nearby park. If you can reach the top of the park's central pagoda, you can snap photos of all of Chan's goons in the act! Drop from your perch and sprint over to the pagoda.

Enter the park and run around the pagoda until you find a grapple point. Zip up and then climb an interior ladder to reach the pagoda's roof.

Excellent! Now use your newfound Camera mode to take pictures of the three gang members. The Wii U GamePad becomes the center of the action while using Camera mode!

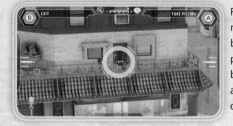

First, find the gang members who are breaking into the pharmacy (red building). Zoom in and snap a picture of them in the act!

Next, look to the left from the pharmacy to find a couple of gang members chatting in an alley. Zoom in again for an incriminating close-up!

Finally, look to the pharmacy's right to find several gang members guarding a yellow sports car near Chang's limo service. The sports car is partially obscured, but take your best picture of the goons.

One Last Shot

You'll need to get closer and grab a picture that shows the stolen car. Chase automatically moves to the ideal spot. Fire up your camera again.

This time, zoom in and take a picture that shows the entire car, along with some of the gang members. Brilliant!

The goons don't take kindly to being photographed and quickly swarm Chase. Use counters and throws to defeat the more powerful thugs as you fight the good fight.

> **NOTE**
>
> Nice work! You've unlocked your communicator's camera function! Now you can snap photos with your Wii U GamePad by pressing ℝ. Just remember to say "cheese!"

INTRODUCTION

POLICE ACADEMY

CHARACTERS AND VEHICLES

WALKTHROUGH

LEGO CITY TOUR

CHECKLISTS

CHAPTER 7:
ONE SMALL JOB FOR CHAN

THANKS TO HIS PHOTOGRAPHY SKILLS, CHASE HAS MANAGED TO PUT SEVERAL OF CHAN'S GANG MEMBERS ON ICE. THIS LEAVES THE SMALL-TIME CRIME BOSS LITTLE OPTION BUT TO CALL ON MCCAIN WHEN HE NEEDS HIS NEXT JOB DONE. GUESS YOU'RE NOT QUITE DONE WITH THIS PETTY CROOK JUST YET!

CITY EXPLORATION

INTRODUCTION

POLICE ACADEMY

CHARACTERS AND VEHICLES

WALKTHROUGH

LEGO CITY TOUR

CHECKLISTS

⭐ OBJECTIVE: GET TO CRESCENT PARK WHARF

Chan has asked you to perform a job for him. Steal some wheels and follow the green studs to reach your destination: Crescent Park Wharf. Exit your vehicle after you arrive and run to the small objective beacon near the jetty.

Press Ⓧ to enter Chan's boat, just as you would any street vehicle. Accelerate and follow the green studs toward Apollo Island, just as you do while driving a car. It's a long trip, so entertain yourself by launching off ramps along the way!

Dock at the objective beacon when you finally reach Apollo Island, then press Ⓧ to exit the boat and step onto the pier. Chan soon calls with further instructions: You're to break into the space center and steal a moon buggy!

⭐ OBJECTIVE: TAKE CHAN'S BOAT TO APOLLO ISLAND

Chan calls again when you arrive at the wharf, furious that his other cronies aren't responding. He instructs you to use his boat to reach Apollo Island, site of LEGO City's space center. Cool!

NOTE

All right, you've unlocked boats for travel! Now you can pilot any boats you find docked around LEGO City.

As you might expect, Apollo Island is locked down pretty tight. Use the control panel near the security gate to open it, then head through.

Hop into the high-tech vehicle beyond the security gate. Follow the green studs around the island as you make for the space center.

⭐ OBJECTIVE: FIND THE SPACE CENTER

After you discover the space center, search nearby for a door that you can pry open with the crowbar. Enter the building and find the bouncing bricks. Use them to form a color swapper.

Fill your color gun with blue energy, then smash the cabinets in the room to find more bricks. Build these into a locker, then open the locker to obtain the Chase McCain (Astronaut) disguise!

Astronaut Antics

Exit the building and run around the left side. Smash a brown crate to discover more bouncing bricks. Build these into a special object called a *space crate*. Switch to your newfound astronaut disguise and activate the space crate.

The space crate's four colored lights blink in a certain order. Pay attention to the lights, then input the same sequence by using ✛ to select the colors and Ⓐ to input each one. Solve this simple puzzle, and the space crate will activate, opening up to reveal a satellite dish that beams in some LEGO bricks nearby.

Nice work! Now simply build the bricks to restore the bottom of the nearby LEGO wall. Blast the wall with blue energy from the color gun, which you recently found by using the color swapper inside the space center. After you color the wall blue and white, you can wall-jump up to the space station's roof.

Swing from a flagpole to reach another section of the roof. Use the grapple gun to zip up to a higher area, where you discover more bouncing bricks.

Build the bricks into a transporter pad, then stand on the pad and switch to the astronaut disguise. Press Ⓐ to activate the pad, and you'll be beamed inside the space center!

SPECIAL ASSIGNMENT 6: ASTRONAUGHTY

INTRODUCTION

POLICE ACADEMY

CHARACTERS AND VEHICLES

WALKTHROUGH

LEGO CITY TOUR

CHECKLISTS

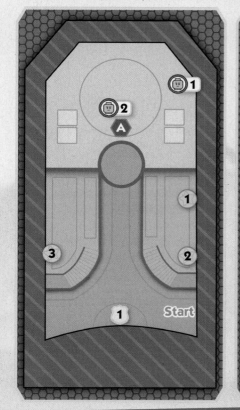

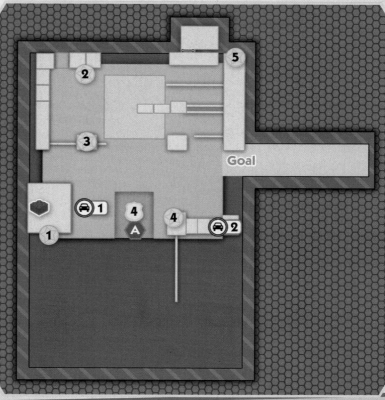

STAGE COLLECTIBLES: "ASTRONAUGHTY"

MAP ICON(S)	TYPE	MODE	NOTES	GOT IT?
1	Police Shield Piece 1	Story	Ride the mechanical rocket in the lobby.	1
1 to 3	Police Shield Piece 2	Story	Smash objects and build three portraits around the lobby.	2
1	"Space Villain" character token	Free Play	Use Rex Fury to rip apart the strength crate in the lobby.	3
2	"Space Scientist" character token	Story	Smash the remaining "planet" after making the solar system diorama fall.	4
1	"L.E.R.V." vehicle token	Free Play	Drill the shaky ground in the hangar.	5
1 to 5	Police Shield Piece 3	Free Play	Smash five space probes around the hangar. Some can be reached only during Free Play.	6
⬡	Red Brick—Super Astro Crate	Free Play	Fix the hangar's background fuse box, ride the lift and get some dynamite, drop and blast the silver floor hatch, beam to another room, chop through the door, and crack the safe.	7
4	Police Shield Piece 4	Free Play	Fix the fuse box in the lower storage room, then return to the floor switch puzzle and solve it again.	8
2	"Garrano" vehicle token	Free Play	Fix the fuse box on the hangar's high walkways, climb the wall, and cross the handholds.	9

LEGO CITY HERO STUD REQUIREMENT: 50,000

⭐ OBJECTIVE: CREATE A DIVERSION

Stealing the moon buggy for Chan won't be easy—the space center is crawling with personnel. You'll need to create a diversion. Begin by activating the space crate on the left, mimicking the crate's color sequence.

POLICE SHIELD PIECE 1

Ride the mechanical rocket in the lobby to earn a shield piece. Far out!

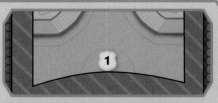

Activating the space crate beams in some bricks. Build these into a transporter pad, then use the pad to beam over to the right side of the lobby's balcony.

You discover some bouncing bricks on the second floor. Build them into a model shuttle. The shuttle blasts off and knocks down some more bricks.

POLICE SHIELD PIECE 2

Smash objects to discover LEGO bricks around the lobby's balconies, then build the bricks into portraits that Chase hangs on the wall. Find and hang all three portraits to score a shield piece! Check the maps for the locations of the three portraits.

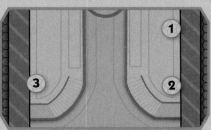

The shuttle knocked down some bricks; build these into a space crate. Activate this to beam in even more bricks nearby.

Build the final batch of bricks into a color swapper. Use the device to fill your color gun with green energy. Head downstairs afterward and use a control panel to open the door back to the lobby.

Move to the lobby's left side and fire the color gun at the red switch on the wall. The switch turns green, and a nearby door opens. Head upstairs to explore the lobby's left balcony.

Use the grapple gun to pull down a large object from the wall. The object smashes apart, leaving some bricks behind. Build these to fill in the missing portion of the nearby checkered track.

With the checkered track repaired, shove the giant battery along the track and into the recess in the background wall. Once the battery is in place, the nearby mechanism powers up, and some dynamite appears. Wild!

Grab the dynamite and head back downstairs. Place the dynamite in the barrel near the silver background wall to blast open the door to the elevator beyond. Stand on the elevator's central button to ride up to the control room above.

Clearing the Control Room

Subdue the security guards in the control room, then smash a white rolling cabinet to discover a scan spot. Follow the footprints over to a small cabinet on the other side of the room.

FREE PLAY
CHARACTER TOKEN 1: SPACE VILLAIN

Use Rex Fury to rip apart the super-strength crate on the right side of the control room. You'll find a character token inside!

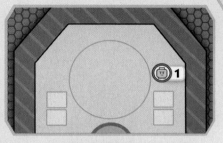

Open the cabinet to find some bricks. Build these into a grapple point that you can pick up and carry over to a nearby machine.

Jump onto the machine and insert the grapple point into one of the three slots on top. One of the three red lights on the wall above turns green. There must be two more grapple points around here!

The second grapple point is visible on another machine to the left. Simply grapple it and pull it out. Carry it over to the machine on the right and insert it to turn another light green.

INTRODUCTION

POLICE ACADEMY

CHARACTERS AND VEHICLES

WALKTHROUGH

LEGO CITY TOUR

CHECKLISTS

The final grapple point is hidden inside a locker. Pry open the lockers around the control room to find some bricks, then build them into the grapple point. Carry it over and insert it into the machine.

With all three grapple points inserted, the machine opens, exposing a transporter pad. Stand on the pad and beam up to a high platform.

Creating a Diversion

There's another model shuttle up near the high platform. Jump over and pull the shuttle's control lever to make it zip along its track. Enjoy the ride as the shuttle carries you over to another platform on the opposite side of the room.

When you come to a stop, jump onto the nearby platform and pull its lever. This causes the hanging model of the solar system to drop from the ceiling, creating a loud racket. If that doesn't distract the workers away from the moon buggy, nothing will!

CHARACTER TOKEN 2: SPACE SCIENTIST

After bringing down the solar system diorama, smash the lone remaining "planet" that lies on the ground (we're pretty sure it's Saturn). Out pops a character token!

Good work! Drop from the high platform and climb the chain from which the model was hanging. Pass through a hole in the ceiling to reach the space center's hangar.

⭐ OBJECTIVE: STEAL THE MOON BUGGY

You've created a diversion and breached the hangar. Now you just need to steal the moon buggy! Unfortunately, the buggy is kept inside the space shuttle—you'll need to open the shuttle somehow. Begin by using the nearby control panel to make the red squares on the floor light up in a special sequence.

Do you remember the pattern? Good! Step on the red squares to make them light up in the same sequence that they did after you used the control panel. If you do it right, all of the squares will turn green, and a color swapper will pop out of the nearby wall.

Fill your color gun with silver energy, then aim and blast the gold dish above the white laser that's shining up from the floor. Paint the dish silver with the color gun, and the laser will be redirected to the left. Neat!

The laser strikes a switch, causing a ladder to lower nearby. Climb up and explore the rest of the hangar.

FREE PLAY
VEHICLE TOKEN 1: L.E.R.V.

Use the construction worker to drill the shaky ground on the hangar's left side. You'll discover a vehicle token beneath the floor!

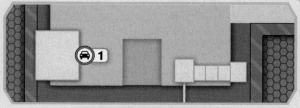

FREE PLAY
POLICE SHIELD PIECE 3

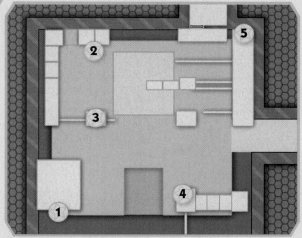

Smash five space probes around the hangar to earn a shield piece! Some are located on the hangar's upper walkways; others are kept in areas you can reach only during Free Play. (You'll need to use the astronaut's jet pack jump to reach one of them.) Check the maps for their locations!

INTRODUCTION

POLICE ACADEMY

CHARACTERS AND VEHICLES

WALKTHROUGH

LEGO CITY TOUR

CHECKLISTS

FREE PLAY
RED BRICK: SUPER ASTRO CRATE

Fix the fuse box on the hangar's left background wall to call an elevator. Ride up to the walkways high above.

Obtain some dynamite from the dispenser above the elevator. Drop down to the hangar's main floor.

Use the dynamite to blast open a silver floor hatch on the hangar's right side. Drop through to reach a small storage room.

Pry open the storage room's door to access a transporter pad. Use the pad to beam up to a higher storage room.

Chop through the higher room's boarded door to enter it. Crack the safe inside the room to score this stage's red brick.

FREE PLAY
POLICE SHIELD PIECE 4

Return to the lower storage room—the one you entered by blasting the silver floor hatch. Fix the fuse box down here to reset the floor switch puzzle you solved when you first entered the hangar.

Return to the floor switch puzzle and use the control panel again. This time, the squares light up in a different pattern. Study the pattern carefully, then step onto the squares in the same order to turn them green. If you do it right, a shield piece will be your prize!

Aligning the Left Laser

To open the shuttle and steal the moon buggy, you've got to restore power by directing two lasers toward the shuttle's power cores. Take out the security guards, then smash the crates near the foreground to discover some bricks. Build these into a space crate, then activate the crate to warp in more bricks.

Build the bricks to assemble a relay dish. Aim and fire your energy gun at the dish to turn it silver.

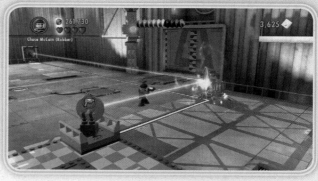

Blast the other nearby dish to paint it silver as well. With both dishes painted silver, the hangar's left laser bounces along the dishes and strikes the shuttle's first power generator. One more to go!

Return to the color swapper and reclaim your silver energy. Blast both of the relay dishes you've built to turn them silver.

Run to the background and smash the remaining crates to unblock the laser that's shining out from the background wall. The laser then bounces from the relay dishes and powers up the shuttle. Nice work!

Aligning the Right Laser

Run around the shuttle's right side and smash a crate to discover some bricks. Build these into a color swapper, then trade your silver energy for red.

Buggin' Out

Look up and spy a nearby green switch. Blast it with your color gun to turn it red. This activates the switch, causing an object to fall from above and smash apart. Build the remains of the object into a relay dish.

Powering the shuttle causes it to open, exposing the moon buggy. Now you just need to reach the crane controls and lower the buggy to the ground. Beat up the guards who ride down the elevator on the right, then use the nearby control panel to call the elevator and ride up to the hangar's upper walkways.

Run into the foreground and smash another large crate to discover more bricks. Build these into another relay dish, then shove the dish along the checkered track as far as it will go.

Cross the balance beam between the walkways and spring off a catapult pad. Keep going until you reach the door to the background office. Pry open the door with the crowbar and enter the storage room beyond.

INTRODUCTION

POLICE ACADEMY

CHARACTERS AND VEHICLES

WALKTHROUGH

LEGO CITY TOUR

CHECKLISTS

FREE PLAY

VEHICLE TOKEN 2: GARRANO

After springing off the catapult pad, fix a fuse box to shut off the electricity that's zapping the nearby climbable wall.

Climb the wall to reach some handholds. Navigate these on your way to a vehicle token that sits atop the elevator you used to get up here.

Crack the safe inside the storage room to discover a key card. Use this to activate the terminal just outside the room. A section of walkway shifts over, allowing you to reach the shuttle's crane controls.

Cross the walkways and activate the crane controls to release the moon buggy. The buggy shatters on the floor, but at least it's within your reach now!

Make a daring leap and land down by the moon buggy's remains. Rebuild the moon buggy, then hop into the driver's seat.

Driving the moon buggy takes a bit of practice. Just use Ⓑ to reverse if you bump into anything. Drive over the red pad on the right to open the hangar door and escape!

★ OBJECTIVE: AVOID APOLLO ISLAND SECURITY

Great work! You've stolen the moon buggy—now you just need to avoid Apollo Island's security force while you wait for Chan's men to arrive with the getaway boat. Speed all around the island, struggling to keep away from the security vehicles that try to ram you.

| TIP |

Make a circuit around the island, looping around to maintain speed as you outrun the security team.

Survive for a whole minute, and Chan's men will arrive at the docks. Hurry over there and drive into the objective beacon to make good your escape!

INTRODUCTION

POLICE ACADEMY

CHARACTERS AND VEHICLES

WALKTHROUGH

LEGO CITY TOUR

CHECKLISTS

CHAPTER 8: THE RESCUE

CHASE HAS SUCCEEDED IN STEALING THE MOON BUGGY FROM APOLLO ISLAND'S SPACE CENTER FOR CHAN—THOUGH HE'S STILL UNSURE WHY THE SMALL-TIME CROOK WOULD WANT SUCH A HIGH-END PIECE OF EQUIPMENT. BEFORE HE FINDS ANY ANSWERS, CHASE RECEIVES AN EMERGENCY CALL FROM CHIEF DUNBY: THE FAMOUS MILLIONAIRE FORREST BLACKWELL HAS BEEN KIDNAPPED!

CITY EXPLORATION

⭐ OBJECTIVE: SAVE BLACKWELL

There's no time to lose! Hop in a car and race through the streets, following the green studs toward your objective.

Blast the LEGO wall with blue energy. That's better! Now climb up to the objective beacon on the roof.

You need to climb a building to reach your objective, but the climbable LEGO wall lacks its traditional blue coloring. There must be a way to activate it!

Rooftop Run

Cross the street and look through the windows of the nearby building—several color swappers are inside. Smash the crate outside the building to find some bricks, then build these into a transporter pad.

Time for a run across the rooftops of LEGO City. Swing across the flagpoles to the left, then tiptoe across the tightrope that follows to reach the next building.

Vault two vents on your way to a catapult pad. Use the pad to soar over to the next building.

Use the transporter pad to beam into the building. Fill your color gun with blue energy and return to the climbable LEGO wall.

After landing, Chase hears the cries of Forrest Blackwell. His abductors have brought him up to a high building. Perhaps they're waiting for a helicopter?

Defeat the goons who soon ambush you, and activate the nearby space crate to beam in some bricks.

Build a LEGO wall out of the bricks, then blast the wall with blue coloring so you may climb up to the roof above.

Run to the right, and make a daring leap over to the blue and white LEGO patch on the wall of the previous building. Climb over to the metal walkway on the right.

Beat up another goon as you circle around the walkway. When you reach a blue and white LEGO pad, jump up and grab it, then jump backward and grab the blue and white drainpipe on the neighboring building.

Climb the pipe to reach the building's roof. Jump along the four thin poles up here to reach a tightrope that leads to another building.

Run to the right and drop to a lower walkway. You discover bouncing bricks on the walkway; build them into a trampoline, then bounce up and grab the overhead LEGO patch.

Shimmy to the right along the LEGO patch, and drop to the neighboring building's walkway. Run toward the foreground to find some handholds, and jump up and to the right to reach a higher walkway.

Use a wall runway to run around the corner of the building and reach another walkway. Skills!

Circle around the walkway to find a blue and white LEGO pad on the wall. You know what to do! Jump up and grab the pad, then perform a backward  jump to reach the roof of the nearby building.

INTRODUCTION

POLICE ACADEMY

CHARACTERS AND VEHICLES

WALKTHROUGH

LEGO CITY TOUR

CHECKLISTS

Vault a vent on your way to a tall blue pole. (Ignore the drain pipe in the foreground.) Climb up the pole to reach a tightrope, then slide down to another rooftop.

Rapidly press Ⓑ to scale the sloped portion of the roof and reach a catapult pad. Use the pad to launch over to another roof, where you finally catch up to Forrest Blackwell's abductors.

Saving Mr. Blackwell

Using counters and overpowering the stronger enemies, beat up the thugs who have captured Mr. Blackwell. Arrest all of the goons to save the day!

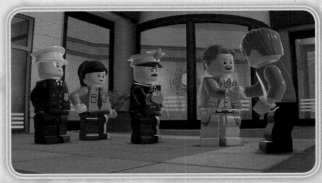

Mr. Blackwell asks you to drive him to the police station, where he'll feel more safe. The ride is uneventful, so just enjoy the trip!

Thrilled to be safe and sound, Mr. Blackwell thanks Chase for all his help. Even Chief Dunby seems relieved that you've rescued LEGO City's richest citizen. Well done!

> **NOTE**
>
> Nice work, you've unlocked free run challenges around LEGO City! Now you can participate in exciting romps around the city's rooftops!

⭐ OBJECTIVE: RESCUE NATALIA FROM CHAN'S SCRAPYARD

Moments after Chase rescues Forrest Blackwell, he receives a call from Natalia. It seems she's been poking around Chan's scrapyard in search of clues about her missing father and now finds herself in dire straits! You'd better find a vehicle and hurry over to the scrapyard, pronto.

Chase's backup arrives just as he reaches the scrapyard. That's right: Officers Studski and Clutch will be accompanying you through the risky mission at hand!

SPECIAL ASSIGNMENT 7: SCRAPYARD SCRAP

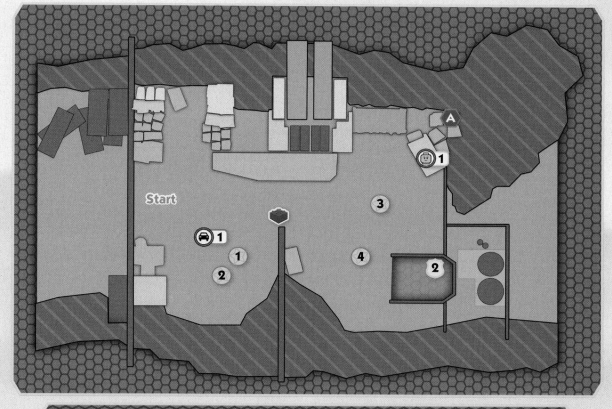

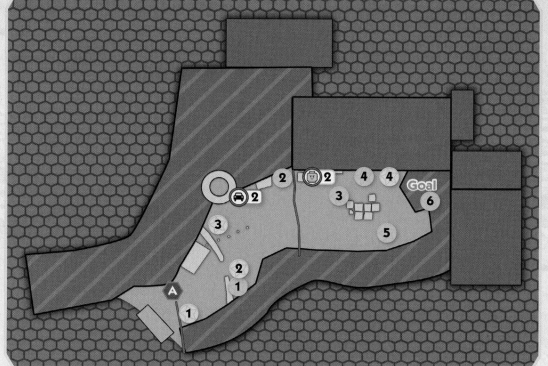

STAGE COLLECTIBLES: "SCRAPYARD SCRAP"

MAP ICON(S)	TYPE	MODE	NOTES	GOT IT?
1 to 4	Police Shield Piece 1	Story	Smash four cars around the scrapyard's first half.	1
🚗 1	"Schmoozer" vehicle token	Free Play	Drill the shaky ground near the start, then ride up the water geyser.	2
👤 1	"Chase Suit" character token	Story	Crack the safe inside the trailer after luring the dog away.	3
2	Police Shield Piece 2	Story	Crack the safe after draining the hazardous pool.	4
⬛	Red Brick—Super Safe Crack	Free Play	Use Rex Fury to rip apart the super-strength crate, then launch off the catapult pad.	5
1 to 4	Police Shield Piece 3	Story	Smash four objects and build four pieces of machinery around the scrapyard's second half.	6
1 to 6	Police Shield Piece 4	Free Play	Douse six barrel fires around the scrapyard's second half.	7
🚗 2	"Jalopy" vehicle token	Free Play	Drill the shaky ground on the scrapyard's right side, place the gear onto the catapult, pull the lever, then beam over and collect the token.	8
👤 2	"Studski" character token	Free Play	Chop through the boarded door on the scrapyard's right side.	9

LEGO CITY HERO STUD REQUIREMENT: 112,000

⭐ OBJECTIVE: SEARCH THE SCRAPYARD

You've got to hurry—Natalia's in trouble! Beat up the gang members in the first area, then run to the foreground to find a generator. Use the nearby gas can to partially fill the generator's tank with fuel.

POLICE SHIELD PIECE 1

Smash four cars around the scrapyard to score a shield piece. Check the maps to see where the four cars are located.

FREE PLAY
VEHICLE TOKEN 1: SCHMOOZER

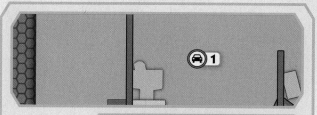

During Free Play, toggle to the construction worker and drill the shaky ground near the start to uncork a water geyser. Ride up the geyser to reach a hovering vehicle token!

You need two more gas cans to fill the generator. Smash a green bin on the left to discover a scan spot, then follow the footprints over to a washer and dryer. Open the washer to discover the second gas can.

Smash another green bin on the right to find the final gas can. Nice work! Now fill the generator and pull its handle to fire up a nearby floor fan. Jump into the fan, which will blow you up to a crane.

Operate the crane to make it drop some large cylinders on the ground. The cylinders smash, leaving a large superbrick behind!

On a Roll

Drop from the crane and collect the superbrick. Press ⊗ to jump onto the lone remaining cylinder, then roll to the right.

Roll the cylinder onto the groove near the fence on the right. After the cylinder slides into place, start rolling it again to open the fence. Now you can explore more of the scrapyard!

Take out more goons on the scrapyard's right side. You need 21,000 bricks to build a car crusher over here. Better look around for more superbricks!

Superbrick 1

Smash some background boulders with the pickax, then shove the nearby fridge to the left along a checkered track. Hey, there's a dynamite dispenser behind the fridge!

INTRODUCTION

POLICE ACADEMY

CHARACTERS AND VEHICLES

WALKTHROUGH

LEGO CITY TOUR

CHECKLISTS

Collect some dynamite from the dispenser, then place it into the small barrel near the silver Dumpster to the right. After the blast, build the remaining bricks into a doghouse.

Building the doghouse lures the guard dog away from the nearby trailer. Pry open the trailer's door and collect the superbrick inside.

Run to the right and jump up a few handholds to reach a blue balance beam. Tiptoe to the edge and pick up the valve wheel. Be careful not to fall—the water below is electrically charged!

CHARACTER TOKEN 1: CHASE SUIT

Backtrack across the beam and drop to solid ground. Insert the valve wheel into the slot near the handholds you used to reach the beam. Turn the wheel afterward to raise a red switch up from the water.

After luring the guard dog away from the trailer, enter the trailer and crack the safe to discover a flashy new civilian outfit for Chase!

Blast the switch with green energy to activate it. This powers the nearby pump, draining the water from the pool. Now you can smash the small cage that was floating in the water and collect the superbrick that's inside!

Superbrick 2

Go left and use the grapple gun to pull down some machinery. The machinery breaks into bricks. Build these into a color swapper, then fill your color gun with green energy.

POLICE SHIELD PIECE 2

Draining the hazardous water from the pool exposes a standing safe. Crack the safe to discover a shield piece!

FREE PLAY
RED BRICK: SUPER SAFE CRACK

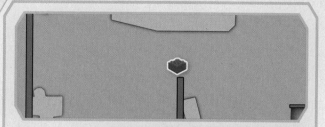

During Free Play, use Rex Fury to rip apart the super-strength crate on the right. This exposes a catapult pad.

Launch off the catapult pad, and you'll soar through the air and collect this stage's red brick, which hovers on high. Nice flying!

Complete the Car Crusher

You now have enough bricks to build the car crusher. Go ahead and do so, then pull its control lever.

The car crusher smashes up the nearby vehicle, turning it into a compact cube. Run back to the scrapyard's left side and use the cube to reach the top of the background junk.

Use balance beams, handholds, and thin ledges as you navigate the junk piles. Climb a blue and white pipe to return to the scrapyard's right side.

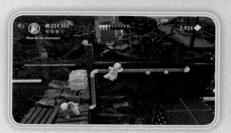

Grinder Time

The pipe leads to a deadly grinder machine. Inch along the thin background ledge to cross without tumbling into the whirling teeth below.

> **CAUTION**
>
> Beware the falling cars as you cross the grinder. Don't let them hit you, or you'll be crushed!

> **TIP**
>
> Press Ⓐ to carefully drop from the thin ledge and the handhold above the grinder. Shimmy right and left to collect several precious studs!

Once you're past the grinder, jump up to a lever and pull it. This causes a crane to drop a pile of bricks onto the platform below.

Drop near the bricks and build them into a climbable LEGO wall. Climb up to vault the high fence and reach the scrapyard's final area.

INTRODUCTION

POLICE ACADEMY

CHARACTERS AND VEHICLES

WALKTHROUGH

LEGO CITY TOUR

CHECKLISTS

⭐ OBJECTIVE: RESCUE NATALIA

You're getting close, but don't relax now! Beat up more thugs in this section of the scrapyard, then smash through the background boulders to discover a crate of LEGO bricks. This should come in handy!

TIP

Use the grapple gun to pull some cars out from the background wall, then jump up the cars to reach the many studs above!

POLICE SHIELD PIECE 3

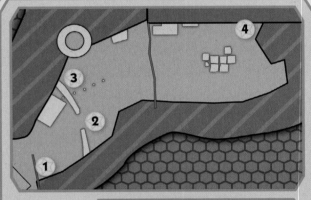

Build four pieces of machinery around the scrapyard's second half to assemble another shield piece. You'll need to smash various objects to find the bricks needed to build each machine. You can't reach one of them until you travel through a transporter. Check the map to see where all four machines are located!

FREE PLAY
POLICE SHIELD PIECE 4

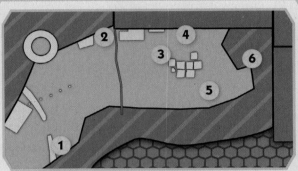

Use the fireman disguise to douse six barrel fires around the scrapyard's second half, and you'll wash off a steamy shield piece. Some of the fires can't be found until you travel through a transporter pad. Check the maps to see where each barrel fire is located!

Carry the crate of bricks over to the green pad on the right. Drop the crate onto the pad, then build the bricks to construct the nearby car's engine.

Repairing the car's engine causes a nearby truck to start up—the vehicles were linked by jumper cables! The truck drives a short distance, exposing a sewer cover that was hidden beneath it. Pry open the sewer cover to discover some dynamite.

More gang members storm out to stop you—beat them down, then collect the dynamite and jump on top of the nearby truck. Jump from the truck's roof and land on the nearby thin pole. Hop across the poles to reach a platform to the left.

Drop the dynamite into the barrel on top of the platform, which sits near a silver plane. The blast blows off the cockpit, causing some bricks to spill out of the fuselage. Build these into a transporter pad, then beam over to the yard's right side.

FREE PLAY
VEHICLE TOKEN 2: JALOPY

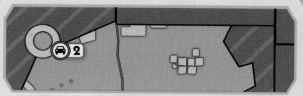

After traveling through the transporter, drill the shaky ground to discover a large gear.

Carry the gear to the left, and place it onto the large catapult. Pull the catapult's lever to send the gear flying over to the yard's left side.

The gear smashes a silver barrel, exposing a character token! Beam back over there and claim your prize.

FREE PLAY
CHARACTER TOKEN 2: STUDSKI

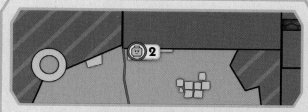

Chop through the boarded door on the yard's right side to enter a small room with a character token. This one's an easy grab!

Rescuing Natalia

More thugs await Chase after he materializes from the transporter. Take them out, then climb the blue background pipe to reach a higher platform.

Use a wall runway to dash across the platform's gap, then flip across a flagpole to reach the platform's end. From here, press Ⓧ to jump into the nearby crane, from which Natalia is desperately hanging. Chase lowers the poor girl to the ground, saving her from captivity!

INTRODUCTION

POLICE ACADEMY

CHARACTERS AND VEHICLES

WALKTHROUGH

LEGO CITY TOUR

CHECKLISTS

CHAPTER 9: BRINGING HOME THE BACON

RESCUING NATALIA FROM CHAN'S SCRAPYARD HAS PUT CHASE ON CHIEF DUNBY'S BAD SIDE—AGAIN! RAIDING THE SCRAPYARD HAS FORCED CHAN INTO HIDING, SO THE VILLAIN WON'T BE ARRESTED ANYTIME SOON. CHIEF DUNBY IS SO UPSET OVER THIS, HE SENDS CHASE TO WORK FOR SHERIFF HUCKLEBERRY OUT IN BLUEBELL NATIONAL PARK. THIS IS ABOUT AS FAR FROM WORKING ON THE REX FURY CASE AS OUR HERO CAN GET!

INTRODUCTION

POLICE ACADEMY

CHARACTERS AND VEHICLES

WALKTHROUGH

LEGO CITY TOUR

CHECKLISTS

 # CITY EXPLORATION

OBJECTIVE: GO TO SHERIFF HUCKLEBERRY

Natalia has been saved, but Chase won't be getting back to the Rex Fury case for a while. Find a fast ride and head out to Chief Huckleberry's without delay.

Chase meets Officer Frank Honey at Sheriff Huckleberry's. After a bit of tomfoolery, the sheriff explains that a local farmer, Jethro Hayes, needs help around his farm. Not exactly the most thrilling assignment for an officer of McCain's talents, but our hero is always ready to lend a helping hand!

OBJECTIVE: GO TO FARMER HAYES'S FARM

Hop onto one of the horses outside Sheriff Huckleberry's station, then trot off toward Farmer Hayes's nearby farm. You'll find that riding a horse is a lot like driving a car—only no turbos!

Chase and Frank arrive just in time to witness Farmer Hayes's pigs break free of their pen and run amok. The poor farmer begs our hero to help him round them up and says he'll loan Chase one of his old farming outfits to help him approach the pigs without startling them. Unfortunately, Farmer Hayes has locked his old outfit in a cabinet and buried the key in his field!

OBJECTIVE: REPAIR FARMER HAYES'S TRACTOR

Farmer Hayes's tractor will help you find the buried key, but the tractor is in need of repair. Build the bouncing bricks near the tractor to patch it up.

You've fixed the tractor. Now you just need to top off its oil. Approach the nearby scan spot and follow Farmer Hayes's footsteps to a light patch of soil. Investigate the dirt to sweep it away, open a hatch, and discover an oil can.

Carry the oil can over to the tractor to fill it with fresh oil. Nice work! Now the tractor is good as new.

OBJECTIVE: PLOW THE FIELD

Drive the tractor over to Farmer Hayes's field. Park at the objective beacon, and Chase will identify four crops of corn around the field.

Simply drive over each patch of corn to plow it with the tractor. Make sure you plow every stalk—the key is buried under one of these crops!

Pick up the key, and carry it back toward Farmer Hayes. Use the key to open the garage, then search the locker inside to discover the Chase McCain (Farmer) disguise!

OBJECTIVE: FIND THE MISSING PIGS

Now that you're properly dressed, you're ready to search for those missing pigs. Approach the nearby planter, which is now marked with a watering can symbol.

Stand on the watering can symbol and press Ⓐ to water the planter's seeds. The seeds quickly sprout into vines—climb the vines to reach a thin ledge above.

Inch across the thin ledge, then drop to a lower roof. Cross the roof and jump up to another thin ledge. Inch around the ledge to reach a rope.

The First Pig

Jump and grab the rope, and climb to the barn's roof. Stand on the chicken symbol you discover up here.

Press Ⓐ while standing on the chicken symbol to activate it. This makes a ring of green studs appear in front of you. Jump up, then press and hold Ⓑ to whip out a chicken and glide through the ring of studs. Chase gains some extra height when he passes through the stud ring, helping him reach the roof of the neighboring barn.

Tiptoe across the balance beam on the second barn's roof to reach another chicken symbol. Again, press Ⓐ to make a ring of green studs appear, then jump and hold Ⓑ to glide through them as you head for another barn.

You land near a red planter. Water it to grow a tall sunflower, then climb up to reach the third barn's roof.

This barn's roof sports a scan spot. Stand there and use Audio Scan mode to detect the telltale oinking of one of Farmer Hayes's missing pigs.

The first pig has somehow managed to get itself stuck on the roof of a nearby shed. Carefully move to the right across the barn's roof, heading for a chicken symbol. Be careful not to fall on your way!

Activate the chicken symbol, then jump up and glide through several rings of studs on your way over to the pig. Make sure to pass through the stud rings to preserve your height as you glide.

Approach the pig after you land on the shed, and press Ⓧ to mount it. Now you can ride the pig just like a horse!

Ride the pig over to Farmer Hayes's pen, and it will jump inside. Two more to go!

The Second Pig

A new scan spot appears after you deliver the first pig to the pen. Follow your objective marker to locate the scan spot—you'll find it atop a hay bale out in Farmer Hayes's field.

Jump onto the hay bale and use Audio Scan mode to detect the oinking of another pig. This one's a lot easier to reach—just run across the field to find it.

Unfortunately, the second pig is fast asleep; you'll need to wake it. Use the nearby scan spot to trace a trail of footprints over to a suspicious patch of soil, then search the earth to discover a valve wheel.

Insert the valve wheel into the pipe near the sleeping pig, and give it a twist. Water spurts up near the pig, rousing it from its slumber. Mount the pig and ride it back to the pen as you did before.

The Third Pig

The final pig takes the most effort to find. Farmer Hayes tells you that Frank has ridden to a nearby castle—he thought he heard some oinking coming from it. Hop onto your horse and follow the studs to locate the castle.

Sure enough, Frank awaits you just outside the castle. Water the nearby planter to grow some vines. Climb them to begin your ascent up the castle's wall.

After climbing the vines, flip across a flagpole to reach a chain. Climb up and then jump to a thin ledge. Inch to the left along the ledge to reach some handholds that lead you over the wall.

Waking the Third Pig

Frank was right—the third pig is fast asleep inside the castle. And only the tantalizing aroma of food will wake it! Turn right and pry open the nearby metal door to discover a planter. Water it to grow an apple tree.

The apple tree drops an apple. Pick it up and bring it to the trough near the sleeping pig. One more piece of food to find!

Run around the castle wall to locate another planter. Water it to grow some vines, then climb up to a thin ledge.

Don't worry—there's a shortcut back to the castle. Simply use the nearby transporter pad to beam back over there.

Place the banana in the trough to at last wake the pig. Now you just need to get it back over to the farm!

Inch along the thin ledge to locate a patch of climbable LEGOs. Jump up and grab these, then scale the wall to reach the top of a tower.

Returning the Third Pig

As luck would have it, there's an easy way to deliver the pig back to its pen. Hop onto the pig, and ride it over to the nearby cannon. Stand on the action symbol in front of the cannon and press Ⓐ to stuff the pig inside.

Hey, there's a chicken symbol up here! Press Ⓐ to activate the symbol, and watch as a series of green stud rings appears in front of you.

Run around the cannon and stand on the other action symbol. Press Ⓐ to wind up the cannon's gears and launch the pig back over to the farm.

Great job! Your good deed for the day is finished.

You know what to do! Jump and glide through those stud rings, heading for the top of the distant train tunnel. Water the seeds you discover up here to grow a banana tree, then collect a banana.

NOTE

Well done! You've unlocked pig rescue events all around LEGO City! Keep on the lookout for more of Farmer Hayes's lost pigs, and blast them back to his pen by way of cannon!

INTRODUCTION

POLICE ACADEMY

CHARACTERS AND VEHICLES

WALKTHROUGH

LEGO CITY TOUR

CHECKLISTS

CHAPTER 10: BACK ON THE CASE

436,650 4,656

Chase McCain (Civilian)

CHASE HAS BEEN SIDETRACKED WITH SOME LESS-THAN-THRILLING ERRANDS OUT IN THE COUNTRYSIDE, BUT AFTER A CALL FROM VINNIE PAPPALARDO, THE REX FURY CASE SUDDENLY PICKS UP AGAIN. VINNIE SAYS HE NEEDS CHASE TO BREAK INTO THE LEGO CITY MUSEUM AND STEAL THE MECHANICAL T-REX EXHIBIT. SOUNDS WILD!

INTRODUCTION

POLICE ACADEMY

CHARACTERS AND VEHICLES

WALKTHROUGH

LEGO CITY TOUR

CHECKLISTS

CITY EXPLORATION

⭐ OBJECTIVE: GO TO THE MUSEUM

At last, you're back on the Rex Fury case! Grab a vehicle and speed off toward the museum.

Chase finds the museum locked up tight—he'll need to find another way inside. Ellie thinks he might be able to enter from the roof, but it will take some effort to get up there.

⭐ OBJECTIVE: CHICKEN-GLIDE FROM THE ART GALLERY

Chase finds several color swappers inside the building. Use one to fill your color gun with green energy, then blast the red switch on the background wall. This opens a door. Head on through!

Mosey over to the art gallery building, which isn't far. Change into the farmer disguise and water the plants along the side of the building to grow some vines. Climb up and shimmy along the overhead patch of LEGOs to reach a handhold.

Climbing the Art Gallery

Shimmy across the handhold and climb up to a ledge. Smash an air conditioner to expose an opening in the side of the building, then press Ⓐ to slide through the hole.

After you emerge from the door, water two planters to grow a pair of flowers. Jump across the flowers to land atop the curved awnings. Run and jump across the awnings to reach the art gallery's roof.

Smash the surrounding fans and build a giant fan out of their bricks. Use the updraft to reach a higher section of roof. Rapidly press Ⓑ to run up the blue and white LEGO patches on the sloped roof and climb even higher.

TIP

As you scale the sloped roof, take breaks by pausing at the narrow flats between the blue and white LEGO patches.

Land on the museum's roof, and climb a patch of blue and white LEGOs to reach a tower.

Use the grapple gun to zip up to a high grapple point. Jump across the blue and white LEGO disks to the right. Hop along them just as if they were thin poles.

Smash another air conditioner after you scale the sloped roof, then build its bricks to add to the blue and white LEGO patch above. Now you can climb up to reach the highest portion of the art gallery's roof.

The disks lead up to a metal door atop the tower. Pry open the door with the crowbar, then head inside to at last enter the museum.

Good work! Now you just need to glide over to the museum. Stand on the chicken symbol and press Ⓐ to activate it. Watch as several green stud rings appear, then jump and chicken-glide through the stud rings to sail all over to the museum's roof.

SPECIAL ASSIGNMENT 8: THE COLOSSAL FOSSIL HUSTLE

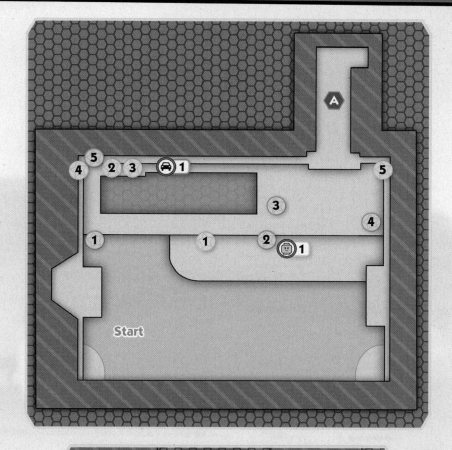

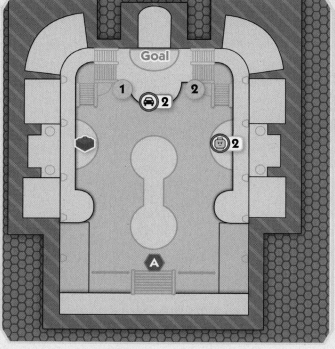

INTRODUCTION

POLICE ACADEMY

CHARACTERS AND VEHICLES

WALKTHROUGH

LEGO CITY TOUR

CHECKLISTS

STAGE COLLECTIBLES: "THE COLOSSAL FOSSIL HUSTLE"

MAP ICON(S)	TYPE	MODE	NOTES	GOT IT?
1 to 5	Police Shield Piece 1	Story	Water five green plant boxes around the museum's first area.	1
1 to 4	Police Shield Piece 2	Story	Smash five T-Rex posters around the museum's first area. One is hidden in the gift shop.	2
1	"Mummy" character token	Free Play	Fix the fuse box near the upper trolly rail.	7
1	"Ancestor" vehicle token	Story	After building the plane, climb the pirate ship's ladder and jump over to its cannon. Blast the background wall.	3
1 to 2	Police Shield Piece 3	Free Play	Use Rex Fury to pull the two super-strength handles near the stairs in the second area.	4
2	"Caveman" character token	Free Play	Use Rex Fury to help you build the Dry Bones exhibit.	5
2	"Silversmith" vehicle token	Free Play	Fix the fuse box near the totem pole exhibit, beam down to the brontosaurus exhibit, climb the tail, grapple up to the pterodactyl, and pull the lever.	6
⬡	Red Brick—Super Break and Enter	Free Play	Use Rex Fury to rip apart the super-strength crate in the unfinished exhibit upstairs, then bring the object down to the triceratops exhibit. Pull the two strength handles near the stairs and bring the other two objects to the triceratops to complete it.	8
—	Police Shield Piece 4	Story	Complete all four upstairs exhibit puzzles (totem, sphinx, archer, caveman) in any order. The first three give you superbricks; the final one gives you the shield piece.	9

LEGO CITY HERO STUD REQUIREMENT:

62,000

⭐ OBJECTIVE: FIND THE T-REX EXHIBIT

You've entered the museum. Now you need to find that mechanical T-Rex. Begin by prying open the door of the gift shop.

POLICE SHIELD PIECE 1

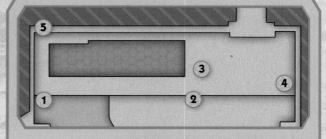

Find and water five green plant boxes in the museum's first area to cultivate a shield piece! Check the map to see where the plant boxes are placed.

POLICE SHIELD PIECE 2

Find and smash five T-Rex posters around this first area of the museum to score another shield piece!

One is hidden in the gift shop; the rest are on the walls in the main area. Check the maps to see where these five posters are affixed.

Off to the Races

Collect the lever handle you find inside the gift shop, then carry it over to the curtained exhibit on the left. Insert the handle into the slot on the wall, then pull the lever to move the curtain and start the race car it was covering.

Latch on to the grapple point on the front of the race car, and give it a good tug. The race car comes loose from its mount and speeds to the right, eventually crashing near the train exhibit.

Take out the security guards who storm forth to investigate the disturbance. Run to the right afterward and build the race car's remains into a dynamite dispenser.

Collect some dynamite from the dispenser, and use it to destroy the nearby silver ingot exhibit. After the blast, build the ingot's remaining bricks to complete the nearby furnace and cause the steam train to roll over to the right.

Crafty Cart

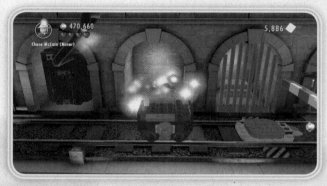

With the train out of the way, you can now explore several background nooks. Smash the machinery in the nook near the furnace to find more bricks; build these into a push cart.

Shove the cart to the right so that it parks on a red button. This lowers some bars, letting you access another nook. Smash the object in the nook to find more bricks. Build these to add a platform to the cart's top.

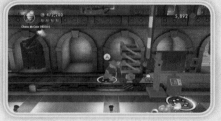

Push the cart to the right again, and it will park on another red button, unbarring another nook. Enter the nook and collect a valve wheel. Fit the wheel onto the front of the cart.

Turn the valve wheel to extend the platform you added to the cart over to the right, creating a set of stairs. Jump up these stairs to reach the balcony above.

INTRODUCTION

POLICE ACADEMY

CHARACTERS AND VEHICLES

WALKTHROUGH

LEGO CITY TOUR

CHECKLISTS

Crafty Key

Smash the large machines you find on the balcony. This reveals some bricks; build these into a color swapper and use it to fill your color gun with green energy.

Blast the red switch in the background nook to activate it; this moves the nearby trolly to the right. Collect the curious crystal you find inside one of the nooks that the trolly had been blocking.

CHARACTER TOKEN 1: MUMMY

During Free Play, fix the fuse box near the upper track to open a nook that sports a character token.

Bring the crystal back down to the main floor and place it into the fabrication machine in one of the lower nooks. The fabrication machine transforms the crystal into a key. Cool!

Insert your newfound key into the nearby lock, and give it a turn to open the final ground-floor nook. Hey, there's a superbrick in there! Grab it and return to the balcony.

Drilling Upward

Next, pick up the box of bricks that sits inside one of the balcony nooks. Carry it over to the left and place the bricks down near the oil derrick exhibit. Build the bricks to add some gears to the oil derrick and start it up.

The oil derrick drills through the ground, causing a geyser of oil to gush up. Jump into the oil geyser to soar up to the walkway that surrounds the pirate ship exhibit.

Sunken Treasure

Run to the left and pull a lever to deploy a salvage craft into the large tank upon which the pirate ship is floating. The camera then pans over to show a sunken superbrick in the water.

Stand on the nearby action symbol and press Ⓐ to take control of the salvage craft. Direct it over to the superbrick, and the craft will automatically grab it with its mechanical arms.

> **TIP**
>
> The salvage craft must be a little higher than the superbrick in order for its arms to grab it.

Bring the superbrick back over to the glowing beacon where the salvage craft was deployed. You will then regain control of Chase.

Pull the lever again to lower the crane, pick up the salvage craft, and drop the superbrick within your reach. Nice work!

Plane to See

Sprint to the right and head upstairs. Collect the large superbrick near the security lasers. Step onto the nearby superbuild pad and press Ⓐ to construct a model airplane—you should have 21,000 bricks by now. The airplane's propeller starts spinning, creating a draft that blows the pirate ship over to the left.

Shipping Off

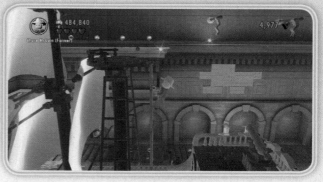

Return to the pirate ship exhibit and cross the gangplank to board the ship. Climb the ship's ladder to reach the high lookout, then leap over to the background ledge.

VEHICLE TOKEN 1: ANCESTOR

Jump off the pirate ship's ladder to land near its cannon. Stand behind the cannon and press Ⓐ to fire it at the background wall. You'll blast free a vehicle token!

Swing along a series of flagpoles to the right and land atop the space exhibit. Drop through the hole in the roof to enter the exhibit.

Use the scan spot inside the space exhibit to track down a buried moon rock. Pick up the rock and place it into the nearby basket. The added weight triggers the button beneath the basket, causing a crate to fall nearby.

INTRODUCTION

POLICE ACADEMY

CHARACTERS AND VEHICLES

WALKTHROUGH

LEGO CITY TOUR

CHECKLISTS

Build the crate's remains into a transporter pad. Step onto the pad to beam over to the mad scientist exhibit.

Turn two valves inside the mad scientist exhibit to align the gauges on the wall. Simply turn each valve so that both gauges' needles land in the green.

Aligning the gauges activates a nearby floor fan. Before jumping into the updraft, pull the lever on the wall near the mad scientist. This causes a color swapper to appear on a high ledge above you.

Now jump into the updraft to float through the mad scientist exhibit's roof. Jump over to the color swapper here, and use it to fill your color gun with red energy.

Good work! Now simply drop from the ledge and blast the green switch beyond the red security lasers. This shuts off the lasers, letting you dash through the background hall and enter the museum's dinosaur exhibit.

⭐ OBJECTIVE: BUILD THE T-REX

You've made it to the dinosaur exhibit, but you must build the T-Rex before you can steal it. This will require 30,000 bricks, and as luck would have it, there are several superbricks located here! Wipe out the first wave of security guards, then begin your search for superbricks.

Security Breach

Run to the left and smash the pterodactyl exhibit's large LEGO egg to discover a scan spot. Follow the footprints over to a patch of soil.

Search the soil to discover a large feather beneath a hatch. How strange!

Pick up the feather and carry it over to the stegosaurus exhibit on the right. Stand on the feather symbol beneath the stegosaurus, and press Ⓐ to tickle the dinosaur with the feather.

The stegosaurus comes to life, waving its tail and smashing the window of the nearby office. Subdue the security guard who storms out, and enter the office. Collect the dynamite you discover inside.

Carry the dynamite over to the right, and use it to blast the silver door of the security office near the pterodactyl exhibit. Defeat the guard and use the control panel to open all of the exhibits on the second floor.

FREE PLAY
POLICE SHIELD PIECE 3

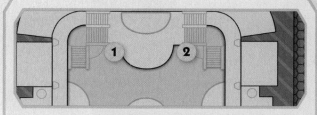

During Free Play, use Rex Fury to pull the two super-strength handles near the background stairs. Rip both handles from the wall to pull out a shield piece!

FREE PLAY
CHARACTER TOKEN 2: CAVEMAN

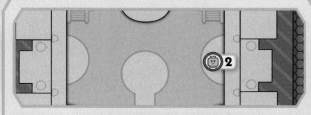

Put Rex Fury's muscles to use again and rip apart the super-strength crate on the right. Build the bricks you discover into a model of Dry Bones, and a character token will appear nearby!

INTRODUCTION

POLICE ACADEMY

CHARACTERS AND VEHICLES

WALKTHROUGH

LEGO CITY TOUR

CHECKLISTS

Superbrick Roundup

Nice work! Now it's time to hunt for superbricks. There are four interactive exhibits around the upper floor—the first three you solve will reward you with large superbricks, while the fourth exhibit you solve will reward you with a collectible shield piece. Good stuff!

Exhibit 1: Totem Poles

Let's begin with the totem pole exhibit. Head upstairs and go right. Use the control panel in front of the totem pole exhibit to spin its three totem poles.

Pay attention to the posters on the background wall. Whenever a totem pole spins and matches the poster behind it, enter the exhibit and step on the red button in front of the totem pole to lock it in place. Now the totem pole won't spin when you use the control panel again!

Just keep spinning the totem poles and locking them in place until you match all three up to the background posters. Once you properly align all three totem poles, your prize will appear! Enter the exhibit and grab it.

> **TIP**
>
> Smash the crate inside the totem pole exhibit to find some bricks. Build these into a robotic tribesman that tosses out studs!

FREE PLAY
VEHICLE TOKEN 2: SILVERSMITH

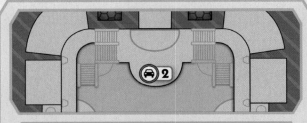

Toggle to the construction worker and fix the fuse box to the right of the totem pole exhibit. This powers up a nearby transporter pad. Use the pad to beam down to the central brontosaurus exhibit.

Smash the pole that's supporting the brontosaurus's mighty tail, and the tail will collapse to the floor. Now you can run up the tail and reach the brontosaurus's back!

Run up the tail and grapple the overhead pterodactyl. Chase zips up onto the pterodactyl's back. Press Ⓐ to pull a lever that sends the creature flying toward a glass display case below.

Drop down to the shattered display case and collect the vehicle token that's now within your grasp. Sweet!

Exhibit 2: Sphinx

Follow the right balcony to its end to locate the sphinx exhibit. Smash the crate here to find some bricks. Build these to complete the sphinx.

Step outside and use the control panel to activate the sphinx exhibit. Two hovering symbols appear over the sphinx's paws, and a timer starts ticking

down. Quickly enter the exhibit again and use the control panels on either side of the sphinx to cycle through the symbols on the walls. Match these symbols to the two above the sphinx's paws to receive your reward!

Exhibit 3: The Archer

Backtrack and run past the T-Rex pad, heading for the exhibits on the left balcony. Ignore the first, unfinished exhibit and smash the crate in the next

one to discover some bricks. Build these into a statue of an archer.

Once you build the archer, the exhibit's background target begins moving back and forth along a track. Use the control panel to make the archer fire

his arrow at the target while the target is over to the right. Score the bull's-eye to make your prize materialize!

FREE PLAY

RED BRICK: SUPER BREAK AND ENTER

Use Rex Fury to rip apart the super-strength crates inside the unfinished exhibit to the left of the T-Rex pad. Pick up the curious object

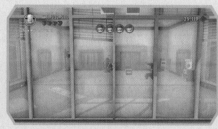

you discover and carry it downstairs, placing it onto the triceratops exhibit.

Use Rex Fury again to pull the two background strength handles (if you haven't already). You'll discover another two pieces of the triceratops exhibit.

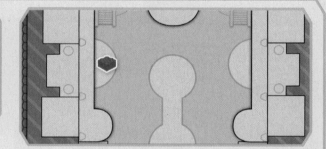

Place all three missing pieces onto the triceratops to make it whole. The great beast roars to life, and you're rewarded with a red brick!

Exhibit 4: Cavemen

Head to the end of the left balcony to locate the caveman exhibit. Smash a crate here to find some bricks. Build these into a club-wielding caveman statue.

Use the exhibit's control panel to make the caveman statue swing his club. Smash the four rough edges of the spinning wheel with the caveman's club to help him "discover" the wheel. More importantly, you'll discover a valuable prize!

INTRODUCTION

POLICE ACADEMY

CHARACTERS AND VEHICLES

WALKTHROUGH

LEGO CITY TOUR

CHECKLISTS

POLICE SHIELD PIECE 4

Find the final shield piece by solving all of the exhibits around the museum's upper balcony. The first three exhibits you solve reward you with superbricks, but the final exhibit you solve gives you a shield piece! Because this shield piece could come from any exhibit, we haven't labeled it on the maps.

Do the Dinosaur

You should now have plenty of bricks, so head on over to the superbuild pad. Stand on the pad and spend 30,000 bricks to build the T-Rex. Chase then hops onto the mechanical monster and smashes his way out of the museum.

CITY EXPLORATION

⭐ OBJECTIVE: DELIVER THE T-REX TO THE AIRPORT

Chase has succeeded in stealing the T-Rex for Vinnie, but he still needs to deliver the mechanical monster to the drop-off point at the airport. Storm through the streets and follow those green studs without delay!

Police will try to stop you from reaching your destination, but they pose little threat to your mighty mechanical T-Rex. Press Ⓐ to make the T-Rex roar and Ⓨ to make it stomp the ground. Both of these attacks are effective at repelling the cops—especially the stomp!

Keep going until you reach the objective beacon inside one of the airport's hangars. This is the drop-off point. Vinnie calls shortly after you

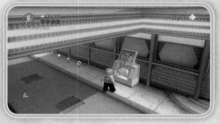

make the drop, pleased with your work. Now he can deliver the T-Rex to his mysterious buyer!

⭐ OBJECTIVE: GO TO THE FIRE DEPARTMENT

You've done well by Vinnie, but the crime boss isn't done with you yet. In fact, he already has a new job for Chase—one that involves stealing a boat from the fire department! Find some wheels and head to the fire department to begin this new job.

SPECIAL ASSIGNMENT 9: HOT PROPERTY

INTRODUCTION

POLICE ACADEMY

CHARACTERS AND VEHICLES

WALKTHROUGH

LEGO CITY TOUR

CHECKLISTS

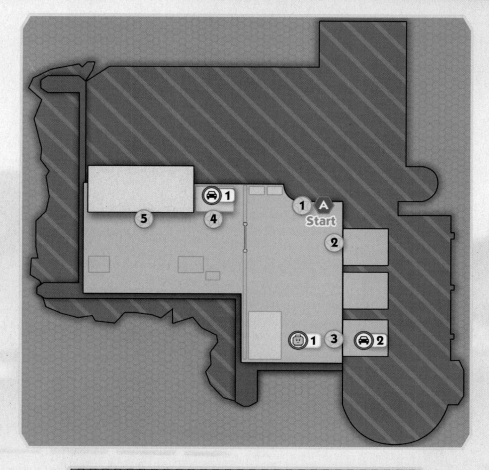

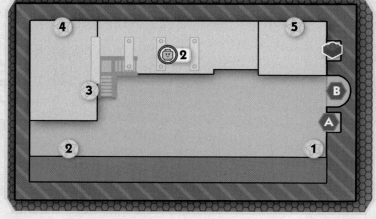

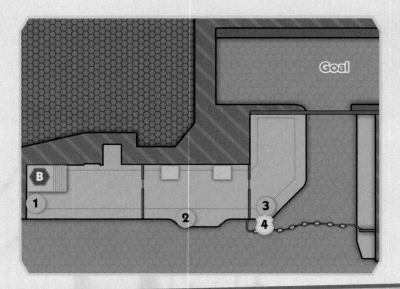

STAGE COLLECTIBLES: "HOT PROPERTY"

MAP ICON(S)	TYPE	MODE	NOTES	GOT IT?
1 to 5	Police Shield Piece 1	Story	Spray five alarm bells atop the garages around the training grounds.	1
1	"Ramon Lopez Delgado" character token	Story	Douse the barrel fire that the firemen are gathered around.	2
1	"Extender" vehicle token	Free Play	Use Rex Fury to rip apart the super-strength crate in the garage beyond the gate.	3
2	"Fire Tracker" vehicle token	Free Play	Use Rex Fury to rip apart the super-strength crate in the burning building. Carry the lever handle over to the garages and pull the lever, then enter the vehicle.	4
1 to 5	Police Shield Piece 2	Story	Smash five piles of gifts around the fire station.	5
	Red Brick—Fancy Dress	Story	Chop through the boarded door on the fire station's right side.	6
2	"Charlotte Hannon" character token	Story	Run on either of the treadmills inside the station.	7
1 to 3	Police Shield Piece 3	Story	Douse three barrel fires around the boathouse.	8
4	Police Shield Piece 4	Story	Pull the lever after using the catapult pad, then ride the raft around the water, collecting the studs.	9

LEGO CITY HERO STUD REQUIREMENT: 50,000

⭐ OBJECTIVE: FIND A UNIFORM

Chase arrives at the fire station just in time to join in the celebration of their chief's 40th birthday. But before our hero can join in the festivities, he needs to complete his training!

Officer Lopez Delgado will walk you through your training. Your first task: Open the garage and find a uniform! Pull the lever near the left garage to open it.

Smash the large crate inside the garage to find some bricks. Build these into a space crate, then solve the sequence to activate it and beam some bricks over to the garage on the right.

Enter the garage and build the bricks into a color swapper. Fill your color gun with red energy and head back outside.

Aim the color gun at the central garage door, and target its four white panels. Fire the color gun to paint all four of its white panels red. Much better! Now simply pull the nearby lever to open the garage.

Enter the central garage and open the locker you find inside. Nice work— you've discovered the Chase McCain (Fireman) disguise!

⭐ OBJECTIVE: COMPLETE FIREMAN TRAINING

Now that you've found the proper attire, Officer Delgado asks you to extinguish the nearby fire. Approach the flames and hold Ⓨ to douse them with your fire extinguisher. Cool!

TIP

Spray water and douse the flaming barrels you find around the fire station to score bonus studs!

POLICE SHIELD PIECE 1

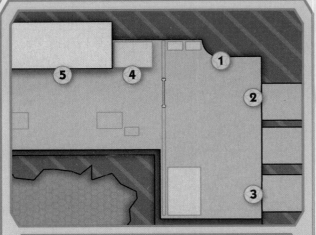

Hold Y to spray water at the red alarm bells around the fire station's grounds. Hit all five alarm bells to receive a shield piece! Some of the bells are located on the left side of the grounds, and you can't reach them until Officer Delgado opens the gate.

CHARACTER TOKEN 1: RAMON LOPEZ DELGADO

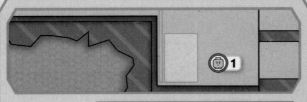

Douse the barrel fire near the garages, which a crew of firemen are standing around. This makes a secret character token appear!

Chop Sticks

Next, Officer Delgado hands you a fire axe, and asks you to smash through the nearby door. Stand on the Axe symbol in front of the door, then rapidly press A to smash through the door's wooden boards.

Nice work! Now collect the valve wheel in the room beyond the door. Carry the wheel over to the fireman who's being tossed around by a squirting hose. Fit the valve wheel onto the fire hydrant, and turn it to shut off the water and rescue the fireman.

Officer Delgado is impressed by your performance and opens a gate that leads to the training area's other half. Head through and step into the glowing objective beacon to begin your next challenge.

FREE PLAY
VEHICLE TOKEN 1: EXTENDER

Use Rex Fury to rip apart the super-strength crate in the garage on the gate's left side. A vehicle token will be your prize!

Towering Inferno

Oh no! Several firemen are trapped inside a burning building! Issue orders to the firemen on the ground, telling them to move either right or left so they can catch the trapped firemen with their net. Simply move the net into the objective beacons that appear, and the trapped firemen will leap down to safety.

You've saved the firemen—now you must douse the building! Jump onto one of the water cannons that Officer Delgado activates for you, and hold

 to spray water at the flames. Just keep spraying until you extinguish all nine flames.

> **TIP**
>
> Feel free to switch cannons if it will help you reach the more distant flames.

Climbing Higher

After you put out the building's fires, Officer Delgado opens a door, revealing a box of bricks. Pick this up and carry it over to the pad on the right. Set the box down on the pad, then build the bricks into a ladder that lets you climb up and enter the building's second floor.

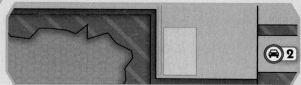

FREE PLAY
VEHICLE TOKEN 2: FIRE TRACKER

After climbing the ladder, toggle to Rex Fury and rip apart the super-strength crate you discover in the building. Pick up the lever handle you find and drop back down to the main grounds.

Run back over to the garages on the right and insert the lever handle into the indicated slot. Pull the lever to lower an emergency vehicle, and hop into the driver's seat to discover a vehicle token!

Cross the building's second floor, and jump out to the exterior scaffolding. Bounce up from a trampoline to reach an overhead handhold, then enter the third floor above.

Use the fire axe to smash through the third floor's boarded door, and carefully tiptoe across the balance beam beyond. Smash another door and head through it.

INTRODUCTION

POLICE ACADEMY

CHARACTERS AND VEHICLES

WALKTHROUGH

LEGO CITY TOUR

CHECKLISTS

Step out onto the scaffolding and jump into the background to reach a lower roof below. Climb the blue pipe here to reach the building's fourth floor.

Chop your way through another boarded door to reach a dynamite dispenser. Switch to the miner disguise and collect some dynamite. Use it to blast through the silver wall on the left.

There's no floor beyond the silver wall, so jump up and grab the overhead LEGO patch instead. Shimmy to the left and drop near another boarded door, then break through.

Use the grapple gun to pull down an overhead ladder beyond the boarded door. Climb the ladder to reach the building's roof.

RC Action

Smash the rooftop crates to discover an action symbol. Press Ⓐ to whip out a controller and take over the nearby RC car. Carefully steer the car through the small opening in the wall on the right.

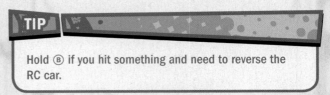

TIP

Hold Ⓑ if you hit something and need to reverse the RC car.

Drive the RC car into the glowing objective beacon, and it will explode, toppling a drum that smashes through the wall. Now you can run over to the little kitty on the right!

The cat is suspicious of you—feed it some fish to win its trust. Fortunately, all LEGO City firemen carry a healthy supply of fish for just such emergencies. Press Ⓐ to present the cat with a fish that sends it leaping into your arms.

Well done! Ramon couldn't be happier with your progress and invites you to join the rest of the crew inside. Head through the indicated door to advance to the next area.

⭐ OBJECTIVE: STEAL THE BOATHOUSE KEY

Your next objective is to steal the boathouse key from the fire chief's office. This won't be easy, because the chief has locked himself in his office—he's really disappointed with the birthday party his fellow firefighters have thrown him!

POLICE SHIELD PIECE 2

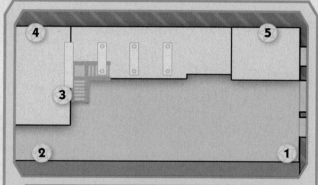

Smash five piles of gift boxes inside the fire station to unwrap a shiny shield piece. Check the maps for the gift boxes' locations!

RED BRICK: FANCY DRESS

This stage's red brick is an easy grab. Just smash through the boarded door on the fire station's first floor, then step into the closet beyond to collect the red brick. Smokin'!

CHARACTER TOKEN 2: CHARLOTTE HANNON

Run on the station's treadmills to score some bonus studs. You'll also reveal a hidden character token!

Luring out the Chief

Approach the party game on the station's ground floor and press Ⓐ to play it. Spray water at the five clown heads, but only after they've spun around to face you. While a clown head is facing you, just keep spraying water at it until a balloon fills up above the clown head. Blow up all five balloons before time runs out to win the game!

When you reach the final overhead light, switch to the farmer disguise and perform a chicken-glide to reach the top of the chief's office. Pry open the skylight atop the office and drop inside.

Hearing the commotion you've caused downstairs, Chief Burns finally leaves his office to join in the fun. Now's your chance! Hurry upstairs and start searching for a way into the chief's office, which he has locked behind him.

Entering the Office

Crack the safe inside the chief's office, then grab the key you discover inside. This must be the boathouse key!

Smash the furniture near the chief's office to discover a hidden scan spot. Follow the footprints from the scan spot to locate a cabinet that contains a key.

Use the control panel on the wall to open the office door, then hurry downstairs. Insert the key into the lock on the right wall. Turn it to open the nearby shutter. Slide down the fireman pole beyond to at last reach the boathouse.

Collect the key from the cabinet and use it to open the nearby door. Enter the room beyond and smash the background objects to discover some bricks that you can build into a trampoline.

Bounce up from the trampoline and grab the overhead flagpole. Flip over to the narrow blue beam on the right, then hop across the overhead lights, heading toward the chief's office.

OBJECTIVE: FIND THE DOCKED FIRE BOAT

You've entered the boathouse—now you just need to steal that fire boat! Smash the hat rack in the entry area to discover a scan spot, then follow the footprints over to a blue bin. Search the bin to discover a valve wheel.

POLICE SHIELD PIECE 3

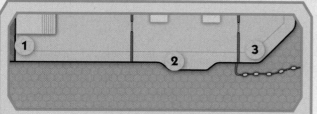

Douse three barrel fires around the boathouse to earn a shield piece. Check the maps for each barrel's location.

Great Gates

Insert the valve wheel into the notch near the lift, and turn the wheel to ride upward. Jump and flip across a pole to soar past the gate to the right.

A trio of whirling fans prevents you from continuing any farther. Drop and smash a large crate to discover some bricks, then build these into a space crate.

Activate the space crate to beam in a dynamite dispenser. Obtain some dynamite, and pry open the door on the left to return to the entry area.

Use the dynamite to blast away the silver bars near the lift, exposing a color swapper. Fill your color gun with red energy.

Run back to the right and blast the green switch on the background wall to deactivate the fans. Nice work! Now ride up the lift again and perform a chicken-glide to slip past the second gate.

Stealing the Fire Boat

A couple of Vinnie's goons await you on the gate's other side. Chat with them, then smash the nearby blue and white object to reduce it to bricks.

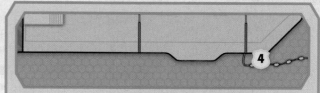

Build the bricks into a catapult pad, and use the pad to fly across the water. Blast the green switch on the wall with the color gun to deactivate the electric fence near the fire boat.

POLICE SHIELD PIECE 4

After launching across the catapult pad, pull the lever on the wall to make a raft fall from the ceiling. Hop onto the raft and follow a trail of studs around the water. Collect every stud to snag a shield piece when you reach the end of the trail!

INTRODUCTION

POLICE ACADEMY

CHARACTERS AND VEHICLES

WALKTHROUGH

LEGO CITY TOUR

CHECKLISTS

 With the electric fence shut off, you can now safely pry open the metal door near Vinnie's goons. Do so, then press ⊗ to pilot the fire boat.

 You're almost out of here! To make good your escape, simply spray the nearby water switch on the wall with one of the fire boat's water cannons. Just keep spraying the switch until it fills with water and the nearby gate opens, allowing Chase to drift off with the fire boat.

CITY EXPLORATION

⭐ OBJECTIVE: GO TO MERCY HEARTS HOSPITAL

Chase has delivered the fire boat to Vinnie, pleasing the crime boss immensely. But before our hero can continue on with his mission, he gets a call from Natalia, who's found herself in trouble again—this time at Mercy Hearts Hospital. Jump into the nearby speedboat and follow the green studs out of the water tunnel and over to the dock near the hospital. Park your speedboat at the dock and run up to the nearby hospital.

⭐ OBJECTIVE: RESCUE NATALIA FROM THE HOSPITAL'S ROOF

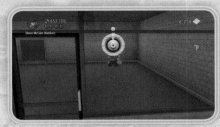 Enter the garage after putting out the fire and beat up the bad guys. Crack the safe inside the garage. Use the key card you find inside the safe to activate the nearby elevator. Collect a superbrick as you board the elevator and ride up to a higher floor.

The hospital is being assaulted by suited goons, and Natalia is trapped on the roof. You've got to save her!

 First things first: Use your fire extinguisher to douse the roaring flames near the hospital's garage.

Subdue a few more goons after you step off the elevator. Collect some dynamite from the nearby dispenser afterward, then put out more flames in the enclosed walkway on the right.

Place the dynamite in the small barrel inside the tunnel. The explosion blasts a hole through the walkway, letting you step out onto the roof.

Rooftop Ruckus

Run back toward the enclosed walkway and jump onto the blue balance beam that runs along its roof. Cross the balance beam to reach the roof on the left.

Spray the flames that surround the left roof's skylight, then use the crowbar to pry open the skylight, and drop inside.

Run toward the foreground and extinguish more flames near some bouncing bricks. Build the bricks into a planter, then water the planter to grow a tall sunflower. Climb up to reach a higher section of roof.

You land near a red color swapper. How convenient! Fill your color gun with red energy, then pry open the nearby door. Make your way back up to the green switch you noticed before.

> **TIP**
>
> Before climbing the sunflower, run along the narrow foreground walkway to discover another superbrick!

> **TIP**
>
> Smash the furniture near the red color swapper to discover another superbrick!

Beat up more goons on the higher roof, then douse the foreground fire so you may approach a green switch. Hang on, you need to find a red color swapper!

Blast the green switch with red energy to activate it and shut off the fan below. Run to the right and vault a pair of low walls to reach another green switch. Blast this one as well to shut off a second fan.

Gotta Keep Climbing

Chase can't reach Natalia, but he thinks he might be able to glide over to her if he can climb all the way up the hospital's tallest tower. Run to the right and bash open a boarded door with the fire axe.

Chop through another boarded door, then cross the balance beam that runs along the enclosed walkway's roof.

Enter the small room beyond the door and use a transporter pad to beam over to another enclosed walkway.

You've reached the base of the tall tower. Jump up the handholds, then wall-jump between the narrow Free Running walls. Just keep going until you reach the tower's apex.

Run to the end of the enclosed walkway and use a color swapper to fill your color gun with blue energy. This will soon come in handy!

Wipe out the suited toughs on the roof, along with the reinforcements that arrive by way of helicopter. A chicken symbol will appear nearby.

Beam back over to the small room and aim the color gun at the patch of white LEGOs on the wall. Blast the white LEGOs with blue energy in three places, and you'll be able to climb up to the room above.

You know what to do! Activate the chicken symbol, then wait for the green stud rings to appear. Jump and chicken-glide through the rings to reach Natalia.

Hasty Escape

Chase swoops up Natalia during his glide, then swings around and lands near a LEGO pad. Spend 20,000 bricks to build a helipad here.

Piloting helicopters couldn't be easier—just move around as you would on foot. Press Ⓐ to fly upward, and press Ⓑ to descend. Refer to the GamePad map to see where Ellie's apartment is located, and fly over there.

Oh no, more goons! Beat them up to secure the helipad, then use the helipad's control panel to call for a helicopter.

You'll see an objective beacon atop Ellie's apartment. Press and hold Ⓐ to fly up to the objective beacon, then simply fly into the beacon to land.

The helicopter arrives moments after you call for it. Press Ⓧ to hop into the pilot's seat, and Natalia will hop aboard as well. Now you just need to fly her over to Ellie's apartment, where she'll be safe from the goons.

Chase and Natalia share a tender moment after they land. Way to go, hero!

> **NOTE**
>
> Helicopters and crash mats are now unlocked! Now you can fly through LEGO City and perform flashy stunt exits from helicopters!

INTRODUCTION

POLICE ACADEMY

CHARACTERS AND VEHICLES

WALKTHROUGH

LEGO CITY TOUR

CHECKLISTS

CHAPTER 11: THE PROOF OF THE PUDDING IS IN THE MEETING

CHASE SUCCESSFULLY RESCUED NATALIA FROM MYSTERIOUS THUGS AT MERCY HEARTS HOSPITAL AND NOW TURNS HIS ATTENTION BACK TO THE REX FURY CASE. MCCAIN HAS ALSO RECENTLY WON VINNIE PAPPALARDO'S TRUST BY COMPLETING SEVERAL DIFFICULT JOBS FOR THE CRIME BOSS AND IS NOW SET TO MEET WITH VINNIE. WITH ANY LUCK, OUR HERO WILL LEARN SOMETHING ABOUT REX FURY'S WHEREABOUTS!

CITY EXPLORATION

⭐ OBJECTIVE: MEET WITH VINNIE AT PAPPALARDO'S

Why drive to Vinnie's when you can fly? Use the helipad atop Ellie's apartment to call for a helicopter. Hop aboard and fly to Pappalardo's—it's marked with a shield icon on your GamePad map. When you arrive, simply fly over the nearby crash mat and press Ⓧ to jump out of the chopper, then walk into the objective beacon.

Chase doesn't find Vinnie at Pappalardo's—only his trusted associate, Moe DeLuca. Moe informs Chase that Vinnie is at a meeting with his mysterious private buyer and expresses concern that something might have gone wrong. You'd better investigate!

⭐ OBJECTIVE: FIND VINNIE IN PARADISE SANDS

Jump up a few handholds to reach a balcony. Run around the balcony and climb a blue drain pipe.

Vinnie's meeting was set to go down at the Paradise Sands Hotel, so find some wheels and head over there. Step into the objective beacon when you arrive.

Follow the trail of studs around the back of the hotel to locate some scaffolding. Climb the scaffolding's ladder to begin your ascent up the building.

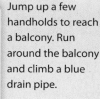

The pipe leads up to a patio with a large mechanical bee. Ignore this curious object for now and pry open the nearby door instead.

Smash up the furniture in the small room beyond the door to discover some bricks. Build these into a color swapper, then fill your color gun with green energy.

Head back outside and blast the red switch in front of the mechanical bee. The bee begins to move up and down like an elevator. Jump onto the bee and ride up, then leap onto a higher patio.

What a Workout

The patio features three different exercise machines. Use all three to "prove" to the nearby gym leader that you're a gym member—only then will he let you pass.

Obtain some dynamite from the dispenser inside the gym, and use it to blast open the patio's silver door. Enter the elevator beyond the door to ride up to a higher patio with a pool.

Pool Fool

Chase finds none other than Officer Frank Honey lazing about the pool patio—along with his horse! This is Frank's parents' hotel, and the well-meaning police officer informs Chase that he saw a sinister-looking helicopter land at the neighboring hotel. That must be where Vinnie has gone!

Jump onto the nearby chicken symbol and activate it, then make the long glide over to the building in the distance, passing through several stud rings and snagging a superbrick on your way there.

Water Work

Your long glide lands you near a flower bed. Water the flowers to grow them, and climb up to the building's roof.

Smash the patio furniture around the roof to discover a red cap. Grab the cap and use it to plug up one of the three spurting geysers in the roof's central fountain.

Break more patio furniture to uncover a scan spot. Trace the footprints to a cabinet that contains another red cap. Use this to plug another of the fountain's geysers.

Next, pry open the background door and enter the small room beyond. Crack the safe here to score another red cap, and use this to plug up a third geyser.

With three of the fountain's four geysers plugged, the pressure causes the remaining geyser to jet up much higher. Jump into the geyser to float upward, then leap over to the background roof.

Roofs and Ropes

Leap from the higher roof and climb up the patch of blue and white LEGOs on the neighboring building. Smash an air conditioner on the roof to discover some bricks. Build these into a climbable wall, and use it to reach a higher roof with a superbrick.

Collect the superbrick on the higher roof, then slide down a tightrope to zip over to the roof of the nearby hotel. Beat up the familiar goons on the rooftop, then pry open a door to score another superbrick. Water two planters afterward to grow a pair of flowers.

Jump up the flowers to reach the blue balance beam above. Tiptoe across the balance beam and background tightrope to reach another section of the hotel's roof.

Smash the blue and white bin atop the next roof to find some bricks. Build these into a color swapper, then fill the color gun with blue energy. Blast the white wall on the left with the color gun so you may climb it.

TIP

Chop through the boarded door near the climbable wall to score another superbrick!

Pool Party

Tiptoe across another tightrope to reach the next building's roof. Pry open a door here to snag a superbrick from the room beyond. Spend 30,000 bricks to build the Paradise Pool superbuild at the nearby LEGO pad.

NOTE

Because you're currently exploring LEGO City, this counts as one of the city's 65 superbuilds and earns you a gold brick!

Nice work! Now change into the fireman disguise and use the extinguisher to fill the pool with water. Just keep spraying the pool until it overflows and the giant beach ball rolls out onto the roof.

Press Ⓧ to jump onto the beach ball and ride it around the roof. Roll to the indicated spot on the right, then jump off the beach ball to reach the high catapult pad. Use the pad to rocket over to the next building.

Colorful Puzzle

Notice the red switch on this building's rooftop. You can't activate it yet, so smash the nearby boulders instead to uncover a transporter pad. Use this to beam over to the neighboring building.

INTRODUCTION

POLICE ACADEMY

CHARACTERS AND VEHICLES

WALKTHROUGH

LEGO CITY TOUR

CHECKLISTS

After teleporting, pick up the small box on the right and place it onto the nearby green pad. Some bricks spill out; build them into an RC car that's loaded with dynamite.

Activate the RC car and drive it through the course on the left, following a trail of studs toward a silver shelf. Ram the shelf with the RC car to destroy it and reduce the shelf to a pile of bricks.

Sprint over to the bricks and build them into a color swapper. Fill your color gun with green energy, then backtrack and beam over to the previous building.

You know what to do! Blast the red switch with the color gun to open the roof and expose a catapult pad. Use the pad to rocket over to yet another building.

Final Climb

Chase smacks into the side of the building and slides down to a handhold. Shimmy to the right and climb the blue and white LEGO patch on the wall to reach a patio.

A locked door catches Chase's eye. Use a wall runway to dash over to the next patio, then chop open a boarded door to access a safe. Crack the safe to claim the key inside.

Wall-run back over to the first patio and use the key to open a locked door. Head inside, and Chase will emerge on the building's roof.

Vinnie and Rex

At last, you've reached your objective: a scan spot! Stand on the scan spot and use Audio Scan mode to eavesdrop on the meeting between Vinnie and Rex Fury in the building across the street.

Chase listens as Vinnie is given orders to steal more goods for the private buyer, who Rex seems to also be working for. Shortly thereafter, Vinnie calls Chase to give him another job—one that involves breaking into millionaire Forrest Blackwell's secret vault!

⭐ **OBJECTIVE: ENTER BLACKWELL'S SEA CAVE**

The entrance to Mr. Blackwell's sea cave isn't far. Follow the green studs to a nearby beach. Swim over to the objective beacon near the sea cave to begin your next assignment.

SPECIAL ASSIGNMENT 10: SMASH 'N' GRAB

INTRODUCTION

POLICE ACADEMY

CHARACTERS AND VEHICLES

WALKTHROUGH

LEGO CITY TOUR

CHECKLISTS

STAGE COLLECTIBLES: "SMASH 'N' GRAB"

MAP ICON(S)	TYPE	MODE	NOTES	GOT IT?
1 to 3	Police Shield Piece 1	Story	Smash three life preserver stands around the sea cave.	1
1 to 4	Police Shield Piece 2	Story	Pry open four red lockers around the sea cave.	2
1	"Moe DeLuca" character token	Free Play	Fix the fuse box on the first ledge, pry open the door, and pull the lever.	3
1	"Buzzer" vehicle token	Story	Grow and climb the vines, jump to the thin ledge, chop through a door, and beam into a small background room.	4
	Red Brick— Attract Studs	Free Play	Flip across the flagpoles above the vines, slide down a tightrope, fix a fuse box, and chop through a boarded door.	5
2	"Scout" vehicle token	Story	Pry open the wall panel on the right side of Blackwell's lounge.	6
3	Police Shield Piece 3	Story	Smash the crate in front of the piano, build the bricks to add the piano keys, and play the piano.	7
4	Police Shield Piece 4	Story	Pry open the lounge's background grate to enter the gym; use the punching bag.	8
2	"Forrest Blackwell Tuxedo" character token	Free Play	Use Rex Fury to rip apart the boards in the lounge's right foreground corner, then fix the fuse box.	9

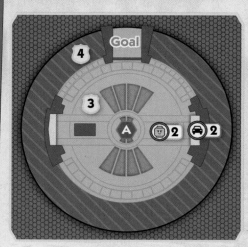

LEGO CITY HERO STUD REQUIREMENT:

60,000

⭐ OBJECTIVE: BREAK INTO BLACKWELL'S LOUNGE

Moe DeLuca awaits Chase within the sea cave and ferries our hero into Mr. Blackwell's secret boathouse by way of the fire boat that Chase stole from the fire department. Moe will wait here for Chase to return with the goods—the rest of the job is up to McCain!

Jump off the fire boat and smash the cabinet on the dock's left side to discover some bricks. Build these to add a handhold to the top of the nearby fence, then jump over.

POLICE SHIELD PIECE 1

Smash three life-preserver stands around the sea cave to soak up a shield piece. Check the maps to see where these stands are stationed!

POLICE SHIELD PIECE 2

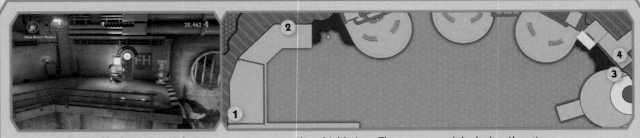

Pry open four red lockers around the sea cave to score another shield piece. The maps reveal the lockers' locations.

The First Ledge

Chop through the boarded door beyond the fence to reach the background ledge. Jump across a thin pole to cross the watery gap that follows.

> **TIP**
>
> Swim around the water to collect some studs if you like. Use the ladder near the fire boat to return to dry land.

Beat up the Blackwell security guards on the next ledge, then douse some fire to expose a pipe with a valve wheel. Spin the wheel to stem the flow of the waterfall to the right.

FREE PLAY
CHARACTER TOKEN 1: MOE DELUCA

During Free Play, use the construction worker disguise to fix the nearby fuse box after beating up the guards. Pry open the background door afterward and pull a lever in the small room beyond to open a nearby wall hatch. Out pops a character token!

The Second Ledge

Use the grapple gun to swing across the gap after shutting off the waterfall. Chop through a boarded door on the ledge you land on to access a lever. Pull the lever to make some bricks tumble out of the nearby wall hatch.

> **TIP**
>
> Smash the spotlight on this ledge to unblock the foreground ladder. Now you can quickly return to the ledge if you happen to fall in the water!

Build the bricks into a fan that creates an updraft. Jump into the updraft to drift up to a thin ledge. Inch around the ledge and drop to the ledge below.

The Third Ledge

Subdue another group of guards on the third ledge, then smash a giant crate to find more bricks. Build these into a space crate that beams in some bricks when activated. Build the bricks to add a few missing gears to the background machinery.

The machinery begins to function after you add the gears. Pull the nearby lever to close the right gate and open the left gate, then collect the valve wheel beyond.

INTRODUCTION

POLICE ACADEMY

CHARACTERS AND VEHICLES

WALKTHROUGH

LEGO CITY TOUR

CHECKLISTS

Pull the lever again to close the left gate and open the right gate. Place the valve wheel onto the pipe beyond the right gate, then turn the wheel to raise a footbridge to the right, which leads to the final ledge.

The Fourth Ledge

Cross the footbridge and wipe out more security guards. Smash a flower barrel to discover a planter. Water the planter to grow some vines, then climb up to reach a ventilation shaft.

VEHICLE TOKEN 1: BUZZER

After climbing the vines, jump over to the left to reach a thin ledge, rather than going right to reach the ventilation shaft. Inch along the thin ledge to reach a boarded door.

Chop through the door to discover a transporter pad. Use the pad to beam down into a small background room.

A vehicle token sits inside the room, along with one of the lockers that pertains to Police Shield Piece 2. Very nice! Use the transporter pad again to exit the room after you've finished looting the place.

FREE PLAY
RED BRICK: ATTRACT STUDS

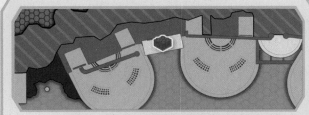

After beaming back out of the small room with the Buzzer vehicle token, flip across the flagpoles to the left to reach a tightrope. Slide down to access another small ledge with a fuse box and a boarded door.

Fix the fuse box to banish the electricity, then chop through the boarded door to enter a small room, where this stage's red brick is located.

Pry open the vent above the vines and step inside to drop into the small room below. Use the color swapper here to obtain some red energy, then shoot the nearby green switch to shut off the electricity so you may pry open the room's metal door.

Pick up the box of bricks near the color swapper, and carry it out of the room and over to the nearby green pad. Set the bricks down, and build them into a control panel. Use the control panel to activate the nearby elevator, then ride up to enter Mr. Blackwell's lavish lounge.

⭐ OBJECTIVE: OPEN BLACKWELL'S TREASURE VAULT

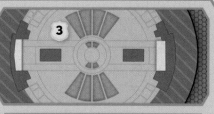

You've snuck into Blackwell's lounge—now you just need to raid his treasure vault! Begin by smashing the right foreground desk to discover a box of bricks. Carry this over to the green pad near the vault.

VEHICLE TOKEN 2: SCOUT

Pry open the wall panel on the right side of Blackwell's lounge. Crack the secret wall safe you discover to score a bunch of studs—plus a vehicle token!

POLICE SHIELD PIECE 3

Smash the crate in front of Mr. Blackwell's piano, then build the remaining bricks to add keys to the piano. Now simply play the piano to waltz away with a shield piece!

POLICE SHIELD PIECE 4

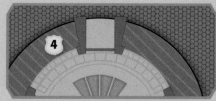

Pry open the sturdy door to the vault's left and enter Mr. Blackwell's personal gym. Beat up the punching bag here to work up a sweat—and score another shield piece in the process!

FREE PLAY
CHARACTER TOKEN 2: FORREST BLACKWELL TUXEDO

During Free Play, use Rex Fury to rip apart the boards against the wall in the right foreground corner. Fix the fuse box on the wall after destroying the crate, and the nearby display case will shatter, exposing a character token!

INTRODUCTION

POLICE ACADEMY

CHARACTERS AND VEHICLES

WALKTHROUGH

LEGO CITY TOUR

CHECKLISTS

Opening the Vault

Set down the bricks, and build them into a control panel. Activate the panel to expose a green switch on the wall above. Now you're getting somewhere!

Next, break the birdcage near the television set, then build the remaining bricks into a color swapper. Fill your color gun with red energy.

You know the drill! Blast the green switch with red energy from the color gun to activate it. This shuts off the vault's security lasers, but the door remains locked tight. You've got to get that thing open!

Wipe out the security guards who storm the room, then go left and jump onto the large display case with the studs inside. Use the grapple gun to pull down the painting above the fireplace. The panel smashes the display case you're standing on, exposing a scan spot.

Use the scan spot to trace some footprints over to a cabinet near the vault. Open the cabinet. Bricks tumble out; use them to build a second control panel. Bingo!

Activate the control panel to expose another green switch. Blast this one with red energy as well to at last open the vault. Now to grab some loot for Vinnie!

CITY EXPLORATION

INTRODUCTION

POLICE ACADEMY

CHARACTERS AND VEHICLES

WALKTHROUGH

LEGO CITY TOUR

CHECKLISTS

⭐ OBJECTIVE: ESCAPE FROM THE SENTINELS

Chase has succeeded in breaking into Blackwell's vault, but he couldn't steal anything for Vinnie before a group of suited goons known as sentinels arrived. McCain managed to escape Blackwell's mansion, but those sentinels are hot on his heels!

You've gotta lose those goons! Hit the gas and speed through the streets on your escape motorcycle. Follow the green studs until you reach an objective beacon.

The sentinels catch up with you when you reach the beacon. There's nothing else for it—you've got to take them out!

⭐ OBJECTIVE: GO TO PAPPALARDO'S ICE CREAM PARLOR

Moe calls after you beat up all of the sentinels. He's worried about Vinnie and asks you to check on him at Pappalardo's. Better hurry over there!

Step into the objective beacon at Pappalardo's, and the camera will pan around to reveal a skylight on the building's roof. Jump up the nearby handholds on the large oil drum to reach a long row of thin poles that lead to the roof.

Hop across the thin poles to reach the roof, then pry open the skylight. Drop inside to begin your next assignment.

SPECIAL ASSIGNMENT 11: THEY ALL SCREAM FOR ICE CREAM

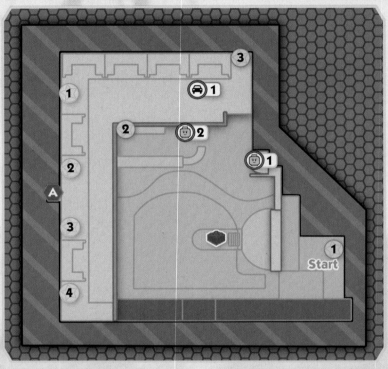

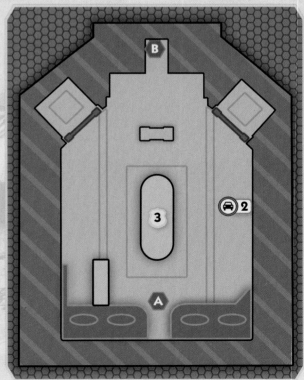

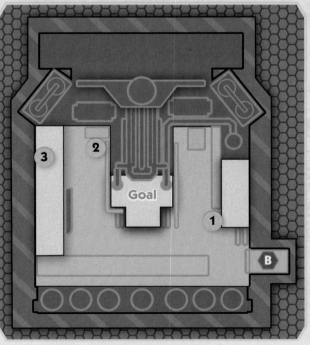

STAGE COLLECTIBLES: "THEY ALL SCREAM FOR ICE CREAM"

MAP ICON(S)	TYPE	MODE	NOTES	GOT IT?
1 to 3	Police Shield Piece 1	Story	Smash three giant sundaes around the ice cream parlor.	1
1	"Jimmy Grossman" character token	Free Play	Fix the fuse box near the piano, build the piano's bricks into a catapult pad, and launch up to the token.	2
2	"Vinnie Pappalardo" character token	Story	Automatically received when you rescue Vinnie from the freezer and rebuild him.	3
	Red Brick—Extra Hearts	Free Play	Use astronaut jet pack to jump up to the balcony above the entry door, activate the space crate, build the color swapper, and blast three switch objects around the parlor.	4
1	"Aceso" vehicle token	Story	Smash the cabinet atop the parlor stairs, build the bricks into an ice cream ball, roll over the red switch to the left, and use the transporter to reach the overhead lights.	5
1 to 4	Police Shield Piece 2	Story	Smash four crates around the parlor's second floor, then build the bricks into four stools.	6
2	"Ironback" vehicle token	Story	Water the planter in Vinnie's office.	7
3	Police Shield Piece 3	Story	Smash all eight chairs around the central table in Vinnie's office.	8
1 to 3	Police Shield Piece 4	Story	Smash three unique machines around the ice cream factory.	9

LEGO CITY HERO STUD REQUIREMENT: 50,000

⭐ OBJECTIVE: RESCUE VINNIE

Chase finds Vinnie in dire straits—he's been locked in a walk-in freezer by Rex Fury's goons! It won't be long before Vinnie is frozen solid, so you'd better hurry and rescue him.

Smash up the entry area if you like, then use the grapple gun to yank open the door to the ice cream parlor.

INTRODUCTION

POLICE ACADEMY

CHARACTERS AND VEHICLES

WALKTHROUGH

LEGO CITY TOUR

CHECKLISTS

POLICE SHIELD PIECE 1

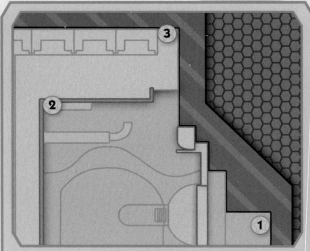

Smash three giant sundaes around the ice cream parlor to receive a tasty shield piece! The sundaes are labeled on the maps to help you find them.

FREE PLAY
CHARACTER TOKEN 1: JIMMY GROSSMAN

Use the construction worker disguise to fix the fuse box near the piano. This causes a spotlight to fall and smash the piano, leaving behind a pile of bricks. Build the bricks into a catapult pad, then use the pad to soar up to a character token on a high balcony.

| TIP |

Search behind the curtain near the piano to discover a purple stud!

Freeing Vinnie

Beat up the thugs around the parlor, then use the grapple gun again to pull down the display above the freezer. The display swings down and breaks the lock on the freezer door, freeing Vinnie.

Unfortunately, Vinnie has already frozen solid and breaks into pieces! Subdue the goons who were guarding him, and build Vinnie's bricks to put him back together.

CHARACTER TOKEN 2: VINNIE PAPPALARDO

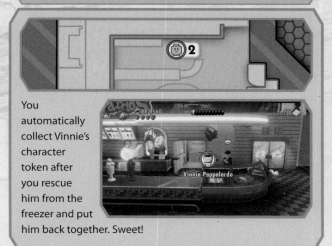

You automatically collect Vinnie's character token after you rescue him from the freezer and put him back together. Sweet!

⭐ OBJECTIVE: ENTER VINNIE'S OFFICE

Vinnie thanks you and says that the gang leader has locked himself inside his ice cream factory, which you can reach via a secret passage in Vinnie's office. Collect the box of bricks in the freezer where Vinnie was trapped, then carry it over to the nearby green pad.

There are two green pads, so you must find more bricks. Go left and smash a small ice cream crate near the counter. Build the remains of the crate into a control panel, and use the panel to make a box of bricks roll out onto the counter.

Nice work! Now carry the second box of bricks over to the other green pad, and set it down. Build the bricks to complete the nearby machine, then turn the machine's wheel to extend some nearby stairs.

FREE PLAY

RED BRICK: EXTRA HEARTS

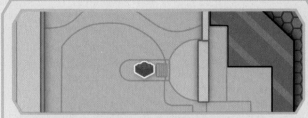

During Free Play, toggle to the astronaut and use a jet pack jump to boost up to the balcony above the ice cream parlor's entry door. Activate the space crate you discover up here to beam in a pile of bricks onto the parlor's second floor.

Head upstairs and build the bricks into a color swapper. Fill your color gun with green energy, then run around  and blast three objects around the parlor that have red switches: the floor buffer, the cash register, and the jukebox.

After blasting all three objects with the color gun and activating their switches, this mission's red brick will appear near the piano stage. Head over and collect your prize!

INTRODUCTION

POLICE ACADEMY

CHARACTERS AND VEHICLES

WALKTHROUGH

LEGO CITY TOUR

CHECKLISTS

Second Floor Smashup

Head upstairs to reach the ice cream parlor's second floor. Nearly everything up here can be smashed to pieces, but all you really need to do to advance is destroy the boulders near the boarded door, then chop your way through to reach Vinnie's office.

VEHICLE TOKEN 1: ACESO

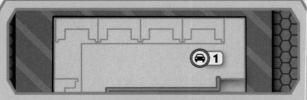

Smash the cabinet atop the stairs, and build its bricks to form a giant ice cream ball. Press Ⓧ to hop onto the ice cream ball and roll to the left.

Smash the table near the left wall to discover a red button on the floor. Ride the ice cream ball onto the button to turn it green and activate the nearby transporter pad.

Jump off the ice cream ball and use the transporter pad to beam onto the nearby overhead light. Jump and grab the blue and white LEGO patch on the ceiling, then shimmy over to the next overhead light, where a vehicle token awaits.

POLICE SHIELD PIECE 2

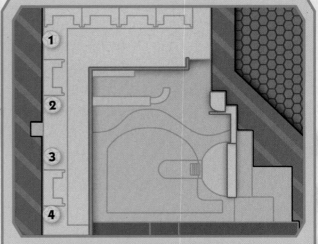

Smash four ice cream crates around the parlor's second floor. Bricks spill out of each crate; build them into stools. Build all four stools to earn a shield piece! Check the maps for the locations of each stool crate.

⭐ OBJECTIVE: FIND THE SECRET PASSAGE

Vinnie's office is crawling with thugs. Arrest them all, then smash the red chair near the planter on the right to discover a scan spot. Follow the footprints to a nearby cabinet that contains a key.

VEHICLE TOKEN 2: IRONBACK

Water the planter on the right side of Vinnie's office to grow a large flower—along with a hidden vehicle token!

POLICE SHIELD PIECE 3

Smash the eight chairs that surround the large table in the middle of Vinnie's office to earn an easy shield piece.

Use the key on the left bookshelf's lock to discover a hidden safe. Crack the safe to find some bricks; build them into a giant ice cream cone. Gee, Vinnie really likes ice cream!

Smash another red chair in the left foreground corner to discover another scan spot. This one's footprints lead to a tall cabinet—open it to discover some bricks that you can form into a color swapper.

Use the color swapper to fill your color gun with red energy, then blast the green switch on the right bookshelf to find another hidden safe. Crack this one to score more bricks that form another giant ice cream cone.

Good work! Now simply shove both of the ice cream cones toward the background until they stop on a pair of green pads. With both green pads depressed, the background portrait of Vinnie shifts, revealing a secret passage to the ice cream factory.

⭐ OBJECTIVE: SUBDUE THE THUG LEADER

The leader of the thugs who are trashing Pappalardo's taunts Chase as he enters the factory. The place is a mess, and it will take some effort to reach the chief goon!

A pair of frosty jets prevents you from exploring the factory's left side. Head into the background instead and use a control panel to make a large box pop out of the nearby wall.

INTRODUCTION

POLICE ACADEMY

CHARACTERS AND VEHICLES

WALKTHROUGH

LEGO CITY TOUR

CHECKLISTS

POLICE SHIELD PIECE 4

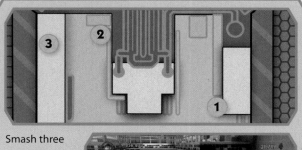

Smash three unique machines around the factory to earn a cool shield piece. Check the maps to see where they're at!

Press Ⓧ to make Chase "put on" the box. Now you can move through those icy jets without being frozen!

Take off the box and beat up the goons beyond the frost jets, then collect some dynamite from the nearby dispenser. Use the dynamite to blast the nearby pile of blocks and expose a large red button.

Step on the button to turn it green and shut off those pesky ice jets. Now you'll have an easier time moving around!

Next, roll a large tube along the checkered floor until it slides into place against the background wall. Jump onto the tube afterward, then hop up onto the factory's left ledge.

Turn the valve at the end of the left ledge to make some red fluid flow into a tube near the central control station. Now you just need to fill that other tube!

Activating the Central Controls

Move toward the foreground and shove a large crate off the ledge, making it fall onto the conveyor belt below. The crate smashes when it hits the belt, and its bricks are delivered to the factory's right side.

Drop from the ledge and head for those bricks. Build them to create a floor fan, then jump into the updraft to reach the right ledge.

Douse the fire on the right ledge, and turn the valve to fill the central control station's other tube with blue fluid. With both tubes filled, the central control station comes online.

Drop to the ground floor and climb a ladder to reach the central control station. Throw the switch to dump a batch of ice cream on the thug leader, at last putting him on ice!

INTRODUCTION

POLICE ACADEMY

CHARACTERS AND VEHICLES

WALKTHROUGH

LEGO CITY TOUR

CHECKLISTS

CHAPTER 12: THE CON IN CONSTRUCTION

WORKING TOGETHER, CHASE AND VINNIE MANAGED TO CAPTURE THE LEADER OF THE THUGS WHO WERE TRASHING PAPPALARDO'S ICE CREAM PARLOR. AFTER A BIT OF INTERROGATION, OUR HERO LEARNS THAT THE HEAD GOON WAS SUPPOSED TO PULL OFF A JOB FOR REX FURY AFTER WRECKING THE PARLOR—ONE THAT WAS SET TO GO DOWN AT THE CONSTRUCTION YARD IN PARADISE SANDS. SEEING A GOLDEN OPPORTUNITY, CHASE DECIDES TO TAKE THE THUG LEADER'S PLACE AND GO UNDERCOVER AT THE CONSTRUCTION YARD.

CITY EXPLORATION

OBJECTIVE: GET TO THE CONSTRUCTION YARD

There's no time to lose! Hop into a vehicle and speed off toward the construction yard.

SPECIAL ASSIGNMENT 12: HIGH STEAL

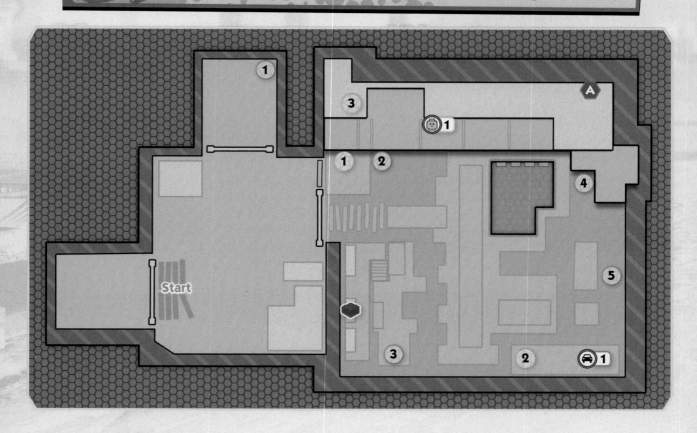

INTRODUCTION

POLICE ACADEMY

CHARACTERS AND VEHICLES

WALKTHROUGH

LEGO CITY TOUR

CHECKLISTS

STAGE COLLECTIBLES: "HIGH STEAL"

MAP ICON(S)	TYPE	MODE	NOTES	GOT IT?
1 to 5	Police Shield Piece 1	Story	Smash five piles of boulders around the construction yard's first area.	1
1 to 3	Police Shield Piece 2	Story	Use three coffee break stations around the construction yard's first area.	2
	Red Brick—Studs x6	Story	Chop through the boarded door of the small shack in the left foreground corner beyond the first gate.	3
1	"Foundation" vehicle token	Story	Use the small cement mixer in the right foreground corner to blast down some bricks, then build an elevator platform and ride up.	4
1	"Construction Foreman" character token	Free Play	Use the astronaut's jet pack jump to reach the small room above the ladder you must pull down with the grapple gun.	5
2	"Roller" vehicle token	Story	Smash the debris in the corner before sliding down the tube in the second area.	6
1 to 3	Police Shield Piece 3	Story	Smash three objects around the second area and build three special objects out of their bricks.	7
4	Police Shield Piece 4	Story	Use the RC crane to dig at four indicated spots around the second area.	8
2	"Patrick Wenham" character token	Story	Fix the fuse box near the right gate, use the color swapper, blast the nearby wall and climb it, and smash the junk on the ledge.	9

LEGO CITY HERO STUD REQUIREMENT: 90,000

⭐ OBJECTIVE: FIND A DISGUISE

Chase needs to disguise himself as a construction worker before he can infiltrate the construction yard. There is a barrel filled with junk near the small background room; shove this to the left to move it out of your way.

With the barrel out of the way, pry open the small room's door. Enter and open the locker inside the room to discover the Chase McCain (Construction) disguise!

⭐ OBJECTIVE: LOCATE REX'S MAN

Now that you're in disguise, you need to find Rex's man on the inside. But now that you're in disguise, the foreman has some work for you, too—he tells you to fix the nearby fuse box. Toggle to the construction worker disguise, then stand near the fuse box and press Ⓐ to tune it up.

Fixing the fuse box exposes a red switch near the background gate. As you exit the small room, a goon who works for Rex Fury will call out to you, informing you that Rex wants you to steal a crane from the construction yard. What could Fury possibly want with a crane?

⭐ OBJECTIVE: OPEN THE GATES

You have your orders—now you just need to find a crane. Run to the area's right foreground corner and smash a large crate to discover some bricks. Build these into a space crate, then activate it.

The space crate beams in some more bricks. Build these into a color swapper, and fill your color gun with green energy.

You know what to do! Blast the red switch that you exposed near the background gate, and the gate will swing open. Go through and press Ⓧ to take control of the steam roller beyond.

POLICE SHIELD PIECE 1

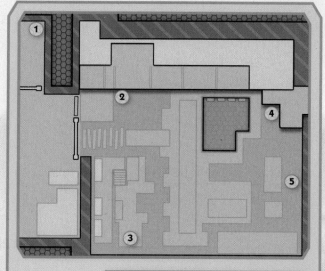

Smash five piles of boulders around the construction yard to dig out a shield piece. Check the maps to see where the five boulder piles lie!

All Steamed Up

Drive the steam roller onto the large red button near the right gate. The button turns green, and the gate opens. Now you can explore more of the yard!

★ OBJECTIVE: FIX THE HOIST CONTROLS

Before the foreman will let you near the crane, he insists that you fix the hoist controls. Unfortunately, the parts you need are submerged in a nearby pool. You'll need to seal off four pipes to drain the pool and get at the parts.

POLICE SHIELD PIECE 2

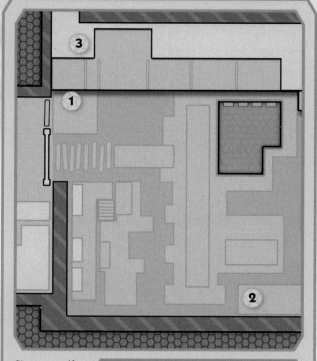

Give yourself a break and use three coffee stations around the construction yard to earn a fresh, hot shield piece. The maps show where each coffee station stands.

INTRODUCTION

POLICE ACADEMY

CHARACTERS AND VEHICLES

WALKTHROUGH

LEGO CITY TOUR

CHECKLISTS

Drill the Pipes

While wearing the construction worker disguise, drill the shaky ground beyond the gate to discover drill symbols. Stand on these and press Ⓐ to drill even deeper, tapping into the water pipes below. Drill all four pipes around the yard to shut off the water supply and drain the pool.

TIP

Use the crowbar to pry into a small shack in the left foreground corner beyond the gate. Fix the fuse box inside the shack to activate a nearby transporter pad. Step onto the transporter pad to beam over to the remote rooftop that's covered in studs!

RED BRICK: STUDS X6

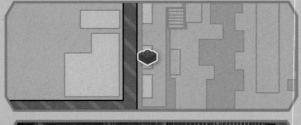

Chop through the boarded door of the small shack in the left foreground corner beyond the gate. The red brick awaits inside the shack.

VEHICLE TOKEN 1: FOUNDATION

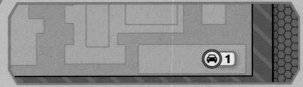

Turn the valve wheel on the side of the small cement mixer in the yard's right foreground corner. The mixer will lob a gob of goo at the nearby tower, knocking some bricks to the ground.

Build the bricks to add a lift to the bottom of the small tower. Step onto the lift's button to ride up and grab the vehicle token that hovers above!

Fixing the Hoist Controls

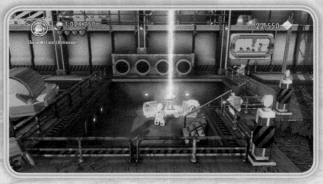

After you've drilled up all four pipes and drained the pool, drop into the empty pool and smash the large crate to uncover a space crate. Activate the space crate to beam in the bricks you need to repair the hoist controls.

Run up to the bricks and build them to repair the hoist controls. Pull the nearby lever to swing the hoist into a wall and knock down a crate that smashes into another pile of bricks. Build these into a ladder, then climb up to begin exploring the background building.

Under Construction

A solid wall blocks the building's first floor and needs to be destroyed. Use the grapple gun to pull down an overhead ladder, then climb up to the second floor.

FREE PLAY
CHARACTER TOKEN 1: CONSTRUCTION FOREMAN

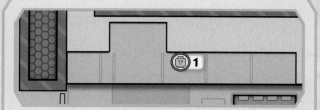

During Free Play, use the astronaut's jet pack jump to boost up to the small room above the ladder that you pull down with the grapple gun. A character token is stashed up here!

Inch across a thin ledge to reach the second floor's right side. Pry open a door over here to access a dynamite dispenser.

Collect some dynamite, then return to the solid wall. Place the dynamite in the small barrel near the wall to blast it to bits.

Elevator Action

The elevator beyond the wall is broken and needs its fuse box repaired. Slide under the blue and white obstacle to the left, then use the grapple gun to zip back up to the second floor.

Step on top of the elevator and fix the fuse box. Drop through the nearby hatch and pull the elevator's lever to ride up to the third floor.

Oh no, the third floor's on fire! Switch to the fireman disguise and douse the flames with the fire extinguisher.

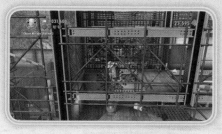

After extinguishing the fire, toggle to the farmer disguise and water the planter on the left. Climb the vines that sprout up to reach the fourth floor.

Painful Gas

Cross a balance beam on your way to a dangerous gas leak. Don't touch the gas—it's deadly! Climb down the nearby ladder instead.

INTRODUCTION

POLICE ACADEMY

CHARACTERS AND VEHICLES

WALKTHROUGH

LEGO CITY TOUR

CHECKLISTS

Smash the red toolbox below the gas leak to discover a valve wheel. Turn the wheel to shut off the gas, then climb up the ladder to return to the fourth floor.

Go right and drop down to the third floor again. Bash through a boarded door with the fire axe, then head through to reach the next section of the construction yard.

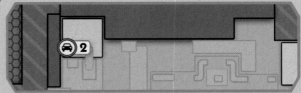

As soon as you enter the construction yard's second area, and before you slide down the long tube, smash the debris in the corner of the small entry room to discover a hidden vehicle token!

⭐ OBJECTIVE: GET THE GATE KEY

You emerge in a small room. Slide down a long tube, and you'll land near a worker in distress—a guard dog has run off with the gate key! Perhaps you can lend a helping hand.

Bring the bone back to the doghouse and place it in the nearby food bowl. This lures the dog away from the doghouse. Hurry and grab the key!

Smash the boulder near the doghouse to discover a scan spot. Follow the doggy tracks over to a pile of debris. Search the debris to uncover a bone.

Use the key to open the nearby gatehouse. Pull the lever inside the gatehouse to open the nearby gate.

⭐ OBJECTIVE: BUILD THE CRANE

Now that you've opened the gate, you just need to build the crane. Unfortunately, this requires 40,000 bricks! Lucky for you, several superbricks are located around the construction yard.

POLICE SHIELD PIECE 3

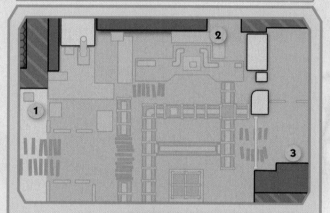

Smash three objects around this portion of the construction yard to discover bricks, then build  the bricks into three special objects. Your hard work will be rewarded with a shield piece! Check the maps to see where the three special objects are located.

Superbrick 1

Jump up the stacked pallets near the crane's superbuild pad to reach a small shack. Pry open the shack's door to enter it and claim the superbrick within.

Superbrick 2

Head to the right, back through the gate, and look for a patch of shaky ground near the foreground. Drill here to uncork a water geyser that boosts you up to a hovering superbrick!

Superbrick 3

Smash a pile of boulders to uncover a scan spot. Follow the footprints to locate a hatch in the ground.

 Open the hatch, and a bunch of bricks will spill out. Build these into a small RC crane that you can control.

Drive the RC crane around the yard and dig at the four indicated spots. You'll discover a superbrick as you go!

INTRODUCTION

POLICE ACADEMY

CHARACTERS AND VEHICLES

WALKTHROUGH

LEGO CITY TOUR

CHECKLISTS

POLICE SHIELD PIECE 4

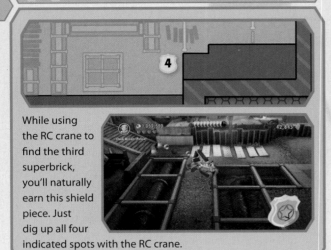

While using the RC crane to find the third superbrick, you'll naturally earn this shield piece. Just dig up all four indicated spots with the RC crane.

CHARACTER TOKEN 2: PATRICK WENHAM

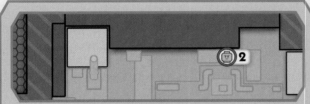

Activate a color swapper by repairing the fuse box near the right gate. Use the color swapper to fill your color gun with blue energy.

Go left and blast the nearby white LEGO wall in the background with the color gun. This adds some blue coloring to the wall, allowing you to climb up to the small ledge above.

Smash the ledge's debris to uncover a hidden character token in the corner. Beauty!

Superbrick 4

Drill another patch of shaky ground near the closed gate on the right. You'll tap into another water geyser that lifts you up, helping you reach the nearby ledge and get past the gate.

The worker on the ledge asks you to help him out by clearing all the junk from the nearby lot. Hey, no problem!

Hold Ⓨ to use the construction worker's pneumatic drill and quickly smash all of the junk in the lot. After you finish clearing out all the junk, the worker will reward you with a superbrick!

Build the Crane

You should now have enough bricks to build the crane. Run to the superbuild pad on the left and press Ⓐ to build it.

INTRODUCTION

POLICE ACADEMY

CHARACTERS AND VEHICLES

WALKTHROUGH

LEGO CITY TOUR

CHECKLISTS

⭐ OBJECTIVE: ALIGN THE PIPES

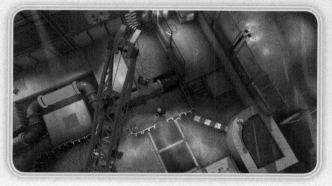

Press ⊗ to take control of the crane, and drive it over to the objective beacon on the right. Use the crane to pick up three colored pipes, and place each pipe on the matching color pad. The gate on the right opens after you properly place all three pipes.

You're all finished here! Drive the crane through the gate and over to the final gate on the right. Rex's inside man greets you when you arrive, then opens the gate so you can make good your escape. Great work!

🛡 CITY EXPLORATION

⭐ OBJECTIVE: GO TO THE OBSERVATORY

Eddie pulls the truck around the building after you clear out the rocks, then gets to work fixing the crane. It seems he damaged the crane on the way up to the observatory. Battle the security guards who arrive while Eddie repairs the crane.

Chase has succeeded in stealing the crane and must now meet up with one of Rex's men, Eddie Jo Jo, at the LEGO City Observatory. You know the drill: Steal some wheels and motor over to the observatory, pronto!

Stealing the Telescope

Eddie awaits you at the observatory and tells you to clear out the nearby rocks so he can pull his truck up close to the building. Use your newfound pneumatic drill to make short work of the rocks—there are 15 to break in all.

After subduing the guards, look around and collect the key that one of them dropped. Use this key to open the observatory's front door.

Enter the observatory and climb the interior ladder to reach a fuse box. Repair the fuse box to open the observatory's roof and expose the telescope.

Eddie has finished repairing the crane. Hop into the driver's seat and use the crane to pick up the telescope. Place the telescope onto the truck that Eddie has parked nearby.

⭐ OBJECTIVE: TAKE THE TELESCOPE TO THE DROP-OFF POINT

Well done! Now you just need to deliver the telescope to the drop-off point. Follow Eddie (and the trail of green studs) to find your way there.

A drawbridge rises as you near your destination, but this doesn't stop Eddie from speeding across. Guess you'll have to do the same! Chase hits the gas and soars over the gap, landing safely on the other side.

CAUTION

The cops will be hot on your tail—don't let them knock you off course!

Continue following Eddie as he drives off-road, ducks into a tunnel, and opens a secret passage. Chase pulls into the secret passage and parks the truck, completing this epic heist like a pro.

CHAPTER 13: SECRETS

CHASE HAS RISKED LIFE AND LIMB BY GOING DEEP UNDERCOVER IN THE HOPES OF BRINGING REX FURY TO JUSTICE. MOST RECENTLY, HE STOLE A GIANT TELESCOPE FROM THE LEGO CITY OBSERVATORY AND DELIVERED IT TO A SECRET BASE HIDDEN INSIDE A REMOTE TRAIN TUNNEL. WHAT COULD REX POSSIBLY WANT WITH SUCH A GRAND TELESCOPE? THE ANSWERS MUST BE CLOSE AT HAND!

INTRODUCTION

POLICE ACADEMY

CHARACTERS AND VEHICLES

WALKTHROUGH

LEGO CITY TOUR

CHECKLISTS

SPECIAL ASSIGNMENT 13: DISRUPTIVE BEHAVIOR

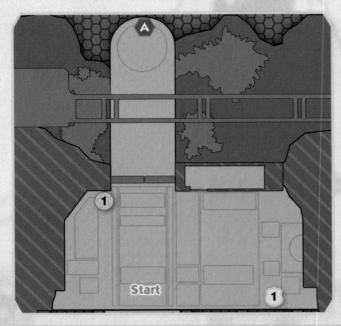

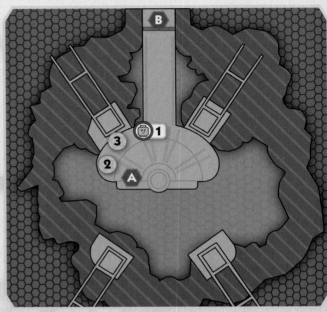

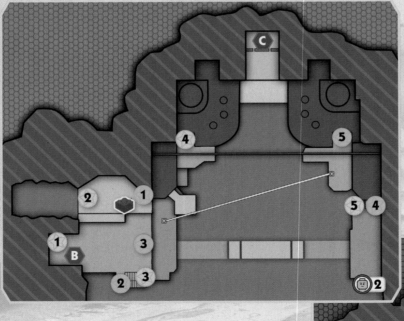

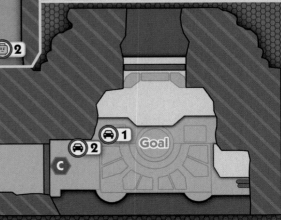

STAGE COLLECTIBLES: "DISRUPTIVE BEHAVIOR"

MAP ICON(S)	TYPE	MODE	NOTES	GOT IT?
1	Police Shield Piece 1	Story	Smash the crate near the basketball hoop, then play and win the basketball game.	1
1 to 3	Police Shield Piece 2	Free Play	Use Rex Fury to rip apart three super-strength crates in the base's first two areas.	2
1	"Henrik Kowalski" character token	Free Play	Fix the fuse box behind one of the super-strength crates near the submarine.	3
1 to 5	Police Shield Piece 3	Story	Pry open five red lockers around the secret base's third area.	4
	Red Brick—Studs x8	Free Play	Use Rex Fury to rip apart the super-strength crate near the security lasers, then activate the space crate and pull the lever.	5
1 to 5	Police Shield Piece 4	Story	Smash five small, brown flower pots around the base's third area.	6
2	"Submarine Captain" character token	Story	After jet pack jumping to the base's right side, inch around the thin ledge.	7
1	"Rex's Brute" vehicle token	Story	Drill through the shaky floor in the base's final area.	8
2	"Jupiter" vehicle token	Free Play	Use Rex Fury to rip apart the super-strength crate in the base's final area.	9

LEGO CITY HERO STUD REQUIREMENT: 50,000

⭐ OBJECTIVE: OPEN THE BAY DOOR

Chase has infiltrated Rex Fury's secret base, but it's not long before his cover is blown. Beat up the thugs who attack you in the entrance, then begin searching around for clues.

POLICE SHIELD PIECE 1

Smash a crate in the base's right foreground corner, and you'll be able to use the nearby basketball net. Shoot hoops and sink three baskets before time runs out to score a shield piece!

INTRODUCTION

POLICE ACADEMY

CHARACTERS AND VEHICLES

WALKTHROUGH

LEGO CITY TOUR

CHECKLISTS

FREE PLAY
POLICE SHIELD PIECE 2

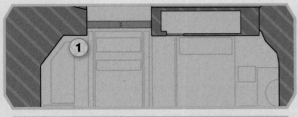

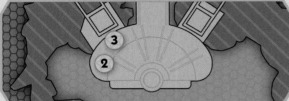

Use Rex Fury to rip apart three super-strength crates around the secret base's entry area. One is located near the mission's starting point; the other two are near the submarine. Destroy all three of these crates to muscle up a shield piece! Check the maps to see where these three crates stand.

Fix the fuse box on the base's right side to disable the electrical current that surrounds a nearby crate. Smash the crate to discover a box of bricks.

Carry the box over to the green pad near the background office. Set the box down, then build the bricks into a control panel.

Use the control panel to open the office door, then head inside. Access the computer inside the office to open the base's bay door. Now you can explore the outdoor helipad!

Run to the end of the helipad and smash the blue satellite dish. Build the remains of the dish into a diving board.

Free Fallin'

Step onto the diving board, take a deep breath, and make a daring leap over the yawning cliff below. Soar through the stud rings to collect them as you plummet ever downward.

> **TIP**
>
> Press Ⓐ to slow down and Ⓑ to speed up as you fall. This will help you collect studs and avoid obstacles!

Avoid the lasers that start firing as you near the opening to a shaft. Just keep diving as you enter the shaft, and do your best to dodge the rotating energy beams within.

OBJECTIVE: GET PAST THE REINFORCED DOOR

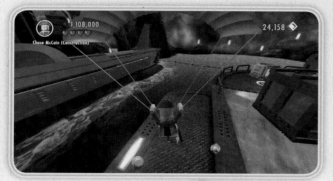

Chase deploys his parachute as he nears the bottom of the shaft. What a rush! Time to explore this section of the base.

Build the bricks to fortify the nearby crane. Smash another crate to find more bricks, then build these as well to complete the crane's upgrade.

Activate the crane's controls, and Chase will use the crane to rip off one of the nearby submarine's engines. Approach the engine and repair its fuse box to fire it up and send it smashing through the reinforced door to the right.

FREE PLAY
CHARACTER TOKEN 1: HENRIK KOWALSKI

Use Rex Fury to rip apart one of the super-strength crates near the submarine as part of obtaining Police Shield Piece 2, and you'll uncover a fuse box. Repair this to open the nearby display case and expose a character token!

Crane Upgrade

Activate the space crate in the background to beam in some dynamite. Use this to blast apart the silver crate near the large crane and discover some bricks.

A gang of astronaut goons arrives moments after you smash the reinforced door. Subdue all of the goons, then sprint through the door to explore more of the base.

OBJECTIVE: RAID THE BASE

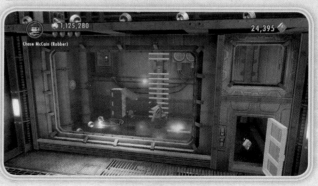

You're doing great! Beat up more baddies to secure this portion of the base, then pry open the background door to enter a small room. Smash a crate in here to find some bricks; build them into a ladder and climb up.

POLICE SHIELD PIECE 3

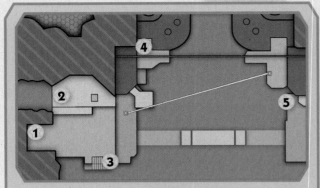

Use the crowbar to open five red lockers in this area of the base, and you'll pry out a shield piece! Look at the maps to see where the five lockers lie.

FREE PLAY
RED BRICK: STUDS X8

Use Rex Fury to rip apart the super-strength crate near the security lasers in this part of the base. You'll discover a space crate. Activate this to beam in a lever.

Pull the lever to shut off the security lasers, then stroll over and collect the red brick the lasers were protecting. Super!

Let's Jet

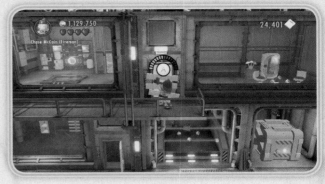

The ladder leads to a higher room with a red switch. Ignore the switch for now and step out onto the balcony. Run right and chop through a boarded door to enter the neighboring room.

Use the color swapper in the neighboring room to fill your color gun with green energy. Return to the red switch and activate it to open the nearby panel, opening the nook with the jet pack.

TIP

Don't miss the purple stud above the jet pack! Jump and boost straight up to collect it.

POLICE SHIELD PIECE 4

Smash five small, brown flower pots around this section of the base to harvest another shield piece! The maps show where the five flower pots are located.

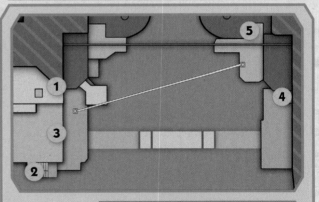

Jet Pack Action

Now that you've found the jet pack, Chase can boost around in his astronaut disguise. Let's give it a try! Return to the balcony and stand on the jet pack symbol. Press Ⓐ to activate the symbol and make two rings of studs appear to the right.

Jump and hold Ⓑ to boost through the stud rings. Keep boosting to the right to pass over the fence and land in a lower area.

NOTE

The jet pack has a limited amount of fuel for each boost. Flying through the stud rings that appear when you activate a jet pack symbol replenishes your fuel, letting you boost for longer durations.

Run to the foreground and jump onto a crate. Jump and boost upward to grab the overhead handhold, then jump onto the ledge above.

Climb a long ladder and take out the goons on the higher ledge above. Move toward the foreground and boost along a line of hovering studs to reach another foreground ledge.

Having a Blast

Boost over to the next ledge to reach a control panel. Use this to send a shuttle flying into some security lasers. The shuttle smashes to bits. Build its bricks into a dynamite dispenser.

Collect some dynamite, and boost back around the ledges. Place the dynamite in the small barrel next to the silver crate on the ledge where you fought the goons. The resulting blast destroys the crate, along with the nearby support column, causing some bricks to fall nearby.

Build the bricks into a transporter pad, then use the pad to beam down into a low room that's sealed by lasers. Grab the lever you discover here, then step on the red button to turn it green and shut off the lasers.

Exit the room and use a nearby jet pack symbol to boost over to a remote ledge on the right. Insert the lever you're carrying into the mechanism here, then pull the lever to drop the giant crate on the right.

Use two more jet pack symbols to boost across two more long gaps to the right. Grab the far handhold, then jump and boost up to another handhold so you may climb onto the ledge above.

INTRODUCTION

POLICE ACADEMY

CHARACTERS AND VEHICLES

WALKTHROUGH

LEGO CITY TOUR

CHECKLISTS

CHARACTER TOKEN 2: SUBMARINE CAPTAIN

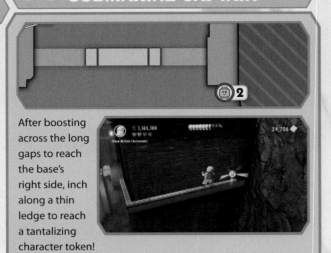

After boosting across the long gaps to reach the base's right side, inch along a thin ledge to reach a tantalizing character token!

Ledges and Ladders

Defeat more goons on the far-right ledge, then boost up to a higher ledge with a transporter pad. Use the pad to beam over to yet another ledge.

Pry open a metal door after using the transporter, and fix the fuse box in the small room beyond to open a hatch above you. Climb a long ladder and pass through the hatch to reach a higher ledge.

Wipe out more thugs on the ledge above the hatch, then pull a lever to lower a walkway. A jet pack symbol appears nearby— activate it and boost through the stud rings to reach the walkway.

One Last Blast

You're nearly finished! Activate the space crate beyond the walkway to beam in a larger crate. Smash this crate to discover some dynamite; use this to blast through the background door.

 ## OBJECTIVE: RESCUE PROFESSOR KOWALSKI

Using his stethoscope, Chase eavesdrops on a conversation in the base's final room between Rex Fury, Forrest Blackwell, and their prisoner,

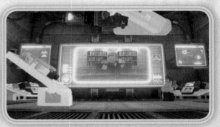

Professor Kowalski. It soon becomes apparent that Mr. Blackwell is the mastermind behind Rex Fury's recent crimes and that he intends to use Professor Kowalski's research to help him fuel his nefarious plot. Worse, Blackwell has managed to capture Professor Kowalski's daughter, Natalia!

VEHICLE TOKEN 1: REX'S BRUTE

Toggle to the construction worker and drill the shaky ground in the base's final area. You'll drop through the floor and claim a hidden vehicle token!

FREE PLAY

VEHICLE TOKEN 2: JUPITER

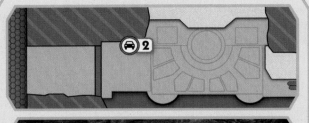

During Free Play, use Rex Fury to rip apart the super-strength crate in the base's final area. This feat of strength scores you another vehicle token!

Laser Tag

You've got to save the professor! Secure the room by beating up all of Rex's goons, then use the grapple gun to pull down the large laser in the left background corner.

Build the laser's bricks into a large energy conduit, and use the nearby control terminal to activate it. This will soon come in handy!

Next, run to the right and smash a large crate to discover a box of bricks. Carry the box over to the green pad on the left. Set it down and build the bricks into another energy conduit. Again, use a nearby control terminal to activate the conduit.

With both energy conduits built and powered, a flying saucer rises from the floor. Wild!

Rescuing Professor Kowalski

You've found your ticket out of this place—now you just need to save Natalia's dad. Pry open the metal door on the right to access a fuse box. Repair the fuse box to power a nearby floor fan.

Use the floor fan's updraft to reach a higher ledge. Smash the crate here to find some bricks, then build them into a transporter pad. Use the pad to beam over to the area where Professor Kowalski is being held.

INTRODUCTION

POLICE ACADEMY

CHARACTERS AND VEHICLES

WALKTHROUGH

LEGO CITY TOUR

CHECKLISTS

Defeat the goons who are guarding the good professor, then use the nearby control terminal to release him. Kowalski thanks Chase and advises that they waste no time in making good their escape.

Heed the professor's advice and drop down to the lower area, where the UFO awaits. Approach the UFO and press Ⓧ to hop aboard. The professor soon joins Chase, and the two fly off, leaving the base far behind!

CITY EXPLORATION

⭐ OBJECTIVE: FLY TO BLACKWELL'S MANSION

There's no time to lose—Blackwell has Natalia! Fly your newfound UFO over to Blackwell's mansion without delay. Simply head for the shield icon on your GamePad map, taking a mountain pass to get there.

Land the UFO on the helipad that's marked by an objective beacon. The gate to Blackwell's mansion is locked, so you'll need to find another way inside. Fortunately, a trail of studs appears to show you the way!

Cliff Jumping

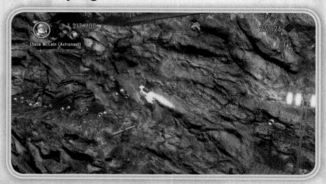

Carefully drop down the stepped cliff to the right of the helipad, following the stud trail. Make your way around the cliff and over to a jet pack symbol. Activate the symbol, then boost over to a distant ledge on the left.

Continue to use the jet pack to boost up the stepped cliff that follows, collecting studs as you go. You eventually reach a fenced-off area filled with guards. Vault the fence and prepare for a fight!

Wipe out all of the guards to secure the area. Approach the nearby control terminal afterward, and Chase and Kowalski will find their way into Blackwell's estate.

SPECIAL ASSIGNMENT 14: BREAKING AND REENTERING

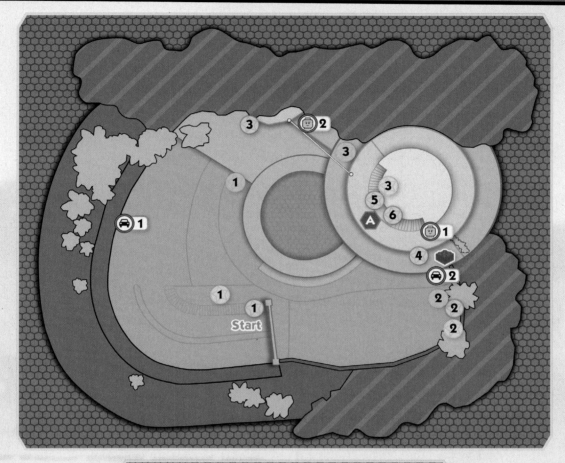

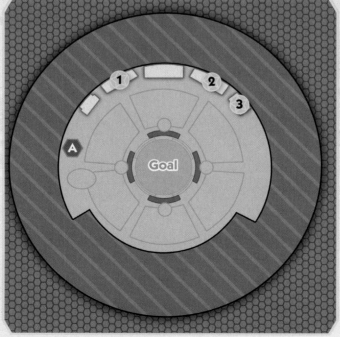

INTRODUCTION

POLICE ACADEMY

CHARACTERS AND VEHICLES

WALKTHROUGH

LEGO CITY TOUR

CHECKLISTS

STAGE COLLECTIBLES: "BREAKING AND REENTERING"

MAP ICON(S)	TYPE	MODE	NOTES	GOT IT?
1 to 6	Police Shield Piece 1	Story	Douse six wall torches around the outer grounds.	1
1 to 3	Police Shield Piece 2	Story	Smash three special boulders around the outer grounds.	2
🚗 1	"Dullahan" vehicle token	Story	Pry open the sewer cover on the grounds' left side.	3
1 to 3	Police Shield Piece 3	Story	Water three green flower boxes around the grounds.	4
🚗 2	"Cloud" vehicle token	Story	Smash the chair on the right side of the small room near the playground.	5
	Red Brick— Attract Bricks	Story	Activate the space crate near the mansion's roof, then smash the red mailbox.	6
👤 1	"Forrest Blackwell Casual" character token	Free Play	Use Rex Fury to rip apart the super-strength crate on the roof.	7
👤 2	"Sentinel Decker" character token	Story	Cross the tightrope on the roof's left side to reach a transporter pad. Beam into a small room and smash the sand castle.	8
1 to 3	Police Shield Piece 4	Story	Blast three red and white targets around Blackwell's study. Two are on the walls; one is hidden behind books.	9

LEGO CITY HERO STUD REQUIREMENT: 50,000

⭐ OBJECTIVE: ENTER BLACKWELL'S STUDY

The grounds surrounding Forrest Blackwell's mansion are crawling with security guards. Wipe out the gang of guards that ambushes you from the start, then begin searching for a way into the mansion.

POLICE SHIELD PIECE 1

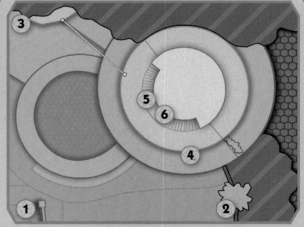

Douse six wall torches around the mansion's outer grounds to soak up a shield piece! Check the maps to see where these six torches are affixed.

POLICE SHIELD PIECE 2

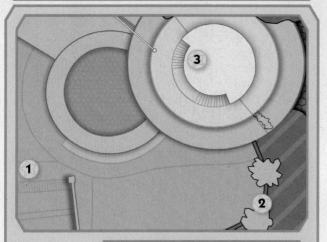

Destroy three special boulders around the mansion's grounds to chip away at another shield piece. Refer to the maps to see where these three boulders stand.

VEHICLE TOKEN 1: DULLAHAN

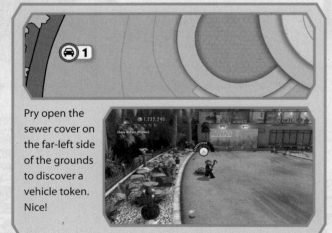

Pry open the sewer cover on the far-left side of the grounds to discover a vehicle token. Nice!

Secret Keyhole

Drill the shaky ground to the left of Blackwell's mansion to discover some dynamite. This should come in handy!

Use the dynamite to blast the silver statue near the mansion's front door. The statue crumbles, revealing a keyhole in the wall behind it.

POLICE SHIELD PIECE 3

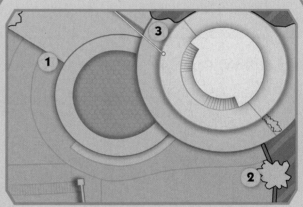

Water three green flower boxes around the mansion's outer grounds to cultivate a shield piece! The maps show where the three flower boxes are located.

Run around the mansion's right side and smash up the playground. Chop through the boarded door over here to enter a small room with a safe. Crack the safe to discover a key.

Fix the fuse box inside the garage to shut off the electric current that's running over to the far stairs. With the current disabled, you can safely scale the stairs and explore the pool area.

VEHICLE TOKEN 2: CLOUD

Smash the chair on the right side of the room beyond the boarded door, and you'll discover a vehicle token! This is the same room that contains the safe and key.

Garage Door Opener

Use the key on the lock you discovered after blasting the silver statue, and the mansion's front door will open. You can explore only a small entry area—go inside and collect the box of bricks.

Carry the box over to the green pad on the left and set it down. Build the bricks into an RC car that's loaded with dynamite.

Take control of the RC car and ram the silver garage door in the background. The explosion destroys the door, letting you investigate the garage.

Pool Party

Wipe out the guards around the pool to secure the area. Smash the patio furniture to discover a scan spot near the background. Follow the footprints to find a buried valve wheel.

Bring the valve wheel to the notch on the pool's right side. Insert the valve wheel, then turn it to drain the pool.

TIP

Jet pack-jump onto the retractable awnings on the right. You'll find a purple stud at the far end!

Drop into the drained pool and use the color swapper to fill your color gun with red energy. Climb the nearby ladder afterward to exit the pool, then blast the green switch on the wall to shut off the electric current that's running along the climbable wall near the switch. Climb up to reach the balcony above.

Run around the balcony and water three planters to grow three large flowers. Now you can jump up the flowers to reach the mansion's roof!

RED BRICK: ATTRACT BRICKS

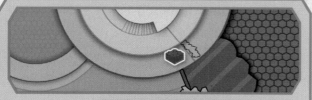

Activate the space crate near the large flower planters to beam in a red mailbox. Smash the mailbox to discover this stage's red brick!

FREE PLAY

CHARACTER TOKEN 1: FORREST BLACKWELL CASUAL

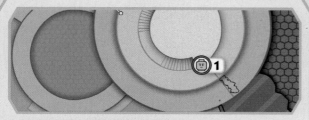

During Free Play, use Rex Fury to rip apart the super-strength crate on the roof's right side. The crate contains a character token!

Rooftop Rampage

Beat up more guards on the roof, then smash the large pile of boulders to uncover a fuse box. Fix the fuse box to raise a shutter on the balcony below and reveal a door that you can pry open.

CHARACTER TOKEN 2: SENTINEL DECKER

Before heading down to the balcony and prying open the door, zip across the tightrope on the roof's left side to reach a transporter pad. Use the pad to beam down into an enclosed area near the pool.

Smash the sand castle inside the enclosed area to discover a hidden character token. Nice!

Use the transporter pad again to beam back out.

After you finish scouring the grounds for goodies, head for the balcony above the pool and pry open the door you've discovered by fixing the rooftop fuse box. Head inside to at last enter the mansion.

INTRODUCTION

POLICE ACADEMY

CHARACTERS AND VEHICLES

WALKTHROUGH

LEGO CITY TOUR

CHECKLISTS

⭐ OBJECTIVE: SEARCH THE STUDY

More guards await you inside Blackwell's lavish study. Bring them all to justice, then use the nearby scan spot to follow a trail of footprints to the left bookshelf. Pull out one of the books to make the nearby light change from red to green.

You must be on to something! Cross the room and smash the furniture to discover another scan spot. Again, follow the footprints—this time to the bookshelf on the right. Pull out another book to turn another red light green.

NOTE

Did you notice the Bell Pepper Emerald inside the study? It seems that rat, Blackwell, has been pulling your strings for quite some time!

POLICE SHIELD PIECE 4

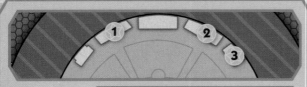

Aim and blast three red and white targets around the study to score a shield piece! Two of the targets are high up on the walls; the last one is hidden behind the books on the right shelf. The astronaut disguise's ray gun works well for blasting these targets!

Revealing Light

With both background lights turned green, the TV between them spins around, revealing a control panel. Sneaky! Activate the panel to open the window shutters on the right, causing sunlight to flood the study.

Beat up the guards who storm the study after you open the shutter. Crack the wall safe afterward to obtain some dynamite, then use the dynamite to destroy one of the three central statues.

With the statue destroyed, there's nothing left to block the sunlight from passing through the Bell Pepper Emerald and striking the remaining statues. This triggers a secret mechanism that causes a grand model to rise from the center of the study. Ingenious!

Professor Kowalski joins Chase in the study shortly after McCain discovers the model. The two suddenly realize Blackwell's scheme: He's turned Blackwell Tower into a giant rocket ship and is planning to travel to the moon!

INTRODUCTION

POLICE ACADEMY

CHARACTERS AND VEHICLES

WALKTHROUGH

LEGO CITY TOUR

CHECKLISTS

CHAPTER 14: SAVINGS AND LOANS

A SUCCESSFUL RAID ON FORREST BLACKWELL'S MANSION HAS REVEALED THE MAD MILLIONAIRE'S VILE PLOT: BLACKWELL HAS SECRETLY TRANSFORMED HIS DOWNTOWN TOWER INTO A ROCKET SHIP AND INTENDS TO BLAST OFF TO THE MOON! NATURALLY, A ROCKET OF SUCH SIZE WOULD LAY WASTE TO LEGO CITY IF IT WERE TO LAUNCH DOWNTOWN. THERE ISN'T MUCH TIME TO SAVE THE DAY!

CITY EXPLORATION

⭐ OBJECTIVE: RECOVER THE SHIELD PROTOTYPES

Time is against you, but Professor Kowalski has a plan. If you hurry, you should be able to contain the rocket blast by using a special shield prototype that the professor has been researching. Race to Kowalski's lab without delay.

Reach the lab before time runs out, and Officer Frank Honey will join you there. Bash down the lab's boarded door with the fire axe and head inside.

⭐ OBJECTIVE: TAKE THE SHIELD PROTOTYPES TO BLACKWELL TOWER

Chase hops into one of the trucks that contains the shield prototypes; Frank drives the other. Now you just need to get to Blackwell Tower and deploy those prototypes before the launching!

It's a long way to Blackwell Tower, so hit the gas and motor over there before time expires. Professor Kowalski and Chief Dunby await you at the tower. The professor tells you to drive to the nearby marker and deploy the first shield prototype.

⭐ OBJECTIVE: BUILD THE SHIELD GENERATORS AROUND BLACKWELL TOWER

Beat up the goons near the first shield prototype's bricks, then build the bricks to assemble the first shield generator. Three more to go!

Continue to drive to each of the markers, defeat the suited goons, and build the shield generators. Keep it up until you've built all four shield generators.

CAUTION

Don't stray too far from Kowalski's truck, or you'll be forced to try again!

Blastoff

With all four shield modulators in place, a powerful force field materializes around Blackwell Tower. Moments later, the tower transforms into a massive rocket ship and launches into outer space. Fortunately, the professor's shield prototypes do their work, and LEGO City is spared from the blast!

McCain has saved a lot of lives this day, but one life still lies in jeopardy—Natalia's! While hacking into the rocket's computer to slow the launch countdown, Professor Kowalski has learned that his daughter was aboard Blackwell's rocket when it took off!

Mayor Gleeson arrives on the scene to congratulate Chase, but our hero's job isn't done just yet. The mayor hints that McCain might be able to find a shuttle at Apollo Island, and Chase sets sail for the island without delay.

INTRODUCTION

POLICE ACADEMY

CHARACTERS AND VEHICLES

WALKTHROUGH

LEGO CITY TOUR

CHECKLISTS

CHAPTER 15: FAR ABOVE THE CALL OF DUTY

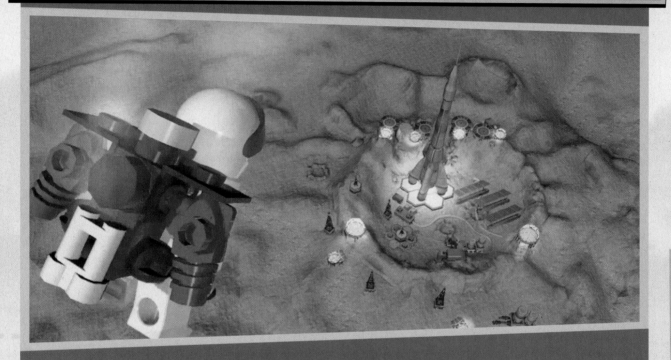

THE REX FURY CASE HAS HAD COUNTLESS TWISTS AND TURNS, AND NOW IT WINDS TO ITS CONCLUSION. CHASE MCCAIN HAS SAVED LEGO CITY FROM DESTRUCTION AT THE HANDS OF THE TRUE MASTERMIND BEHIND REX FURY, MILLIONAIRE FORREST BLACKWELL. BUT THE VILE MILLIONAIRE HAS MANAGED TO ESCAPE JUSTICE—AND LEGO CITY—BY WAY OF ROCKET SHIP. CHASE ISN'T ABOUT TO LET BLACKWELL AND FURY ESCAPE, HOWEVER, ESPECIALLY NOT WITH NATALIA IN THEIR CLUTCHES!

CITY EXPLORATION

⭐ OBJECTIVE: GET TO THE LAUNCH PAD

There's no time to lose! Rush to the objective beacon on Apollo Island, climbing a ladder to reach it. The beacon marks a superbuild, where you can build a space shuttle. The shuttle requires 50,000 bricks to construct—luckily, the nearby launch tower is filled with superbricks!

Superbrick 1

Climb a ladder to begin exploring the launch tower. Use the grapple gun to zip up to the platform above.

 Perform a couple of jet pack jumps to clear the next two gaps to the left.

You land near a space crate. Activate it to beam in a superbrick nearby.

Flip across the flagpole to the right to reach a handhold. Climb up to the walkway above, then run left and slide under a low beam to reach the superbrick you've just beamed in.

Superbrick 2

After collecting the first superbrick, perform a series of jet pack jumps to climb the background ledges and reach a blue balance beam.

Tiptoe around the balance beam to reach another superbrick.

Superbrick 3

Run to the right from the balance beam and wall-jump to a higher platform.

Climb a long, blue and white drainpipe to reach a superbrick at the very top of the launch tower.

Superbrick 4

Drop from the tower and return to the blue balance beam. Drop again to the walkway below, then run up the ramp on the right.

You soon reach a transporter pad. Beam up to a small room above, where a superbrick sits.

Superbrick 5

Beam back down to the lower platform and run down the ramp on the left. Jump off the side of the ramp to land in a lower area with a skylight.

Pry open the skylight and drop into the room below. Claim a superbrick and then use the control panel on the background wall to open the room's door so you may exit.

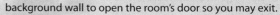

Building the Shuttle

You've got plenty of bricks now, so let's get a move on! Drop from the launch tower and return to the superbuild pad. Spend 50,000 bricks to build the space shuttle.

NOTE

Because you're currently exploring LEGO City, constructing this superbuild earns you a gold brick. You also unlock the Spaceman character token. Cool!

Boarding the Shuttle

You've built the space shuttle—now you just need to enter the cockpit! Climb back up the launch tower, using the grapple gun to zip upward. Jet pack-jump to the left, then flip across the flagpole on the right to reach the ramp. Run up the ramp and cross the foreground walkway to reach the objective beacon near the shuttle's cockpit. Step into the beacon to begin the final mission.

SPECIAL ASSIGNMENT 15: FLY ME TO THE MOON

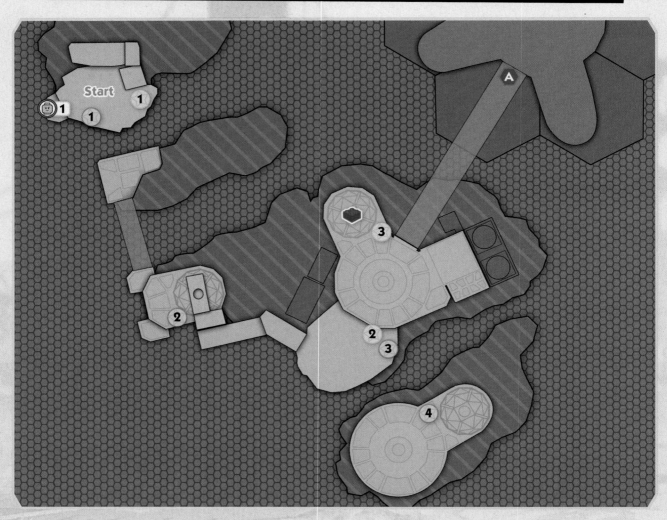

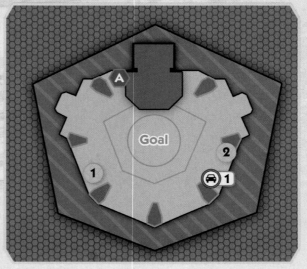

STAGE COLLECTIBLES: "FLY ME TO THE MOON"

MAP ICON(S)	TYPE	MODE	NOTES	GOT IT?
1	"Ben Sharples" character token	Story	Fix the fuse box above the lift near the start, then use the color swapper. Drop to the foreground ledge and blast the switch.	1
1 to 4	Police Shield Piece 1	Story	Smash four space probes around the moon base.	2
1 to 3	Police Shield Piece 2	Free Play	Use Rex Fury to rip apart three strength crates around the moon base.	3
⬢	Red Brick—Studs x10	Free Play	After ripping apart the final strength crate, blast the switch you uncover and enter the nearby dome.	4
1 to 2	Police Shield Piece 3	Story	Crack two standing safes in the rocket's loading bay.	5
1	"Payload" vehicle token	Free Play	Use Rex Fury to rip apart the strength crate in the rocket's loading bay.	6
—	Police Shield Piece 4	Story	Smash three crates during the final battle against Rex Fury.	7
—	"Rex's Tempest" vehicle token	Story	Smash the remains of the T-Rex during the final battle against Rex Fury.	8
—	"Rex Fury" character token	Story	After falling past the spinning energy beams and exiting the rocket, pass through the first stud ring you see.	9

LEGO CITY HERO STUD REQUIREMENT: 26,000

⭐ OBJECTIVE: STORM THE BASE

The shuttle has delivered Chase to the moon, where Forrest Blackwell has secretly erected an impressive base. Time to raid this moon base and rescue Natalia!

First things first: smash the crates near the starting point to discover some bricks, then build them into a red button. Step onto the button to ride up a lift.

INTRODUCTION

POLICE ACADEMY

CHARACTERS AND VEHICLES

WALKTHROUGH

LEGO CITY TOUR

CHECKLISTS

CHARACTER TOKEN 1: BEN SHARPLES

After riding up the lift, climb a blue pipe to reach a fuse box. Fix the fuse box to supply power to the color swapper below.

Use the color swapper to obtain some red energy, then drop back down to the starting point. Run to the foreground and drop off the edge to land on a small ledge below. Blast the green switch down here to shut off the nearby security lasers that guard a character token.

POLICE SHIELD PIECE 1

Smash four space probes around the base's exterior to detect a shield piece! See the maps for the probes' locations.

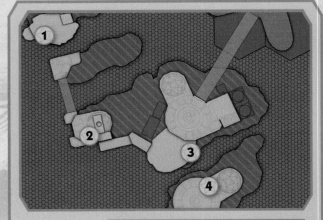

FREE PLAY
POLICE SHIELD PIECE 2

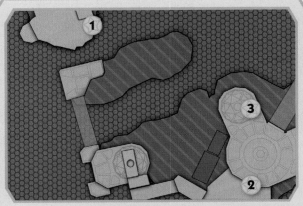

During Free Play, use Rex Fury to rip apart three super-strength crates around the moon base. These feats of strength will score you a shield piece! Check the maps to see where the three strength crates stand.

Gaps and Goons

The lift hoists you up to a platform. Activate the jet pack symbol here, then boost through the stud rings to reach another platform.

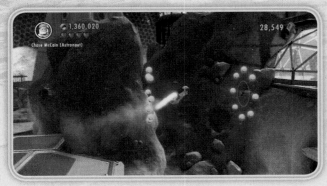

Beat up the astronaut goons who try to stop you, then activate another jet pack symbol and boost to the next platform on the right.

Swing from a chain to reach the next platform. Use a control panel over here to lower a lift. Step onto the lift and pull the lever to ride up to the platform above.

Dome Damage

Smash the crates on the higher platform to discover some dynamite. Use this to blast the nearby silver door so you may enter the hydroponic dome.

Smash the plants inside the dome to uncover some shaky flooring. Use the construction worker's pneumatic drill to tear up the floor and cause a water geyser to froth up. Use the geyser to reach a higher platform.

Elevator Activator

Run to the right until you reach an elevator that's locked by a pair of red switches. Subdue the many astronaut goons who ambush you here, then boost over to the platform on the right.

Smash the platform's large crates to discover some bricks. One pile of bricks forms a space crate; the other forms a color swapper. Fill your color gun with green energy, and activate the space crate to beam in more bricks.

The bricks you beamed in aren't bouncing, so you can't build them just yet. Ignore them for the moment and blast the background dome's red switch to open the dome's door. Head inside and collect a box of bricks.

Bring the box over to the bricks that you recently beamed in via the space crate. Set the box down on the green pad—you'll then be able to build all of the bricks into a moon buggy.

Carefully drive the moon buggy onto the large red button on the ground to the left, and an energy bridge will appear. Drive across the bridge to return to the elevator with the two red switches.

Hop out of the moon buggy and blast both red switches to access the elevator. Hop back into the moon buggy, then drive onto the elevator and ride up to the platform above.

INTRODUCTION

POLICE ACADEMY

CHARACTERS AND VEHICLES

WALKTHROUGH

LEGO CITY TOUR

CHECKLISTS

FREE PLAY
RED BRICK: STUDS X10

During Free Play, after you rip apart the final strength crate with Rex Fury as part of obtaining Police Shield Piece 2, you'll uncover a red switch. Your color gun will already be loaded with green energy by this point, so simply blast the switch to open the nearby dome, where this stage's red brick is located.

Buggy Button

After riding up the elevator, jump off the moon buggy and run to the right. Jump up and grab a handhold, then climb to the platform above.

Pry open the nearby door and enter the small room beyond, which houses a lever. Pull the lever to make a large red button pop up from the ground back near the elevator.

Return to the moon buggy and drive onto the red button to turn it green. This extends an energy bridge into the background, all the way toward Blackwell's rocket. Speed down the bridge and enter the rocket. Natalia must be in there somewhere!

⭐ OBJECTIVE: FIND REX FURY

Chase finds himself in a large loading bay inside Blackwell's rocket. Run to the left and hammer a fuse box to supply power to the green switch on the wall above.

POLICE SHIELD PIECE 3

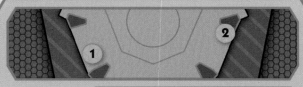

Crack two standing safes in the loading bay to pilfer a shield piece! Check the maps to see where the two safes stand.

FREE PLAY
VEHICLE TOKEN 1: PAYLOAD

During Free Play, use Rex Fury to rip apart the super-strength crate in the loading bay's right foreground corner. You'll discover a vehicle token!

Head to the warehouse's left side and smash a crate to expose a color swapper. Fill your color gun with red energy.

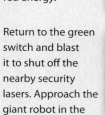

Return to the green switch and blast it to shut off the nearby security lasers. Approach the giant robot in the nook beyond the lasers and press Ⓧ to jump into the pilot's seat.

Heavy Metal

Cool, your very own robot! Stomp over to the background control panels and press Ⓐ to make your robot take control of either one.

When you use the control panels, your view changes to show a network of pipes running across green and red tiles. Depending on the control panel you're using, you'll be able to rotate either the red tiles or the green tiles. Your goal is to spin the tiles and connect the pipes so that the flow of energy is sent to the conduit on the right, as shown.

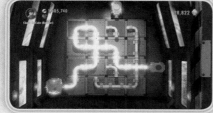

Naturally, Mr. Blackwell is not happy about Chase's meddling. He wastes little time ordering Rex Fury to finish Chase off.

Rex arrives on cue, riding the giant mechanical T-Rex that Chase stole from the museum. Looks like it's time for a robot showdown!

T-Wrecks

You know how dangerous that T-Rex can be, so waste no time stomping over and pressing Ⓐ to pick up one of the loading bay's giant metal barrels. While holding a barrel, aim at the T-Rex and press Ⓨ to hurl the barrel at it.

> **NOTE**
>
> The metal barrels reappear after you throw them, so you'll never run out of "ammo."

Nailing Fury's T-Rex with a metal barrel stuns the monster for a brief moment. Hurry over to the T-Rex and press Ⓐ to grab it. Keep tapping Ⓐ to overpower the T-Rex and knock it to the ground.

⭐ OBJECTIVE: DEFEAT REX FURY

Reconfiguring the flow of energy causes Blackwell's rocket to blast off. Its new destination: LEGO City!

Now's your chance! Hurry over to the action symbol that appears near the T-Rex while it's down. Press Ⓐ to pick up the T-Rex, then keep tapping Ⓐ to swing it around by its tail.

Chase throws the T-Rex into one of the energy tanks that line the loading bay's walls. This damages Blackwell's rocket, along with the T-Rex. Do this three times to destroy the T-Rex and advance the plot.

With his evil scheme undone, Blackwell decides to cut his losses, flee to his rocket's command module, and set his rocket to self-destruct.

The sequence can't be stopped, and Chase soon finds himself plummeting to Earth aboard the broken remains of the loading bay!

⭐ OBJECTIVE: DEFEAT REX FURY—AGAIN!

As if falling to your doom wasn't enough, you must also contend with Rex Fury and his astronaut goons. Defeat the enemy astronauts until two sections of your plummeting platform break off and Rex makes his grand entrance.

TIP

Tiptoe along the platform's outer balance beams to reach valuable studs!

POLICE SHIELD PIECE 4

Smash three small crates around the falling platform, and you'll earn a shield piece. There's no map

for this final battle area, but the crates are easy to spot. Two of them are on the left side of the falling platform; the other is on the right.

VEHICLE TOKEN 2: REX'S TEMPEST

Smash the remains of the T-Rex, which lie in a heap on the platform's right foreground corner, and

you'll discover a hidden vehicle token!

Besting Rex

Rex is protected by a bubble shield, and there's only one way to penetrate it. Grab one of his goons, then hold Ⓨ to aim. Target Rex Fury, and release Ⓨ to toss the goon at Rex.

CAUTION

Careful: More sections of the platform will break off as you battle Rex.

Hitting Rex with a thrown goon causes his shield to falter. Rex lands and decides to fight you, man to man. Don't get too close to Fury, or he'll pick you up

and throw you. Instead, wait until you see an Ⓧ icon appear above Rex's head, then press Ⓧ to counter his attack and hurt him.

After you counter Rex, he flees and reactivates his bubble shield. Toss another goon at him, then counter Rex again by pressing Ⓧ when

the Ⓧ icon appears. Keep this up until you at last defeat Rex Fury. Be sure to slap on the handcuffs while he's down!

Deal the final blow to Rex Fury, and Blackwell's evil scheme will at last be undone. The vile millionaire is sent careening off into space in his escape pod, and the remains of his rocket are stuck in a free fall to Earth.

⭐ OBJECTIVE: REACH THE COMMAND CAPSULE

You have defeated the bad guys, but Natalia is still in jeopardy! Try to fly through the stud rings during this epic final fall to Earth—they'll help you attain LEGO City Hero status. Avoid debris as you plummet, and press Ⓐ to slow down and Ⓑ to speed up your descent.

CHARACTER TOKEN 2: REX FURY

After falling past spinning energy beams and exiting through the bottom of Blackwell's rocket, pass through the first stud ring you see to collect this stage's final goodie—a very valuable character token!

A timer appears as you near the end of your descent. Hold Ⓑ to fall faster than normal, and catch up to the rocket's falling command capsule before time runs out.

Day: Saved

Chase lands on the command capsule just in time to pull a lever and deploy a giant parachute. The capsule gently touches down in LEGO City, and Natalia is saved!

McCain returns to a hero's welcome. The Rex Fury case is closed, and LEGO City has been saved. Natalia falls into his arms, and even Chief Dunby has to congratulate Chase on a job well done. Way to go, hero!

NOTE

Congratulations, you've beaten Story mode! There's still plenty to see and do in LEGO City, though. You've unlocked all of Chase's abilities now, so feel free to revisit those Special Assignments and use McCain's myriad skills to collect all of the Free Play goodies you couldn't claim before. LEGO City itself is also filled with all sorts of treasures and adventures. Check out the next chapter to discover everything the city has to offer!

INTRODUCTION

POLICE ACADEMY

CHARACTERS AND VEHICLES

WALKTHROUGH

LEGO CITY TOUR

CHECKLISTS

LEGO CITY TOUR

INTRODUCTION

WELCOME, CITIZEN, TO YOUR OFFICIAL GUIDED TOUR OF LEGO CITY! THIS CHAPTER FULLY EXPOSES EACH OF LEGO CITY'S MANY DISTRICTS, HELPING YOU TRACK DOWN ALL THOSE HIDDEN GOODIES WITH EASE. THERE'S LOTS TO SEE AND DO, SO LET'S GET STARTED!

TOUR PREP

Before you begin exploring LEGO City, consider completing the following tasks. You'll have an easier time navigating the city after you accomplish the following:

Beat Story Mode! When you clear Story Mode and save LEGO City, you unlock all of Chase McCain's disguises and outfits. This gives you nearly every skill you need to fully explore the city!

Unlock Rex Fury! Only Rex Fury is strong enough to open objects that sport orange strength handles. This makes Rex invaluable while exploring LEGO City. You likely collected Rex Fury's character token during the final Story mode mission, so go ahead and drop a whopping 1,000,000 studs to purchase him at the Police Station as soon as you're able. Then use the Police Station's disguise booth to set Rex Fury as your robber disguise.

Get the Super Color Gun red brick! This special red brick upgrades your robber disguise's color gun so that it automatically fires the proper color at whatever object you're targeting. Find and purchase this red brick, and you won't have to bother with searching for color swappers anymore! This red brick is located in Uptown.

Get the Unlimited Dynamite red brick! With this red brick, your miner disguises will carry an unlimited supply of dynamite, eliminating the need for dynamite dispensers. Handy! Find this red brick in Special Assignment 3, "Miner Altercation."

Get the Super Fast Travel red brick! This red brick lets you instantly travel between LEGO City's many different zones. This comes in handy while exploring the city, so track down this red brick at LEGO City Airport. You'll need Rex Fury's help to claim it.

Get a Stud Multiplier red brick! These red bricks multiply the value of every stud you collect, making them extremely desirable. You'll be grabbing plenty of studs while exploring the city, so these red bricks will pay for themselves in no time. You likely collected one of these red bricks during the later Story mode missions.

NOTE

Beating Story mode gives you the abilities you need to fully explore LEGO City and causes many of the city's special feats to appear. For instance, Farmer Hayes's lost pigs won't appear around the city until after you help him at his farm during Story mode. It's impossible to see and do everything around the city until you've beaten Story mode, so focus on that first!

CITY ZONES

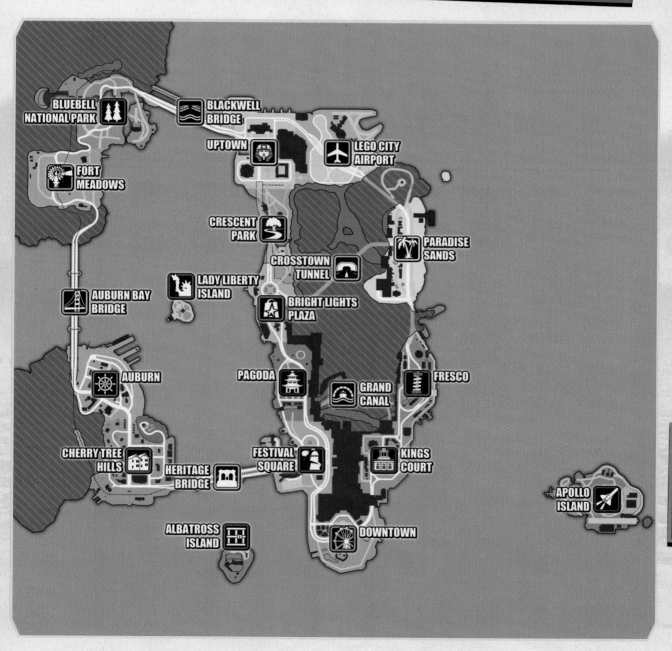

INTRODUCTION

POLICE ACADEMY

CHARACTERS AND VEHICLES

WALKTHROUGH

LEGO CITY TOUR

CHECKLISTS

LEGO City is so massive, it's divided into several districts, or "zones." This lets you "divide and conquer" as you explore the city one district at a time.

The name of your current district is shown at the top of the GamePad. Notice how the name changes as you move through the city. Knowing which zone you're in is important, for each one features its own special surprises and collectibles. Make good use of the GamePad map as you explore!

Here's a complete alphabetical listing of LEGO City's 22 zones:

NOTE

Though it's not technically a district, the Police Station is a unique area that contains its own hidden goodies. The Police Station is also a hub of great importance to Chase, so we cover it in full detail here in the LEGO City Tour chapter. It's the first zone we expose!

POINTS OF INTEREST

Each city district features unique points of interest. Some of these are fairly obvious, like Fort Meadows's imposing castle, while others are more discreet, like the entrance to Auburn's unassuming metro station. Knowing a district's intricacies is helpful and important, so every zone's section begins with an overview of its particular points of interest.

FEATS AND COLLECTIBLES

All of LEGO City's districts have special feats for you to accomplish—even the smaller areas like islands and bridges. Achieve these feats to unlock fabulous rewards, such as gold bricks and character or vehicle tokens!

NOTE

Complete all feats of a certain type (Aliens Caught, Boulders Destroyed, etc.) across the entire city to unlock special characters! See the "Characters and Vehicles" chapter for details.

Check your progress in each zone by tapping the small "i" icon that appears at the top of the GamePad. This displays a menu that reveals all of the zone's available feats and how many you've accomplished. Tap the "i" icon again to close the menu.

Let's look at each of the many different feats and events you're likely to find in any given zone of the city.

? BLOCKS

Amount: 5
Reward: "Super Wrestler" character token (after all ? Blocks in the city have been found)

These special objects should look very familiar to fans of classic gaming. There are only five ? Blocks in all of LEGO City—and you know what to do when you find one! Stand beneath the block and jump to bump it from below. Studs will fly out of the block—keep jumping and bumping until it breaks apart! Something good will happen when you smash all five ? Blocks in the city.

ALIENS CAUGHT

Amount: 17
Reward: Gold bricks

Many zones feature special space crates that cause alien invaders to appear when activated. Hurry and chase after these freaky creatures; then press Ⓐ to knock them down when you get close and the Ⓐ icon appears. Slap on the handcuffs afterward to arrest the alien and earn a gold brick!

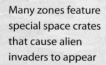

Fire the grapple gun to wrap up fleeing aliens and make them easier to catch!

ATMS SMASHED

Amount: 18
Reward: Gold bricks

While any character can use ATMs to withdraw fast studs, only robber characters can smash up ATMs for fun and profit. Toggle to your robber disguise, then rapidly tap Ⓐ to bust up every ATM you see in the city. You'll score even more studs—along with a gold brick!

TIP

Double your payday by withdrawing studs from an ATM before you wreck it!

BBQ FIRES EXTINGUISHED

Amount: 17
Reward: Gold bricks

Open flames are dangerous when left unattended. Whenever you see a BBQ fire blazing away, toggle to a fire fighter disguise and hold Ⓨ to douse the flames with your extinguisher. You'll cook up a gold brick each time you put out a BBQ fire!

BOULDERS DESTROYED

Amount: 22
Reward: Gold bricks

Boulders are common objects, but did you know there are a few special boulders hidden around LEGO City? Destroy these rare, crystal-covered boulders with the miner disguise's pickax to extract lots of studs and some precious gold bricks!

⭐ 🐱 CATS RESCUED

Amount: 17
Reward: Gold bricks

A number of innocent kitties have gotten themselves stuck in precarious places around LEGO City. Search for these forlorn felines whenever you hear their telltale meowing; then toggle to a fire fighter disguise and press Ⓐ to rescue them from their plight.

⭐ 👤 CHARACTER TOKENS

Amount (in the city): 260
Reward: New character disguises

A vast number of character tokens have been sprinkled throughout LEGO City. Some of these tokens are fairly easy to find, while others will appear only after you complete special feats, such as erecting a superbuild or blasting a certain number of objects with a robber's color gun. Collect character tokens to unlock bonus characters for purchase back at the Police Station.

TIP

Flip back to the "Characters and Vehicles" chapter for a complete list of all character disguises and info on where you can find their tokens.

⭐ ☕ COFFEE BREAKS COMPLETED

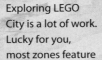

Amount: 20
Reward: Gold bricks

Exploring LEGO City is a lot of work. Lucky for you, most zones feature special coffee stations where you can relax and take a breather. Toggle to the construction worker disguise, and press Ⓐ to use these special stations, where you'll slurp up a gold brick.

⭐ 🌸 DISGUISE BOOTHS

Amount: 17
Rewards: Gold bricks, additional disguise booths

Whenever you see a special blue crate with a police shield logo, smash it and build its bricks into a disguise booth. These work just like the one in the Police Station's basement—step inside to customize the disguise wheel with your favorite disguises. Remember: you must purchase disguises at the Police Station before you can use them.

⭐ 🏙 DISTRICTS CONQUERED

Amount: 20
Reward: Gold bricks

Nearly every zone features a special stand where you can raise a flag. Toggle to the astronaut disguise and press Ⓐ to raise the flag and conquer a gold brick! These special flag stands are usually found someplace high and require a little effort to reach.

⭐ ⚒ DRILL THRILLS COMPLETED

Amount: 17
Reward: Gold bricks

Whenever you spot a sizzling fuse box in the city, switch to the construction worker disguise and press Ⓐ to fix it with your hammer. There's a good chance you'll fire up a drill thrill event!

During drill thrills, you have a limited amount of time to destroy several nearby shaky plates with the construction worker's pneumatic drill. Hold Ⓨ and drill all of those plates before time runs out to dig up a gold brick. Don't worry—if you don't succeed on your first effort, you can always try again!

INTRODUCTION

POLICE ACADEMY

CHARACTERS AND VEHICLES

WALKTHROUGH

LEGO CITY TOUR

CHECKLISTS

⚓ FERRY ROUTES ACTIVATED

Amount: 3
Reward: Gold bricks, fast travel, vehicle tokens

Ferry routes let you quickly travel between LEGO City's mainland and its outlying islands. While there are only three ferry routes to find, each one you activate earns you a gold brick!

🌼 FLOWERS WATERED

Amount: 20
Reward: Gold bricks

Use the farmer disguise's watering can to soak green flower boxes you see around the city. Each one you water will sprout some flowers—along with a gold brick!

🏃 FREE RUNS

Amount: 19
Rewards: Gold bricks, character tokens

Free runs are unique events that require a bit of explanation. First, before you can attempt a zone's free run, you must often locate a free run token within the zone. Collect the token, and a free run beacon will appear somewhere in the zone. Step into the beacon to begin the free run event!

During a free run, you must race through an obstacle course on foot, traveling a short distance around the zone. Collect time tokens as you go to add precious seconds to the clock. If time runs out, you'll have to try again!

Run hard and reach the goal before time runs out to complete the free run event. You earn a gold brick each time you beat a free run, and you often unlock character tokens as well!

👮 GANGS ARRESTED

Amount: 16
Reward: Gold bricks

Even after Chase saves LEGO City, a few troublemakers still lurk about. Look for audio scan points around the city and use the GamePad to listen in on nearby conversations, just as you did in Story mode. One of these will reveal a gang of hooligans that's about to stir up trouble!

After you overhear the troublemakers' scheme, a special beacon will appear in the zone. Hurry over to the beacon before time runs out or you'll miss your chance to make the bust!

Reach the beacon, and the troublemakers will appear. Beat up all of these goons and arrest each one!

The final thug often flees the scene on foot. Race after him and press Ⓐ to knock him down when you get close. Slap on the cuffs while he's down. Your crime-fighting efforts will score you a shiny gold brick!

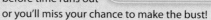

TIP

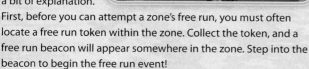

Use the grapple gun to tie up fleeing goons and make catching them a little easier.

⭐ PIGS RETURNED

Amount: 22 **Reward:** Gold bricks

Poor Farmer Hayes has lost his prized pigs, and the little hogs have gotten themselves stuck in all sorts of crazy places around LEGO City. Whenever you find a lost pig, toggle to the farmer disguise and press Ⓧ to hop onto the pig's back.

A trail of green studs appears after you mount a pig, leading you toward the nearest pig cannon. Ride the little piggy over there and press Ⓐ

to stuff it into the cannon. Move around to the side and press Ⓐ again to launch the pig back to Farmer Hayes's pen. Your swine-finding efforts will rustle you up a gold brick!

⭐ RED BRICKS

Amount (in the city): 25
Reward: Red bricks

Red bricks are rare prizes that grant special benefits.
Each one has its own power—for example, some will multiply the value of studs you collect. Search high and low for red bricks, and collect them to make them available for purchase back at the Police Station.

TIP

Spend your hard-earned studs on red bricks before anything else, especially the ones that multiply the value of studs. You need lots of moolah to purchase all those character disguises and vehicles!

⭐ SILVER STATUES DESTROYED

Amount: 17
Reward: Gold bricks

Rex Fury had such a grip on LEGO City that his goons managed to erect several silver statues in the scoundrel's honor. Destroy the miscreant's monuments by using dynamite to blast each silver statue to bits. You'll need to locate a dynamite dispenser, of course—unless you've found and purchased the Unlimited Dynamite red brick! (It's hidden in Special Assignment 3, "Miner Altercation.")

⭐ SUPERBRICKS

Amount: Lots! **Rewards:** Bricks

Superbricks are big, colorful bricks that are hidden all over LEGO City. Next to studs, these are the most plentiful goodies in the game. Small superbricks are worth 1,000 bricks; large superbricks are worth a whopping 10,000! Collect superbricks to quickly amass the bricks you need to construct superbuilds.

NOTE

There are so many superbricks in LEGO City that you shouldn't have trouble finding all the bricks you need. In a pinch, tap the Data Scan button on the Wii U GamePad and search your surroundings for nearby superbricks. Or simply drive recklessly and smash into lots of LEGO objects to jack up your brick multiplier!

⬤ SUPERBUILDS

Amount (in the city): 65
Rewards: Gold bricks, character tokens, vehicle tokens, and more!

Superbuilds are special objects and monuments that Chase can erect around LEGO City. Look for large, flat LEGO pads, stand on them, and then press Ⓐ to see what the superbuild is called and how many bricks it will cost you to construct.

Superbuilds require a significant amount of bricks to build and often provide special benefits once they've been constructed. Some of the most useful superbuilds are helipads and vehicle call-in points—these let you order any aircraft or vehicle you've unlocked and purchased at the Police Station. Train stations and ferries are also handy superbuilds, as they'll help you travel around the city.

You earn a gold brick each time you complete a superbuild, and many superbuilds also reward you with bonus character or vehicle tokens. Other superbuilds can help you reach special areas of the city that you couldn't reach without their help. It pays to complete superbuilds, so spend those hard-earned bricks and build every one you see!

⭐ SUPER STARS

Amount: 5
Reward: "Pop Star" character token (after you have found all Super Stars in the city)

Five special Super Stars are scattered across LEGO City. Search high and low for their bright, bouncing bricks, then build them to make the Super Stars whole again. Unfortunately, they won't make Chase sparkly and invincible, but you'll earn a special prize if you track down and build all five!

🏁 TIME TRIALS

Amount: 16
Rewards: Gold bricks, vehicle tokens

Some parked vehicles in the city are highlighted by light beacons. Hop into one of these highlighted rides to begin a thrilling race around LEGO City! Simply follow the green studs and pass through each checkpoint to extend your time. Use turbos if you've got them, and keep speeding around the course until you reach the goal.

🚆 TRAIN STATIONS

Amount: 14
Rewards: Gold bricks, fast travel

Train stations are special terminals that let Chase rapidly travel LEGO City. You must activate each train station before you can use it. Chase activates two train stations during Story mode: one in Cherry Tree Hills and another in Bluebell National Park. Activate more train stations to make navigating the city much easier!

Some train stations are activated by constructing superbuilds. Other train stations are activated by smashing an object on the station platform and then building its bricks into a ticket machine. You receive a gold brick each time you activate a new train station.

Using a train station couldn't be easier—just stand in front of the station's ticket machine and press Ⓐ to use it. Look at your GamePad afterward and tap on the train station to which you'd like to travel. You'll then automatically board the train and speed off to your destination.

INTRODUCTION

POLICE ACADEMY

CHARACTERS AND VEHICLES

WALKTHROUGH

LEGO CITY TOUR

CHECKLISTS

VEHICLE ROBBERIES COMPLETED

Amount: 13
Rewards: Gold bricks, vehicle tokens

Vehicle robberies are intense events in which you must steal a vehicle and then avoid the police as you race to reach a distant chop shop. These events often lead you a good distance around the city, and the police won't rest until you reach your destination, or they smash your vehicle to bits. Follow the green studs toward the chop shop and use turbos to stay ahead of the cops.

VEHICLE ROBBERS ARRESTED

Amount: 12
Rewards: Gold bricks, vehicle tokens

Some zones feature criminal scan spots. Move to these spots and use the GamePad to scan your surroundings for criminal activity, just as you did in Story mode. There's bound to be a crook around somewhere!

The moment you discover the nearby criminal, he speeds off in a stolen vehicle. Lucky for you, a police helicopter delivers an emergency vehicle right nearby for you to use! Hurry into the driver's seat and race after the thief.

Ram the car thief's vehicle until it loses its hearts and you destroy it. The robber then flees on foot. Leap out of your vehicle and chase after him!

Press Ⓐ when you get close to knock the robber to the ground, then slap on the handcuffs to bring the chase to an end. All vehicle robber events reward you with gold bricks, and many offer bonus vehicle tokens as well.

VEHICLE TOKENS

Amount (in the city): 80   **Reward:** New vehicles

Vehicle tokens are similar to character tokens. Collect them to purchase cool new vehicles at the Police Station! Unlike the ones hidden in Special Assignments, vehicle tokens in LEGO City are obtained only by completing other feats, such as constructing superbuilds or completing time trials. You'll never find loose vehicle tokens around the city.

TIP

Flip back to the "Characters and Vehicles" chapter for a complete list of every vehicle, with details on where to find their tokens.

WARP PIPES

Amount: N/A   **Reward:** Fast travel

Warp pipes are super-secret goodies that are commonly hidden inside of objects with orange strength handles. Only Rex Fury can rip open objects with orange strength handles and discover what might be hidden inside. Purchase Rex Fury at the Police Station and set him as your robber disguise. Use him to rip open these objects and discover the warp pipes. Each warp pipe links to another warp pipe elsewhere in the city, letting you quickly travel vast distances!

LEGO CITY POLICE STATION

INTRODUCTION

POLICE ACADEMY

CHARACTERS AND VEHICLES

WALKTHROUGH

LEGO CITY TOUR

CHECKLISTS

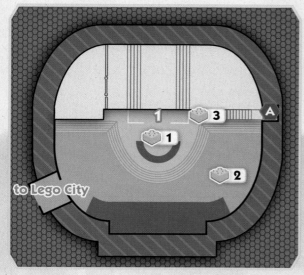

LOBBY

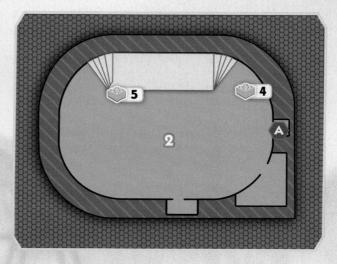

BRIEFING ROOM

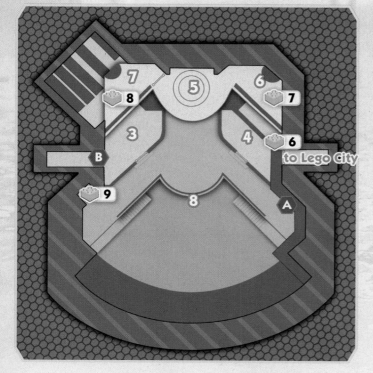

BASEMENT

LINEUP ROOM

MAP LEGEND

MAP ICON(S)	FEAT/COLLECTIBLE	REWARD(S)	LOCATION/HOW TO REACH	GOT IT?
1	Gold Brick 1	Gold brick	Smash objects around the lobby to find bricks, then build three wall portraits.	1
2	Gold Brick 2	Gold brick	Smash the objects in the lobby's right foreground corner, then build and get on the amusement ride.	2
3	Gold Brick 3	Gold brick	Obtain dynamite from the lobby's dispenser, then blast the lobby's silver cabinet.	3
4	Gold Brick 4	Gold brick	Use the popcorn cart in the briefing room.	4
5	Gold Brick 5	Gold brick	Pry open the briefing room's closet, carry the bricks over to the pad, build the donut table.	5
6	Gold Brick 6	Gold brick	Smash the crate near Chuck's vehicle requisitions desk.	6
7	Gold Brick 7	Gold brick	Smash the crate near the red brick station.	7
8	Gold Brick 8	Gold brick	Smash the crate near the gold brick station.	8
9	Gold Brick 9	Gold brick	Use the fire fighter disguise to chop through the boarded door near Ellie's desk.	9
10	Gold Brick 10	Gold brick	Smash the crate in the suspect lineup room near Ellie's desk.	10

POINTS OF INTEREST

1 MAIN COMPUTER

The Police Station's main computer (or main "compuper," as Frank would call it) is a marvel of modern crime-fighting technology. Use the main computer to review your total game time and progress percentage and to input cheat codes.

2 PROJECTOR

Ride the Police Station's elevator to the top floor briefing room, and you'll find a film projector all set up for Chase to use. Start the projector at any time to review Chase's past trials and tribulations while working the Rex Fury case. All Story mode cutscenes you've viewed can be watched and enjoyed again here.

3 ELLIE'S REQUISITIONS DESK

Take the elevator down to the basement to visit several important stations. Officer Ellie Phillips runs the requisitions desk here and is happy to help Chase by providing him with all sorts of goodies, like communicator upgrades and new disguises. After you discover character tokens, visit Ellie and spend studs to purchase new disguises for Chase.

⭐ 4 CHUCK'S VEHICLE REQUEST DESK

The vehicle requests desk is located right next to Ellie's and is run by Chuck, the station's mechanic. Chase can spend his hard-earned studs here to purchase new vehicles after he discovers their vehicle tokens. After making a purchase, Chase can order his new vehicles at any call-in point (for land vehicles) or helipad (for aircraft).

Chase can't visit Chuck's desk until he acquires the grapple gun in Story mode. Once Chase has the grapple gun, he can zip up onto the vent above the basement's elevator and drop down near Chuck's desk.

⭐ 5 BASEMENT LIFT

After you unlock the Chase McCain (Robber) disguise during Story mode, crack the wall safe behind the vehicle requisitions desk to discover a key card. Use this to activate the nearby lift, which hoists you up to the basement's upper level.

⭐ 6 RED BRICK TERMINAL

Activate the lift that lies between Chuck's and Ellie's desks. Ride it to another pair of important stations. The station on the right lets Chase spend studs to purchase red bricks he's discovered. Once you purchase a red brick, its special power can be turned on and off at any time through the Pause menu.

⭐ 7 GOLD BRICK TERMINAL

Across from the red brick terminal is the gold brick terminal, where Chase can turn excess studs into prized gold bricks. You can purchase 16 gold bricks here, but it takes a lot of studs to buy them all! Unlike red bricks, gold bricks don't bestow any powers, so purchase red bricks first and exploit their special benefits.

⭐ 8 DISGUISE BOOTH

Sprint downstairs to the basement's lowest floor, where plenty of exercise equipment is located. There's a disguise booth down here—the same one that Chase uses at the start of Story mode. Like all other disguise booths around the city, Chase can use this booth to pick which disguises he'll carry with him.

⭐ 9 LINEUP ROOM

This room is set aside for witnesses to identify suspects. Move Chase onto the big red button here to get a closer view of the suspects. You can actually customize their appearance! The lineup room serves as your create-a-disguise tool at the Police Station. Go ahead and see what sorts of crazy custom disguises you can make!

INTRODUCTION

POLICE ACADEMY

CHARACTERS AND VEHICLES

WALKTHROUGH

LEGO CITY TOUR

CHECKLISTS

FEATS AND COLLECTIBLES

NOTE

Unlike in all other areas of the city, you can find gold bricks only in the Police Station. A few superbricks are hidden in the station as well, but no other major collectibles are hidden here.

GOLD BRICK 1

Build four portraits around the Police Station's lobby to make a gold brick appear in the center of the room. This requires no special disguise skills—simply smash objects around the lobby to discover the bricks you need.

GOLD BRICK 2

Smash the objects on the lobby's right side, then build the remaining bricks into a police car. Hop on and enjoy the ride!

GOLD BRICK 3

After you unlock the Chase McCain (Miner) disguise in Story mode, return to the Police Station and collect some dynamite from the dispenser in the lobby. Use the dynamite to blast the lobby's silver filing cabinet and uncover a hidden gold brick!

GOLD BRICK 4

Pop by the briefing room's popcorn cart and grab a handful of buttery goodness. You'll make Chase's day—and you'll discover a gold brick in the process!

GOLD BRICK 5

After you've found the Chase McCain (Robber) disguise in Story mode, visit the Police Station's briefing room and pry open the door near the elevator to access a storage closet.

Pick up the box of bricks you discover inside the closet, then carry it over to the green pad across the briefing room. Set down the box and build the bricks into a table with donuts for fellow officers to enjoy. Your good deed is soon rewarded by the sudden appearance of a gold brick!

GOLD BRICK 6

Down in the basement, smash the crate near Chuck's vehicle requisitions desk to discover a gold brick. You need the grapple gun in order to reach Chuck's desk—just keep playing through Story mode until you get it.

GOLD BRICK 7

Next, activate and ride up the central lift to reach the red brick and gold brick terminals above. Smash a box near the red brick terminal to discover another gold brick.

GOLD BRICK 8

After riding up the central lift, smash a crate near the gold brick terminal to find another gold brick. Score!

GOLD BRICK 9

After you unlock the Chase McCain (Fireman) disguise in Story mode, use the fire axe to chop open the boarded door near Ellie's desk. You'll discover a hidden gold brick inside a small closet!

GOLD BRICK 10

Enter the suspect lineup room near Ellie's desk. Smash the crate in the far corner here to claim another easy gold brick.

ALBATROSS ISLAND

POINTS OF INTEREST

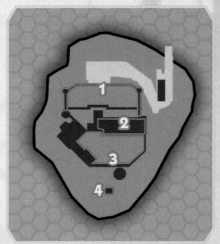

Wall-hug around the ledge until you reach a handhold. Use it to hop over the fence.

A grapple point hangs off the vent shaft two stories up. Use your grapple gun to ascend to the roof.

Head to the right and you'll find yourself underneath the numerous guard towers along the prison wall.

⭐ 1 GUARD WALL

Surrounding the prison grounds are a series of guard towers. Don't worry, these guards are too sleepy to be bothered.

Behind the road that leads up to the prison is this little alcove with LEGO walls you can jump off. Wall-bounce to get up to the slope.

⭐ 2 UPPER PRISON YARD

The really good prisoners can use a fenced yard at the top of the prison, which has a nice view of the city. Not surprisingly, Chase McCain is the only "good" prisoner on Albatross Island.

From the prison's south side, go to the building with the greenish blue roof. Use the astronaut's jetpack to get onto the roof.

Quickly run up the slopes and then hop onto the thin ledge.

Boost up to the next building and grab the handhold. Climb up.

Use the robber's crowbar to break into the prison offices.

Along the way, you'll come across a dynamite dispenser. Grab some if you like.

Keep heading right until you're outside again. There are handholds along the building. Grab on and make your way up the building.

Hop the fence to reach the upper prison yard.

⭐ ③ SOUTH SIDE OF THE PRISON

Not surprisingly, LEGO City's prison has its own gated community that not everyone can enter.

The prison's southern side isn't easily accessible. To reach it, you'll need a transporter pad. From the pier, face the prison and head left along the beach until you find an astronaut crate. Break it open and build the transporter pad.

Use the pad to get into the locked-off section of Albatross Island.

⭐ ④ TOP OF THE TOWER

At the back end of Albatross Island is an imposing lighthouse/guard tower. Thanks to this impressive tower, no one can escape the island. The best you can hope for is getting on top of the tower.

Go to the prison's south side. Head toward the back and go upstairs to the large tower overlooking the water.

On the tower's right side are some plants to water with the farmer. Use these to get up to the next level.

There are some handholds that spiral all the way up to the tower's top. Take these and you'll end up on top of the world...or at least on top of the tower.

INTRODUCTION

POLICE ACADEMY

CHARACTERS AND VEHICLES

WALKTHROUGH

LEGO CITY TOUR

CHECKLISTS

FEATS AND COLLECTIBLES

MAP LEGEND

MAP ICON(S)	FEAT/COLLECTIBLE	REWARD(S)	LOCATION/HOW TO REACH	GOT IT?
	Alien Caught	Gold Brick	On top of the entrance to the prison cells.	1
	ATM Smashed	Gold Brick	In the upper corner of the south side of the prison.	2
	BBQ Fire Extinguished	Gold Brick	Underneath a walkway on the west side of the prison yard.	3
	Boulder Destroyed	Gold Brick	On the beach at the south end of the island.	4
	Cat Rescued	Gold Brick	On a balcony near the prison roof.	5
1 to 3 / 1	Character Token 1	Tribal Hunter	Find three pallets spread across the beach; smash each one and build sand castles from their broken blocks.	6
2	Character Token 2	Press Photographer	Hidden inside a boulder next to the small lagoon at the beach.	7
3	Character Token 3	Hot Tub Harry	Use the transporter pad under the guard tower, then use the super jetpack rings to get across to the correct tower.	8
1 to 3 / 4	Character Token 4	Boxer	Paint the three silver punching bags yellow.	9
5	Character Token 5	Verne	On a guard tower, up the stairs from the helicopter superbuild.	10
6	Character Token 6	Butcher	On the way toward the prison, hug the fenced wall and move around to the other side.	11
7	Character Token 7	Beefy Baker	Hidden in a pallet near the prison offices.	12
	Coffee Break Completed	Gold Brick	Behind the basketball court.	13
	Disguise Booth	Gold Brick, "Prison Guard" character token	Near the beginning of the pier.	14
	District Conquered	Gold Brick	Astronaut boost when at the top of the tower.	15
	Drill Thrill Completed	Gold Brick	Against a fence in the upper prison yard.	16
	Flowers Watered	Gold Brick	In the south side of the prison, near some dancing inmates.	17
	Free Run	Gold Brick, "Warden Stonewall" character token	In the upper prison yard.	18
	Gang Arrested	Gold Brick	Chicken glide from the top of the tower onto a water tower.	19
	Pig Returned	Gold Brick	Inside the fenced area next to the docks, break into the boarded door and climb the ladder to the roof.	20
	Red Brick	Police Siren Hat	Break into the door at the bottom of the prison tower.	21
	Silver Statue Destroyed	Gold Brick	Use the transporter pad in the upper prison yard to teleport to the statue.	22
	Superbuild: Helipad	Gold Brick, "Chopper" vehicle token	On the west side of the prison yard, near the guard towers.	23

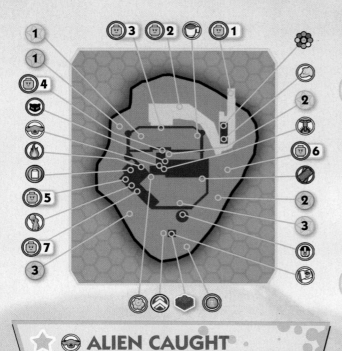

BOULDER DESTROYED

Reward: Gold brick

A special boulder sits on the beach on the south side of the island.

CAT RESCUED

Reward: Gold brick

Stand at the bottom of the stairs next to the helipad superbuild. Use your grapple gun to yank down an air conditioner. Crooks don't deserve such perks!

Build the broken pieces into a trampoline, then bounce up to the handhold.

Follow the handholds to the left until you can hop onto a small platform, where a cat waits for a brave fireman to come to the rescue.

ALIEN CAUGHT

Reward: Gold brick

You'll find a space crate atop the entrance to the prison cells. Activate it to beam in an alien invader!

ATM SMASHED

Reward: Gold brick

This unlawful ATM stands in the prison yard on the prison's south side. It's in the upper east corner.

BBQ FIRE EXTINGUISHED

Reward: Gold brick

The blazing BBQ is against a wall, underneath a walkway on the west side of the prison yard.

INTRODUCTION

POLICE ACADEMY

CHARACTERS AND VEHICLES

WALKTHROUGH

LEGO CITY TOUR

CHECKLISTS

⭐ 🔘1 CHARACTER TOKEN 1

Reward: Tribal Hunter

Find three pallets spread across the beach. Smash each one and build sand castles from their broken blocks to unlock the Tribal Hunter.

You'll find the character token atop some crates on the pier.

⭐ 🔘2 CHARACTER TOKEN 2

Reward: Press Photographer

This token is hidden inside this boulder. Look for the small lagoon just west of the pier.

⭐ 🔘3 CHARACTER TOKEN 3

Reward: Hot Tub Harry

Make your way along the guard wall. On the front side of the prison, you'll find a transporter pad underneath one of the guard towers. Use it to reach the tower's top.

Stand on the jetpack symbol and activate it. Use the super jetpack rings to get to the far tower.

Land and that token is all yours.

⭐ 🔘4 CHARACTER TOKEN 4

Reward: Boxer

Start at the upper prison yard. In the far corner is a color swapper. Switch to yellow paint.

Drop to the ground level and find the three unpainted punching bags. Once you've turned all three yellow, the character token appears.

You'll find the token in front of the entrance to the prison cells.

⭐ 5 CHARACTER TOKEN 5

Reward: Verne

From the helipad superbuild, run up the stairs. The token is sitting on the edge of the guard tower. Leap to the handhold and grab the token.

⭐ 6 CHARACTER TOKEN 6

Reward: Butcher

You can grab this on your way toward the guard wall. When you're hugging the thin ledge, instead of leaping over the fence, keep heading left.

The token is just around the corner. See the "Points of Interest" section if you're unsure of the path to take.

⭐ 7 CHARACTER TOKEN 7

Reward: Beefy Baker

On your way toward the upper prison yard, just before you break into the prison offices, you'll see a pallet on the ground. Smash it to score the character token. Check the "Points of Interest" for details on how to reach the upper prison yard.

⭐ ☕ COFFEE BREAK COMPLETED

Reward: Gold brick

The cup o' joe is stashed behind the basketball court.

⭐ ✿ DISGUISE BOOTH

Reward: Gold brick, "Prison Guard" character token

The disguise booth is at the beginning of the pier, on the beach.

⭐ 🏴 DISTRICT CONQUERED

Reward: Gold brick

From the top of the tower, use the astronaut's jetpack to boost to the very top of the tower. Plant your flag and claim this district for the LEGO City Police. See the "Points of Interest" section to find out how to reach the tower's top.

⭐ 🔧 DRILL THRILL COMPLETED

Reward: Gold brick

The fuse box for the drill thrill challenge is next to the fence where you enter the upper prison yard. See the previous "Points of Interest" section to learn how to get there.

INTRODUCTION

POLICE ACADEMY

CHARACTERS AND VEHICLES

WALKTHROUGH

LEGO CITY TOUR

CHECKLISTS

⭐ 🌼 FLOWERS WATERED

Reward: Gold brick

The flower bed is on the prison's south side, against the upper west wall near some dancing inmates.

Use your chicken to reach the top of the water tower, where you can spy on some thugs. Five gang members appear in the prison yard below you. Use your fists to bring them down.

⭐ 🔺 FREE RUN

Reward: Gold brick, "Warden Stonewall" character token

The free run token is right next to the fence used to get into the upper prison yard.

⭐ 🐷 PIG RETURNED

Reward: Gold brick

To nab this piggie, you'll need the fireman. Break open the boarded door and climb the ladder.

The free run course starts at the bottom of the prison tower. See the "Points of Interest" section to learn how to reach these two places.

Grab the handhold so you can get on the roof. Drop down on the other side to find the pig.

⭐ 🎯 GANG ARRESTED

Reward: Gold brick

At the top of the tower, head around the walkway to find a spot to chicken-glide.

Ride the pig up the nearby hill and get him to the cannon.

INTRODUCTION

POLICE ACADEMY

CHARACTERS AND VEHICLES

WALKTHROUGH

LEGO CITY TOUR

CHECKLISTS

⬡ RED BRICK

Reward: Police Siren Hat

From the prison's south side, go through the open gate at the back and to the bottom of the tower. Use the robber's crowbar to break into the bottom of the tower and claim your prize.

🗿 SILVER STATUE DESTROYED

Reward: Gold brick

The dynamite dispenser is in the prison offices, which you pass through on your way to the upper prison yard. Fortunately, you'll pass this on your way to the Rex statue. Use the "Points of Interest" section for help getting there.

In the center of the upper prison yard is a transporter pad. Use it to teleport up to the Rex statue. Time for a glorious explosion!

🏛 SUPERBUILD: HELIPAD

Reward: Gold brick, "Chopper" vehicle token

Drill the shaky ground on the west side of the prison yard to uncover the drill spot.

Ride the water spout up and run along the walkway.

Follow the stairs to the helipad superbuild. Now you can "get to the choppah" whenever you want!

APOLLO ISLAND

POINTS OF INTEREST

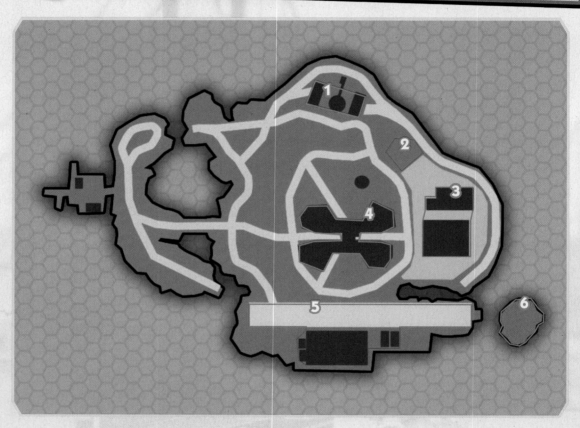

⭐ 1 RESEARCH BUNKER

This small bunker is closed off to the public, but that isn't going to stop an intrepid detective like Chase McCain.

You need to construct the super satellite superbuild before you can access the research bunker. Once that's built, walk up the stairs and pull the switch.

This activates the satellite, which creates a transporter pad nearby. Use the pad to zap yourself into the research bunker.

Inside the bunker, you want to open the blast door. See those red buttons on the floor? They open the door, but they require power. Find the crate near the door and smash it; then use the pieces inside to build a transporter pad.

Teleport into the locked room and snag some dynamite. With dynamite in hand, hop back onto the transporter pad and return to the main bunker.

Next to the red buttons on the floor is a silver door just waiting to be blown to smithereens. Place your dynamite and back away.

Inside the newly opened room is an fuse box. Give it a few taps with the construction worker's hammer to activate the buttons on the bunker floor.

Back in the bunker, one of the floor buttons has turned yellow. Step on it and another button turns yellow. Go from one yellow button to the next until all are activated.

And watch as the doors finally open! This activates Time Trial 2.

⭐ ② ASTRONAUT CARNIVAL

In the grassy area to the right of the space center is a playground where astronauts train in how to have fun. These games are a quick way to earn some studs.

⭐ ③ SPACE CENTER ROOFTOPS

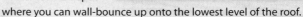

The main attraction of Apollo Island is the Space Center, where astronauts do lots of astronaut things. On the roof of the Space Center, you'll do all sorts of Chase McCain things.

There are a few things you can do on the Space Center's rooftops. To get up there, walk along the left side of the Space Center to find a spot where you can wall-bounce up onto the lowest level of the roof.

To get higher, swing along the flagpoles. Eventually you'll reach a rooftop with a flower pot. Water it to grow a plant, enabling you to climb higher.

On the other end of the roof is a tightrope you can slide down.

INTRODUCTION

POLICE ACADEMY

CHARACTERS AND VEHICLES

WALKTHROUGH

LEGO CITY TOUR

CHECKLISTS

From here you need to move along a series of wall runways. Keep at it until you find yourself on a new rooftop.

There are handholds on the nearby wall. Climb them and follow another wall runway to yet more handholds leading you up.

Run up the slope and hop onto the trampoline at the top.

After you climb one more wall, you'll be at the top of the Space Center. Enjoy the view!

⭐ 4 LAUNCH PAD

This is where LEGO men and women prove they have the right stuff. If you've completed Story mode, then a space shuttle sits on the launch pad.

⭐ 5 RUNWAY

Space shuttles may lift off at the launch pad, but they land on the runway. You can find the large runway and its garages on the island's east side.

To get on top of the garage, find this spot of shaky ground. Drill it and ride the water spout up.

From there, it's just a simple climb to the top.

⭐ 6 THE LIL' ISLAND

Easily missed, this tiny spot of land is north of the runway.

FEATS AND COLLECTIBLES

INTRODUCTION

POLICE ACADEMY

CHARACTERS AND VEHICLES

WALKTHROUGH

LEGO CITY TOUR

CHECKLISTS

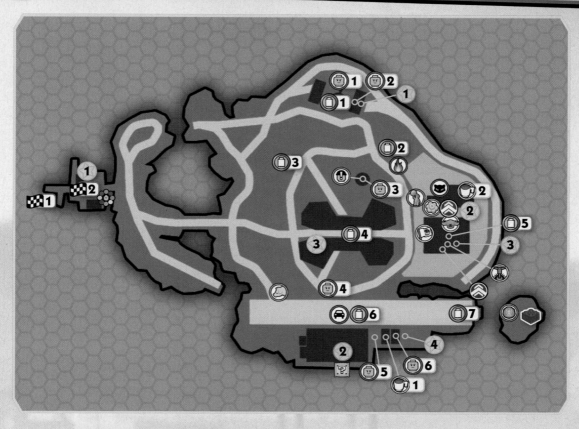

MAP LEGEND

MAP ICON(S)	FEAT/COLLECTIBLE	REWARD(S)	LOCATION/HOW TO REACH	GOT IT?
? Block	? Block	"Super Wrestler" character token (after all ? Blocks in the city have been found)	Behind the garages that are along the runway.	1
	Alien Caught	Gold Brick	On the Space Center roof.	2
	BBQ Fire Extinguished	Gold Brick	Near the picnic tables at the astronaut carnival.	3
	Boulder Destroyed	Gold Brick	On the lil' island.	4
	Cat Rescued	Gold Brick	Near the start of the free run course.	5
1 to 3 / 1	Character Token 1	Radio DJ	Build the three mini-satellites spread around the island.	6
2	Character Token 2	Classic Alien	Directly above the transporter pad when you teleport into the research bunker.	7
3	Character Token 3	Forrest Blackwell	Use Rex Fury to rip open the barrier and get underneath the water tower.	8
4	Character Token 4	Jonlan Regnix	Super jetpack hover from the roof of the garage to the tightrope above the rusty pipes. Slide down the tightrope.	9
1 to 4 / 5	Character Token 5	Garbage Man	Paint the four silver troughs yellow.	10
6	Character Token 6	Jenny Rathbone	On the roof of the runway garage.	11

MAP LEGEND CONTINUED

MAP ICON(S)	FEAT/COLLECTIBLE	REWARD(S)	LOCATION/HOW TO REACH	GOT IT?
1	Coffee Break Completed 1	Gold Brick	Inside the garage. Fix the fuse box to open the door.	12
2	Coffee Break Completed 2	Gold Brick	Under an overhang toward the back of the Space Center.	13
	Disguise Booth	Gold Brick, "Brantford Cubbery" character token	By the island's front gate.	14
	District Conquered	Gold Brick	On the roof of the Space Center.	15
	Drill Thrill Completed	Gold Brick	On the Space Center roof.	16
	Flowers Watered	Gold Brick	Inside the ground floor office of the Space Center.	17
	Free Run	Gold Brick, "Bud Hawkins" character token	At the top of the Space Center.	18
	Gang Arrested	Gold Brick	Use the catapult pad on the roof of the Space Center to get on top of the water tower.	19
	Pig Returned	Gold Brick	Atop the rusty pipes near the runway.	20
	Red Brick	Super Ray Gun	Activate the four switches around the lil' island bunker.	21
	Silver Statue Destroyed	Gold Brick	At the front of the Space Center roof.	22
1	Superbuild 1: Super Satellite	Gold Brick	Near the research bunker.	23
2	Superbuild 2: The Spinning Shuttle Programme	Gold Brick, "Dutch Danish" character token	In the center of the astronaut carnival.	24
3	Superbuild 3: Vehicle Call-in	Gold Brick, "Wanderer" vehicle token	Along the dirt road in front of the launch pad.	25
4	Super Build 4: Space Shuttle	Gold Brick, "Spaceman" character token	At the base of the launch pad.	26
5	Super Build 5: Helipad	Gold Brick, "UFO" vehicle token	At the top of the Space Center roof, walk up the last set of stairs.	27
6	Super Build 6: Loop de Loop	Gold Brick	Smack dab in the center of the runway.	28
7	Super Build 7: Stunt Ramp	Gold Brick, "Chat Show Host" character token	At the end of the runway.	29
1	Time Trial 1	Gold Brick, "Atlas" vehicle token	Look for the boat at the docks.	30
2	Time Trial 2	Gold Brick, "Cocoon" vehicle token	Open the research bunker doors first, then go back to the front gate.	31
	Vehicle Token	Wash Wagon	Build the Loop de Loop on the runway, then drive up it.	32

⭐ ? BLOCK

Reward: "Super Wrestler" character token (after all ? Blocks in the city have been found)

One of LEGO City's five ? Blocks is hidden behind the garages. Head back here from the runway and smash open the big ? Block.

⭐ ALIEN CAUGHT

Reward: Gold brick

The space crate used to reveal this alien menace is found on the Space Center rooftops.

The alien appears far below you. Don't be afraid—Chase won't take damage from the fall! Jump down there and get after that rascally alien.

⊛ BBQ FIRE EXTINGUISHED

Reward: Gold brick

There's a little picnic area at the astronaut carnival. It's along the dirt road. The BBQ rages next to some picnic tables.

⊛ BOULDER DESTROYED

Reward: Gold brick

Get to the lil' island to find Apollo Island's special boulder hiding among a pile of regular boulders.

🐱 CAT RESCUED

Reward: Gold brick

Make your way up to the Space Center rooftops. After climbing the plant, you'll be right in front of a spot to rescue a cat. Use the "Points of Interest" section for a step-by-step guide on getting to the Space Center roof.

⊡1 CHARACTER TOKEN 1

Reward: Radio DJ

Build the three satellites spread around the island by smashing brown crates and assembling the pieces inside.

Once complete, the character token appears here.

⊡2 CHARACTER TOKEN 2

Reward: Classic Alien

This token is directly above the transporter pad when you teleport into the research bunker. To learn how to get inside, see the "Points of Interest" section.

⊡3 CHARACTER TOKEN 3

Reward: Forrest Blackwell

As Rex Fury, head to the water tower and grab the orange handle on this crate.

Slide under the beam to grab the token.

INTRODUCTION

POLICE ACADEMY

CHARACTERS AND VEHICLES

WALKTHROUGH

LEGO CITY TOUR

CHECKLISTS

 ④ **CHARACTER TOKEN 4**

Reward: Jonlan Regnix

Use the "Points of Interest" section to get onto the garage rooftop. There, you'll find this jetpack symbol.

Use the super jetpack rings to boost onto the large, rusty pipes on the runway's other side.

Drop onto the tightrope, and as you slide down, you'll snatch this token.

The character token appears next to the garages by the runway once you're finished.

 ⑥ **CHARACTER TOKEN 6**

Reward: Jenny Rathbone

Go to the runway, and use the "Points of Interest" section to help you reach

the roof of the building next to the garages. You'll find a chicken symbol here.

Chicken-glide to the roof of the garage.

Walk across the beam to reach the character token.

 ⑤ **CHARACTER TOKEN 5**

Reward: Garbage Man

To earn this upstanding sanitation worker, you'll need to do some painting. You can find the yellow color swapper in this garage.

Paint the four silver troughs on the island to unlock this token.

 ① **COFFEE BREAK 1 COMPLETED**

Reward: Gold brick

Find the broken fuse box in front of this garage. Fix it and the garage door opens.

This provides you a chance to step inside and take a coffee break while no one's looking.

☆ 🫖2 COFFEE BREAK 2 COMPLETED

Reward: Gold brick

This one can be tricky to spot. It's located toward the back of the Space Center, on the left side, under an overhang. Look for the orange traffic cone.

☆ 🌸 DISGUISE BOOTH

Reward: Gold brick, "Brantford Cubbery" character token

The disguise booth is next to the front gate of the island.

☆ DISTRICT CONQUERED

Reward: Gold brick

You'll find this toward the front of the Space Center roof. See the "Points of Interest" section to find out how to reach the top of the Space Center.

☆ 🔧 DRILL THRILL COMPLETED

Reward: Gold brick

This is easy to find once you reach the top of the Space Center rooftops. See the "Points of Interest" section if you need help reaching the top.

☆ 🌼 FLOWERS WATERED

Reward: Gold brick

If you've finished Story mode, then this door is already open. If not, use the robber to open the door and get inside the building.

The flower bed is at the end of the room.

☆ FREE RUN

Rewards: Gold brick, "Bud Hawkins" character token

You'll find the free run token at the top of the Space Center. Check out the "Points of Interest" section to learn how to get up there.

The free run challenge starts lower on the Space Center rooftops, at the top of the tightrope.

The free run ends when you step on a catapult pad and launch to the top of a water tower.

GANG ARRESTED

Reward: Gold brick

From the Space Center rooftops, run onto this catapult pad. It will launch you onto the water tower.

Here you can listen in on criminal activity. The bad guys appear behind the Space Center.

PIG RETURNED

Reward: Gold brick

Follow the directions to claim the "Jonlan Regnix" character token. After sliding down the tightrope, walk along this plank to the end of the pipes.

The pig is sitting here, eager to be taken to a cannon.

The cannon is nearby, on the lawn overlooking the lagoon.

RED BRICK

Reward: Super Ray Gun

Go to the lil' island. Most of the island is just a big blast door. There are four switches surrounding the door. Step on each to open the door.

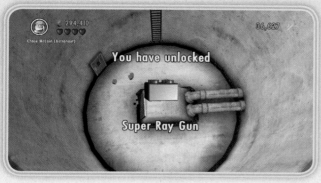

Drop down and grab the red brick below.

SILVER STATUE DESTROYED

Reward: Gold brick

After getting up onto the Space Center rooftops, head to the front of the building to find the Rex statue.

SUPERBUILD 1: SUPER SATELLITE

Reward: Gold brick

This massive platform is tough to miss. Build a super satellite here so mankind can search for signs of alien life.

SUPERBUILD 2: THE SPINNING SHUTTLE PROGRAMME

Reward: Gold brick, "Dutch Danish" character token

The superbuild is right in the center of the games at the astronaut carnival.

SUPERBUILD 3: CALL-IN POINT

Reward: Gold brick, "Wanderer" vehicle token

This superbuild is along the dirt road in front of the launch pad area.

SUPERBUILD 4: SPACE SHUTTLE

Reward: Gold brick, "Spaceman" character token

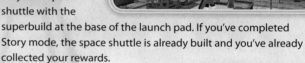

You can build your very own space shuttle with the superbuild at the base of the launch pad. If you've completed Story mode, the space shuttle is already built and you've already collected your rewards.

SUPERBUILD 5: HELIPAD

Reward: Gold brick, "UFO" vehicle token

At the top of the Space Center rooftops, walk up the final steps to find this superbuild.

SUPERBUILD 6: LOOP DE LOOP

Reward: Gold brick

Found in the center of the runway on the south side of Apollo Island. Once you build it, a vehicle token appears at the top of the loop de loop.

INTRODUCTION

POLICE ACADEMY

CHARACTERS AND VEHICLES

WALKTHROUGH

LEGO CITY TOUR

CHECKLISTS

⬡⑦ SUPERBUILD 7: STUNT RAMP

Reward: Gold brick, "Chat Show Host" character token

You'll find this superbuild at the end of the runway on the island's south side.

🏁② TIME TRIAL 2

Reward: Gold brick, "Cocoon" vehicle token

You'll need to open the research bunker doors to unlock this time trial. See the "Points of Interest" section to see how to open the doors. It starts at the front gate and takes you across the bumpy roads around Apollo Island.

🏁① TIME TRIAL 1

Reward: Gold brick, "Atlas" vehicle token

This challenge is at the docks where you first arrive at Apollo Island. The water race takes you along the outer edge of the island and through its lagoon.

🚗 VEHICLE TOKEN

Reward: "Wash Wagon" vehicle token

Build the loop de loop to get this token to appear. Now, grab a vehicle and head toward this beautiful construct.

Drive through the loop de loop to snag the token.

AUBURN

POINTS OF INTEREST

INTRODUCTION

POLICE ACADEMY

CHARACTERS AND VEHICLES

WALKTHROUGH

LEGO CITY TOUR

CHECKLISTS

⭐ 1 NORTH DOCKS

The docks feature a number of goodies for Chase to track down, and most are located around its northern area.

You can climb one of the docks' eastern cranes by leaping up several handholds, starting from the base. Use the grapple gun to swing across a gap at one point, then scamper up a steep slope to reach a character token atop the crane's arm.

With a little effort, it's also possible to reach the top of the docks' northern cranes. Begin by driving toward the Auburn Bay Bridge and looking for a stone column that has some blue and white LEGOs on one side. Jetpack-jump up to the LEGO patch, landing on the bridge's orange support to reach it.

Activate the chicken symbol atop the column, then glide through the stud rings to reach the top of the first northern crane.

Run to the end of the first crane to discover a jetpack symbol. Activate this as well, then boost through more stud rings to reach the other northern crane, where you can raise Auburn's flag.

⭐ 2 NORTH-CENTRAL BUILDINGS

Many items of interest are found around the north-central buildings. This is where Auburn's free run event plays out, so it's important to know how to navigate the buildings.

Before you can fully explore the north-central buildings, you must blast the northeast fence's silver gate. Search the large crates near the loading docks to discover a dynamite dispenser in the one near the banana pallets.

Bring the dynamite to the silver gate, then blast it to bits. Now you can begin exploring the north-central buildings.

Fix the fuse box on the garage to open it and score a superbrick if you like, then circle around the nearby Octan drum to spy a low handhold. Grab the handhold to begin your ascent up the north-central buildings' rooftops.

Vault a pair of vents to reach a blue balance beam that leads to the next building.

Chop through a boarded door to enter a small room with a lever. Pull the lever to open the nearby garage door.

Enter the garage and douse the flames at the base of the wall-jump pads. Leap between the pads to reach the roof above.

Next, use a wall runway to zip around the building's corner. Climb a LEGO wall afterward, then use another wall runway to round another corner.

Climb a ladder to reach a small superbuild pad and a planter. Water the planter to grow a sunflower that stretches up to the higher roof above.

Climb the sunflower to reach a chicken symbol. Activate the symbol and then glide across to the far building.

Vault several rooftop supports to reach a tightrope that leads to the final building. Slide down to reach the end of the run. Whew!

⭐ ③ METRO STATION

Auburn's train station is located in a tunnel underneath a bridge, making it tricky to locate. Drive up to the north side of town and look for a red metro station with a small parking lot out front. The metro station is right near the bridge—head inside to visit Auburn's underground train station!

⭐ ④ SOUTH-CENTRAL BUILDINGS

Traverse this block of buildings to reach a number of goodies.

North Access Point

Drill the shaky pavement on the sidewalk along the street that runs north of the buildings. Drilling the pavement here uncorks a geyser that boosts you over the tall fence.

Climb a ladder, then run to the right and vault another tall fence. Head through the next fence's open door and then shimmy along a blue drainpipe, heading up to a fenced-off roof.

Vault the roof's fence, then use a wall runway to sprint over to the neighboring roof. Run left and slide under the next fence you encounter.

Water a planter to grow some vines, then climb the vines to reach a higher roof. From here, you can either use a transporter pad to reach a distant roof or perform a jetpack jump to reach the blue and white LEGO patch that runs up the nearby building on the right.

The transporter pad leads to a "dead-end" roof with an audio scan symbol. The LEGO patch leads up to a smaller roof, from which you can jump and scale a series of handholds that run up a thick chimney.

If you climb the chimney, the smoke stack will boost you skyward. You can drift over to the neighboring chimney if you like, above which floats a character token.

INTRODUCTION

POLICE ACADEMY

CHARACTERS AND VEHICLES

WALKTHROUGH

LEGO CITY TOUR

CHECKLISTS

South Access Point

Drive around the southeast corner of the south-central buildings, looking for a blue and white LEGO patch that you can climb to reach a half-filled pool.

Use the fireman disguise's extinguisher to fill the pool the rest of the way. Swim across and leap up to a thin ledge. Jump from the ledge to reach a handhold, then scamper up the steep roof above.

Slide down the roof and vault a tall fence. Slide under a vent and then look left to spy an opening in the railing. Leap to the left and land on a large water tank.

Activate a jetpack symbol on the rim of the tank, then boost over to the taller tank ahead. You can reach a hovering character token up here, where this rooftop run ends.

⭐ 5 HANK'S GARAGE AND GAS STATION

This section of Auburn sports a gas station and a storage garage. A wooden ramp leads up to the freeway, which in turn leads north toward the Auburn Bay Bridge.

⭐ 6 SOUTH BUILDINGS

You can climb the southern collection of crates and buildings to reach a few goodies across the street.

Use the grapple gun to pull down a ladder along the south side of the south buildings, then climb up.

Run left after climbing up the ladder to locate a skylight. Pry this open and drop through to land in a small room with a safe that contains a character token.

Or run right and climb a few more ladders to reach the building's roof. Use a scan spot up here and trace some footsteps to a shed with a box of bricks.

Set down the box and build the bricks into an RC car. Race the car through the electrified cage, scaling two ramps to reach two buttons and shut off the electricity.

After shutting off the electricity, it's safe to jump onto the cage and boost onto the nearby roof. From there, you can boost over to a character token or drop and explore the lower ground.

INTRODUCTION

POLICE ACADEMY

CHARACTERS AND VEHICLES

WALKTHROUGH

LEGO CITY TOUR

CHECKLISTS

TIP

Collect a token with the RC car to make a trail of studs appear. Reach the end of the line to make a large superbrick appear atop the cage!

Water the planter near the large water tank to grow a sunflower. Climb to the top of the nearby crate.

Leap to the left crate and smash a blue and white barrel to find some bricks. Build these into a trampoline, then bounce up to the tin roof above.

Run northwest along the tin roof to reach a long pipe that stretches across the street. The pipe is on fire—douse the flames and then run across to reach the roofs to the northwest.

Use a transporter to beam up to a higher roof, then slide down a tightrope to reach another building. Fix a fuse box up here to activate a fan, then use the updraft to reach a higher roof.

Scamper up a steep slope to reach a catapult pad that sends you soaring over to a large water tank near Hank's Garage.

Use the transporter pad atop the water tank to beam over to another tin roof. You've come full circle; you're now back near the roof with the electrified cage and RC car.

⭐ 7 EAST BUILDINGS

This group of buildings to the southeast features several goodies. The image of Natalia's father, Professor Henrik Kowalski, dominates one of the buildings here—his private lab!

North Access Point

Run around the north end of the east buildings, looking for a boarded door you can chop open. Head up the interior stairs to reach the building's roof.

The roof sports a superbuild pad and a space crate. Activate the crate to beam in some bricks that form a catapult pad.

Use the catapult pad to launch over to a water tower, where a scan spot that triggers a vehicle robber event is located.

Central Access Point

Climb the building next to Professor Kowalski's lab by scaling the blue and white LEGO patch on one corner of the building.

Chop open the boarded door above the blue and white LEGO patch to discover some bricks. Build these into a wall runway, then zip over to a flagpole and flip onto an eve.

Run around the building and climb a blue and white LEGO wall. Dash across a wall runway to reach a roof.

Sprint up some stairs and use a scan spot to track down a valve wheel. Use the wheel to extend a nearby platform.

> **TIP**
>
> You can also use a jetpack symbol to reach a higher roof, where you can pull a lever to reveal several valuable studs.

Cross the blue balance beams and platforms to reach another building. You can leap up the chimneys here to reach a character token before sliding down a tightrope to reach the final building.

The final building features a skylight. Pry it open and drop through to land inside a garage. Crack a safe here to find a superbrick.

⭐ 8 BEACH

Auburn's scenic beach is a happening spot. Stroll through the sizzling sands and hop along the thin poles that stretch out to the water to reach some valuable superbricks.

FEATS AND COLLECTIBLES

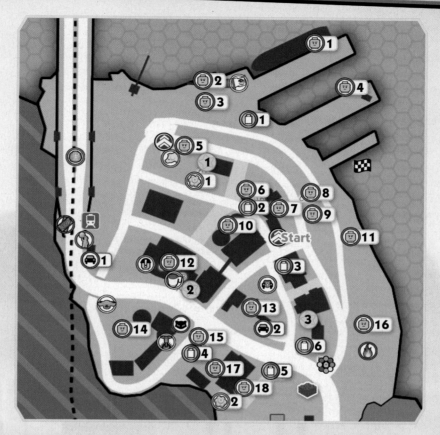

MAP LEGEND

MAP ICON(S)	FEAT/COLLECTIBLE	REWARD(S)	LOCATION/HOW TO REACH	GOT IT?
Alien Caught	Alien Caught	Gold brick	Underneath a wooden ramp near the gas station.	1
ATM Smashed	ATM Smashed	Gold brick	In the train tunnel, at the train station platform.	2
BBQ Fire Extinguished	BBQ Fire Extinguished	Gold brick	On the beach.	3
Boulder Destroyed	Boulder Destroyed	Gold brick	Underneath the Auburn Bay Bridge (smash piles of boulders to discover).	4
Cat Rescued	Cat Rescued	Gold brick	Climb the south buildings, then cross the flaming pipe to reach a rooftop billboard.	5
Character Token 1	Character Token 1	Sarah Horner	Atop the large cargo ship at the docks.	6
Character Token 2	Character Token 2	Clown Robber Max	Pry open the metal door at the base of one of the docks' north crane.	7
Character Token 3	Character Token 3	Tow Truck Driver	Complete the timed stud run around the crates at the north docks.	8
Character Token 4	Character Token 4	Docks Crane Driver	Climb the docks' eastern crane; the token is at the top.	9
Character Token 5	Character Token 5	Louie Mitchell	Hidden in a nook beneath the final leg of the free run course. Smash a blue barrel, build a trampoline, then bounce up and shimmy along the overhead LEGO patch to reach.	10
Character Token 6	Character Token 6	Hazmat Guy	Build the Auburn Chimney atop the north-central buildings, then use the chimney's updraft to reach the hovering token.	11
Character Token 7	Character Token 7	Deborah Graham	Navigate the north-central buildings, cross the blue balance beam, circle around the right side of the building, and search behind the Octan gas tank.	12

MAP LEGEND CONTINUED

MAP ICON(S)	FEAT/COLLECTIBLE	REWARD(S)	LOCATION/HOW TO REACH	GOT IT?
1 to 3 / 8	Character Token 8	Violet de Burgh	Paint three crates of cherries red around Auburn.	13
9	Character Token 9	Samson Crow	Paint the bananas yellow on the pallets along the east road near the docks.	14
10	Character Token 10	Henrik Kowalski	Navigate the south-central buildings using the southeast access point; leap to the water towers and use a jetpack jump to reach the hovering token.	15
11	Character Token 11	Hot Tub McCreedy	Paint five buoys red in the water by the beach.	16
12	Character Token 12	Lance Linberger	Navigate the south-central buildings, using the chimney updrafts to reach the hovering token.	17
13	Character Token 13	Allie Jaekshe	At the east buildings, climb the building near Professor Kowalski's lab, then jump up the three chimneys to reach the hovering token.	18
14	Character Token 14	Stephen Rhodes	Inside the gas station near Hank's Garage.	19
15	Character Token 15	Mechanic	Build the Sky Glide superbuild atop the water tower near the south buildings, then use the updraft to reach the hovering token.	20
16	Character Token 16	Garage Worker	Smash four objects around the beach and build their bricks into palm trees and other objects.	21
17	Character Token 17	Bobby Hammer	Navigate the south buildings, starting from the flower pot; the token is on a high crate at the end of the run.	22
18	Character Token 18	Chris Parry	Pull down the ladder near the south buildings, pry open the skylight, drop inside, and open the safe.	23
	Coffee Break	Gold brick	Navigate the south-central buildings.	24
	Disguise Booth	Gold brick, "Harbour Worker" character token	Near Professor Kowalski's lab.	25
	District Conquered	Gold brick	Climb the Auburn Bay Bridge's southern supports, slide down its east support rail, climb up a stone column, glide over to Auburn's north docks' crane, jetpack jump over to the neighboring crane, and raise the flag there.	26
	Drill Thrill	Gold brick	Climb the south buildings, then cross the flaming pipe to reach a rooftop fuse box.	27
1	Flowers Watered 1	Gold brick	Among the north-central buildings.	28
2	Flowers Watered 2	Gold brick	Behind the south buildings.	29
	Free Run	Gold brick, "Docks Foreman" character token	Navigate the north-central buildings to reach the free run token, then return to the beacon and navigate the buildings again.	30
	Gang Arrested	Gold brick	Navigate the south-central buildings to reach a transport pad that leads to the roof with the audio scan point.	31
	Pig Returned	Gold brick	Navigate the north-central buildings to reach the pig at the end of the rooftop run.	32
	Red Brick	Data Scan Upgrade— Character Challenges	Smash a small green trash bin across the street from the disguise booth, then follow the footprints to the hidden red brick.	33
	Silver Statue	Gold brick	Atop a stone column near the Auburn Bay Bridge (smash boulders and build a trampoline to reach).	34
1	Superbuild 1: Call-in Point	Gold brick, "Dragger" vehicle token	At the north docks.	35
2	Superbuild 2: Auburn Chimney	Gold brick	Navigate the north-central buildings to find the small circular superbuild pad.	36
3	Superbuild 3: Helipad	Gold brick, "Hera" vehicle token	Atop a roof of the east buildings (chop through a boarded door and climb the interior stairs).	37
4	Superbuild 4: Sky Glide	Gold brick	In the large water tank near the south buildings (fix the fuse box to drain the water).	38
5	Superbuild 5: Call-in Point	Gold brick, "Trasher" vehicle token	Near the south buildings.	39
6	Superbuild 6: Stunt Ramp	Gold brick, "Race Car Driver" character token	Near Professor Kowalski's lab.	40

MAP LEGEND CONTINUED

MAP ICON(S)	FEAT/COLLECTIBLE	REWARD(S)	LOCATION/HOW TO REACH	GOT IT?
	Time Trial	Gold brick, "Brawn" vehicle token	Boat docked along the eastern docks.	41
	Train Station	Gold brick, fast travel	In the train tunnel beneath the Auburn Bay Bridge (smash the green cabinets on the station platform).	42
1	Vehicle Robbery Completed 1	Gold brick, "Rex's Riot" vehicle token	Use Rex Fury to rip apart the superstrength crate near the garage north of the gas station, then pry open the door.	43
2	Vehicle Robbery Completed 2	Gold brick, "Enberg" vehicle token	Among the east buildings (douse the fire in front of a door, then pry it open).	44
	Vehicle Robber Arrested	Gold brick, "Sphinx" vehicle token	Atop a water tower among the east buildings (chop through the boarded door, climb the interior stairs, activate a space crate, catapult-pad over to the water tower).	45

⊙ ALIEN CAUGHT

Reward: Gold brick

Slide underneath a wooden ramp near the gas station to discover a space crate that triggers this zone's alien pursuit.

⊙ ATM SMASHED

Reward: Gold brick

The ATM is found in the metro tunnel, near the train station platform. Simply use the metro station entrance (POI 3) to enter the tunnel, then smash up the ATM.

⊙ BBQ FIRE EXTINGUISHED

Reward: Gold brick

A BBQ fire has been left unattended on Auburn's east beach. Douse it to ensure the public's safety.

⊙ BOULDER DESTROYED

Reward: Gold brick

Smash a pile of boulders beneath the bridge to discover and destroy Auburn's special boulder.

⊙ CAT RESCUED

Reward: Gold brick

Climb the south buildings (POI 6) and cross the flaming pipe that stretches across the street. Run across the rooftop beyond to find a hapless cat trapped atop a large billboard.

⊙ 1 CHARACTER TOKEN 1

Reward: Sarah Horner

Climb to the top of the large cargo ship that's moored at the north docks—you'll find a character token way up on the crow's nest. Leap from the nearby crates to land on the ship's deck.

INTRODUCTION

POLICE ACADEMY

CHARACTERS AND VEHICLES

WALKTHROUGH

LEGO CITY TOUR

CHECKLISTS

② CHARACTER TOKEN 2

Reward: Clown Robber Max

Pry open the metal door at the base of one of the docks' northern cranes to get at this character token.

③ CHARACTER TOKEN 3

Reward: Tow Truck Driver

While exploring the north docks, notice a time token near a group of crates. Collect the token, then race through the crates and collect the studs that suddenly appear! Reach the end of the stud run before time runs out to make a character token appear nearby as well.

④ CHARACTER TOKEN 4

Reward: Docks Crane Driver

Climb the north docks' eastern crane to reach a character token way up at the top.

⑤ CHARACTER TOKEN 5

Reward: Louie Mitchell

This character token hovers beneath the small building that features the lost pig and free run token on its roof. Smash a barrel and build a trampoline out of its bricks, then bounce up and grab the overhead LEGO patch. Shimmy over to the token and collect your prize!

⑥ CHARACTER TOKEN 6

Reward: Hazmat Guy

Navigate the north-central buildings (POI 2) and build the Auburn Chimney superbuild atop one of the roofs. Climb up and use the chimney's updraft to reach a character token that hovers high above.

⑦ CHARACTER TOKEN 7

Reward: Deborah Graham

While navigating the north-central buildings (POI 2), after crossing the blue balance beam, circle around the right side of the building and search behind an Octan oil tank to discover a hidden character token that can't be seen until you collect it.

⑧ CHARACTER TOKEN 8

Reward: Violet de Burgh

Find and blast three small crates full of cherries around Auburn, coloring them all red. Check the map for the crates' locations. You can find a red color swapper in the east buildings (POI 7) by chopping through a boarded door on the side of the building near Professor Kowalski's lab.

After you color all three crates of cherries red, a character token appears near the banana pallets that line the east road near the docks. Go on and grab it!

9 CHARACTER TOKEN 9

Reward: Samson Crow

While driving up Auburn's east road, heading toward the docks, spy a group of pallets with piles of bananas stacked on them. Pry open a nearby crate to discover a yellow color swapper, then blast and paint the white bananas yellow. Paint them all yellow to make a character token appear nearby!

10 CHARACTER TOKEN 10

Reward: Henrik Kowalski

Drive around the southeast corner of the south-central buildings (POI 4), climbing a blue and white LEGO patch and filling a pool full of water. Keep following the rooftop run, leaping over to some nearby water tanks. A character token hovers above the taller tank—use a jetpack jump to reach it.

11 CHARACTER TOKEN 11

Reward: Hot Tub McCreedy

While visiting the beach, take aim and blast five distant floating buoys with the robber's color gun. Paint all five buoys red to make a character token wash up nearby! You can find a red color swapper in the nearby east buildings (POI 7), near Professor Kowalski's lab.

12 CHARACTER TOKEN 12

Reward: Lance Linberger

Make your way across the south-central buildings (POI 4), starting from the north drill geyser and eventually using a jetpack jump to reach a patch of blue and white LEGOs on the side of one of the buildings. Climb the handholds on the giant chimney that follows, then use the chimney's updraft to reach a high hovering character token.

13 CHARACTER TOKEN 13

Reward: Allie Jaekshe

While exploring the east buildings (POI 7), climb the building near Professor Kowalski's lab and cross the rooftops to reach a roof with three chimneys. Jump up the chimneys to reach a hovering character token.

14 CHARACTER TOKEN 14

Reward: Stephen Rhodes

Pry open the gas station's door near Hank's Garage, then enter the station and collect the character token within.

15 CHARACTER TOKEN 15

Reward: Mechanic

After constructing the Sky Glide superbuild atop the southern water tank, use the giant fan's updraft to reach a character token that hovers high above.

INTRODUCTION

POLICE ACADEMY

CHARACTERS AND VEHICLES

WALKTHROUGH

LEGO CITY TOUR

CHECKLISTS

16 CHARACTER TOKEN 16

Reward: Garage Worker

Smash four objects around the beach and build four different objects out of their bricks.

After you build all four objects, a character token appears here.

17 CHARACTER TOKEN 17

Reward: Bobby Hammer

Jetpack jump from the tin roof near the electrified cage atop the south buildings (POI 6) to reach this token, which hovers atop the stacked southern crates.

18 CHARACTER TOKEN 18

Reward: Chris Parry

While exploring the south buildings (POI 6), pull down the ladder and pry open the skylight. Drop through and crack the safe to score a character token.

COFFEE BREAK COMPLETED

Reward: Gold brick

Navigate the south-central buildings (POI 4), starting from the north drill geyser, to reach a coffee break station. Pour yourself a hot cup of joe before venturing onward.

DISGUISE BOOTH

Reward: Gold brick, "Harbour Worker" character token

Auburn's disguise booth is located down south, right near Professor Kowalski's lab. Smash the blue police crate and build the booth at your convenience.

DISTRICT CONQUERED

Reward: Gold brick

Raising Auburn's flag requires significant effort, as you must reach the top of the docks' north cranes. See the "North Docks" section under the Points of Interest for details.

DRILL THRILL COMPLETED

Reward: Gold brick

Climb the south buildings (POI 6) and cross the flaming pipe that stretches across the street. Fix the fuse box on the following rooftop to begin a drill thrill event. You'll need to use a ladder and transporter pad to reach all of the shaky patches of roofing during this frantic challenge!

⓵ FLOWERS WATERED 1

Reward: Gold brick

This first flower box is nestled amongst Auburn's north-central buildings (POI 2). Run along the central alley and hop the north wall to find it sitting near a garage.

⓶ FLOWERS WATERED 2

Reward: Gold brick

Circle around Auburn's south buildings (POI 6) to spy another flower box tucked away just a short distance from the vehicle call-in point.

FREE RUN

Rewards: Gold brick, "Docks Foreman" character token

Cross the rooftops of the north-central buildings (POI 2) to reach this zone's free run token. Collect the token to make a free run beacon appear back where you began your ascent of the north-central buildings.

Return to the free run beacon and begin the event. Rush back along the north-central buildings' rooftops, following the studs that appear. Keep going until you reach the finish!

GANG ARRESTED

Reward: Gold brick

Navigate the south-central buildings (POI 4), starting from the north drill geyser, to reach a rooftop with a transporter pad. Beam over to reach a distant roof with an audio scan spot that triggers this event. Eavesdrop on the nearby gang members, then hurry all the way over to the beach and bust up those punks!

PIG RETURNED

Reward: Gold brick

Auburn's lost pig is stuck on the final roof at the end of the north-central buildings (POI 2). Make your way to the end of the rooftop run to find the pig, then ride the little guy to the nearby cannon that's set up at the docks.

⬡ RED BRICK

Reward: Data Scan Upgrade—Character Challenges

Smash a small trash bin across the street from Professor Kowalski's lab to discover a blue scan spot. Trace the footprints over to a suspicious pile of leaves, where a bit of inspection exposes Auburn's red brick!

INTRODUCTION

POLICE ACADEMY

CHARACTERS AND VEHICLES

WALKTHROUGH

LEGO CITY TOUR

CHECKLISTS

⭐ 🌐 SILVER STATUE DESTROYED

Reward: Gold brick

Drive north up the freeway, heading for the Auburn Bay Bridge. As you go, spy a pile of boulders near a stone column on the right. Smash the boulders, then build a trampoline out of their bricks. Bounce up to the top of the stone column, where a silver statue awaits destruction.

TIP

Find some dynamite in the train tunnel beneath the freeway—stroll through the metro station entrance (POI 3) to get there.

⭐ 🎟① SUPERBUILD 1: CALL-IN POINT

Reward: Gold brick, "Dragger" vehicle token

For a mere 8,000 bricks, you can build a vehicle call-in point near the north docks.

⭐ 🎟② SUPERBUILD 2: AUBURN CHIMNEY

Reward: Gold brick

While navigating the rooftops of the north-central buildings (POI 2), keep an eye out for a small, circular superbuild pad. Here you can spend 12,000 bricks to build a tall chimney next to two others. This not only rewards you with a gold brick, but also causes a character token to appear above the chimney!

⭐ 🎟③ SUPERBUILD 3: HELIPAD

Reward: Gold brick, "Hera" vehicle token

Chop through the boarded door at the north end of the east buildings (POI 7) and head up the stairs to reach a roof where a helipad can be built for 20,000 bricks.

⭐ 🎟④ SUPERBUILD 4: SKY GLIDE

Reward: Gold brick

Climb the long ladder on the side of the large water tank near the south buildings (POI 6); then fix the fuse box atop the tank to drain the water and expose a superbuild. Construct a giant fan here for 12,000 bricks, and you'll be blown up to a high hovering character token!

⭐ 🎟⑤ SUPERBUILD 5: CALL-IN POINT

Reward: Gold brick, "Trasher" vehicle token

Another vehicle call-in point can be assembled here, at the south end of Auburn. Drop 8,000 bricks and build this valuable asset.

 ## SUPERBUILD 6: STUNT RAMP

Reward: Gold brick, "Race Car Driver" character token

Drop 10,000 studs to build a stunt ramp here, right next to Professor Kowalski's lab. This ramp comes into play while racing to complete the Time Trial that begins in Cherry Tree Hills.

TIME TRIAL

Reward: Gold brick, "Brawn" vehicle token

Hop into the boat docked along Auburn's east piers to begin an exciting nautical race. Carefully pass through the wooden posts near the beach as you move from checkpoint to checkpoint, speeding toward the finish.

 ## TRAIN STATION

Reward: Gold brick, fast travel

Use the metro station entrance (POI 3) to reach Auburn's underground train station, which runs north below the Auburn Bay Bridge. You'll eventually come to a platform with a dynamite dispenser, an ATM, and a couple of green cabinets. Bash the cabinets to discover some bricks, then build these into the train station's ticket dispenser, thus activating the station.

  ## VEHICLE ROBBERY COMPLETED 1

Reward: Gold brick, "Rex's Riot" vehicle token

Use Rex Fury to rip apart the superstrength crate near the garage that stands north of the gas station (POI 5). This exposes a door you can crowbar; pry it open to begin a vehicle robbery challenge!

VEHICLE ROBBERY COMPLETED 2

Reward: Gold brick, "Enberg" vehicle token

While exploring the east buildings (POI 7), look for a ground-level door that's blocked by fire. Douse the flames, then pry open the door to begin another fast-paced vehicle robbery event!

 ## VEHICLE ROBBER ARRESTED

Reward: Gold brick, "Sphinx" vehicle token

Scale the east buildings (POI 7) by chopping through the boarded door and going upstairs. Build the catapult pad and soar to the water tower, where the scan spot that triggers Auburn's vehicle robber event is located.

INTRODUCTION

POLICE ACADEMY

CHARACTERS AND VEHICLES

WALKTHROUGH

LEGO CITY TOUR

CHECKLISTS

AUBURN BAY BRIDGE

 ## POINTS OF INTEREST

⭐ 1 TOP OF THE BRIDGE

LEGO City's faithful re-creation of San Francisco's Golden Gate Bridge may only have few collectibles, but it offers one heck of a view. Getting to the top of the bridge is quite a challenge, but it should be no problem for a pro like you.

Start out on the right side of the south tower. Perform a jetpack jump up to the handholds and then climb up to the first platform.

From here, you can cross the tightrope for a red brick. If you want to get to the bridge's top, though, take the next set of handholds up.

You'll reach a long handhold. Shimmy along that until you see more handholds above. Leap up to grab the next handhold and keep ascending.

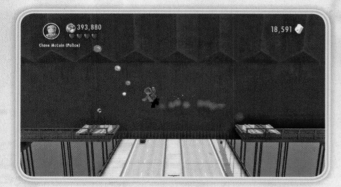

Now for the fun part. There's a wall runway up ahead. Take it to cross the gap and run to the catapult pad.

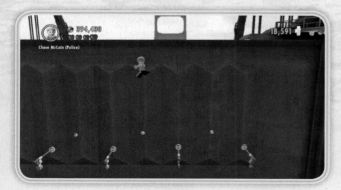

The pad launches you back to the other side of the bridge, up to a higher platform. Another catapult pad shoots you back the opposite way, again sending you even higher.

You're halfway there! See the wall that you can run up? Do so and then jump off the wall to reach a flagpole. Swing across the flagpoles that follow to reach the bridge's other side. Hop onto the tall ladder and climb up.

You soon come to some handholds. Grab these and make your way over to the gap by the next ladder. Navigate the series of handholds and ladders that follows.

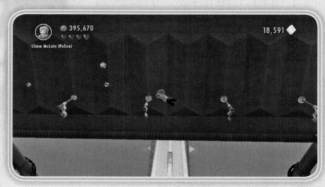

Eventually, you'll reach another set of catapult pads (wheeeee!) and another series of flagpoles. Tackle these just as you did before.

A drain pipe leads to the top of the bridge. Your long journey is over—take a moment to enjoy the view!

INTRODUCTION POLICE ACADEMY CHARACTERS AND VEHICLES WALKTHROUGH LEGO CITY TOUR CHECKLISTS

FEATS AND COLLECTIBLES

MAP LEGEND

MAP ICON(S)	FEAT/COLLECTIBLE	REWARD(S)	LOCATION/HOW TO REACH	GOT IT?
	? Block	Super Wrestler	On the support beams, under the bridge.	1
	Boulder Destroyed	Gold Brick	On the foundation, at the base of the bridge.	2
	Character Token 1	DaMumbo	Above the drainpipe at the top of the bridge.	3
	District Conquered	Gold Brick	Atop the bridge tower.	4
	Free Run	Gold Brick, "Fitness Instructor" character token	On a beam at the top of the bridge tower.	5
	Red Brick	Data Scan Upgrade: Red Bricks	Suspended over a tightrope along the bridge tower.	6
	Time Trial	Gold Brick, "Wrath" vehicle token	At the north end of the bridge.	7

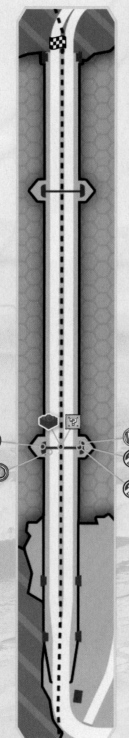

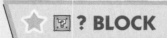

? BLOCK

Reward: Super Wrestler" character token (after all ? Blocks in the city have been found)

This one is a tough find, but it's easy to get to once you know how. Drop down to the base of the bridge's support leg.

Walk around the base until you see some handholds on the wall. Climb up and make your way across a narrow walkway to a sloped support beam.

Run up the slope, but be careful not to go over the crest and down the other side.

The ? Block is at the top of the slope, just waiting to be smashed.

BOULDER DESTROYED

Reward: Gold brick

This boulder is located at the bridge's base, along the water. To get here, go to the left side of the southern tower and drop over the edge.

CHARACTER TOKEN 1

Reward: DaMumbo

You'll find this token floating above the drainpipe that leads to the bridge's top. Use the astronaut's jetpack jump to snatch it. Check the "Points of Interest" section to learn how to climb up the bridge.

DISTRICT CONQUERED

Reward: Gold brick

You'll find this flag stand at the very top of the bridge. Check out the "Points of Interest" section if you need help getting up here.

FREE RUN

Rewards: Gold brick, "Fitness Instructor" character token

Climb to the top of the bridge to find the free run token sitting way up top. See the previous "Points of Interest" section to learn how to get up here.

The free run starts all the way back at the base of the bridge. The route is the same one you took to get to the free run token at the top—just keep an eye out for time tokens as you go!

RED BRICK

Reward: Data Scan Upgrade: Red Bricks

As you begin to climb the bridge, stop after you reach the first platform. Cross a tightrope to pick up a red brick.

TIME TRIAL

Reward: Gold brick, "Wrath" vehicle token

You'll find this time trial at the bridge's north end. The race takes you on a thrill ride back and forth along the Auburn Bay Bridge. Enjoy the trip!

INTRODUCTION

POLICE ACADEMY

CHARACTERS AND VEHICLES

WALKTHROUGH

LEGO CITY TOUR

CHECKLISTS

BLACKWELL BRIDGE

POINTS OF INTEREST

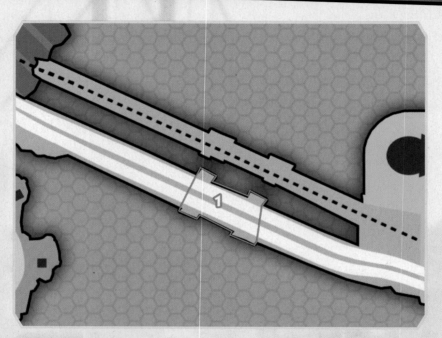

⭐ 1 UNDER THE BRIDGE

Most of the good stuff is hidden underneath Blackwell Bridge, so leap off any point on the bridge and get Chase a little wet. (Don't worry, he's an excellent swimmer!) Several of the bridge's support legs rise out of the water, and many of these legs feature something worthwhile.

FEATS AND COLLECTIBLES

INTRODUCTION

POLICE ACADEMY

CHARACTERS AND VEHICLES

WALKTHROUGH

LEGO CITY TOUR

CHECKLISTS

MAP LEGEND

MAP ICON(S)	FEAT/ COLLECTIBLE	REWARD(S)	LOCATION/HOW TO REACH	GOT IT?
	Boulder Destroyed	Gold Brick	Under the bridge, on a support leg.	1
	Character Token 1	Titus Winkleman	On a support leg under the bridge.	2
	District Conquered	Gold Brick	Atop the freeway sign.	3
	Red Brick	Nitrous for All	On one of the other support legs under the bridge.	4

⭐ BOULDER DESTROYED

Reward: Gold brick

Head under the bridge and find this support leg. Run up the slope and smash the boulders you discover.

⭐ DISTRICT CONQUERED

Reward: Gold brick

The green section of the bridge has a traffic sign with a climbable drainpipe. Make your way up the pipe, then walk along some beams to eventually reach a spot where you can raise a flag.

⭐ CHARACTER TOKEN 1

Reward: Titus Winkleman

Go under the bridge and find this support leg. Just run up the slope and this character token will be all yours.

⭐ RED BRICK

Reward: Nitrous for All

This is another goodie hidden on one of the support legs. Search under the bridge to find this prize.

BLUEBELL NATIONAL PARK

POINTS OF INTEREST

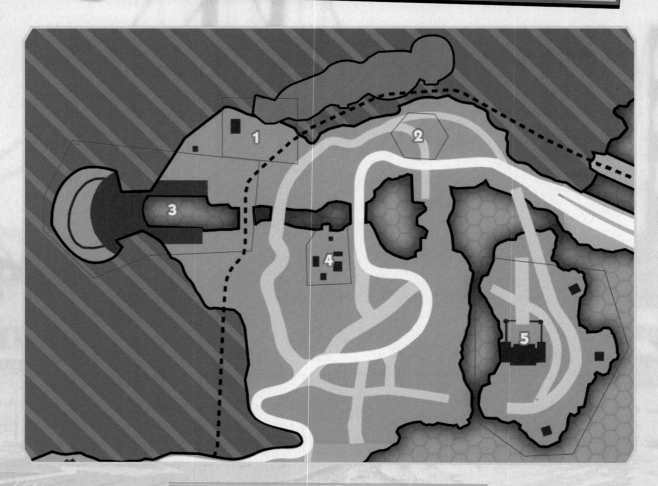

⭐ 1 BLUEBELL MINE

The Bluebell Mine is located on the park's north end. Chase visits this place during one of his Special Assignments. There are several interesting goodies to be found near the mine's entrance, but there's no reason to enter the mine during your romp through the park.

You can traverse the rocks near the mine—you just need some dynamite to blast the large pile of silver boulders that get in the way. Find some dynamite at the dispenser near the mine shack.

When it seems you can go no farther, use the grapple gun to pull down an overhead platform. The platform smashes into a pile of bricks—build these into a ladder that lets you climb to the top of the nearby train tunnel.

⭐ ② NORTHERN ROCK FORMATION

This rock formation holds several treats but seems impossible to scale. Not so! Simply smash the nearby rocks to discover some bricks, then build a large, rideable boulder out of them.

Hop onto the boulder and ride to the indicated spot near one end of the the boulder in place, you can leap up the rock formation and get at the goodies above!

⭐ ③ BLUEBELL DAM

The Bluebell Dam is a large structure located on the park's west side. It features a north walkway, a south walkway, and a watery reservoir that lies between them.

To explore the north walkway, grow vines from a planter near the dam's north wall. Climb the vines to reach a thin ledge, then drop from the ledge to land on the north walkway.

> **TIP**
>
> You can also jetpack jump over the north walkway's fence if you're in a rush.

The south walkway is a little easier to reach. Just swim through the reservoir and climb a ladder to reach it. Or use the north walkway's catapult pad to launch yourself straight over to the south walkway.

Navigate the south walkway's thin ledges and climbable walls to reach a rock atop the wall. Smash the rock to discover some bricks, then build a transporter pad that beams you way up to the dam's top.

> **CAUTION**
>
> Be careful not to move past the dam's transistors while they're glowing with energy. Wait for them to calm down, then hurry past!

⭐ ④ SHERIFF HUCKLEBERRY'S POLICE STATION

Several goodies are found around this humble police station, a few of which are located on (or accessed by exploring) the roof. Climb up to the roof by growing a tall sunflower from the planter around back. Pry open the skylight to enter the station.

The police station's guard tower takes a little more effort to enter. First, find a sleeping bear in a campsite to the north. The bear is dreaming of a fish dinner—discovering this triggers the appearance of a scan spot on the dock back near the guard tower!

INTRODUCTION

POLICE ACADEMY

CHARACTERS AND VEHICLES

WALKTHROUGH

LEGO CITY TOUR

CHECKLISTS

Return to the guard tower and use the scan spot to trace some footprints that lead to a hidden key. Use this key to open the guard tower's door.

⑤ BARRY SMITH'S KUNG-FU DOJO

This impressive temple dojo stands just east of the park, across a deep ravine. You must construct the Serenity Bridge superbuild in order to reach the dojo, and this is accomplished during Story mode. The dojo serves as the site of a Special Assignment, so there's no need to enter it while searching for city-based collectibles. However, a few items of interest are found around the dojo's tranquil grounds.

The road near the dojo is impressive. You can jump the gap at the south end when you're traveling in a vehicle. On foot, you can slip around behind the dojo by running around to the right of the entry steps and crossing a wall runway and a treacherously thin ledge.

⭐ FEATS AND COLLECTIBLES

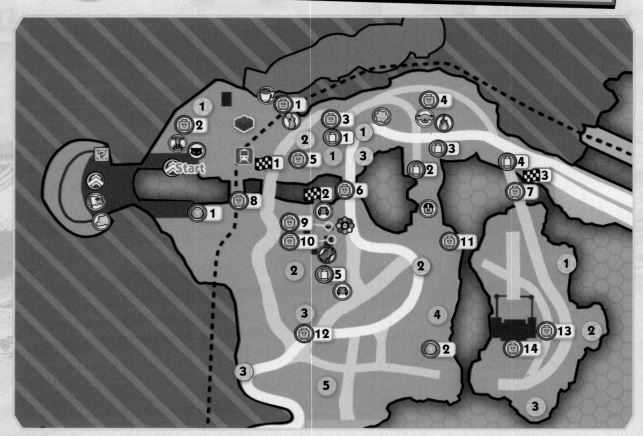

MAP LEGEND

MAP ICON(S)	FEAT/COLLECTIBLE	REWARD(S)	LOCATION/HOW TO REACH	GOT IT?
	? Block	"Super Wrestler" character token (after you find all ? Blocks in the city)	Beam up to the top of the dam, chop through the boarded door, and climb the ladder.	1
	Alien Caught	Gold brick	Build and use the rolling boulder to climb up the large rock formation.	2
	ATM Smashed	Gold brick	Near Sheriff Huckleberry's police station.	3
	BBQ Fire Extinguished	Gold brick	Out in the open, near a couple of tents.	4
1	Boulder Destroyed 1	Gold brick	Hidden under a pile of regular boulders near the dam.	5
2	Boulder Destroyed 2	Gold brick	Hidden under a pile of regular boulders to the west of Barry Smith's Kung-Fu Dojo.	6
	Cat Rescued	Gold brick	At the end of the dam's north walkway.	7
1	Character Token 1	Rex Fury Bare Chest	Use Rex Fury to rip open the superstrength handle crate near the north train tunnel.	8
2	Character Token 2	Bill Derby	Astronaut boost up onto the small shack west of the Bluebell Mine.	9
3	Character Token 3	Forestman	Construct the Bluebell Tree superbuild, then climb up to the tree house.	10
4	Character Token 4	Todd Graywacke	Astronaut boost near the alien space crate.	11
5	Character Token 5	Ben Moseley	Use a fish to lure the bear away from the large campsite, then color the two tents to match their blankets.	12
1 to 3, 6	Character Token 6	Snowboarder	Paint three road signs yellow around the main road that runs through the park.	13
7	Character Token 7	Karate Guy	Appears over the Serenity Bridge after you construct the superbuild.	14
8	Character Token 8	Sam Penn	Climb to the top of the metal bridge east of the dam.	15
9	Character Token 9	Ranger Lewis	Pry open the skylight atop Sheriff Huckleberry's police station, then drop inside.	16
10	Character Token 10	Karate Champ	Grapple and pull the two radar dishes atop Sheriff Huckleberry's police station.	17
1 to 3, 11	Character Token 11	Elf	Smash three LEGO trees around the park and build three birdhouses from their bricks.	18
1 to 5, 12	Character Token 12	Jessie Weingartner	Douse five small campfires around the park.	19
1 to 3, 13	Character Token 13	Samurai Warrior	Ring the three gongs along the trail east of Barry Smith's Kung-Fu Dojo.	20
14	Character Token 14	Trouserless Barry	Behind Barry Smith's Kung-Fu Dojo. Trick the Piranha Plant into burning away the spiderweb.	21
	Coffee Break	Gold brick	Climb the rocks to the east of the Bluebell Mine entrance.	22
	Disguise Booth	Gold brick, "Ranger Barber" character token	Near Sheriff Huckleberry's police station.	23
	District Conquered	Gold brick	Beam up to the top of the dam, drill the shaky ground, then climb up to the flag stand.	24
	Drill Thrill	Gold brick	The shack near the Bluebell Mine.	25
	Flowers Watered	Gold brick	The shack across the street from Barry's Kung-Fu Dojo.	26
	Free Run	Gold brick, "Brickett" character token	Find the token at the top of the dam, then free run around the dam.	27

INTRODUCTION

POLICE ACADEMY

CHARACTERS AND VEHICLES

WALKTHROUGH

LEGO CITY TOUR

CHECKLISTS

MAP LEGEND CONTINUED

MAP ICON(S)	FEAT/COLLECTIBLE	REWARD(S)	LOCATION/HOW TO REACH	GOT IT?
	Gang Arrested	Gold brick	Audio scan point atop a platform near the waterfall—gang appears near the Bluebell Mine.	28
	Pig Returned	Gold brick	Beam up to the top of the dam, drill the shaky ground, then climb up and chicken-glide over to the pig.	29
	Red Brick	Data Scan Upgrade: Clues	Use dynamite to destroy the silver crate near the Bluebell Mine.	30
	Silver Statue Destroyed	Gold brick	Scale the rocks to the east of the mine entrance.	31
1	Superbuild 1: Bluebell Tree	Gold brick	Scale the rocks east of the mine entrance, then chicken-glide over to the superbuild (30,000).	32
2	Superbuild 2: Stunt Ramp	Gold brick, "Duke Huckleberry" character token	Atop the roof of the restaurant near the waterfall (10,000).	33
3	Superbuild 3: Call-in Point	Gold brick, "Vigilant" vehicle token	Near the road near the bridge to Barry Smith's Kung-Fu Dojo.	34
4	Superbuild 4: Serenity Bridge	Gold brick	Near the road across the river from Barry Smith's Kung-Fu Dojo.	35
5	Superbuild 5: Helipad	Gold brick, "Skybringer" vehicle token	Chop through the door near Sheriff Huckleberry's police station, then go upstairs (20,000).	36
1	Time Trial 1	Gold brick, "Tracker" vehicle token	Near the entrance to the Bluebell Mine.	37
2	Time Trial 2	Gold brick, "Oldster" vehicle token	Near the docks near Sheriff Huckleberry's police station.	38
3	Time Trial 3	Gold brick, "Chan's Ironback" vehicle token	Near the road by the Serenity Bridge leading to Barry Smith's Kung-Fu Dojo.	39
	Train Station	Gold brick, fast travel	Near the entrance to the Bluebell Mine. Automatically built during Story mode.	40
	Vehicle Robber Arrested	Gold brick, "Hero" vehicle token	Criminal scan spot atop the guard tower near Sheriff Huckleberry's police station.	41

? BLOCK

Reward: "Super Wrestler" character token (after you find all ? Blocks in the city)

Teleport to the top of the dam, then chop through a boarded door to enter a small room with a ladder. Climb up to reach a ? Block.

ATM SMASHED

Reward: Gold brick

Search around Sheriff Huckleberry's police station to discover an ATM that's just begging to be smashed.

ALIEN CAUGHT

Reward: Gold brick

The space crate that summons this alien is located atop the northern rock formation (POI 2). See the previous "Points of Interest" section to learn how to scale the rock formation and reach the space crate.

BBQ FIRE EXTINGUISHED

Reward: Gold brick

This zone's BBQ fire sits out in the open in the center of a small campsite.

INTRODUCTION

POLICE ACADEMY

CHARACTERS AND VEHICLES

WALKTHROUGH

LEGO CITY TOUR

CHECKLISTS

1 BOULDER DESTROYED 1

Reward: Gold brick

Bluebell National Park features two special boulders. The first is hidden under a large pile of regular boulders near the dam's south end.

2 BOULDER DESTROYED 2

Reward: Gold brick

Bluebell National Park features two special boulders. The first is hidden under a large pile of regular boulders near the dam's south end.

The other special boulder is hidden under another large pile of regular boulders across the ravine from Barry Smith's Kung-Fu Dojo.

CAT RESCUED

Reward: Gold brick

This poor kitty is stuck on a tall pillar on the dam's north walkway. To reach it, grow vines from the planter near the dam's north wall, then climb the vines and drop from the thin ledge.

1 CHARACTER TOKEN 1

Reward: Rex Fury Bare Chest

Explore near the north train tunnel and notice a crate with an orange handle. Use Rex Fury's great strength to rip open this crate and claim the character token within.

2 CHARACTER TOKEN 2

Reward: Bill Derby

Use the astronaut's jetpack jump to boost onto the roof of the tiny shack to the west of the Bluebell Mine, where this zone's drill thrill plays out. Boost up again and claim the character token that hovers above the shack.

3 CHARACTER TOKEN 3

Reward: Forestman

After constructing the Bluebell Tree superbuild, use the grapple gun to pull down a ladder, then climb up to the tree house. A character token is tucked within!

4 CHARACTER TOKEN 4

Reward: Todd Graywacke

Scale the northern rock formation (POI 2) and approach the space crate on top of it. This is the same space crate that summons this zone's alien. Look up, and spy a character token hovering above. Boost up and claim the token with the aid of the astronaut's jetpack.

⭐ 5 CHARACTER TOKEN 5

Reward: Ben Moseley

This character token takes a bit of effort to claim. Begin by exploring the large campsite across the river to the north of Sheriff Huckleberry's police station. There's a sleeping bear here that's dreaming of a fish dinner.

Build the bouncing bricks into a colorless tent. Peek inside the tent and notice the color of the blanket inside—it's orange. Blast the tent with the color gun to turn it orange. You can find an orange color swapper inside Sheriff Huckleberry's police station if need be (enter through the skylight).

Examining the sleeping bear causes a scan spot to appear near the dock across the river. Swim over to the scan spot and use it to track down a lost key.

There's one other colorless tent. This one has a purple blanket inside of it. Blast the tent with purple energy to color it as well. With both tents colored, a character token at last appears!

Use the key to open the nearby guard tower. Climb the ladder and collect the box of bricks on the lookout loft.

⭐ 6 CHARACTER TOKEN 6

Reward: Snowboarder

Fill your color gun with yellow energy using the swapper near the helipad, then begin driving along Bluebell Park's main road. Look for three colorless road signs as you go, and blast each one to paint it yellow.

Carry the bricks down and place them on the green LEGO pad on the dock. Build the bricks into a fishing pole, then take a moment to catch a fish.

Swim back over to the campsite and give the fish you've caught to the bear. The big beast races off to enjoy its meal, leaving a pile of bouncing bricks behind!

After you paint all three signs yellow, a character token appears here.

7 CHARACTER TOKEN 7

Reward: Karate Guy

This character token appears after you construct the Serenity Bridge superbuild. There's a good chance you collected it on your way to Barry Smith's Kung-Fu Dojo during Story mode.

8 CHARACTER TOKEN 8

Reward: Sam Penn

Scale the handholds on the side of the metal bridge that lies just east of the Bluebell Dam. Tiptoe across the top of the bridge to reach several superbricks—along with a character token!

9 CHARACTER TOKEN 9

Reward: Ranger Lewis

Break into the skylight atop Sheriff Huckleberry's police station, then drop down to reach a small room with a character token.

 10 CHARACTER TOKEN 10

Reward: Karate Champ

Use the grapple gun to pull the two radar dishes on the roof of Sheriff Huckleberry's police station so that both are made to stand upright. A character token appears right nearby.

11 CHARACTER TOKEN 11

Reward: Elf

Find and smash three special LEGO trees around the park to discover bricks, then build the bricks into three birdhouses. Check the map to learn the birdhouses' locations.

After you build the third birdhouse, a character token appears here.

12 CHARACTER TOKEN 12

Reward: Jesse Weingartner

Douse five small campfires around the park with the fireman's extinguisher. Review the map to see where these campfires are found.

INTRODUCTION

POLICE ACADEMY

CHARACTERS AND VEHICLES

WALKTHROUGH

LEGO CITY TOUR

CHECKLISTS

After the fifth campfire has been extinguished, a character token appears here.

13 CHARACTER TOKEN 13

Reward: Samurai Warrior

Ring the three gongs around the east path of Barry Smith's Kung-Fu Dojo. Each gong is located inside a small tower, and there's a mallet lying near each gong.

A character token appears atop another small tower after you've rung all three gongs. Climb up and claim your reward!

14 CHARACTER TOKEN 14

Reward: Trouserless Barry

Make your way to the back of Barry Smith's Kung-Fu Dojo using the wall runway to the right of the dojo's entry stairs. You'll find a character token stashed inside of a small, web-covered rock formation back here, along with a large pipe that you can water.

Water the pipe to grow a monstrous Piranha Plant. Yikes! The Piranha Plant spits fireballs, so find some cover. To collect the character token, you must trick the Piranha Plant into burning away the web with a fireball. Stand in front of the web, then dodge just before the fireball strikes!

COFFEE BREAK COMPLETED

Reward: Gold brick

Climb the rocks to the east of the Bluebell Mine entrance to reach this coffee break station. See the "Bluebell Mine" section near the start of this zone chapter for details on how to climb the rocks.

DISGUISE BOOTH

Reward: Gold brick, "Ranger Barber" character token

This disguise booth sits right near Sheriff Huckleberry's police station. You can't miss it!

 DISTRICT CONQUERED

Reward: Gold brick

Use the transporter pad atop the dam's south walkway to beam up to the dam's top. Drill the shaky ground you discover up here to uncork a geyser that hoists you up to a few handholds. Climb up to reach a lofty platform where you can raise a flag.

DRILL THRILL COMPLETED

Reward: Gold brick

Fix the fuse box on the outside wall of the tiny shack west of the Bluebell Mine, then step on the nearby button to begin a drill thrill event. Drill all of those shaky tiles before time expires to win a gold brick!

FLOWERS WATERED

Reward: Gold brick

Find this flower box near the shack across the street from Barry Smith's Kung-Fu Dojo.

FREE RUN

Rewards: Gold brick, "Brickett" character token

Beam up to the dam's top, then use a scan spot to follow a trail of footprints to a bin that contains dynamite. Use the dynamite to blast open the nearby silver crate, then build the remaining bricks into a trampoline. Bound up to the top of the tower above, then slide down a tightrope to reach another tower, where this zone's free run token is located.

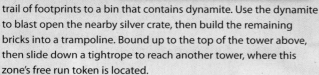

Collect the free run token, then use the nearby catapult pad to rocket back down to the dam's reservoir. Make your way to the dam's north walkway, where the free run starting point now appears.

Before starting the free run, crowbar your way into a small nearby room and obtain some dynamite from the dispenser within. Use this to blast open the silver door to the right, then enter the small room beyond and use the color swapper within to fill your color gun with blue energy.

Exit the room and blast the nearby white LEGO wall to add some blue coloring. Now you can wall-jump to the top of the dam's north wall. This means you're ready to take on the free run!

Start the free run and begin by wall-jumping to the top of the dam's north wall. Go left and carefully hop between the thin poles while the transistors aren't sizzling with dangerous energy.

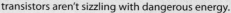

Use a catapult pad to sail over to the dam's south wall, then maneuver past more dangerous transistors on your way to the top. Use the transporter pad to beam up to the top of the dam.

Bound up from the trampoline you recently built up here to reach the top of a tall tower, then slide down a tightrope to reach the goal. Nice run!

GANG ARRESTED

Reward: Gold brick

Use the audio scan point on the platform here to eavesdrop on the gang members inside the restaurant that overlooks the waterfall. The thugs are planning to stir up trouble over at the Bluebell Mine. Hurry over there and bust 'em all before it's too late!

PIG RETURNED

Reward: Gold brick

Beam up to the top of the dam, then drill the shaky ground to uncork a geyser that boosts you to the tower's top. Perform a chicken-glide from up here to reach the pig on the lower nearby tower. The pig cannon is right nearby.

INTRODUCTION

POLICE ACADEMY

CHARACTERS AND VEHICLES

WALKTHROUGH

LEGO CITY TOUR

CHECKLISTS

⬢ RED BRICK

Reward: Data Scan Upgrade—Clues

This red brick is hidden inside a silver crate near the entrance to the Bluebell Mine. Obtain some dynamite from the dispenser at the nearby shack, then blast the crate to bits to reveal the red brick.

🔘 SILVER STATUE DESTROYED

Reward: Gold brick

Grab some dynamite from the dispenser near the Bluebell Mine, then scale the rocks to the east. Make your way to the top of the train tunnel, where this zone's silver Rex Fury statue stands.

1 SUPERBUILD 1: BLUEBELL TREE

Reward: Gold brick

Scale the rocks east of the Bluebell Mine to reach the top of the nearby train tunnel, where the silver statue is located. Perform a chicken-glide from the edge of the tunnel's roof to land atop a high hill, right near a superbuild.

Spend 30,000 bricks to erect the towering Bluebell Tree.

⬛2 SUPERBUILD 2: STUNT RAMP

Reward: Gold brick, "Duke Huckleberry" character token

Spend a mere 10,000 bricks to build a stunt ramp here, on the roof of the restaurant near the waterfall. This ramp comes into play during one of Bluebell National Park's time trial events.

🔘3 SUPERBUILD 3: CALL-IN POINT

Reward: Gold brick, "Vigilant" vehicle token

Drop 8,000 bricks to build a vehicle call-in point along the roadside here.

4 SUPERBUILD 4: SERENITY BRIDGE

Reward: Gold brick

This superbuild is erected during the course of Story mode—it's the bridge that leads across the river and over to Barry Smith's Kung-Fu Dojo. Constructing this superbuild causes the "Karate Guy" character token to appear over the bridge.

⑤ SUPERBUILD 5: HELIPAD

Reward: Gold brick, "Skybringer" vehicle token

Chop through the boarded door near Sheriff Huckleberry's police station, then scale the stairs beyond to discover a superbuild. Part with 20,000 bricks to construct a helipad here.

①TIME TRIAL 1

Reward: Gold brick, "Tracker" vehicle token

This time trial begins near the entrance to the Bluebell Mine and takes you all around Bluebell National Park. Before attempting this time trial, make sure that you've built the stunt ramp atop the roof of the restaurant near the waterfall—it comes in handy!

②TIME TRIAL 2

Reward: Gold brick, "Oldster" vehicle token

This nautical time attack takes you on a quick trip through Bluebell Park's eastern waters. It kicks off with a massive jump over the waterfall and leads you underneath Blackwell Bridge.

③ TIME TRIAL 3

Reward: Gold brick, "Chan's Ironback" vehicle token

Hop into the truck parked near the Serenity Bridge to begin Bluebell National Park's final time trial. This one leads you across Blackwell Bridge and all around Uptown.

TRAIN STATION

Reward: Gold brick, fast travel

The train station is located just outside the entrance to the Bluebell Mine. This station is automatically built during the course of Story mode, so there's no need for you to activate it. How convenient!

VEHICLE ROBBER ARRESTED

Reward: Gold brick, "Hero" vehicle token

Enter the guard tower near Sheriff Huckleberry's police station, then climb the ladder to reach the lookout. Switch to the astronaut disguise and boost up to the tower's roof, where a criminal scan spot is located. Zero in on the criminal in the police station garage, then hurry after him and make the bust!

INTRODUCTION

POLICE ACADEMY

CHARACTERS AND VEHICLES

WALKTHROUGH

LEGO CITY TOUR

CHECKLISTS

BRIGHT LIGHTS PLAZA

POINTS OF INTEREST

To reach the roof, find this spot of shaky ground near the front doors of the luxury apartments.

Drill until the water spouts up, allowing you to get on top of the overhang. There's a tightrope to the right. Make the long walk across it.

Run across the overhang until you reach some handholds. Climb up and around the "Quentins" billboard.

This will get you to another glass overhang, where you'll find a transporter pad. Teleport to another overhang with a catapult pad that launches you to another section of the apartment building.

Once you're on the next overhang, climb the drainpipe onto the roof for a nice view of Lady Liberty Island and the Auburn Bay Bridge.

⭐ 1 LUXURY APARTMENTS

Chances are Chase McCain doesn't make enough studs per month to afford a high-rise apartment in the heart of Bright Lights Plaza. At least he can climb all over this one for free!

⭐ 2 ATLAS STATUE

This impressive statue stands just north of the shopping mall. Drive any car off the ramp in front of the statue to fly through the "world" supported on Atlas's shoulders!

⭐ 3 ELLIE'S APARTMENT

Ellie's apartment is quite something. You won't want to visit it until you've rescued Natalia from Mercy Hearts Hospital during Story mode.

To get inside, find the keypad outside of the ground-floor elevator.

Once inside, head to the right to find a doorway leading to some stairs. Head upstairs to find yourself on the roof of Ellie's pad.

⭐ 4 WEST SIDE SHOPS

Along the waterfront, there are plenty of things to keep you occupied. Along with a giant toy store, there's a gym and a theater. You'll want to get to the toy store and all the way around the shops and inside the gym.

Go into the middle section of the shopping mall, with the disco lights on the floor. Head north and go out back, behind Wheatley's Bakery. Hop up some handholds that lead to a series of thin poles.

Continue along the narrow path until you reach a wall runway. Run along the wall to get past the gap.

Keep going until you reach a handhold on the wall. Grab it and drop down to a thin ledge.

Wall-hug the ledge and head left until you are back on more solid ground. Now it's time to race forward for a while. Keep heading around the glass overhang, eventually crossing a tightrope.

INTRODUCTION

POLICE ACADEMY

CHARACTERS AND VEHICLES

WALKTHROUGH

LEGO CITY TOUR

CHECKLISTS

Keep going until you reach a jetpack symbol. Activate it and then boost over the water and onto the theater's marquee.

Slide down the tightrope that follows and then leap across a flagpole to reach another marquee.

You're almost at the end of your run. Get to the transporter pad and teleport into the gym. Now you've seen everything the west side shops have to offer!

Between the LEGO store and the Rex statue is a ladder. It's too high to grab on to normally, so you'll need to boost up to it with the astronaut's jetpack.

Climb the ladder and hop across a series of posts until you reach a climbable wall.

Scale the wall to reach a higher platform. Run to the left until you reach some handholds. Scale these as well to reach higher ground.

⑤ SHOPPING MALL

An impressive shopping mall lies at the heart of Bright Lights Plaza. Its most notable feature is a giant Disco Dude statue at the front. There's quite a lot to do around the mall, which has a few Points of Interest of its own.

Run to the right, sliding under and vaulting over several beams. When you reach the end, you'll find a billboard with a balance beam you can cross. Do so to reach a tightrope.

⑥ TOP OF THE MALL

Want a nice view of the tourist section of LEGO City? Then you'll want to make a jaunt to the top of the mall. Start in front of the LEGO store.

Slide down the tightrope to reach another billboard. See those handholds? Time to climb!

Climb the drainpipe above the handholds, then use a wall runway to sprint past a gap.

Climb the handhold wall and you're there. Phew!

FEATS AND COLLECTIBLES

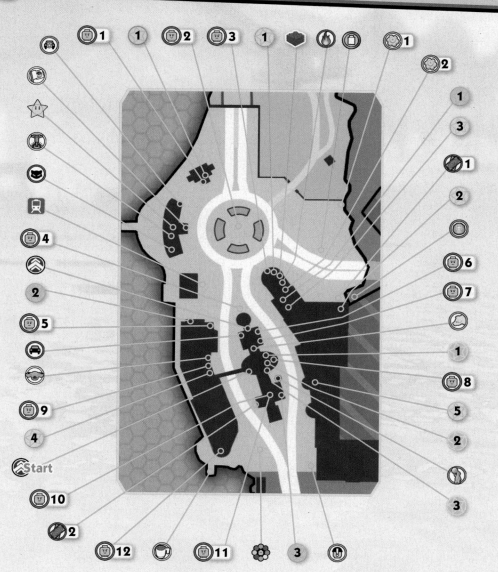

INTRODUCTION

POLICE ACADEMY

CHARACTERS AND VEHICLES

WALKTHROUGH

LEGO CITY TOUR

CHECKLISTS

MAP LEGEND

MAP ICON(S)	FEAT/COLLECTIBLE	REWARD(S)	LOCATION/HOW TO REACH	GOT IT?
	Alien Caught	Gold brick	Inside the west side shop's gym.	1
1	ATM Smashed 1	Gold brick	Outside Ellie's apartment.	2
2	ATM Smashed 2	Gold brick	Next to the shopping mall.	3
	BBQ Fire Extinguished	Gold brick	On the roof of Ellie's apartment.	4
	Boulder Destroyed	Gold brick	Near Ellie's pad, on the far east corner of the lawn.	5
	Cat Rescued	Gold brick	Hanging out on the roof of the luxury apartments.	6
1 1	Character Token 1	Pat Patterson	Paint the "L" of the hotel sign yellow.	7
2	Character Token 2	Spartan Warrior	Smash a car through the Atlas statue.	8
3	Character Token 3	Luke Cashmore	Inside the room with the locked door, at the top of Ellie's apartment.	9
1 to 5 4	Character Token 4	Ryan McLaughlin	Build the five watercoolers around Bright Lights Plaza to unlock.	10
1 to 3 5	Character Token 5	Eddie JoJo	Earned after painting the three ice cream dispensers pink.	11
6	Character Token 6	Chris Wyatt	Along the R&J sign near the top of the shopping mall.	12
7	Character Token 7	Zombie	At the top of the mall.	13
1 to 3 8	Character Token 8	Lizard Man	Collect after building the LEGO sets in the LEGO store.	14
9	Character Token 9	Magician	Above the transporter pad inside the west side shops' gym.	15
10	Character Token 10	Disco Dude	Over the disco ball on top of the giant Disco Dude statue.	16
11	Character Token 11	James Curry	On the ceiling of the lower level of the shopping mall.	17
12	Character Token 12	Clockwork Robot	On the stage next to the giant toy statue of the west side shops.	18
	Coffee Break Completed	Gold brick	Near the water in the south end of Bright Lights Plaza.	19
	Disguise Booth	Gold brick, "Paparazzo" character token	Next to the main street.	20
	District Conquered	Gold brick	Climb the ladder on the roof of the luxury apartments.	21
	Drill Thrill Completed	Gold brick	On the roof of the luxury apartments.	22
1	Flowers Watered 1	Gold brick	In the northeast corner of the plaza.	23
2	Flowers Watered 2	Gold brick	On the roof of Ellie's sweet apartment.	24
	Free Run	Gold brick, "Cheerleader" character token	Atop the billboard on the top of the mall.	25
	Gang Arrested	Gold brick	Located on an awning above a shop near Pagoda.	26
	Pig Returned	Gold brick	Chilling on an overhang at the top of the mall, reachable by a catapult pad.	27
	Red Brick	Instant Vehicles	In the hallway of Ellie's apartment.	28

MAP LEGEND CONTINUED

MAP ICON(S)	FEAT/COLLECTIBLE	REWARD(S)	LOCATION/HOW TO REACH	GOT IT?
	Silver Statue Destroyed	Gold brick	In a locked room next to the LEGO store.	29
	Superbuild 1: Vehicle Call-in	Gold brick, "Chaser" vehicle token	Along the street on the north end of the plaza.	30
	Super Star	"Pop Star" character token (after you've found all Super Stars in the city)	At the very top of the luxury apartments.	31
	Train Station	Gold brick, Fast Travel	South of the Atlas statue.	32
	Vehicle Robbery Completed	Gold brick, "Cetan" vehicle token	Inside the Autos shop at the north end of the shopping mall.	33
	Vehicle Robber Arrested	Gold brick, "Gersemi" vehicle token	In the far corner of the luxury apartments roof.	34

INTRODUCTION

POLICE ACADEMY

CHARACTERS AND VEHICLES

WALKTHROUGH

LEGO CITY TOUR

CHECKLISTS

 ALIEN CAUGHT

Reward: Gold brick

Follow the route along the west side shops (POI 4) until you beam into the gym. Activate the gym's space crate and open it to reveal an alien! Hurry out to the street and arrest the invader.

 ATM SMASHED 2

Reward: Gold brick

Found on the side of the shopping mall next to some vending machines.

 ATM SMASHED 1

Reward: Gold brick

The ATM is outside Ellie's apartment, on the east side of Bright Lights Plaza.

 BBQ FIRE EXTINGUISHED

Reward: Gold brick

Head to the roof of Ellie's apartment to find this BBQ fire.

BOULDER DESTROYED

Reward: Gold brick

This is buried under a bunch of black boulders at the far east corner of Ellie's apartment.

CAT RESCUED

Reward: Gold brick

Use the previous "Points of Interest" section to reach the roof of the luxury apartments (POI 1). The trapped cat is on the roof's left side.

1 CHARACTER TOKEN 1

Reward: Pat Patterson

Paint the "L" of the hotel sign yellow to unlock this token, which appears right in front of the hotel.

2 CHARACTER TOKEN 2

Reward: Spartan Warrior

To nab this token, you'll need a fast car. Find one, then drive off the ramp in front of the Atlas statue. You'll fly through the statue, destroying the globe and grabbing the token as you go!

3 CHARACTER TOKEN 3

Reward: Luke Cashmore

On the roof of Ellie's apartment, look for the locked door. Break in with the robber's crowbar, then walk around to the back of the room to find your prize.

4 CHARACTER TOKEN 4

Reward: Ryan McLaughlin

Find and smash five brown crates in Bright Lights Plaza, then build watercoolers from their bricks. Each of these crates is located inside a shop or building—check the maps to see where the five crates lie.

After you build all five watercoolers, a character token appears at the back of the shopping mall.

5 CHARACTER TOKEN 5

Reward: Eddie JoJo

Paint the area's three silver ice cream carts pink. You can find a pink color swapper near the theater's entrance.

After you paint all three ice cream carts pink, a character token appears in front of the theater.

Inside the LEGO store are three large boxes with LEGO pieces inside. Smash the boxes and build a space shuttle, a pirate ship, and a crocodile. The character token appears in the center of the store after you do this.

⭐ 🔘6 CHARACTER TOKEN 6

Reward: Chris Wyatt

Make your way toward the top of the mall (POI 6). When you reach the R&J sign, don't climb up the handholds. Instead, follow the path to the right to find this token!

⭐ 🔘9 CHARACTER TOKEN 9

Reward: Magician

Use the "Points of Interest" section to get around the west side shops (POI 4) and enter the gym. The token is right above the transporter pad used to get inside.

⭐ 🔘7 CHARACTER TOKEN 7

Reward: Zombie

Follow the instructions in the "Points of Interest" section to reach the top of the mall (POI 6). You'll automatically grab this token as you reach the top.

⭐ 🔘10 CHARACTER TOKEN 10

Reward: Disco Dude

From the front of the shopping mall, you'll see a drainpipe. Climb it.

⭐ 🔘8 CHARACTER TOKEN 8

Reward: Lizard Man

With dynamite in hand, head over to the LEGO store. The door is locked, but that's nothing a little dynamite can't fix. You can find a dispenser in the walkway under the shopping mall.

Head right and you'll find some handholds so you can get right up to the Disco Dude statue.

Head behind the statue and to the other side where there are some handholds you can grab and shimmy along.

Follow the path to a wall runway and use it to get across the gap.

Climb the ladder beyond the gap to enter a tube. Slide under and vault a series of beams until you reach a transporter pad.

Use the transporter to get atop the giant disco ball. The token hovers above the disco ball—just jump up and grab it!

⑪ CHARACTER TOKEN 11

Reward: James Curry

On the ground floor of the shopping mall, look for some handholds on the ceiling. Smash the nearby phone and build a trampoline, then bounce up to the token.

⑫ CHARACTER TOKEN 12

Reward: Clockwork Robot

Follow the route around the west side shops (POI 4). After you pass the giant toy doll statue, look for a character token in the background—it's easy to spot. Use the nearby handhold to climb up to the token.

☕ COFFEE BREAK COMPLETED

Reward: Gold brick

This break spot is by the water on the south end of Bright Lights Plaza.

✿ DISGUISE BOOTH

Reward: Gold brick, "Paparazzo" character token

This is right out in the open, next to the main street.

DISTRICT CONQUERED

Reward: Gold brick

Go to the rooftop of the luxury apartments (POI 1). Climb the ladder on the roof's right side to reach the spot where you can raise a flag.

DRILL THRILL COMPLETED

Reward: Gold brick

The fuse box that fires up this event is found on the right side of the luxury apartments rooftop (POI 1). If you need help getting up there, see the "Points of Interest" section.

FLOWERS WATERED 1

Reward: Gold brick

The dry flower bed is in the northeast corner of the plaza. Get to watering!

② FLOWERS WATERED 2

Reward: Gold brick

You'll find the flower bed on the roof of Ellie's apartment.

⬆ FREE RUN

Rewards: Gold brick, "Cheerleader" character token

Get to the top of the mall (POI 6) by following the directions in the "Points of Interest" section. Once there, you'll see that you can actually get a little bit higher. Climb a blue and white LEGO wall to reach the top of a billboard, where the free run token is located.

The free run challenge starts in front of the LEGO store, so head on down there.

TIP

When you start the free run, switch to the astronaut and boost up as you pass under the first overhead time clock, collecting it without having to actually use the overhead handholds. You may then boost up onto the ladder that follows and complete the run.

🎙 GANG ARRESTED

Reward: Gold brick

You'll actually start this event in Pagoda, right near the border to Bright Lights Plaza. Drill the shaky ground at this spot and ride the water blast up to a drainpipe.

Climb up the drainpipe and then slide under a beam. Climb the scaffolding that follows to reach an audio scan spot, which reveals that a gang is about to start trouble in the shopping mall. Hurry over there and show those gang members why Chase McCain is the greatest detective ever!

🐷 PIG RETURNED

Reward: Gold brick

Make your way to the top of the mall (POI 6). Climb onto the billboard and use the catapult pad to launch yourself toward a distant ledge with a lost pig.

Once on the pig, take a big leap off the building. Don't worry, that pig is tough enough to handle a 10-story drop! Just head for the cannon, which you'll find in the northwest section of Bright Lights Plaza.

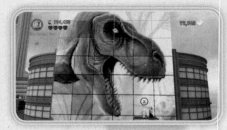

RED BRICK

Reward: Instant Vehicles

After taking the elevator into Ellie's apartment, follow the hall left to find this red brick.

SILVER STATUE DESTROYED

Reward: Gold brick

The Rex statue is next to the LEGO shop in the shopping mall, but it's kept in a locked room! Use the nearby scan spot to track down the key you need.

Unlock the door, then head left and grab some dynamite from the nearby dispenser. Plant your dynamite and step back!

SUPERBUILD: VEHICLE CALL-IN

Reward: Gold brick, "Chaser" vehicle token

You'll find this superbuild east of the Atlas statue.

SUPER STAR

Reward: "Pop Star" character token (after you find all Super Stars in the city)

The Super Star is on the rooftop of the luxury apartments. Climb the ladder on the roof's right side to reach it. If you're not sure how to get to the roof, check out the "Points of Interest" section.

TRAIN STATION

Reward: Gold brick, fast travel

Bright Lights Plaza's train station lies south of the Atlas statue. To activate it, smash the green object at the bottom of the metro stairs, then build the bricks into the station's ticket machine.

VEHICLE ROBBERY COMPLETED

Reward: Gold brick, "Cetan" vehicle token

Look for the Autos shop at the north end of the shopping mall. Break into the door to take the Cetan for a joy ride.

VEHICLE ROBBER ARRESTED

Reward: Gold brick, "Gersemi" vehicle token

Get up to the rooftop of the luxury apartments (POI 1). Climb the ladder to the right and then drop off the right side to the roof's other half. Find the scan spot that starts this event in the roof's far corner.

CHERRY TREE HILLS

POINTS OF INTEREST

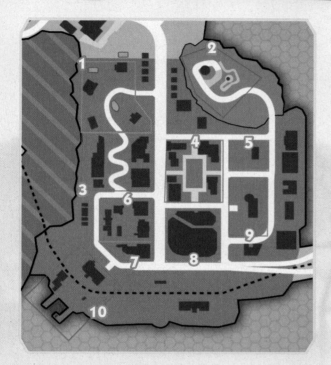

INTRODUCTION

POLICE ACADEMY

CHARACTERS AND VEHICLES

WALKTHROUGH

LEGO CITY TOUR

CHECKLISTS

⭐ 2 RADIO TOWER AND LOOKOUT POINT

Travel up a winding road to reach this tall hill, where a high-tech radio tower stands. Head inside the tower to discover a dynamite dispenser. Continue following the road up to a scenic lookout, where you can enjoy beautiful views of LEGO City.

Activate the chicken symbol on the lookout, then glide over to the radio tower. Vault a few obstacles to reach a transporter pad that beams you to the dome atop the tower.

⭐ 1 MANSIONS

A collection of impressive mansions stands near the northwest corner of Cherry Tree Hills. Chase can climb around these shmancy dwellings to reach several special goodies. Reaching the mansions' roofs is easy—most simply require Chase to grow plants and climb up or zip up with the grapple gun.

Slide out from the dome, then quickly run around the edge of the tower's apex, stepping on several red buttons. Quickly run across all of the buttons to activate them before the first one pops back up. If you're fast, you'll activate a fan inside the dome. Slide back inside and use the updraft to reach a few secrets at the tower's top.

⭐ ③ NORTHWEST ROOFTOPS

Chase must navigate these roofs to reach a few special goodies. To get here, cross the north tightrope after climbing onto the roof near the Red Café (POI 7), then traverse the southwest rooftops (POI 6), working your way north.

When you reach the southwest rooftops' final roof, ignore the catapult pad and slide down the north tightrope to cross the street and reach the first building of the northwest rooftops area.

Climb a ladder and then use a wall runway to reach another ladder, which leads up to a lavish rooftop pool.

Go upstairs and slide under an obstacle. Wall-jump onto a thin blue ledge, then tiptoe around the ledge to reach a flagpole. Flip over to the next building.

Flip across a series of flagpoles, heading for a wall that you can jump off to reach the balcony above.

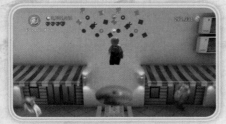

Two people are enjoying a meal at a picnic table on the balcony. Jump onto the table to give them a panic, then leap up to the roof.

This final roof sports a luxurious tennis court. Cross the court to explore the roof and discover a few goodies. The catapult pad up here will send you flying over to the baseball billboard in the distance.

⭐ ④ NORTHEAST ROOFTOPS

These roofs contain many goodies, and unlike the other rooftops mentioned in these Points of Interest sections, you don't reach the northwest rooftops by starting near the Red Café. Instead, you reach them by climbing up from the street level around the vicinity. There are two access points.

Wall-Jump Access Point

To begin your ascent to the northeast rooftops, first locate the 500 Hotel. Simply run west along the street from the auto shop (POI 9). You

can't miss the 500 Hotel, thanks to its big red signs.

Use the transporter pad near the 500 Hotel sign to beam inside the hotel. Collect some dynamite from the dispenser in the small room, then beam back out.

Cross the street and use your dynamite to blast a silver garage door. Build the remaining bricks to complete the blue and white wall-jump pads above you, then wall-jump up to a ledge.

Use a wall runway to circle around the building and reach a balcony. Bounce off a trampoline to reach the roof above.

You now face a choice: either pry open the nearby door and grow a plant to reach a character token and a catapult pad that takes you to the east rooftops, or climb a blue and white LEGO wall to explore the rooftops to the north, which lead to a Super Star.

Going for the Token

Ignore the blue and white LEGO wall, and pry open the door of the nearby glass enclosure instead. Grow a tall sunflower from the planter within, then climb up.

Tiptoe across a tightrope to reach the neighboring rooftop, which sports a sweet DJ stage. Smash a blue and white barrel here, then build its bricks into a trampoline that lets you bounce on top of the stage.

Collect the character token atop the DJ stage, then step onto the nearby catapult pad to soar over to the next group of buildings, where your run ends.

Pursuing the Super Star

Instead of prying into the glass enclosure, ignore it and climb the nearby blue and white LEGO wall instead. Sprint up a sloping solar panel, then make a daring leap over to the next building, aiming to grab the blue and white LEGO patch that runs up its side.

Climb up the LEGO patch, then slide under a fence. Vault the fence and hop up three thin poles to reach a wall-jump pad. Use the pad to wall-jump over to the next roof.

Make another risky leap to the lower rooftop on the left, grabbing the handhold to avoid falling. Follow a trail of studs to a catapult pad that launches you to the next building.

Use a wall runway to reach a thin ledge that runs atop a fence. Cross the thin ledge to reach a handhold, then leap up to a high patio.

Wall-jump up to the next patio, then climb a blue and white LEGO patch to reach another thin ledge. Inch along the ledge to reach another wall-jump pad that's stuck to the back of a small billboard.

INTRODUCTION

POLICE ACADEMY

CHARACTERS AND VEHICLES

WALKTHROUGH

LEGO CITY TOUR

CHECKLISTS

Wall-jump to the roof above, then vault an obstacle and slide down a tightrope. Slide under some vents on your way to a series of thin poles.

Hop along the thin poles to at last reach the final rooftop. Here you discover a yellow box that contains this zone's Super Star.

Grapple Access Point

Look for a spot where you can grapple up from the street level and climb onto a roof with a space crate. You'll find this grapple point around the east side of this POI.

Activate the space crate to beam in some bricks, then build a ladder and climb up to the nearby roof. Pry open a door up here, then head through to emerge on a higher roof.

Smash an air conditioner to find some more bricks, then build a trampoline. Bounce up to the next roof, then inch along a thin ledge.

The thin ledge leads to a handhold. Leap up to reach the final roof, where you find an audio scan spot that lets Chase eavesdrop on the illicit plans of a local gang.

⭐ 5 JENNY'S DINER

This small burger stand is renown around LEGO City for its yummy fast food. Chase can climb up to the roof using his grapple gun and can assemble a red color swapper up there after smashing some stuff.

⭐ 6 SOUTHWEST ROOFTOPS

These roofs feature a few goodies and allow Chase to reach the aforementioned northwest rooftops (POI 3).

Reach these rooftops by climbing to the roof of the building near the Red Café (POI 7) and then crossing the north tightrope.

Scamper up the sloped roof that follows, then drop down to a grassy yard, where a blazing BBQ fire is located.

Climb the nearby blue and white LEGO wall to reach a balcony, then climb some vines to reach the balcony above.

Run around and shimmy across an overhead patch of LEGOs to reach a blue drainpipe. Climb the pipe to reach the next balcony above.

Cross a wall runway to round the corner, then climb more LEGOs to reach a handhold that leads up to the roof.

You now have a choice: either use the north tightrope to slide over to the northwest rooftops (which continues at POI 3), or use the roof's catapult pad to soar over to the buildings to the west and continue exploring the current rooftops.

The catapult pad sends you soaring westward, over to a nearby building. Climb a drainpipe to reach the building's narrow roof.

Smash the antenna at the end of the roof to remove the obstacle, then jump to the next roof below.

Slide down a tightrope to reach the final rooftop, where a transporter pad is located. This will beam you inside the Red Café (POI 7), where you'll find a character token.

⭐ 7 RED CAFÉ

This popular hangout serves as Chase's main access point for exploring many of the rooftops around Cherry Tree Hills. It also happens to be Chief Dunby's primary source of donuts!

Head upstairs to visit the Red Café's patio and discover a dynamite dispenser. Climb the nearby blue and white LEGO patch to reach the top of the red awning. From there, use the grapple gun to zip up to the adjacent building's roof.

From the roof of the building near the Red Café, you can either go north along a tightrope or glide east via a chicken symbol. The tightrope leads to the southwest rooftops (POI 6), which in turn lead to the northwest rooftops (POI 3). On the other hand, chicken-gliding will land you on the southeast rooftops (POI 8), covered in the next section.

⭐ 8 SOUTHEAST ROOFTOPS

A few more goodies are hidden atop these roofs, including a lost pig and a character token.

Chase can reach these rooftops by chicken-gliding from the top of the building near the Red Café (POI 7).

INTRODUCTION

POLICE ACADEMY

CHARACTERS AND VEHICLES

WALKTHROUGH

LEGO CITY TOUR

CHECKLISTS

Climb the stairs after landing from your glide, then glide again to reach the next roof. If you brought some dynamite with you, use it to blast the silver door atop the stairs and score a superbrick.

After your second glide, use a transporter pad to beam inside a glass enclosure. Grow a sunflower from a planter here, then climb up onto the enclosure. Proceed across a balance beam.

Vault a low wall and locate a ladder. Climb up to reach a space crate, then activate it to beam in some bricks. Build these into a catapult pad, then soar over to another roof.

Sprint up a slope and cross a tightrope to reach another roof. Jump down to a lower roof and climb a blue drainpipe to reach a chicken symbol atop a tall drum, which leads to a lost pig—the main reason to traverse these eastern rooftops.

⑨ AUTO SHOP

This luxury auto shop stands on the east side of Cherry Tree Hills. Chase can reach its roof by way of helicopter, for the roof sports a crash mat!

⑩ LEGO CITY POLICE STATION

LEGO City's primary police station is found in Cherry Tree Hills. This is the very station that Chase works out of during Story mode. Several secrets are found near here—some are hidden around its grounds, while others are found by climbing the building.

You can climb up to the police station's roof by scaling its exterior stairs to reach a white LEGO wall. Chop through the nearby door to find a blue color swapper, then blast the white wall with blue coloring so you may climb up to the roof.

TIP

Flip back to the "LEGO City Police Station" section near the start of our LEGO City Tour for an overview of the police station's many interior areas and secrets.

FEATS AND COLLECTIBLES

INTRODUCTION

POLICE ACADEMY

CHARACTERS AND VEHICLES

WALKTHROUGH

LEGO CITY TOUR

CHECKLISTS

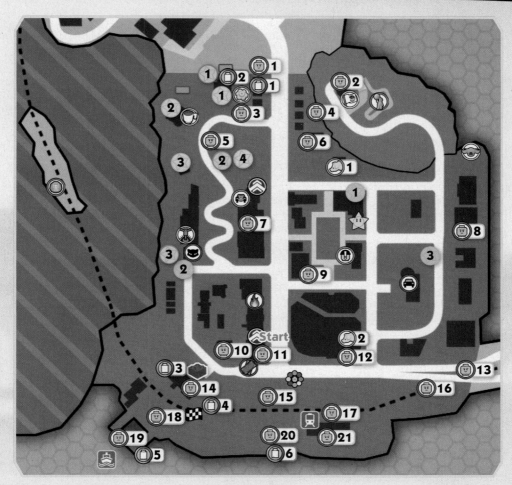

MAP LEGEND

MAP ICON(S)	FEAT/COLLECTIBLE	REWARD(S)	LOCATION/HOW TO REACH	GOT IT?
	Alien Caught	Gold brick	Space crate near the northeast buildings, close to the water.	1
	ATM Smashed	Gold brick	Near the Red Café.	2
	BBQ Fire Extinguished	Gold brick	In a yard among the southwest rooftops.	3
	Boulder Destroyed	Gold brick	Follow the train tracks into the northwest tunnel. The boulder is on the left side of the tracks.	4
	Cat Rescued	Gold brick	On a western rooftop. Perform a pair of chicken-glides from the roof of the southwest mansion.	5
1	Character Token 1	Sleepyhead	Appears on the front steps of the Hillside House superbuild (must construct the superbuild).	6
2	Character Token 2	Anchor Man	Atop the radio tower (chicken-glide from the lookout point; activate the updraft fan).	7
1 to 3 / 3	Character Token 3	Werewolf	Smash three LEGO trees and build three doghouses out of their bricks.	8
4	Character Token 4	Detective	Use the scan spot near the large billboard near the radio tower.	9

MAP LEGEND CONTINUED

MAP ICON(S)	FEAT/COLLECTIBLE	REWARD(S)	LOCATION/HOW TO REACH	GOT IT?
1 to 4 5	Character Token 5	TV Reporter	Build four satellite dishes on the roofs of the northwest mansions.	10
1 to 3 6	Character Token 6	Mail Man	Paint three mailboxes red around Cherry Tree Hills. A red color swapper is found on the roof of Jenny's Diner.	11
7	Character Token 7	Tennis Player	Drill one of the two patches of shaky roofing atop the roof with the tennis court (cross the southwest and northwest rooftops to reach).	12
8	Character Token 8	Dave Something	Grapple up to the transport pad atop the Security building's entry steps, then beam over to the token.	13
9	Character Token 9	Rapper	Above the rooftop DJ stage (navigate the northeast rooftops to reach).	14
10	Character Token 10	Shaky Harry	Inside the Red Café (navigate the southwest rooftops to reach a transport pad, then beam over).	15
11	Character Token 11	George Fartarbensonbury	Paint two pieces of furniture red inside the shop near the Red Café.	16
12	Character Token 12	Clown Robber Lou	Atop the LEGO City Bank. Navigate the southeast rooftops to reach.	17
13	Character Token 13	Troublemaker Phil	Paint three white trees near the southeast road green. A green color swapper is located around a building to the north (Herbert Hotel).	18
14	Character Token 14	Grubby Grubster	Scale the police station's exterior stairs and pry open the exterior jail cell.	19
15	Character Token 15	Taxi Driver	Bounce off the train station's patio tables to reach its roof, then beam over to the archway with the token.	20
16	Character Token 16	Louise Andrew	Inside the southeast train tunnel.	21
17	Character Token 17	Street Racer	Build five bubble gum dispensers around the train station and waterfront (smash crates to find their bricks).	22
18	Character Token 18	Security Guard	Inside the police booth behind the police station.	23
19	Character Token 19	Butch Patterson	Inside the police booth near the ferry.	24
20	Character Token 20	Ice Skater	Appears near the Wishing Fountain after you complete the superbuild.	25
21	Character Token 21	Train Driver Bill	Pry open the train station's second-floor door, then crack the safe inside the station.	26
	Coffee Break	Gold brick	On the roof of the west mansion's porch (wall-jump to reach).	27
	Disguise Booth	Gold brick, "Maintenance Worker" character token	Near the train station.	28
	District Conquered	Gold brick	Atop the radio tower (chicken-glide from the lookout point; activate the updraft fan).	29
	Drill Thrill	Gold brick	Atop a western building's roof (chicken-glide from the roof of the southwest mansion to reach).	30
	Ferry Route	Gold brick, fast travel, "Pumpkin" vehicle token	Pier behind the police station.	31
	Flowers Watered	Gold brick	In the backyard of one of the north townhomes (near the mansions).	32
	Free Run	Gold brick, "Baseball Player" character token	Get the token at the end of the northwest rooftops run, then navigate the rooftops again.	33
	Gang Arrested	Gold brick	Scan spot atop the northeast rooftops.	34
1	Pig Returned 1	Gold brick	Atop the car wash (grow a sunflower to reach).	35
2	Pig Returned 2	Gold brick	Atop the southeast rooftops (chicken-glide from a tall drum to reach).	36

MAP LEGEND CONTINUED

MAP ICON(S)	FEAT/COLLECTIBLE	REWARD(S)	LOCATION/HOW TO REACH	GOT IT?
	Red Brick	Data Scan Upgrade: City Challenges	Scale the police station's exterior stairs and pry open the exterior jail cell.	37
	Silver Statue	Gold brick	At the lookout point (dynamite dispenser is in the nearby radio tower).	38
1	Superbuild 1: Hillside House	Gold brick	Along the north road leading to Auburn.	39
2	Superbuild 2: Emergency Crash Mat	Gold brick, "Revolver" vehicle token	On the roof of the northernmost mansion.	40
3	Superbuild 3: Helipad	Gold brick, "Responder" vehicle token	Atop the police station (paint the white LEGO wall blue to reach; the blue color swapper is located behind the nearby boarded door).	41
4	Superbuild 4: Call-in Point	Gold brick, "Imprisoner" vehicle token	Near the police station.	42
5	Superbuild 5: Ferry	Gold brick, "Pumpkin" vehicle token	Pier behind the police station.	43
6	Superbuild 6: Wishing Fountain	Gold brick	Along the waterfront, near the train station.	44
☆	Super Star	"Pop Star" character token (after you have found all Super Stars in the city)	Run around the northeast rooftops until you reach the gold box at the end.	45
	Time Trial	Gold brick, "Lantos" vehicle token	Near the police station.	46
	Train Station	Gold brick, fast travel	Along the waterfront.	47
	Vehicle Robbery Completed	Gold brick, "Valkyrie" vehicle token	Leap from a helicopter onto the crash mat atop the auto shop, then pry open the skylight.	48
	Vehicle Robber Arrested	Gold brick, "Grassman" vehicle token	Drill one of the two patches of shaky roofing atop the roof with the tennis court (cross the southwest and northwest rooftops to reach).	49

ALIEN CAUGHT

Reward: Gold brick

Explore around the northeast buildings to discover a space crate near the water. Activate it and then chase down that alien invader!

ATM SMASHED

Reward: Gold brick

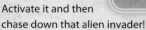

This zone's one and only ATM stands on the sidewalk near the Red Café (POI 7). Switch to your robber and have at it!

BBQ FIRE EXTINGUISHED

Reward: Gold brick

Climb up to the roof near the Red Café (POI 7), then cross the north tightrope to reach the west rooftops. It won't be long before you discover this blazing BBQ fire, which you should douse for safety.

BOULDER DESTROYED

Reward: Gold brick

Starting at the train station, follow the train tracks west and then north, heading into an elevated tunnel. After passing through the first section of tunnel, look for a special gem-covered boulder on the left side of the tracks.

INTRODUCTION

POLICE ACADEMY

CHARACTERS AND VEHICLES

WALKTHROUGH

LEGO CITY TOUR

CHECKLISTS

⭐ 🐱 CAT RESCUED

Reward: Gold brick

This poor kitty is trapped on a western rooftop. To reach it, grapple up to the roof of the southwest mansion (POI 1), then perform a pair of chicken-glides.

⭐ ①1 CHARACTER TOKEN 1

Reward: Sleepyhead

Complete the Hillside House superbuild up north, and a character token will appear on the Hillside House's front steps. Run up and claim your prize!

⭐ ②2 CHARACTER TOKEN 2

Reward: Anchor Man

Reach the top of the radio tower and activate the fan, then use the updraft to reach the character token that hovers above the tower.

⭐ ③3 CHARACTER TOKEN 3

Reward: Werewolf

Smash three special LEGO trees around Cherry Tree Hills to discover bricks, from which you can build three doghouses.

After you build all three doghouses, a character token appears here, in one of the backyards of the townhomes near the mansions (POI 1).

⭐ ④4 CHARACTER TOKEN 4

Reward: Detective

Head up to the radio tower (POI 2), and locate a scan spot near the large billboard. Follow the footprints to a suspicious pile of debris, where a character token is hidden.

⭐ ⑤5 CHARACTER TOKEN 5

Reward: TV Reporter

Scale the mansions in the northwest corner of Cherry Tree Hills, and build four satellite dishes atop the mansions' roofs. You'll need to smash crates on the roofs to discover some of the dishes' bricks.

After you build all four dishes, a character token appears in the duck pond near the mansions (POI 1).

⑥ CHARACTER TOKEN 6

Reward: Mail Man

Find and blast three mailboxes around Cherry Tree Hills with the robber's color gun to paint them all red, and a character token will appear. Check the map for the mailboxes' locations. You can find a red color swapper on the roof of Jenny's Diner (POI 5).

After coloring all three mailboxes red, a character token appears on the roof of the building near the giant baseball billboard. Climb a drainpipe to reach it.

⑦ CHARACTER TOKEN 7

Reward: Tennis Player

Navigate the southwest rooftops (POI 6) and northwest rooftops (POI 3) until you reach a roof with a tennis court. This roof features two patches of shaky roofing. Cross the court and then run around the court's right side to reach one patch of shaky roofing, then drill to discover a hidden token.

⑧ CHARACTER TOKEN 8

Reward: Dave Something

To reach this character token, first locate the security building, which stands west of the auto shop (POI 9). Grapple up to the transporter pad atop the security building's entry steps, then beam into a small room, where the token is kept.

⑨ CHARACTER TOKEN 9

Reward: Rapper

Scale the northeast rooftops (POI 4), prying open the glass enclosure's door at the junction and growing a plant to help you reach the roof with the DJ stage. Smash a barrel and build a trampoline here, then bounce up and collect the character token atop the stage.

⑩ CHARACTER TOKEN 10

Reward: Shaky Harry

This character token is stashed inside the Red Café (POI 7), but reaching it takes some doing. Scale the building near the Red Café, then cross the north tightrope to reach the southwest rooftops (POI 6). When you reach the roof with the catapult pad, use the pad to rocket over to the west buildings. Cross a few more roofs to reach a transporter pad that beams you into the Red Café.

⑪ CHARACTER TOKEN 11

Reward: George Fartarbensonbury

Fill your color gun with red energy, then enter the shop near the Red Café (POI 7) by passing through one of its revolving doors. Inside the shop, paint two pieces of furniture red to make a character token appear above the flagpoles outside. There's a red color swapper at Jenny's Diner (POI 5).

INTRODUCTION

POLICE ACADEMY

CHARACTERS AND VEHICLES

WALKTHROUGH

LEGO CITY TOUR

CHECKLISTS

Now you just need to reach that token! Stroll outside, climb a blue drainpipe, and then flip across the flagpoles until you claim your prize.

⭐ 12 CHARACTER TOKEN 12

Reward: Clown Robber Lou

This character token hovers near the roof of the LEGO City Bank. Navigate the southeast rooftops (POI 8) to reach it, just as if you were heading for the second lost pig. Step out onto the eve above the bank's front steps and claim the token.

⭐ 13 CHARACTER TOKEN 13

Reward: Troublemaker Phil

Paint three white LEGO trees green around the building near the road that leads east toward the Heritage Bridge. After you do this, a character token appears nearby.

TIP

Find a green color swapper at the nearby Herbert Hotel, which stands just north of the building with the colorless trees.

⭐ 14 CHARACTER TOKEN 14

Reward: Grubby Grubster

Scale the police station's exterior stairs to find a pair of exterior jail cells. One contains a red brick; the other contains this character token. Simply pry open the cell doors to claim these prizes.

⭐ 15 CHARACTER TOKEN 15

Reward: Taxi Driver

Head up the train station's rear stairs to reach its second-floor patio, then bounce off the picnic tables on the left (west) side to reach the station's roof. Use the transporter pad atop the train station to beam over to a nearby archway, where a character token awaits.

⭐ 16 CHARACTER TOKEN 16

Reward: Louise Andrew

Follow the train tracks east from the train station, heading into an underground tunnel. It won't be long before you spy this character token hovering near the top of the tunnel. Perform a wall-jump off the nearby LEGO pad to grab it.

⭐ 🔘17 CHARACTER TOKEN 17

Reward: Street Racer

Find and build five bubble gum dispensers around the waterfront to make a character token appear. You'll need to smash crates to discover some of the dispensers' bricks. One of the dispensers is stashed inside the train station—blast open the station's silver gate with dynamite to reach it. There's a dynamite dispenser near the train station.

After you've built all five bubble gum dispensers around the waterfront, a character token appears here.

⭐ 🔘18 CHARACTER TOKEN 18

Reward: Security Guard

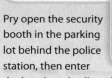

Pry open the security booth in the parking lot behind the police station, then enter the booth and collect this goodie.

⭐ 🔘19 CHARACTER TOKEN 19

Reward: Butch Patterson

Head out to the jetty behind the police station and pry open the security booth near the ferry. Enter the booth and collect the character token within.

⭐ 🔘20 CHARACTER TOKEN 20

Reward: Ice Skater

This character token appears within easy reach after you complete the Wishing Fountain superbuild down by the waterfront.

⭐ 🔘21 CHARACTER TOKEN 21

Reward: Train Driver Bill

Scale the train station's rear stairs to reach its right (east) upper patio, then pry open the station's second-floor door. Head inside and crack a safe inside the station to swipe a hidden character token!

⭐ ☕ COFFEE BREAK COMPLETED

Reward: Gold brick

Perform a wall-jump to reach the roof of the west mansion's elaborate porch. Run around the porch's roof to discover a coffee break station that's creatively set up in an open window.

⭐ ✿ DISGUISE BOOTH

Reward: Gold brick, "Maintenance Worker" character token

Smash the big, blue police crate along the side of the road near the train station, then build its bricks to form a handy disguise booth.

INTRODUCTION

POLICE ACADEMY

CHARACTERS AND VEHICLES

WALKTHROUGH

LEGO CITY TOUR

CHECKLISTS

DISTRICT CONQUERED

Reward: Gold brick

Make your way to the top of the radio tower, then activate the fan and step into the updraft to reach the very top, where you can raise a flag.

DRILL THRILL COMPLETED

Reward: Gold brick

After gliding from the roof of the southwest mansion and rescuing the trapped cat, fix the rooftop's fuse box to fire up this zone's drill thrill event.

FERRY ROUTE ACTIVATED

Reward: Gold brick, fast travel, "Pumpkin" vehicle token

Cherry Tree Hills features a ferry route that leads to Albatross Island—check behind the police station to find it. Chase activates this ferry route during the course of Story mode, so there's a good chance you've already obtained this gold brick.

FLOWERS WATERED

Reward: Gold brick

Explore the backyards of the townhomes to the east of the mansions. Chase can vault the picket fences to move from one yard to the next. One of yards on the street's east side sports a flower box that's begging to be watered.

FREE RUN

Rewards: Gold brick, "Baseball Player" character token

Navigate the southwest rooftops (POI 6) and northwest rooftops (POI 3) until you reach a roof with a tennis court. Cross the court and slide under a vent to snatch this zone's free run token.

The free run begins back at the roof of the building near the Red Café (POI 7). Make your way back over to the Red Café and climb up to the nearby roof. Next, move into the free run beacon to begin the event, which leads you back across the same rooftops.

GANG ARRESTED

Reward: Gold brick

Navigate the northeast rooftops (POI 4), using the grapple gun access point from the street level as you head over to this high audio scan spot. Listen in on some gang activity in the area, then hurry down to the basketball court and beat up the punks before they make a mess.

PIG RETURNED 1

Reward: Gold brick

This little piggy has gotten itself stuck atop the roof of the car wash just south of the radio tower and lookout point (POI 2). Grow a tall sunflower in the planter near the car wash, then climb up to reach the pig. Ride the little fellow down to the waterfront and use the pig cannon there to launch him back to Farmer Hayes.

PIG RETURNED 2

Reward: Gold brick

Another lost pig is stuck atop the southeast rooftops (POI 8). Chicken-glide from the roof near the Red Café (POI 7) to reach the southeast rooftops, then work your way around the roofs until you find a tall drum with a drainpipe. Climb the pipe to reach a chicken symbol atop the drum, then glide over to the piggy.

RED BRICK

Reward: Data Scan Upgrade—City Challenges

This red brick is an easy grab—just head up the police station's exterior stairs and pry open the jail cell door on the right to claim it.

SILVER STATUE DESTROYED

Reward: Gold brick

Head up to the lookout point near the radio tower (POI 2) to discover a silver statue of Rex Fury glimmering in the sunlight. Grab some dynamite from the dispenser inside the radio tower and blast that crummy statue to bits!

SUPERBUILD 1: HILLSIDE HOUSE

Reward: Gold brick

This superbuild lies way up north, near the road that leads out to Auburn. It's a little pricey, but it makes for a lovely addition to the neighborhood.

SUPERBUILD 2: EMERGENCY CRASH MAT

Reward: Gold brick, "Revolver" vehicle token

Climb up to the roof of the northernmost mansion to discover a superbuild pad. Part with a few bricks to assemble a crash mat up here.

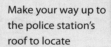 SUPERBUILD 3: HELIPAD

Reward: Gold brick, "Responder" vehicle token

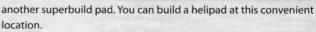

Make your way up to the police station's roof to locate another superbuild pad. You can build a helipad at this convenient location.

SUPERBUILD 4: CALL-IN POINT

Reward: Gold brick, "Imprisoner" vehicle token

Build the vehicle call-in point near the police station, and you won't have to venture very far to order the vehicles you've unlocked.

INTRODUCTION

POLICE ACADEMY

CHARACTERS AND VEHICLES

WALKTHROUGH

LEGO CITY TOUR

CHECKLISTS

⬛5 SUPERBUILD 5: FERRY

Reward: Gold brick, "Pumpkin" vehicle token

During Story mode, Chase must construct this superbuild in order to reach Albatross Island by way of ferry. This means there's a good chance you've already built this one.

⬛6 SUPERBUILD 6: WISHING FOUNTAIN

Reward: Gold brick

Complete the superbuild down by the waterfront to add a tranquil fountain for citizens and tourists to enjoy. Your good deed also causes a character token to appear nearby!

⭐ SUPER STAR

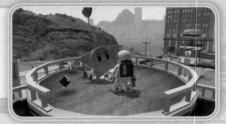

Reward: "Pop Star" character token (after you've found all Super Stars in the city)

Make your way around the northeast rooftops (POI 4) until you discover a yellow box. Smash it and build its bricks into a sparkly Super Star!

🏁 TIME TRIAL

Reward: Gold brick, "Lantos" vehicle token

This wild time trial begins near the police station and takes you around the north half of Cherry Tree Hills, eventually leading you into Auburn. It helps if you've built the stunt ramp in Auburn, but it's not necessary—you can just veer left and go around the stunt ramp's superbuild pad.

🚆 TRAIN STATION

Reward: Gold brick, fast travel

The Cherry Tree Hills train station is automatically activated during the course of Story mode—Chase catches a train here to hasten his journey up to the Bluebell Mine. Ergo, this gold brick is obtained during Story mode.

🚗 VEHICLE ROBBERY COMPLETED

Reward: Gold brick, "Valkyrie" vehicle token

Reaching this vehicle robbery requires the aid of a helicopter. Build the helipad atop the police station, then fly east, aiming to make a daring leap onto the crash mat atop the auto shop (POI 9). After you land, pry open the nearby skylight to begin the real challenge!

🚓 VEHICLE ROBBER ARRESTED

Reward: Gold brick, "Grassman" vehicle token

Reaching the criminal scan spot that triggers this event takes some doing. Starting from the Red Café (POI 7), head north and make your way across the southwest rooftops (POI 6) and northwest rooftops (POI 3) until you reach a roof with a tennis court. Cross the court and then drill the shaky patch of roofing on the left to discover the scan spot you need. Scan for a vehicle thief in a nearby garage, then drop from the roof and use the provided police car to ram that robber off the road!

CRESCENT PARK

POINTS OF INTEREST

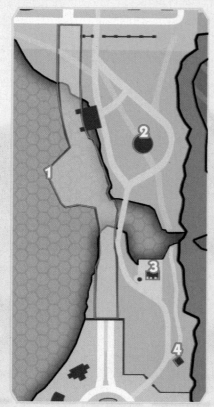

2 GAZEBO

Chase McCain hasn't been lucky in love, otherwise this picturesque gazebo in the heart of Crescent Park would make the perfect spot for the hero of LEGO City to get hitched.

3 FANCY HOUSE

This posh house sits on the water near Crescent Park's lovely waterfall. Along with cozy accommodations, it sports a beautiful array of color swappers.

4 TREE HOUSE

At the park's far southeast end is a mighty tree house. There's a ladder leading up to the top. You'll need to do an astronaut boost up to the ladder, but that should be no problem for LEGO City's greatest detective.

1 TUNNEL

At either entrance of the park is a tunnel allowing cars to drive under Crescent Park and keep it unspoiled.

The tunnel actually takes you under the ocean. Here you can see a glass panel view of the ocean. Step on the button if you want to see a big shark get an even bigger surprise!

INTRODUCTION

POLICE ACADEMY

CHARACTERS AND VEHICLES

WALKTHROUGH

LEGO CITY TOUR

CHECKLISTS

FEATS AND COLLECTIBLES

MAP LEGEND

MAP ICON(S)	FEAT/COLLECTIBLE	REWARD(S)	LOCATION/HOW TO REACH	GOT IT?
	Alien Caught	Gold brick	Hidden behind the waterfall.	1
	ATM Smashed	Gold brick	Behind the fancy house.	2
	BBQ Fire Extinguished	Gold brick	Under a tree, along the main bike path.	3
	Boulder Destroyed	Gold brick	On Crescent Park's small beach.	4
	Cat Rescued	Gold brick	At the resting area east of the giant gazebo.	5
1 to 3 1	Character Token 1	Zookeeper	Build the three birdhouses in the park.	6
1 to 3 2	Character Token 2	Musketeer	Build the three sandcastles along the beach.	7

MAP LEGEND CONTINUED

MAP ICON(S)	FEAT/COLLECTIBLE	REWARD(S)	LOCATION/HOW TO REACH	GOT IT?
3	Character Token 3	Fisherman	Use the fishing rod on the pier. The fish you catch drops the token.	8
1 4	Character Token 4	Lifeguard	Go to the pier and paint the three life preservers red.	9
1 5	Character Token 5	Carlo Cone	Paint the balloons on the gazebo the correct colors.	10
6	Character Token 6	Maximilian Jarvik	Teleport onto the top of the gazebo.	11
7	Character Token 7	Otto Hornfells	Floating near the shark poster inside the tunnel.	12
1 8	Character Token 8	Paramedic	Paint the four silver posts in the tunnel yellow.	13
1 9	Character Token 9	Nurse	Create matching sets of flowers on the bridge with the color gun.	14
1 to 3 10	Character Token 10	Sailor	Paint the fancy house's three ship wheels orange.	15
11	Character Token 11	Chef	Drive a car off the ramp and launch over the giant coffee cup near the fancy house.	16
12	Character Token 12	Patty Hayes	Behind the boarded up door inside the tree house.	17
	Coffee Break Completed	Gold brick	Underneath the giant tea cup near the fancy house.	18
	Disguise Booth	Gold brick, "Waitress" character token	Behind the fancy house.	19
	District Conquered	Gold brick	Climb the ladder inside the tree house.	20
	Drill Thrill Completed	Gold brick	Against a divider at the south edge of the park.	21
	Flowers Watered	Gold brick	On the back deck of the fancy house.	22
	Free Run	Gold brick, "Skater" character token	In the center of the playground.	23
	Gang Arrested	Gold brick	The scan spot is on a hill behind the fancy house.	24
	Pig Returned	Gold brick	Atop the castle-like wall at the north end of the park.	25
	Red Brick	Super Ram	In a small cave along the ocean.	26
	Silver Statue Destroyed	Gold brick	Atop the giant gazebo.	27
	Train Station	Gold brick, Fast Travel	Just north of the giant gazebo.	28
	Vehicle Robbery Completed	Gold brick, "T.R.E.V." vehicle token	Inside the garage next to the tree house.	29

INTRODUCTION · POLICE ACADEMY · CHARACTERS AND VEHICLES · WALKTHROUGH · LEGO CITY TOUR · CHECKLISTS

⭐ ALIEN CAUGHT

Reward: Gold brick

Hiding behind Crescent Park's waterfall is a space crate. Match the color sequence to reveal the alien.

⭐ ATM SMASHED

Reward: Gold brick

The ATM is behind the fancy house (POI 3).

★ BBQ FIRE EXTINGUISHED

Reward: Gold brick

This BBQ fire blazes dangerously under a tree, along the main bike path.

★ BOULDER DESTROYED

Reward: Gold brick

Find this special boulder on the beach, covered by regular boulders.

★ CAT RESCUED

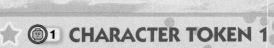

Reward: Gold brick

From the gazebo with the Rex statue (POI 2), head east up the steps to find this troubled kitty.

★ 1 CHARACTER TOKEN 1

Reward: Zookeeper

Destroy the small trees around the park and use their pieces to build three birdhouses.

The token shows up near the playground.

★ 2 CHARACTER TOKEN 2

Reward: Musketeer

Build the three sandcastles along the beach to reveal this token.

Once you build the sandcastles, the token appears here.

★ 3 CHARACTER TOKEN 3

Reward: Fisherman

Use the fishing rod at the end of the pier to catch a Cheep Cheep. The Cheep Cheep spits out a character token. Gross...and awesome!

★ 4 CHARACTER TOKEN 4

Reward: Lifeguard

To gain this token, paint the three silver life preservers at the pier red. The token appears right nearby.

INTRODUCTION

POLICE ACADEMY

CHARACTERS AND VEHICLES

WALKTHROUGH

LEGO CITY TOUR

CHECKLISTS

5 CHARACTER TOKEN 5

Reward: Carlo Cone

Paint the silver balloons at the gazebo so there is an alternating pattern of red and yellow balloons. Once all three balloons are properly colored, you can grab the token in the center of the gazebo.

6 CHARACTER TOKEN 6

Reward: Maximilian Jarvik

Use the transporter pad near the gazebo to beam up to the gazebo's roof, where a token floats.

7 CHARACTER TOKEN 7

Reward: Otto Hornfells

There's a parking lot inside the tunnel (POI 1), where you'll find a blue and white barrel. Smash it and build a trampoline, then bounce up to the LEGO patch on the nearby wall.

Climb onto the ceiling until you are hanging right over a token. Simply drop and collect it.

8 CHARACTER TOKEN 8

Reward: Paramedic

Head down into the tunnel (POI 1). Paint the four silver parking posts yellow to reveal this token.

9 CHARACTER TOKEN 9

Reward: Nurse

To reveal this token, paint the flowers on the bridge to match the color of the flowers on the bridge's opposite side. Lucky for you, the fancy house (POI 3) and its color swappers are right nearby!

10 CHARACTER TOKEN 10

Reward: Sailor

Reveal this token by painting the three ship wheels on the fancy house orange. The token appears on the house's deck.

11 CHARACTER TOKEN 11

Reward: Chef

Find a fast car and boost off the ledge that overlooks the fancy house (POI 3). Aim to snatch the token that hovers high above the giant teacup.

⊡12 CHARACTER TOKEN 12

Reward: Patty Hayes

This token is secured behind a boarded door at the top of the tree house. Break down the door, and the token is yours.

☕ COFFEE BREAK COMPLETED

Reward: Gold brick

You can take a load off at the coffee stand underneath the giant teacup. It's right next to the fancy house. Well, where else would you expect to take a coffee break?

❀ DISGUISE BOOTH

Reward: Gold brick, "Waitress" character token

Find a disguise booth behind the fancy house.

☐ DISTRICT CONQUERED

Reward: Gold brick

Climb to the top of the tree house (POI 4), chop through the boarded door, then climb a ladder to reach the spot where you can raise this district's flag.

⛏ DRILL THRILL COMPLETED

Reward: Gold brick

The fuse box that fires up this event is attached to a short stone pillar at the south end of Crescent Park.

❁ FLOWERS WATERED

Reward: Gold brick

Go to the back of the fancy house and jetpack-jump onto the color swappers. Boost again to reach a patio, where you can water some thirsty flowers.

⌂ FREE RUN

Rewards: Gold brick, "Skater" character token

This might be the easiest free run in all of LEGO City. The token is in the center of the playground, and the free run course starts inside the playground, not far from where you grab the token.

ⓜ GANG ARRESTED

Reward: Gold brick

The hill behind the fancy house is a perfect spot to scan for criminal activity. Eavesdrop on a gang of troublemakers, then hurry to the gazebo and bust up the punks.

PIG RETURNED

Reward: Gold brick

Find the wall at the north edge of the park, and climb up the handholds at the far east end of the wall.

Cross the tightrope and perform chicken-glides to cross the top of the wall.

A pig is stuck on the wall's highest point. Hop onto the piggy and ride it to the nearby cannon.

SILVER STATUE DESTROYED

Reward: Gold brick

The Rex statue is on top of the gazebo in the middle of Crescent Park. Use the gazebo's transporter pad to reach the roof. You can find some dynamite at the fancy house (POI 3).

TRAIN STATION

Reward: Gold brick, fast travel

The train station is just north of the gazebo (POI 2). Smash the green cabinet and build the ticket machine to activate it.

RED BRICK

Reward: Super Ram

This red brick is tucked inside a shallow cave along the water. Chase will need to get a little wet to claim it. Hop into the ocean from the south side of the park, then swim until you find the cave.

VEHICLE ROBBERY COMPLETED

Reward: Gold brick, "T.R.E.V." vehicle token

The garage right next to the tree house (POI 4) has a sweet ride inside. Drop from the tree house and land on the garage's roof, then pry open the skylight to begin the challenge.

INTRODUCTION

POLICE ACADEMY

CHARACTERS AND VEHICLES

WALKTHROUGH

LEGO CITY TOUR

CHECKLISTS

CROSSTOWN TUNNEL

NOTE

There are no points of interest for this long tunnel, which serves as a shortcut through LEGO City's mainland.

FEATS AND COLLECTIBLES

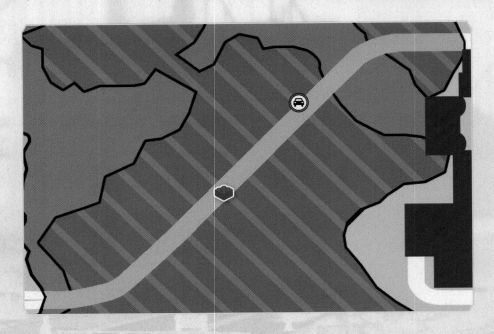

MAP LEGEND

MAP ICON(S)	FEAT/COLLECTIBLE	REWARD(S)	LOCATION/HOW TO REACH	GOT IT?
	Red Brick	Super Drill Ride	Behind a door only Rex Fury can open, along the maintenance walkway.	1
	Vehicle Token	Rex's Galican	Along the north walkway, behind a door only Rex Fury can rip open.	2

⭐ ⬢ RED BRICK

Reward: Super Drill Ride

You'll need Rex Fury for this one. Follow the walkway about halfway through the Crosstown Tunnel until you reach this spot.

Use Rex Fury to grab the orange handle and rip open the door. A red brick awaits inside.

⭐ 🚗 VEHICLE TOKEN

Reward: Rex's Galican

You need Rex Fury to get this token. Follow the walkway at the northern end of the Crosstown Tunnel to this door.

Have Rex grab the orange handle and use his mighty strength to tear the door free. A rare loose vehicle token is found inside the nook beyond.

INTRODUCTION

POLICE ACADEMY

CHARACTERS AND VEHICLES

WALKTHROUGH

LEGO CITY TOUR

CHECKLISTS

DOWNTOWN

POINTS OF INTEREST

⭐ 1 BANK

At the north end of downtown is a prestigious bank. To reach the top of the bank, you'll actually need to start far away.

Go to the alley behind the R.F.A. building, which is right behind the bull statue. Drill the shaky ground there and ride the water spout up to a ladder that leads to the roof.

Make your way onto the roof and toward the large billboard. Grab the handholds and ascend to the top of the billboard.

There's a chicken symbol here, which means it's time to chicken-glide. It's a long way to the bank, so hold on tightly to that chicken! After a long flight, you're on top of the bank.

⭐ 2 X AND Y BUILDINGS

In the northeast section of downtown, there are two buildings you'll use to get several the area's goodies.

Getting onto the X building is pretty easy. Head to the north corner of the X building and look for the shaky ground. Drill here to create a water spout.

There are a bunch of locked doors up here, most of which contain superbricks. Use the robber's crowbar to pad your brick bank account.

To reach the top of the Y building, water the planter out front, then climb up the sunflower. This won't get you onto the roof, though—that takes a little more effort.

To reach the Y building's roof, you'll actually have to go down in order to go up. Find the skylight and break into it with the robber's crowbar.

Drop through the skylight to land on the bottom floor of the Y building. Use the transporter pad down here to beam up to the Y building's roof.

⭐ 3 GLASS TOWER

The glass tower may be the most impressive-looking skyscraper in downtown. It's also one of the most useful.

At the base of the tower is a brown crate. Smash it and build a transporter pad.

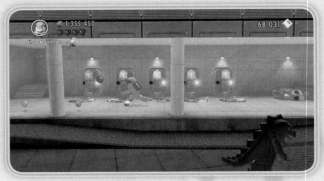

Use the transporter pad to beam into the glass tower's lobby. Here you'll find every color swapper imaginable, along with a dynamite dispenser. Handy!

The Top of the Tower

You'll also want to reach the top of this glass behemoth. To do this, you'll actually start on the roof of the tourist center. See the following "Tourist Center" section to learn how to get up there.

From the tourist center, make your way to this transporter pad. Use it and you'll appear above a tightrope.

When you fall onto the tightrope, you'll automatically slide across to a nearby billboard. Jetpack-jump to the roof across the street. Don't worry, you can make it!

Boost up to the higher section of rooftop and scale the scaffolding of a big billboard.

Make your way onto the tightrope and walk across to the glass building.

⭐ 4 TOURIST CENTER

From the air, this brick area, with two huts in the center, looks like a pig's snout. A dynamite dispenser is located here.

Run around the exterior brick wall and water a planter to grow a tall sunflower. Climb up to reach the roof. From there, you can jetpack-jump onto the huts or use a chicken symbol or a transporter pad to venture to new areas, such as the top of the Glass Tower (POI 3).

FEATS AND COLLECTIBLES

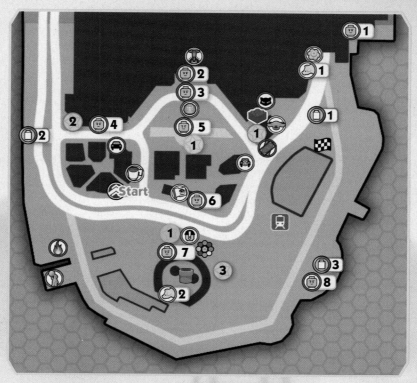

MAP LEGEND

MAP ICON(S)	FEAT/COLLECTIBLE	REWARD(S)	LOCATION/HOW TO REACH	GOT IT?
	Alien Caught	Gold brick	On the roof of the X building.	1
	ATM Smashed	Gold brick	In front of the X building.	2
	BBQ Fire Extinguished	Gold brick	Near the cannon, on the west end of downtown.	3
	Boulder Destroyed	Gold brick	Next to a tree, close to the bull statue.	4
	Cat Rescued	Gold brick	On top of the Y building.	5
1	Character Token 1	Jo Chalkley	Behind the Y building, in a little nook by a decorative cannon.	6
2	Character Token 2	Cacey	Near the top of the bank.	7
1 to 3 3	Character Token 3	Traffic Cop	Paint the three silver traffic post tops near the back yellow.	8
4	Character Token 4	Mime	On a ledge along the side of the bank.	9
1 5	Character Token 5	Minotaur	Paint the bull statue gold.	10
6	Character Token 6	Weather Girl	Next to the astronaut flag symbol atop the glass tower.	11
1 7	Character Token 7	Artist	Color the artist statue's painting.	12

INTRODUCTION

POLICE ACADEMY

CHARACTERS AND VEHICLES

WALKTHROUGH

LEGO CITY TOUR

CHECKLISTS

MAP LEGEND CONTINUED

MAP ICON(S)	FEAT/COLLECTIBLE	REWARD(S)	LOCATION/HOW TO REACH	GOT IT?
8	Character Token 8	Ringmaster	Superbuild the Ferris wheel to get this token to appear. Then drive a car through the center of the Ferris wheel.	13
	Coffee Break Completed	Gold brick	Found along the path of the free run course.	14
	Disguise Booth	Gold brick, "Hugh Hunter" character token	Near the artist statue.	15
	District Conquered	Gold brick	At the top of the glass tower.	16
	Drill Thrill Completed	Gold brick	On top of the bank.	17
	Flowers Watered	Gold brick	Right next to the Y building.	18
	Free Run	Gold brick, "Ninja" character token	The free run course is unlocked in Story mode. The course starts west of the glass tower.	19
	Gang Arrested	Gold brick	On the palette of the artist's statue.	20
1	Pig Returned 1	Gold brick	On the awnings that you reach by chicken-gliding from the Y building.	21
2	Pig Returned 2	Gold brick	Sitting on the roof of the tourist center.	22
	Red Brick	Wonder Whistle	Behind a locked door on the Y building.	23
	Silver Statue Destroyed	Gold brick	Right by the water on the west side of downtown.	24
1	Superbuild 1: Call-in Point	Gold brick, "Patrollo" vehicle token	On the east side of downtown, near the main street.	25
2	Superbuild 2: Call-in Point	Gold brick, "Earwig" vehicle token	On the far west side of downtown, along the water.	26
3	Superbuild 3: Ferris Wheel	Gold Brick	In the center of an empty plaza, by the bouncy castle.	27
	Time Trial	Gold brick, "Drakonas" vehicle token	On the east side, near the jetty.	28
	Train Station	Gold brick, fast travel	North of the Ferris wheel.	29
	Vehicle Robbery Completed	Gold brick, "Bearer" vehicle token	Inside a building just west of the bull statue.	30
	Vehicle Robber Arrested	Gold Brick, "Narym" vehicle token	On top of the billboard of a building near the glass tower.	31
	Warp Pipe	Fast Travel	Use Rex Fury to rip open the crate in the tourist center.	32

⭐ 🛸 ALIEN CAUGHT

Reward: Gold brick

Get to the roof of the Y building (POI 2), following the tips in the "Points of Interest" section. You'll find the alien invader space crate on the roof.

⭐ ⦿ ATM SMASHED

Reward: Gold brick

This is in front of the Y building, and easy to find.

⬢ BBQ FIRE EXTINGUISHED

Reward: Gold brick

The BBQ is all the way on the west end of downtown, near the cannon.

⬤ BOULDER DESTROYED

Reward: Gold brick

The special boulder is next to a tree near the bull statue.

🐱 CAT RESCUED

Reward: Gold brick

Get onto the X building (POI 2) with help from the "Points of Interest" section. Move left, past the numerous locked doors until you see a climbable wall.

Climb the wall and then use a wall runway to cross a gap and reach the kitty in need.

👤1 CHARACTER TOKEN 1

Reward: Jo Chalkley

This token is hidden behind the X building (POI 2), right at the border of Kings Court. There's a green cannon in front of the token, so look for that if you're having trouble spotting this one.

👤2 CHARACTER TOKEN 2

Reward: Cacey

Follow the steps in the "Points of Interest" section to get on top of the bank's roof. You'll collect this token after you land from your long chicken-glide.

👤3 CHARACTER TOKEN 3

Reward: Traffic Cop

Paint the tops of three silver traffic posts yellow to make this token appear. Check the map to see where the traffic posts are located.

INTRODUCTION

POLICE ACADEMY

CHARACTERS AND VEHICLES

WALKTHROUGH

LEGO CITY TOUR

CHECKLISTS

After you paint all three posts yellow, a character token appears in front of the bank.

⭐ 🪙4 CHARACTER TOKEN 4

Reward: Mime

Along the side of the bank is a climbable wall. Scale it to reach a narrow ledge.

Cross the ledge and climb another wall to reach a thin ledge. Inch over to some thin poles and hop across them.

Keep going until you reach a small nook with a character token. Score!

⭐ 🪙5 CHARACTER TOKEN 5

Reward: Minotaur

Blast the bull statue in downtown with gold coloring, and this token will appear right in front of it. Remember, every color swapper you could ever need is in the lobby of the glass tower (POI 3).

⭐ 🪙6 CHARACTER TOKEN 6

Reward: Weather Girl

Follow the instructions in the "Points of Interest" section to reach the top of the glass tower, where this token awaits.

⭐ 🪙7 CHARACTER TOKEN 7

Reward: Artist

Near the tourist center (POI 4), finish the artist statue's painting with the color gun. Paint the head yellow and the shirt red to make a character token appear nearby.

⭐ 🪙8 CHARACTER TOKEN 8

Reward: Ringmaster

You must construct the Ferris wheel superbuild to make this token appear. Once you build the Ferris wheel, hop into a car and launch off the ramp in front of it. You'll soar through the center of the wheel, nabbing a character token!

COFFEE BREAK COMPLETED

Reward: Gold brick

Getting a quick coffee break takes quite a lot of work in downtown. Start at the free run challenge marker, where you'll see a climbable wall and some handholds. Make your way up.

Leap from flagpole to flagpole as you head left.

Cross a tightrope, vault a few beams, then step onto a catapult pad to launch yourself up to the next building.

Scale the climbable wall up to the next level of this building and head to the right. See that brick wall full of handholds? Leap over to it.

Run around a metal ledge and perform a wall-jump to reach the drainpipe on the adjacent building.

Once on the roof, hop up a series of thin poles to reach a tightrope that leads to the final building.

Keep heading right to at last find the most well-hidden coffee spot in all of LEGO City!

DISGUISE BOOTH

Reward: Gold brick, "Hugh Hunter" character token

Downtown's disguise booth is located near the artist statue and tourist center (POI 4).

DISTRICT CONQUERED

Reward: Gold brick

Use the previous "Points of Interest" section to learn how to reach the top of the glass tower (POI 3). Follow those instructions and you'll find a perfect spot to plant your flag.

DRILL THRILL COMPLETED

Reward: Gold brick

Use the "Points of Interest" section to learn how to glide onto the bank (POI 1), then shimmy across the handhold on the right and climb the wall to reach the bank's roof.

INTRODUCTION

POLICE ACADEMY

CHARACTERS AND VEHICLES

WALKTHROUGH

LEGO CITY TOUR

CHECKLISTS

The fuse box that kick-starts this drill thrill event is located on the bank's roof.

FLOWERS WATERED

Reward: Gold brick

Downtown's flower bed is in the upper north part of the zone, next to the X building.

FREE RUN

Rewards: Gold brick, "Ninja" character token

There's no need to collect a free run token in downtown—playing through Story mode unlocks this district's free run course. Find the free run's starting point by a group of buildings just west of the glass tower.

GANG ARRESTED

Reward: Gold brick

Get onto the roof of the tourist center and find the chicken symbol. Glide onto the artist statue's palette, where you find the audio scan symbol that triggers this event.

PIG RETURNED 1

Reward: Gold brick

Using the "Points of Interest" section to guide you, get onto the roof of Y building (POI 2). Activate a chicken symbol up here and make a long glide toward a series of awnings.

Carefully cross the awnings to reach the pig. The closest cannon is actually north, in Kings Court, but you can always stick to downtown and return the pig via the cannon on the zone's west side.

PIG RETURNED 2

Reward: Gold brick

Get onto the roof of the tourist center (POI 4) by growing a sunflower from a planter, then make your way around until you spot this zone's other lost pig.

RED BRICK

Reward: Wonder Whistle

Get up onto the X building (POI 2) with the help of the "Points of Interest" section. The red brick is behind a door with a crowbar symbol. Crack it open to grab your goody.

SILVER STATUE DESTROYED

Reward: Gold brick

Head into the lobby of the glass tower (POI 3) and get some dynamite out of the dispenser. Mosey over to the west side of downtown, toward the water, and blow up the Rex statue.

SUPERBUILD 1: CALL-IN POINT

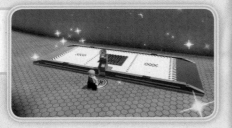

Reward: Gold brick, "Patrollo" vehicle token

The superbuild is on the east side of downtown, near the main street.

SUPERBUILD 2: CALL-IN POINT

Reward: Gold brick, "Earwig" vehicle token

This superbuild is on the far west side of downtown, along the water.

SUPERBUILD 3: FERRIS WHEEL

Reward: Gold brick

This superbuild is in the center of a very empty plaza. Drop a ton of bricks and add something of interest to go with the bouncy castle.

TIME TRIAL

Reward: Gold brick, "Drakonas" vehicle token

The time trial is on the east side, near the jetty. The race takes you all around downtown.

TRAIN STATION

Reward: Gold brick, fast travel

Downtown's train station lies north of the plaza where you build the Ferris wheel. Smash the green cabinet and build its bricks into a ticket machine to activate downtown's train station. Now you can quickly travel here and access the vast array of color swappers found within the glass tower (POI 3)!

INTRODUCTION

POLICE ACADEMY

CHARACTERS AND VEHICLES

WALKTHROUGH

LEGO CITY TOUR

CHECKLISTS

VEHICLE ROBBERY COMPLETED

Reward: Gold brick, "Bearer" vehicle token

Pry open the door of the garage west of the bull statue to begin this frantic vehicle robbery event.

VEHICLE ROBBER ARRESTED

Reward: Gold brick, "Narym" vehicle token

To reach this event, start out like you're going to glide over to the bank rooftop (POI 1), using the "Points of Interest" section for help. But instead of climbing the billboard with the chicken-glide symbol, head left and cross a tightrope.

Once across, wall-jump up the narrow walls that follow, heading to a roof with a crash mat.

Ignore the crash mat and instead climb a few handholds to reach the top of the nearby billboard. Activate the chicken symbol up there and glide over to another building.

Climb up to another billboard with handholds that lead to a criminal scan spot. Use the scan spot and then hurry after that vehicle thief!

WARP PIPE

Reward: Fast travel

Use the incredible strength of Rex Fury to rip open the crate in the tourist center.

Bricks spill out from the crate—build them into a warp pipe. Neat-o! Hop into the warp pipe to travel to (and unlock) Lady Liberty Island.

FESTIVAL SQUARE

POINTS OF INTEREST

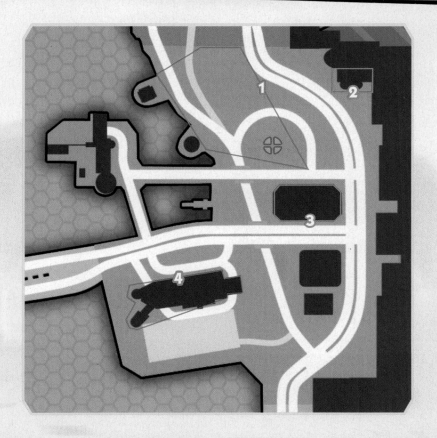

INTRODUCTION

POLICE ACADEMY

CHARACTERS AND VEHICLES

WALKTHROUGH

LEGO CITY TOUR

CHECKLISTS

☆ 1 CARNIVAL GAMES

It wouldn't be a festival without some carnival games. Merry-go-rounds, bouncy castles, and much more await!

☆ 2 LEGO CITY GYM

You won't get much of a workout at the LEGO City Gym, which is located just north of the carnival games, but you will find some extracurricular activities.

To get into the gym, you'll need to find this trio of pig balloons on the lawn. Smash the blue barrel on the ground nearby and build a trampoline, then bounce up onto the first pig balloon.

Bounce your way from one pig balloon to the next until you reach a roof. Go to the back ledge and follow it to the right, leaping onto the weight-lifter sign as you circle around the building.

Flip from a flagpole to reach the final ledge. From here, you can leap down to the lower roof with a lost pig and skylight. Pry open the latter to enter the gym.

Bounce up to a ledge, then go either left or right, circling around the building until you reach a planter. Water the pot and make your way up the vines to the climbable wall.

Use a drainpipe to climb even higher up the mega building. Circle around the building again and build another trampoline to bound up higher still.

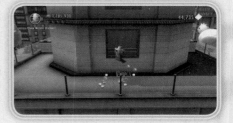

After a bit more climbing, you can hop onto the roof of one of Festival Square's tallest buildings.

⭐ ③ MEGA BUILDING

Festival Square doesn't have much in the way of tall buildings, so this impressive structure really stands out. As impressive as it is to look at from the ground, it's even more so from the roof.

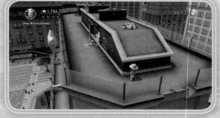

From the ground floor of the mega building, look for this fenced off construction area. Vault the fence and smash a barrel, then build a trampoline from its bricks.

⭐ ④ MERCY HEARTS HOSPITAL

Even the best of the boys in blue get sick in LEGO City. Fortunately, there's a big hospital in Festival Square for recovery. There's plenty to do around the hospital, even if you're not ill.

Look for this open garage door and head to the elevator. This is the elevator that Chase activates during Story mode while racing to save Natalia.

The elevator takes you to the second floor, where there's a dynamite dispenser. Go right and climb a tall sunflower to get up to the third floor.

Go left, across the top of the glass tunnel, and you'll reach the hospital tower. Wall-bounce your way to the top, just as you did in Story mode.

Vault a few beams as you continue to the right. Climb the blue and white LEGO patch on the far wall to reach the fourth floor.

Now you're king of the world! Or, at least, this hospital.

INTRODUCTION

POLICE ACADEMY

CHARACTERS AND VEHICLES

WALKTHROUGH

LEGO CITY TOUR

CHECKLISTS

FEATS AND COLLECTIBLES

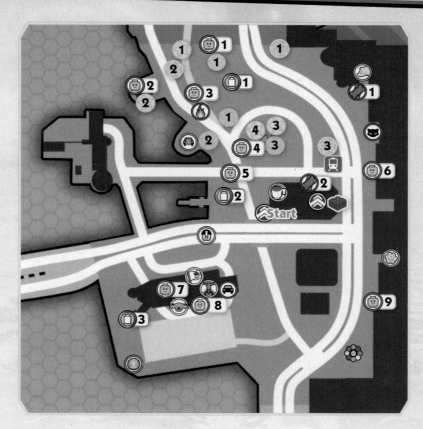

MAP LEGEND

MAP ICON(S)	FEAT/COLLECTIBLE	REWARD(S)	LOCATION/HOW TO REACH	GOT IT?
Alien Caught	Gold brick	On a ledge above the first floor of the hospital.	1
1 ATM Smashed 1	Gold brick	Near the LEGO City Gym.	2
2 ATM Smashed 2	Gold brick	On the north side of the mega building.	3

MAP LEGEND CONTINUED

MAP ICON(S)	FEAT/COLLECTIBLE	REWARD(S)	LOCATION/HOW TO REACH	GOT IT?
	BBQ Fire Extinguished	Gold brick	Along the street, near the carnival games.	4
	Boulder Destroyed	Gold brick	In the back corner of the hospital parking lot.	5
	Cat Rescued	Gold brick	Close to the LEGO City Gym.	6
1 1	Character Token 1	Sumo Wrestler	Jump five times inside the bouncy castle to make this token appear.	7
2	Character Token 2	Vinnie Clown	Inside the clock tower.	8
1 to 4 3	Character Token 3	Circus Clown	Paint the balloons red and yellow to unlock this token.	9
1 to 3 4	Character Token 4	Weight lifter	Show you're a strong man by ringing the three bells in the carnival games.	10
1 to 3 5	Character Token 5	Gorilla Suit Guy	Paint the three basketball backboards red, then win nine games of hoops.	11
6	Character Token 6	Doctor Jones	On top of the theater awning.	12
7	Character Token 7	Natalia Kowalski	Behind the boarded up door on the hospital rooftop.	13
8	Character Token 8	Surgeon	Grapple to get above the front door of the hospital.	14
9	Character Token 9	Tribal Chief	Inside the bookstore.	15
	Coffee Break Completed	Gold brick	At the ground floor of the mega building, near where you build the trampoline.	16
	Disguise Booth	Gold brick, "Doctor Smith" character token	Near the main street, in the southeast end of Festival Square.	17
	District Conquered	Gold brick	At the top of the hospital tower.	18
	Drill Thrill Completed	Gold brick	Next to the glass walkway on the second floor of the hospital.	19
	Flowers Watered	Gold brick	In an alley at the far east end of Festival Square.	20
	Free Run	Gold brick, "Robot" character token	At the very top of the mega building.	21
	Gang Arrested	Gold brick	On the snout of the alligator balloon floating over Festival Square.	22
	Pig Returned	Gold brick	Next to the skylight entrance to get into the LEGO City Gym.	23
	Red Brick	Larger Vehicle Boost	Hidden on the far end of the roof of the mega building, out of sight.	24
1	Superbuild 1: Deep Sea Spin	Gold brick, "Deep Sea Diver" character token	In the center of the carnival games.	25
2	Superbuild 2: Call-in Point	Gold brick, "Douser" vehicle token	Near the water, next to the freeway.	26
3	Superbuild 3: Helipad	Gold brick	This helipad, at the hospital, is unlocked in Story mode.	27
	Train Station	Gold brick, Fast Travel	To the north of the mega building.	28
	Vehicle Robbery Completed	Gold brick, "Panacea" vehicle token	The garage is at the east end of the hospital.	29
	Vehicle Robber Arrested	Gold brick, "Inferno" vehicle token	At the top of the lighthouse.	30

INTRODUCTION

POLICE ACADEMY

CHARACTERS AND VEHICLES

WALKTHROUGH

LEGO CITY TOUR

CHECKLISTS

★ ◉ ALIEN CAUGHT

Reward: Gold brick

Find the low grapple point over the front door of the hospital (POI 4). Grapple up to a low ledge and run to the left to find a space crate. Enter the pattern shown to reveal the alien menace.

★ ⦾1 ATM SMASHED 1

Reward: Gold brick

This ATM is tucked in a corner next to the LEGO City Gym (POI 2).

★ ⦾2 ATM SMASHED 2

Reward: Gold brick

Go to the north side of the mega building (POI 3) to find this ATM.

★ ◉ BBQ FIRE EXTINGUISHED

Reward: Gold brick

The BBQ is along the street near the carnival games (POI 1). People are probably using it to cook food, but fires are dangerous. Best to put this one out.

★ ◉ BOULDER DESTROYED

Reward: Gold brick

The special boulder is in the southwest corner of the hospital parking lot (POI 4).

★ ◉ CAT RESCUED

Reward: Gold brick

This one's a cake walk. Find the kitty on the east side of Festival Square, near the LEGO City Gym (POI 2).

★ ◉1 CHARACTER TOKEN 1

Reward: Sumo Wrestler

Jump five times inside this bouncy castle, and a character token will appear overhead. Hold down the Jump button to get high jumps, just like you would on a trampoline.

★ ◉2 CHARACTER TOKEN 2

Reward: Vinnie Clown

Before you start this, make sure you have gold paint loaded in your color gun. Find some inside the glass tower in the downtown district. Once your color gun's loaded, head to the giant clock tower and climb the ladder at its base.

Use the transporter pad behind the tower to teleport to the top of the nearby tented lighthouse—and right onto a chicken-glide symbol. Make a long glide over to the clock tower's top.

Paint the silver clock face gold and it will open up, exposing a shaft. Jump into the tower and fall down the shaft to land right atop the character token!

⭐ 🔲3 CHARACTER TOKEN 3

Reward: Circus Clown

Notice the bunches of balloons around the carnival games area (POI 1). Most of them have a red, green, yellow, and blue balloon, except for four bunches that have an odd silver balloon. Paint each of these silver balloons either red, blue, yellow, or green to make them more colorful. If you don't have the Super Color Gun red brick, you can find every color swapper in the glass tower in downtown.

After you color all four balloons, a character token appears above the steps here.

⭐ 🔲4 CHARACTER TOKEN 4

Reward: Weightlifter

Ring the three strongman bells around the carnival games (POI 1) to flex Chase's muscles.

A character token appears here after you ring all three strongman bells.

⭐ 🔲5 CHARACTER TOKEN 5

Reward: Gorilla Suit Guy

There are three sets of three basketball hoops around the carnival games area (POI 1). Paint the three silver basketball backboards red so that you can use them, then play and win all three games at all three sets (nine games in total).

After winning all nine games of hoops, the character token appears under the freeway. Wall-jump onto the overhead LEGO patch, then shimmy over and snatch it.

⬤6 CHARACTER TOKEN 6

Reward: Doctor Jones

It takes some work to reach this token. Start by heading to the east side of Festival Square and looking for these narrow LEGO walls. Bounce between the walls and up to a handhold.

Navigate the series of beams and thin ledges as you deftly maneuver around the building.

Keep going until you reach a drainpipe that takes you up to solid ground.

Vault over and slide under the beams as you sprint to the left, heading for a tightrope. Slide down to reach an awning, where the character token awaits.

⬤7 CHARACTER TOKEN 7

Reward: Natalia Kowalski

Go to the roof of the hospital's main tower (POI 4) and chop through a boarded door to discover a hidden token. Check the "Points of Interest" section for help on navigating the hospital.

⬤8 CHARACTER TOKEN 8

Reward: Surgeon

Go to the front door of the hospital (POI 4), on the side with the parking lot. There's a grapple point just above the door. Use the policeman's grapple gun to get up, then go right to find this token out in the open.

⬤9 CHARACTER TOKEN 9

Reward: Tribal Chief

Use the robber to break into the bookstore on the east side of Festival Square. The token is at the store's other end, visible through the window.

☕ COFFEE BREAK COMPLETED

Reward: Gold brick

Vault over the fence that blocks off the construction at the foot of the mega building (POI 3), and you'll find a coffee break spot where you build the trampoline.

⚙ DISGUISE BOOTH

Reward: Gold brick, "Doctor Smith" character token

Look for the disguise booth near the main street in the southeast end of Festival Square.

INTRODUCTION

POLICE ACADEMY

CHARACTERS AND VEHICLES

WALKTHROUGH

LEGO CITY TOUR

CHECKLISTS

PRIMA OFFICIAL GAME GUIDE

DISTRICT CONQUERED

Reward: Gold brick

Follow the instructions in the "Points of Interest" section to reach the top of the hospital tower (POI 4). The flag spot is above a boarded door—use an astronaut to boost up and place your flag.

DRILL THRILL COMPLETED

Reward: Gold brick

Following the instructions in the "Points of Interest" section, make your way to the second floor of the hospital (POI 4). Fix the fuse box near the shattered glass walkway, then have fun drilling!

FLOWERS WATERED

Reward: Gold brick

Find this flower box in an alley at the far east end of Festival Square.

FREE RUN

Rewards: Gold brick, "Robot" character token

Get to the top of the mega building (POI 3), using the "Points of Interest" section to guide you. Once there, chop through a boarded door and step onto the transporter pad inside.

Teleport and then run forward, vaulting beams and hopping across thin poles on your way to the free run token.

The free run challenge starts way down below, in front of the fenced-off area at the mega building's base.

GANG ARRESTED

Reward: Gold brick

Start on the roof of the mega building (POI 3). Activate a chicken-glide symbol up here, then make a long glide onto a giant chicken balloon.

Giant balloons are bouncy—be careful not to fall, or you'll have to start all over again! Walk the tightrope from the chicken balloon to the shark balloon, then keep bouncing from one giant balloon to the next, using another tightrope and a handhold as you go.

Get to the alligator balloon, then bounce up to its head, where an audio scan spot is located. Eavesdrop on the gang activity, then hurry to the carnival games (POI 1) and bust up the punks.

342 primagames.com

PIG RETURNED

Reward: Gold brick

Get to the secret entrance into the LEGO City Gym (POI 2), using the "Points of Interest" section to guide you. Right next to the skylight entrance is the pig. Ride the little guy over to the cannon near the carnival games (POI 1).

RED BRICK

Reward: Larger Vehicle Boost

Use the "Points of Interest" section to reach the top of the mega building (POI 3). You can see the red brick, but just run around behind the brick enclosure with the free run token on top, and you'll collect it.

SUPERBUILD 1: DEEP SEA SPIN

Reward: Gold brick, "Deep Sea Diver" character token

In the center of the carnival games (POI 1) is an important superbuild. After all, it's not a carnival without an octopus ride!

SUPERBUILD 2: CALL-IN POINT

Reward: Gold brick, "Douser" vehicle token

This superbuild is near the water, next to the freeway.

SUPERBUILD 3: HELIPAD

Reward: Gold brick

This superbuild is constructed during Story mode. Chase builds this helipad atop the hospital (POI 4) and then uses a helicopter to fly Natalia to safety.

TRAIN STATION

Reward: Gold brick, fast travel

The train station is just north of the mega building.

VEHICLE ROBBERY COMPLETED

Reward: Gold brick, "Panacea" vehicle token

Look for this garage on the east end of the hospital. Pry open the door and make off with those wheels!

VEHICLE ROBBER ARRESTED

Reward: Gold brick, "Inferno" vehicle token

Near the carnival games, along the water, is a festive-looking lighthouse. Walk into the front door to reach the top of the lighthouse stairs, where you'll find a scan spot. Search for the car thief, then race to stop him.

INTRODUCTION

POLICE ACADEMY

CHARACTERS AND VEHICLES

WALKTHROUGH

LEGO CITY TOUR

CHECKLISTS

FORT MEADOWS

POINTS OF INTEREST

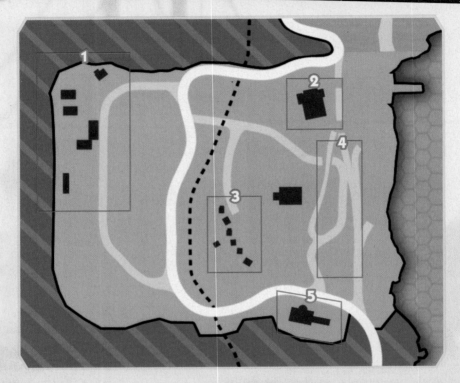

⭐ 1 JETHRO HAYES'S FARM

Farmer Hayes tends a pretty impressive farm here in Fort Meadows. Chase visits Jethro during Story mode and spends quite a bit of time here on the farm, chasing down lost pigs.

Several secrets can be found around this place, including a pair of useful color swappers (a blue one and a yellow one) that are stashed in the barn. You can also climb around the rooftops just as you did in Story mode.

⭐ 2 CASTLE

This towering old castle has stood watch over Fort Meadows for ages. Chase can use this great structure as a playground, scaling it to reach a number of goodies hidden atop its high walls. Simply climb the vines at the castle's base to begin your ascent, just like you did during Story mode.

⭐ ③ CABINS

A collection of cabins covers the hilltop here. Chase can climb onto their roofs by performing jetpack jumps or by growing plants and climbing them. Tightropes connect many of the cabins, letting Chase cross from one roof to the next. Chase can also break into some of the cabins using a robber disguise's crowbar or the firefighter's axe.

⭐ ④ SPIDERWEB CAVE

Secrets are concealed within this webby cave. To enter the cave, collect some dynamite from the dispenser near the gas station, then use it to blast away the rubble at the cave's south entrance.

Use the scan spot inside the cave to discover more dynamite, then blast the nearby silver boulders to create another opening that leads out to the east beach. Return for more dynamite and blast the silver boulders at the cave's north end to create yet another opening out to fresh air.

⭐ ⑤ GAS STATION

This colorful gas station doubles as a diner and is the same one that Chase visits early on in Story mode. You can find a number of goodies around the station.

Smash the small blue bike rack near the vehicle call-in point, then build its bricks to add a patch of blue and white LEGOs to the back of the nearby billboard.

Climb the LEGOs to reach a chicken symbol atop the billboard. Activate the symbol, then glide over to the gas station's roof. This is the only way to reach the goodies up here.

INTRODUCTION

POLICE ACADEMY

CHARACTERS AND VEHICLES

WALKTHROUGH

LEGO CITY TOUR

CHECKLISTS

FEATS AND COLLECTIBLES

MAP LEGEND

MAP ICON(S)	FEAT/COLLECTIBLE	REWARD(S)	LOCATION/HOW TO REACH	GOT IT?
	Alien Caught	Gold brick	Inside the spiderweb cave.	1
	ATM Smashed	Gold brick	Near the gas station.	2
	BBQ Fire Extinguished	Gold brick	North of Jethro Hayes's Farm	3
	Boulder Destroyed	Gold brick	Inside the spiderweb cave.	4
	Cat Rescued	Gold brick	Build the Lumberjack's Log Cabin superbuild, then climb onto the roof and cross the tightrope.	5
1 to 3 / 1	Character Token 1	Highland Battler	Paint three wheelbarrows blue around the zone.	6
2	Character Token 2	The Monster	Climb to the top of the castle, chop through the boarded door, build the catapult pad, launch to the flagpole.	7
3	Character Token 3	Rooster	Jetpack jump up and climb the blue and white LEGO patch on the wall under the elevated train tracks.	8
4	Character Token 4	Cave Woman	Smash a rock inside the spiderweb cave.	9
5	Character Token 5	Farm Worker Bob	Water a planter near the sawmill, then climb the sunflower to reach the token on its roof.	10
1 to 3 / 6	Character Token 6	Stinky Fletcher	Paint three hay bales yellow around the farm and fields.	11
7	Character Token 7	Dougy Dungarees	Inside the cabin with the crowbar door.	12

MAP LEGEND CONTINUED

MAP ICON(S)	FEAT/COLLECTIBLE	REWARD(S)	LOCATION/HOW TO REACH	GOT IT?
1 to 3 8	Character Token 8	Bea Heckerson	Smash three yellow hay bales around Farmer Hayes's fields, then build their bricks into scarecrows.	13
9	Character Token 9	Lumberjack	Inside the Lumberjack's Log Cabin (must construct the superbuild).	14
10	Character Token 10	Buddy Weingartner	Inside the cabin with the boarded door.	15
11	Character Token 11	Farm Worker Bill	Jetpack jump onto a cabin's roof, then cross a tightrope to reach the token in the nearby tree.	16
12	Character Token 12	Train Driver Bob	Inside the train station's waiting booth (must build the train station).	17
1	Coffee Break 1	Gold brick	In the middle of Farmer Hayes's field.	18
2	Coffee Break 2	Gold brick	Near the sawmill.	19
	Disguise Booth	Gold brick, "Gas Station Manager" character token	Near the gas station.	20
	District Conquered	Gold brick	Atop the gas station (glide from the billboard).	21
	Drill Thrill	Gold brick	At the sawmill.	22
	Flowers Watered	Gold brick	Behind Farmer Hayes's barn (west side).	23
	Free Run	Gold brick, "Vampire" character token	Start at the base of the castle and climb to the top. No free run token—the event is unlocked during Story mode.	24
	Gang Arrested	Gold brick, "Vampire" character token	Scan spot atop the hay bales near Jethro Hayes's Farm.	25
	Pig Returned	Gold brick	Atop the gas station (glide from the billboard).	26
	Red Brick	Data Scan Upgrade: Tokens	Hidden in a pile of boulders inside the spiderweb cave.	27
	Silver Statue Destroyed	Gold brick	Atop the south train tunnel entrance (chicken-glide from the roof of a cabin to the north).	28
1	Superbuild 1: Call-in Point	Gold brick, "Torsion" vehicle token	Along the north road.	29
2	Superbuild 2: Lumberjack's Log Cabin	Gold brick	Among the cabins on the hill.	30
3	Superbuild 3: Fort Meadows Train Station	Gold brick	Along the train tracks, to the south.	31
4	Superbuild 4: Emergency Crash Mat	Gold brick, "Slicker" vehicle token	Atop the south train tunnel entrance (chicken-glide from the roof of a cabin to the north).	32
5	Superbuild 5: Call-in Point	Gold brick, "Trooper" vehicle token	Near the gas station (built during Story mode progression).	33
	Time Trial	Gold brick, "Armadillo" vehicle token	The tractor near Farmer Hayes's field.	34
	Train Station	Gold brick, fast travel	Along the train tracks, to the south.	35

INTRODUCTION

POLICE ACADEMY

CHARACTERS AND VEHICLES

WALKTHROUGH

LEGO CITY TOUR

CHECKLISTS

ALIEN CAUGHT

Reward: Gold brick

Blast your way into the spiderweb cave (POI 4) to find the space crate that summons this zone's alien invader.

ATM SMASHED

Reward: Gold brick

Smash up the ATM near the gas station (POI 5) to score lots of studs and a shiny gold brick.

BBQ FIRE EXTINGUISHED

Reward: Gold brick

A BBQ fire is burning away at the north end of Jethro Hayes's farm (POI 1). This open flame is unsafe with so much hay around, so douse the BBQ fire with a spurt from a firefighter's extinguisher.

BOULDER DESTROYED

Reward: Gold brick

Blast your way into the spiderweb cave (POI 4). You'll find a special boulder hidden inside.

CAT RESCUED

Reward: Gold brick

Construct the Lumberjack's Log Cabin superbuild at the cabins (POI 3), then grow a tall sunflower out of a planter that sits on the porch. Climb up to the cabin's roof, then step onto the branch of the nearby tree and help a hapless kitty climb down to safety.

1 CHARACTER TOKEN 1

Reward: Highland Battler

Visit Farmer Hayes's farm (POI 1) and fill your color gun with blue energy, then blast three colorless wheelbarrows around Fort Meadows to paint them all blue. One of the wheelbarrows is atop the castle (POI 2).

After you paint all three wheelbarrows blue, a character token appears at the farm (POI 1).

2 CHARACTER TOKEN 2

Reward: The Monster

Climb to the top of the castle (POI 2), then chop through a boarded door and build a catapult pad from the bricks that tumble out. Use the pad to launch over to the nearby flagpole, which Chase slides down in heroic fashion, collecting a character token as he goes.

⭐ 🔵3 CHARACTER TOKEN 3

Reward: Rooster

This character token hovers on high beneath the elevated train tracks to the west of the castle. To reach it, perform a jetpack jump to grab the blue and white LEGO patch on the wall under the elevated tracks, then climb up to the token.

⭐ 🔵4 CHARACTER TOKEN 4

Reward: Cave Woman

Blast open the spiderweb cave (POI 4), then smash a rock near the north silver boulders to discover a hidden character token.

⭐ 🔵5 CHARACTER TOKEN 5

Reward: Farm Worker Bob

Water a planter near the sawmill to grow a tall sunflower, then climb up to reach the mill's tin roof. Snatch the character token you discover up here.

⭐ 🔵6 CHARACTER TOKEN 6

Reward: Stinky Fletcher

Visit Farmer Hayes's farm (POI 1) and fill your color gun with yellow energy, then blast three colorless hay bales around the farm to color them all yellow.

After you paint all three hay bales yellow, a character token appears in a field here.

⭐ 🔵7 CHARACTER TOKEN 7

Reward: Dougy Dungarees

Crowbar your way into one of the cabins on the hill (POI 3). You'll find a character token inside.

⭐ 🔵8 CHARACTER TOKEN 8

Reward: Bea Heckerson

Smash three yellow hay bales around Farmer Hayes's fields, then build their bricks into scarecrows.

After you build all three scarecrows, a character token appears near a couple of trees in a field.

INTRODUCTION

POLICE ACADEMY

CHARACTERS AND VEHICLES

WALKTHROUGH

LEGO CITY TOUR

CHECKLISTS

9 CHARACTER TOKEN 9

Reward: Lumberjack

After constructing the Lumberjack's Log Cabin superbuild, pry open the cabin's door and claim the character token that's stashed inside. This token doesn't appear until you build the Lumberjack's Log Cabin.

10 CHARACTER TOKEN 10

Reward: Buddy Weingartner

Chop through the boarded door of one of the cabins (POI 3), then enter the cabin and claim the character token within.

11 CHARACTER TOKEN 11

Reward: Farm Worker Bill

Perform a jetpack jump to reach the roof of one of the cabins (POI 3). Head south and tiptoe across a tightrope to reach a character token that hovers above a tree.

12 CHARACTER TOKEN 12

Reward: Train Driver Bob

Complete the Fort Meadows Train Station superbuild, then walk into the small waiting booth to claim a character token. You can't collect this token until you construct the superbuild.

1 COFFEE BREAK COMPLETED 1

Reward: Gold brick

This first coffee station stands in the middle of one of Farmer Hayes's fields. Stroll right up and enjoy a hot cup.

2 COFFEE BREAK COMPLETED 2

Reward: Gold brick

The zone's second coffee station is located near the sawmill. Take another break and earn another gold brick in the process.

DISGUISE BOOTH

Reward: Gold brick, "Gas Station Manager" character token

Smash the police crate near the gas station, then build its bricks into a disguise booth.

⭐ DISTRICT CONQUERED

Reward: Gold brick

Climb to the top of the gas station's roof, where you can raise this zone's flag.

⭐ DRILL THRILL COMPLETED

Reward: Gold brick

Fix the fuse box at the sawmill to fire up this zone's drill thrill event.

⭐ FLOWERS WATERED

Reward: Gold brick

Check behind Farmer Hayes's farm to find a plant box that can be watered to grow some flowers.

⭐ FREE RUN

Rewards: Gold brick, "Vampire" character token

This free run is unlocked during Story mode—there's no free run token to collect. Head to the castle (POI 2) and make your way to the top, climbing the vines and handholds as you did during Story mode to reach one of Farmer Hayes's pigs.

⭐ GANG ARRESTED

Reward: Gold brick

Climb to the top of the hay bales near Jethro Hayes's farm (POI 1) to reach an audio scan spot. Listen in on some scheming wackos who are planning to smash up the sawmill. Hightail it over there and teach those creeps a lesson!

⭐ PIG RETURNED

Reward: Gold brick

Glide to the top of the gas station's roof to discover a pig in distress. There's no way to bring the little piggy up to the cannon atop the castle, but that's okay—just ride over to Jethro Hayes's farm and drop off the pig at the pen!

⭐ ⬢ RED BRICK

Reward: Data Scan Upgrade—Tokens

Blast your way into the spiderweb cave, then smash a pile of boulders inside the cave to discover this zone's red brick.

⭐ SILVER STATUE DESTROYED

Reward: Gold brick

A silver Rex statue stands atop the south train tunnel. To reach it, perform a long chicken-glide from the roof of one of the cabins to the north (POI 3). Just make sure to bring some dynamite with you!

INTRODUCTION

POLICE ACADEMY

CHARACTERS AND VEHICLES

WALKTHROUGH

LEGO CITY TOUR

CHECKLISTS

SUPERBUILD 1: CALL-IN POINT

Reward: Gold brick, "Torsion" vehicle token

Build a call-in point here, and you'll be rewarded with a gold brick and a vehicle token.

SUPERBUILD 2: LUMBERJACK'S LOG CABIN

Reward: Gold brick

Build a lovely cabin that fits in with the rest of the cabins atop the hill (POI 3). Afterward, you can break into the cabin to claim a character token and use its roof to reach a trapped cat.

SUPERBUILD 3: FORT MEADOWS TRAIN STATION

Reward: Gold brick

Part with some bricks and construct a train station at the superbuild along the train tracks. As a bonus, you can enter the station's waiting booth afterward and claim a character token.

SUPERBUILD 4: EMERGENCY CRASH MAT

Reward: Gold brick, "Slicker" vehicle token

This superbuild lies atop the zone's south train tunnel. To reach it, perform a long chicken-glide from the roof of one of the cabins to the north. Then drop a few bricks to build a crash mat up here.

SUPERBUILD 5: CALL-IN POINT

Reward: Gold brick, "Trooper" vehicle token

This superbuild is constructed early in Story mode—it's the call-in point that Chase builds near the gas station (POI 5).

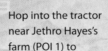 TIME TRIAL

Reward: Gold brick, "Armadillo" vehicle token

Hop into the tractor near Jethro Hayes's farm (POI 1) to partake in a wild race around Fort Meadows. You'll see all the zone's most scenic spots as you speed from one checkpoint to the next.

TRAIN STATION

Reward: Gold brick, fast travel

Activate this train station by completing a superbuild in Fort Meadows. Now it won't take you so long to get here the next time you want to visit Farmer Hayes!

FRESCO

INTRODUCTION

POLICE ACADEMY

CHARACTERS AND VEHICLES

WALKTHROUGH

LEGO CITY TOUR

CHECKLISTS

⭐ POINTS OF INTEREST

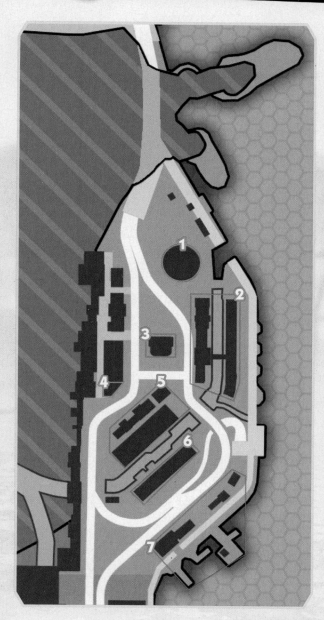

⭐ 1 LEANING TOWER

Who needs Pisa? LEGO City has its own magnificent leaning tower. As long as you're not scared of heights or things that lean, be sure to head up the spiraling walkway to the top.

⭐ 2 LITTLE VENICE: NORTH APARTMENTS

To get to the roofs of the north apartments, you first need to find the flower pot across the street from the disguise booth. Water it and climb up the sunflower to reach a balcony.

Cross the balcony and traverse a thin ledge, leaping through the far window.

Run down the hall and use the far transporter pad.

This teleports you onto the roof of the north apartments. You'll find plenty to do on these rooftops.

Head left along a thin ledge, until you reach a drainpipe. Climb the pipe to reach the roof.

To get inside the greenhouse, go right until you see a space crate. Ignore that for now, and jump onto the nearby awnings instead to reach the higher section of roof.

Head left and cross a tightrope to reach the roof of the greenhouse. Use the transporter pad to teleport inside the greenhouse, where you can snag a red brick.

⭐ ③ PAPPALARDO'S ICE CREAM PARLOUR

Pappalardo put Fresco on the map with his delicious Italian ice cream. You can't get a scoop, but you can at least admire the building. There are pink and brown color swappers on either side of the building as well.

⭐ ④ GREENHOUSE

This large apartment block has an expansive roof, highlighted by a large greenhouse.

To reach the roof, you'll need to find this flower pot on the south end of the building. Use the farmer to water the flower and climb it to get onto the awning.

⭐ ⑤ LITTLE VENICE: SOUTH APARTMENTS A

The south apartments have so much going on that they have two totally different access points. Block A is on the west side of the canal.

To get onto the rooftop, find this flower pot and water it to reach a small deck with a locked door.

Use the robber to break inside, where you'll find a blue color swapper. Use it, then blast the nearby LEGO wall to activate it. Wall-jump up to the thin ledge and handhold above.

Shimmy around the building and leap up through an opening in the fence to reach the roof.

Climb up and you'll see a wall runway ahead. Use it to make your way around the corner.

If you head right, you'll find this transporter pad. This is where you can split off in a few different paths to find city challenges and character tokens.

Enter the building and take the stairs up. You're soon back outside; climb a drainpipe to reach the roof.

⭐ 6 LITTLE VENICE: SOUTH APARTMENTS B

On this sun-drenched deck is another flower pot. Water it and scale the sunflower.

Take a fun little slide down this tightrope to the next roof and continue to your right. This path will take you to the edge of the south apartments.

One of Fresco's most notable tourist spots is this quaint re-creation of the Italian city of Venice. A canal separates some apartments here. You'll find some interesting things along the rooftops of both the south and north apartments.

Find this flower pot on the south apartments of Little Venice. Water it and climb up to the awning.

⭐ 7 DOCKS

Most of Fresco's residents are in the import and export business, probably because of the docks at the south side. Plenty of shipments go in and out of here in the middle of the night.

Make your way across a few more awnings until you reach this climbable wall.

To get onto the dock roofs, look for this bit of shaky ground. Drill it and use the water spout to get on top of the warehouse.

INTRODUCTION

POLICE ACADEMY

CHARACTERS AND VEHICLES

WALKTHROUGH

LEGO CITY TOUR

CHECKLISTS

Scale slopes and handholds on your way across the rooftops, heading for a catapult pad.

Use the pad to launch to another set of buildings, then run up a slope and slide down a rope. Good thing Chase McCain cross-trains in the winter. His legs are unstoppable!

FEATS AND COLLECTIBLES

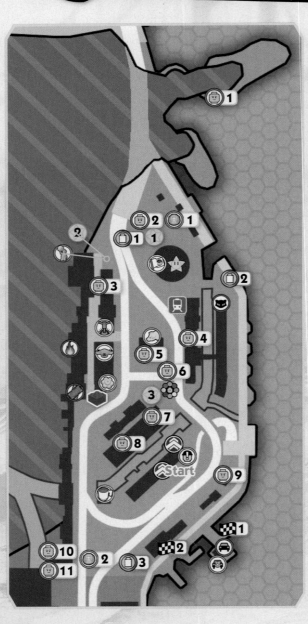

ALIEN CAUGHT

Reward: Gold brick

Get to the greenhouse (POI 4), using the "Points of Interest" section if you need help. Once there, head right to find this space crate. The alien appears on the street below.

ATM SMASHED

Reward: Gold brick

South of the greenhouse building (POI 4) is an ATM just waiting to be pummeled.

MAP LEGEND

MAP ICON(S)	FEAT/COLLECTIBLE	REWARD(S)	LOCATION/HOW TO REACH	GOT IT?
	Alien Caught	Gold brick	Right of the greenhouse.	1
	ATM Smashed	Gold brick	On the street level, near the greenhouse building.	2
	BBQ Fire Extinguished	Gold brick	Tucked in an alley on the west side of Fresco.	3
1	Boulder Destroyed 1	Gold brick	Just north of the leaning tower.	4
2	Boulder Destroyed 2	Gold brick	Close to the main street, at the south end of Fresco.	5
	Cat Rescued	Gold brick	Near a pair of chimneys on the roof of the north apartments.	6
1	Character Token 1	Tim Welch	Hidden in a rock near the helipad behind Blackwell's (vault the fence to reach).	7
2	Character Token 2	Soccer Player	Rip the ball free from the soccer player statue to reveal this token.	8
3	Character Token 3	Tony One-Time	Inside a fenced area past the greenhouse.	9
4	Character Token 4	Bryony Muska	In the sunroom on the roof of the north apartments.	10
5	Character Token 5	Vinnie Tracksuit	After completing the ice cream statue puzzle, paint the ice cream to unlock this token.	11
1 to 3 / 6	Character Token 6	Carlo Jerome	Build the ice cream statue by rolling the three metal scoops onto the bowl outside Pappalardo's.	12
7	Character Token 7	Salvatore Calzone	Behind a boarded up door on the roof of south apartments A.	13
8	Character Token 8	Paulie Blindfolds	On a sunroof at the highest point of south apartments A.	14
9	Character Token 9	Lucky Pete	Behind a locked door on the roof of the garage on the docks.	15
10	Character Token 10	Sentinel Channard	Grapple up to the balcony on the south apartments.	16
11	Character Token 11	Forrest Blackwell Tuxedo	Behind a block only Rex Fury can destroy, in the corner room of a building along Fresco's west edge.	17
	Coffee Break Completed	Gold brick	Along the water on the canal's west end.	18
	Disguise Booth	Gold brick, "Gangster" character token	In between Pappalardo's and Little Venice.	19
	District Conquered	Gold brick	Atop the Leaning Tower.	20
	Drill Thrill Completed	Gold brick	To the right of the greenhouse, after sliding down the tightrope.	21
	Flowers Watered	Gold brick	Just outside the greenhouse.	22
	Free Run	Gold brick, "Snowboarder Guy" character token	Climb up the drainpipe at the far end of south apartments B.	23
	Gang Arrested	Gold brick	On top of the tower on south apartments B.	24
	Pig Returned	Gold brick	On the roof of Pappalardo's.	25
	Red Brick	Fall Rescue	Inside the greenhouse.	26
	Silver Statue Destroyed	Gold brick	In an open plaza on the north side of Fresco.	27
1	Superbuild 1: Call-in Point	Gold brick, "Crater" vehicle token	Along the freeway, near the Leaning Tower.	28
2	Superbuild 2: Stunt Ramp	Gold brick, "Mickey Spoilers" character token	At the north end of the canal.	29

INTRODUCTION

POLICE ACADEMY

CHARACTERS AND VEHICLES

WALKTHROUGH

LEGO CITY TOUR

CHECKLISTS

MAP LEGEND CONTINUED

MAP ICON(S)	FEAT/COLLECTIBLE	REWARD(S)	LOCATION/HOW TO REACH	GOT IT?
3	Superbuild 3: Call-in Point	Gold brick, "Squeaky" vehicle token	At the far south end of Fresco, near the freeway.	30
☆	Super Star	"Pop Star" character token (after you find all Super Stars in the city)	At the very top of the Leaning Tower.	31
1	Time Trial 1	Gold brick, "Squadmobile" vehicle token	Find the speedboat at the docks.	32
2	Time Trial 2	Gold brick, "Muncher" vehicle token	The Pappalardo's Ice Cream truck is parked on the docks.	33
🚆	Train Station	Gold brick, Fast Travel	South of the Leaning Tower.	34
🚗	Vehicle Robbery Completed	Gold brick, "Falchion GT" vehicle token	The locked garage is on the docks.	35
🚗	Vehicle Robber Arrested	Gold brick, "Transfer" vehicle token	Atop one of the buildings on the docks.	36

☆ 🔥 BBQ FIRE EXTINGUISHED

Reward: Gold brick

It can be tough to see this BBQ from the street. Walk along the building on Fresco's far west end. Look for this alleyway, which has some steep stairs.

The BBQ is at the top of the stairs.

☆ 1 BOULDER DESTROYED 1

Reward: Gold brick

From the Leaning Tower (POI 1), head north onto this grassy knoll to find the special boulder.

2 BOULDER DESTROYED 2

Reward: Gold brick

You'll find this special boulder at the south end of Fresco, close to the main street.

☆ 🐱 CAT RESCUED

Reward: Gold brick

Get to the rooftops of the north apartments (POI 2). If you're not sure how to get up there, see the "Points of Interest" section for help. Once on the roof, head forward until you see a chance to turn and cross over the canal.

Go right and follow the roof until you reach a pair of chimneys. The cat is on top, awaiting a savior.

★ ① CHARACTER TOKEN 1

Reward: Tim Welch

Fly to the high helipad at the north end of Fresco—the one near the entrance to Forrest Blackwell's mansion, which Chase visits near the end of Story mode.

Land and navigate the narrow ledge trail, heading for Blackwell's mansion.

Once you reach the fence, vault it just as you did in Story mode.

Go right and look for a spot where you can vault the fence again, landing on a small ledge with a rock. Smash the rock to score a hidden token.

★ ② CHARACTER TOKEN 2

Reward: Soccer Player

North of the Leaning Tower (POI 1) is a statue of a soccer player. To get this character token, use the grapple gun to yank the ball away. With the ball free, you'll score this token.

★ ③ CHARACTER TOKEN 3

Reward: Tony One-Time

Make your way toward the greenhouse (POI 4). You can use the "Points of Interest" section to help you. Instead of going left to reach the inside of the greenhouse, head to the right and take a tightrope down to this rooftop.

Continue to the right, using a catapult pad to launch over to the next building. Keep heading to the right and enter a window with a handhold.

Head to the left to find a transporter pad. Use it to teleport inside the fenced area behind you, where a character token floats.

★ ④ CHARACTER TOKEN 4

Reward: Bryony Muska

Go to the rooftop of the north apartments (POI 2), using the "Points of Interest" section if you need a guiding hand. From here, head straight along the rooftops to find a character token just sitting inside this stone gazebo.

5 CHARACTER TOKEN 5

Reward: Vinnie Tracksuit

After assembling the ice cream statue at Pappalardo's (see the next section for details), paint the giant ice cream balls pink and brown to make a Neapolitan delight. Another character token then appears right nearby! As luck would have it, you can find pink and brown color swappers on either side of the Pappalardo's building.

6 CHARACTER TOKEN 6

Reward: Carlo Jerome

Find, assemble, and then hop on and roll three silver scoops of ice cream over to the empty ice cream bowl in front of Pappalardo's (POI 3). One of these is hidden beneath the silver statue. When all three scoops have been placed, a token appears in front of the statue.

7 CHARACTER TOKEN 7

Reward: Salvatore Calzone

Use the "Points of Interest" section to make your way to the rooftops of south apartments A (POI 5). Instead of using the transporter pad, head to the right and chop through a boarded door to enter a small room with a character token.

8 CHARACTER TOKEN 8

Reward: Paulie Blindfolds

Go to the rooftops of the south apartments A (POI 5) and go along the same path as you would to get the Salvatore Calzone token. See the big crate here? Smash it.

Build a catapult pad from the pieces, then launch yourself onto a sunny spot with a character token.

9 CHARACTER TOKEN 9

Reward: Lucky Pete

Follow the instructions in the "Points of Interest" section to reach the rooftops along the docks (POI 7). At the end of your little trek is a locked door. Use the robber's crowbar to break in and claim a token.

10 CHARACTER TOKEN 10

Reward: Sentinel Channard

There are some buildings on the southwest end of Fresco. Look for these handholds and climb up.

Navigate a thin ledge to reach a small balcony. Use the grapple gun to zip up to the character token above. You'll eventually find yourself on top of a balcony.

11 CHARACTER TOKEN 11

Reward: Forrest Blackwell Tuxedo

Follow the same path to get the Sentinel Channard character token. Reach the balcony with that token, then head left until you can enter a building. Inside, there's an orange handle that only Rex Fury can rip free. Do so and claim another character token.

COFFEE BREAK COMPLETED

Reward: Gold brick

Go to the west end of the canal in Little Venice. You'll find this spot for a coffee break right against the water where the canal ends.

DISGUISE BOOTH

Reward: Gold brick, "Gangster" character token

The disguise booth is in between Pappalardo's and Little Venice.

DISTRICT CONQUERED

Reward: Gold brick

Go to the entrance of the Leaning Tower (POI 1) and run up its winding walkway. Go to the top, and you'll find a spot to fly your flag.

DRILL THRILL COMPLETED

Reward: Gold brick

Make your way toward the inside of the greenhouse (POI 4), using the "Points of Interest" section to guide you. After bouncing from the awnings to reach the upper roof, head right and find a tightrope you can slide down to reach a roof with a fuse box. You know the drill!

FLOWERS WATERED

Reward: Gold brick

Get to the greenhouse (POI 4) with the help of the "Points of Interest" section. The flower bed is right outside the greenhouse—you can't miss it.

FREE RUN

Rewards: Gold brick, "Snowboarder Guy" character token

Get onto the rooftops of the south apartments B in Little Venice (POI 6). The "Points of Interest" section can guide you there. At the far end of the roofs, you'll see this drainpipe. Climb up and grab the free run token.

INTRODUCTION   POLICE ACADEMY   CHARACTERS AND VEHICLES   WALKTHROUGH   LEGO CITY TOUR   CHECKLISTS

The free run challenge's starting point appears here.

GANG ARRESTED

Reward: Gold brick

Follow the directions in the "Points of Interest" section to reach the end of the rooftop along the docks (POI 7). Climb a wall to find a catapult pad.

The pad sends you flying over to a distant roof with a scan spot. Listen in on gang activity in the area, then hurry back to the docks to bust up the goons.

PIG RETURNED

Reward: Gold brick

Head over to Pappalardo's (POI 3) and find this tall tank. Climb the handholds on its side to reach the tank's top, then hop across several thin poles to reach Pappalardo's roof.

Water a planter on the roof and climb the sunflower to find a pig in need. Hop on and ride the little oinker to the cannon over by the canal.

RED BRICK

Reward: Fall Rescue

Follow the instructions on how to get inside the greenhouse (POI 4) in the "Points of Interest" section. Once inside the greenhouse, the red brick will be right in front of you.

SILVER STATUE DESTROYED

Reward: Gold brick

Find a dynamite dispenser behind a locked door near where you start your journey up to the greenhouse (POI 4). With dynamite in hand, head to the Rex statue at the north end of Fresco.

SUPERBUILD 1: CALL-IN POINT

Reward: Gold brick, "Crater" vehicle token

This call-in spot is along the freeway, to the west of the Leaning Tower (POI 1).

SUPERBUILD 2: STUNT RAMP

Reward: Gold brick, "Mickey Spoilers" character token

Need some epic jumps in Fresco? Be sure to build this stunt ramp, which you can find at the canal's north end.

⭐ 🎴3 SUPERBUILD 3: VEHICLE CALL-IN

Reward: Gold brick, "Squeaky" vehicle token

This superbuild is at the far south end of Fresco, near the freeway.

⭐ ☆ SUPER STAR

Reward: "Pop Star" character token (after you find all Super Stars in the city)

Run to the top of the Leaning Tower (POI 1) and find the yellow box on the roof. Smash the box and then build the pieces to create a super-rare Super Star!

⭐ 🏁1 TIME TRIAL 1

Reward: Gold brick, "Squadmobile" vehicle token

Find the speedboat on the docks (POI 7) and hop in to start a time trial. You'll make some tight turns as you speed through the canal in this race. This one will test your boating skills!

⭐ 🏁2 TIME TRIAL 2

Reward: Gold brick, "Muncher" vehicle token

This time trial won't appear until you've built the stunt ramp superbuild in Paradise Sands. Once that's done, you can find the Pappalardo's Ice Cream truck on the docks (POI 7).

⭐ 🚆 TRAIN STATION

Reward: Gold brick, fast travel

This station lies just south of the Leaning Tower (POI 1). Head downstairs and smash the green cabinet, then build the ticket machine to activate the station.

⭐ 🚗 VEHICLE ROBBERY COMPLETED

Reward: Gold brick, "Falchion GT" vehicle token

This garage is on the docks, against the water. Break inside and take a sweet ride for a test drive.

⭐ 🚓 VEHICLE ROBBER ARRESTED

Reward: Gold brick, "Transfer" vehicle token

Head to the docks and find a garage with a blue and white LEGO patch running up its wall. This is the same garage you break into to begin Fresco's vehicle robbery event. Climb up to reach a scan spot that helps you discover a car thief on the run!

INTRODUCTION

POLICE ACADEMY

CHARACTERS AND VEHICLES

WALKTHROUGH

LEGO CITY TOUR

CHECKLISTS

GRAND CANAL

> **NOTE**
>
> There are no points of interest in the Grand Canal. This underground waterway simply serves as a convenient means of crossing LEGO City's mainland.

⭐ FEATS AND COLLECTIBLES

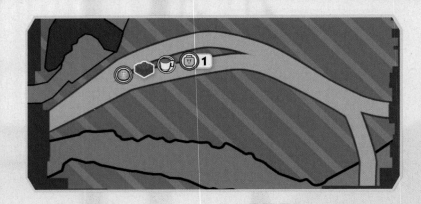

MAP LEGEND

MAP ICON(S)	FEAT/COLLECTIBLE	REWARD(S)	LOCATION/HOW TO REACH	GOT IT?
◎	Boulder Destroyed	Gold brick	On a walkway on the west end of the canal.	1
◎1	Character Token 1	Brad Hoggle	Behind a boarded up door on the canal walkway.	2
☕	Coffee Break Completed	Gold brick	On the canal walkway, near the character token.	3
⬡	Red Brick	Ring Tone—Pig	Behind a locked door on the canal walkway.	4

◎ BOULDER DESTROYED

Reward: Gold brick

Along the canal are some walkways. Find the one toward the west end of the canal that's covered in boulders. The special boulder is hidden in the corner pile.

①1 CHARACTER TOKEN 1

Reward: Brad Hoggle

With the firefighter's axe in hand, you're going to rescue this character token. Chop through the boarded door on one of the canal's walkways and claim your prize.

☕ COFFEE BREAK COMPLETED

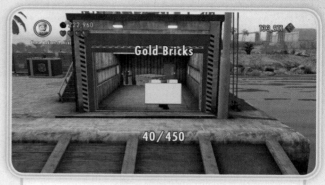

Reward: Gold brick

There's nothing like a damp canal to make you want a warm cup o' joe. This coffee break spot sits on a walkway near the aforementioned character token. Smash a few construction cones to reach it.

⬢ RED BRICK

Reward: Ring Tone—Pig

Along the walkway, west of where you take a coffee break, is a locked door. Use the robber's crowbar to open the door and collect the red brick beyond.

INTRODUCTION

POLICE ACADEMY

CHARACTERS AND VEHICLES

WALKTHROUGH

LEGO CITY TOUR

CHECKLISTS

HERITAGE BRIDGE

POINTS OF INTEREST

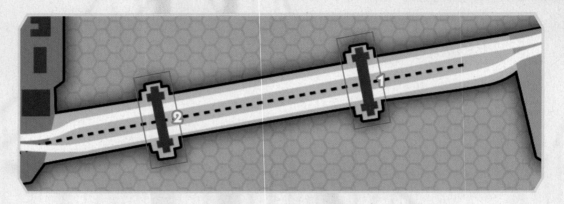

⭐ 1 EAST TOWER

You'll gain a better appreciation for the size of LEGO City from atop the Heritage Bridge. This bridge features two towers, one on the west end and one on the east end.

Leap up the handholds to reach a thin ledge. Inch over to a longer handhold and shimmy across.

Continue making your way around the tower, using ledges, handholds, and wall runways as you go.

Keep going until you reach a blue and white LEGO patch. Climb this to at last reach the east tower's apex.

Reaching the top of the east tower starts, not surprisingly, from the bottom. Look for some shaky ground around the back side of the tower. Drill it and ride the water spout up to some handholds.

⭐ ② WEST TOWER

Start at the base of the west tower, where you'll see this grapple point. Use the grapple gun to yank down some LEGO pieces.

Maneuver onto a thin ledge and shimmy to another blue and white LEGO patch. Use this to climb even higher.

Build a trampoline from the pieces and bounce up to the blue and white LEGO patch above.

When you can climb no higher, drop to a small stone ledge and then leap across a couple flagpoles.

You'll end up in a rather precarious position, barely standing on the narrow curve of an arch. Notice the grapple point above, and use it to swing across.

Keep going, crossing more thin ledges and flagpoles on your way to the final LEGO patch that leads up to the tower's top. Take a bow, then get back to cleaning up the streets of LEGO City!

INTRODUCTION

POLICE ACADEMY

CHARACTERS AND VEHICLES

WALKTHROUGH

LEGO CITY TOUR

CHECKLISTS

FEATS AND COLLECTIBLES

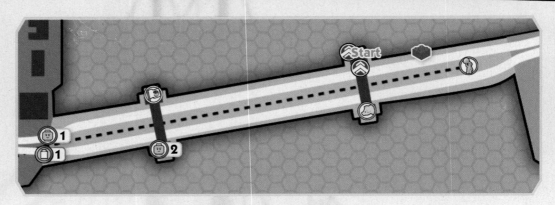

MAP LEGEND

MAP ICON(S)	FEAT/COLLECTIBLE	REWARD(S)	LOCATION/HOW TO REACH	GOT IT?
1	Character Token 1	Frank Honey	Appears after you superbuild the Model Citizen statue.	1
2	Character Token 2	Ted Baxter	Atop the bridge's west tower.	2
	District Conquered	Gold brick	On top of the west tower.	3
	Free Run	Gold brick, "Skier" character token	At the top of the east tower.	4
	Pig Returned	Gold brick	Waiting for you at the top of the east tower.	5
	Red Brick	Collect Sat Nav Studs	From the top of the east tower, slide down the tightrope.	6
	Silver Statue Destroyed	Gold brick	On a platform on the east side of the bridge.	7
1	Superbuild 1: The Model Citizen	Gold brick	Find the empty platform at the bridge's west end.	8

⭐ 1 CHARACTER TOKEN 1

Reward: Frank Honey

Construct the Model Citizen statue superbuild, and this token will appear right at its feet.

⭐ 2 CHARACTER TOKEN 2

Reward: Ted Baxter

Get to the top of the west tower (POI 2), using the "Points of Interest" section if necessary. Once there, you'll see this character token sitting out to the left.

DISTRICT CONQUERED

Reward: Gold brick

Follow the directions in the "Points of Interest" section to reach the top of the west tower (POI 2). Once there, run to the right and raise your flag.

FREE RUN

Rewards: Gold brick, "Skier" character token

Use the "Points of Interest" section to learn how to reach the top of the east tower (POI 1). Head left to find the free run token.

The free run challenge starts where you first drilled into shaky ground, at the bottom of the east tower. The route is the same as the one you took to reach the top of the east tower. Slide down the tightrope to reach the finish.

PIG RETURNED

Reward: Gold brick

Reach the top of the east tower (POI 1) to find this poor lost pig. Hop on and ride the little guy to the left to find the cannon, which is also on top of the tower.

RED BRICK

Reward: Collect Sat Nav Studs

Go to the top of the east tower (POI 1). Once at the top, head left, toward the pig cannon. Slide down the nearby tightrope to collect a red brick. Note that you can't collect this red brick during the free run challenge—that'd be too easy!

SILVER STATUE DESTROYED

Reward: Gold brick

There's no dynamite dispenser in this zone, so you'll need to find one in another location. (The one inside the hospital in Festival Square to the east is a good option.) The Rex statue stands atop a platform on the bridge's east side—smash the nearby phones and build a trampoline from the bricks, then bounce up to the statue.

SUPERBUILD 1: THE MODEL CITIZEN

Reward: Gold brick, "Frank Honey" character token

There's some shaky ground on the bridge's west end, near one of the supports. Drill it and ride the water spout up to a series of handholds.

The handholds lead to a superbuild pad, where you can construct a monument to LEGO City's ultimate citizen.

INTRODUCTION

POLICE ACADEMY

CHARACTERS AND VEHICLES

WALKTHROUGH

LEGO CITY TOUR

CHECKLISTS

KINGS COURT

POINTS OF INTEREST

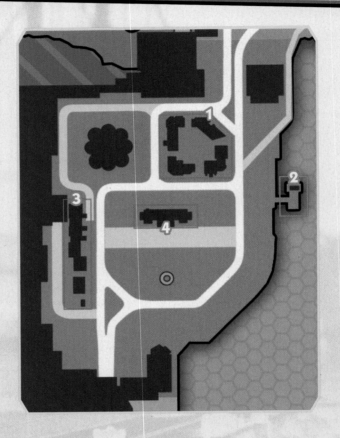

⭐ 1 PLAYGROUND

Kings Court isn't just for politicians and art snobs. It's also for kids! And bored cops.

Of course, it's not all fun and games. You can leave the playground and get to the rooftops of the surrounding buildings. Start by finding this green trash bin next to Jenny's Diner. Jump onto it and use an astronaut boost to get up onto the overhang.

Make your way around the overhang until you can boost up to this handhold.

Use the wall runway to scamper along the "Jenny's Diner" sign. Climb up the far wall and enjoy the smell of pancakes coming from inside.

⭐ ② THE DOCKS

The Kings Court docks are small and easily overlooked, but anyone who wants to find all of LEGO City's secrets should be sure to check it out.

⭐ ③ OFFICE BUILDINGS

On the west side of Kings Court is a long series of connected office buildings, featuring tall arches with walkways and posters advertising artwork you could see at the museum. There's a lot you can do in and around the office buildings, so it's definitely worth checking out.

Exploring the Rooftops

Your first goal is to get on top of these buildings. Isn't that what all the cool cops are doing these days? Start at the south side of the office buildings, where you'll see a climbable wall.

Climb the wall, walk along a tightrope, and then climb the next wall ahead. Grab on to the handhold and pull yourself onto the first office roof. Wall-jump up to a catapult pad, which slings you to the side of the next building.

Race up a sloped rooftop, then hop across a few thin poles. Vault a fence, then run to the foreground and look to drop down to this ledge, landing near a wall runway.

Use the runway to cross the gap, then climb up the handhold to reach the end of the office building rooftops.

Entering the Offices

Aside from exploring the roofs of these buildings, you can actually enter some of the offices here. Start by looking for these brick arches. There's a drainpipe here you can climb.

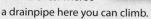

At the top is a locked door, primed for the robber to break into with his crowbar. Once inside, you'll see plenty of goodies that make your short trip worthwhile, including a red color swapper that comes in handy.

INTRODUCTION

POLICE ACADEMY

CHARACTERS AND VEHICLES

WALKTHROUGH

LEGO CITY TOUR

CHECKLISTS

⭐ 4 CITY HALL

Smack dab in the center of Kings Court is City Hall. Here, the most important men and women of LEGO City meet to discuss what to have for lunch. As with most important buildings in LEGO City, you'll want to get up top.

Start by locating and watering a planter in front of City Hall. Climb up the sunflower and onto the balcony.

Head right, hugging the wall as you inch around a thin ledge. Leap across the long series of flagpoles that follows, making your way to the building's other side.

Inch around another thin ledge to reach another planter. Water it and climb the sunflower to reach the roof. You'll find a variety of goodies atop City Hall!

FEATS AND COLLECTIBLES

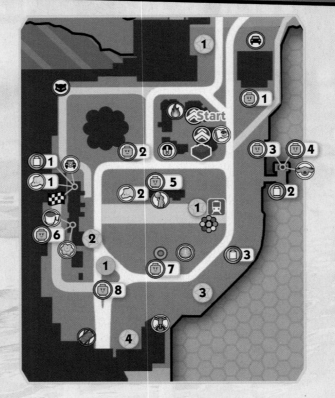

MAP LEGEND

MAP ICON(S)	FEAT/COLLECTIBLE	REWARD(S)	LOCATION/HOW TO REACH	GOT IT?
	Alien Caught	Gold brick	Atop a building on the docks.	1
	ATM Smashed	Gold brick	Next to the south entrance into Kings Court.	2

MAP LEGEND CONTINUED

MAP ICON(S)	FEAT/COLLECTIBLE	REWARD(S)	LOCATION/HOW TO REACH	GOT IT?
	BBQ Fire Extinguished	Gold brick	At the back of the playground.	3
	Boulder Destroyed	Gold brick	In the south gardens, near City Hall.	4
	Cat Rescued	Gold brick	On the awning of the Herbert Hotel.	5
1 1	Character Token 1	Mayor Gleeson	Get Bullet Bill to follow you to the cage. Once he blows up the cage, you can grab the token.	6
2	Character Token 2	Royal Guard	Above a statue near Blackwell Tower.	7
3	Character Token 3	Cal Wainwright	Behind the boarded up door on the docks.	8
4	Character Token 4	Drew Calhoun	Floating above a sign at the docks.	9
5	Character Token 5	Farmer Bales	Behind the Rex statue on the roof of City Hall.	10
6	Character Token 6	Graduate	Inside an office on the west side of Kings Court.	11
1 to 4 7	Character Token 7	Doorlock Holmes	Paint four phone boxes red to unlock this token.	12
1 8	Character Token 8	Dr. Whatsit	Paint the LEGO brick statue to reveal this character token.	13
	Coffee Break Completed	Gold brick	Inside the office building.	14
	Disguise Booth	Gold brick, "Horace Crone" character token	Near the train station.	15
	District Conquered	Gold brick	At the top of Jenny's Diner.	16
	Drill Thrill Completed	Gold brick	On the roof of the building with the gold doors.	17
	Flowers Watered	Gold brick	Inside the office building.	18
	Free Run	Gold brick, "Street Skater" character token	On top of the roof of the building by the playground.	19
	Gang Arrested	Gold brick	On the roof of the Tinebury restaurant.	20
1	Pig Returned 1	Gold brick	On the rooftop of the office building.	21
2	Pig Returned 2	Gold brick	On the roof of City Hall.	22
	Red Brick	Invincibility	Behind a door only Rex Fury can pry open, on the roof of Jenny's Diner.	23
	Silver Statue Destroyed	Gold brick	Standing atop City Hall.	24
1	Superbuild 1: Crash Mat	Gold brick, "Kowalski's Shifter" vehicle token	At the end of the office building rooftops.	25
2	Superbuild 2: Ferry	Gold brick, "Sevila" vehicle token	Go to the end of the docks.	26
3	Superbuild 3: Call-in Point	Gold brick, "Bristler" vehicle token	Along the street, at the south end of Kings Court.	27
	Time Trial	Gold brick, "Taxi Cab" vehicle token	In an alleyway north of the office buildings.	28
	Train Station	Gold brick, Fast Travel	On the east end of City Hall.	29
	Vehicle Robbery Completed	Gold brick, "Downforce" vehicle token	Inside a gated parking lot.	30
	Vehicle Robber Arrested	Gold brick, "Arbalest" vehicle token	On the far end of the office building rooftop.	31

INTRODUCTION

POLICE ACADEMY

CHARACTERS AND VEHICLES

WALKTHROUGH

LEGO CITY TOUR

CHECKLISTS

⭐ 🚗 ALIEN CAUGHT

Reward: Gold brick

The space crate is on top of this building, near the docks (POI 2). Use a climbable wall to reach it, then activate the crate to expose the alien threat.

⭐ 🚫 ATM SMASHED

Reward: Gold brick

Find this ATM standing next to Kings Court's south entrance.

⭐ 🔥 BBQ FIRE EXTINGUISHED

Reward: Gold brick

This blazing flame's an easy find, near the back of the playground (POI 1).

⭐ ◎ BOULDER DESTROYED

Reward: Gold brick

You'll find this special boulder in the south gardens of City Hall (POI 4).

⭐ 🐱 CAT RESCUED

Reward: Gold brick

There have been a number of complaints from the guests at the Herbert Hotel about a cat crying for help. The hotel is in the far northwest corner of Kings Court. Find the shaky ground by the entrance and drill into it to create a water spout.

Ride the spout onto the awning. The poor lost kitty is trapped behind the hotel sign.

⭐ 1 CHARACTER TOKEN 1

Reward: Mayor Gleeson

This token is locked behind a seemingly unbreakable cage. Only Bullet Bill can destroy the cage. Good thing Kings Court has its very own cannon that fires Bullet Bills!

On the walkway on the east side near City Hall (POI 4), there are some green cannons. One cannon, right near the train station, fires off a Bullet Bill when you pass by.

Bullet Bill chases after you; lure him toward the distant cage. There are a lot of pedestrians and objects in the way, so if Bullet Bill hits any of them, you'll have to start over!

You'll grab the token as you fall, so relax for a moment and let gravity do its thing!

TIP

Destroy everything in your way if you do have to restart, and you'll have a clearer path.

Lead Bullet Bill north, back to the cage. Switch to the astronaut and boost onto the cage, watching for Bullet Bill. Jump or drop off the cage, away from Bullet Bill, just as he's about to reach you. This causes Bullet Bill to strike the cage, destroying it and exposing the token!

⭐ 🎫2 CHARACTER TOKEN 2

Reward: Royal Guard

This token is on top of a statue near Blackwell Tower. But to reach it, you actually need to go to this nearby building. Next to a dynamite dispenser is a flower pot. Water it and climb up the plant.

Hop onto the transporter pad and you'll be teleported above the statue.

⭐ 🎫3 CHARACTER TOKEN 3

Reward: Cal Wainwright

At the docks (POI 2), look for the boarded up door. Use the firefighter's axe to break it down. The character token is right inside the building.

⭐ 🎫4 CHARACTER TOKEN 4

Reward: Drew Calhoun

This one is hard to spot. At the docks (POI 2), go to the pier that has the space crate. Near the crate is a sign with a beam on top that you can stand on. Jetpack jump onto this sign, then do another boost—the token is right above you!

⭐ 🎫5 CHARACTER TOKEN 5

Reward: Farmer Bales

This token is on the roof of City Hall (POI 4), right behind the Rex statue. See the "Points of Interest" section for details on how to reach the top of City Hall.

INTRODUCTION

POLICE ACADEMY

CHARACTERS AND VEHICLES

WALKTHROUGH

LEGO CITY TOUR

CHECKLISTS

⭐ 🔵6 CHARACTER TOKEN 6

Reward: Graduate

Climb the drainpipe and break into the office buildings on the west side of Kings Court (POI 3). The token is there for the taking.

⭐ 🔵7 CHARACTER TOKEN 7

Reward: Doorlock Holmes

Paint four silver phone booths red around Kings Court to unlock this token. You can find a red color swapper inside the office buildings (POI 3). Then check the map to see where the four phone booths are located.

The token appears near the fountain.

⭐ 🔵8 CHARACTER TOKEN 8

Reward: Dr. Whatsit

Paint the silver LEGO brick statue's three blocks red, blue, and yellow to make a character token appear right nearby.

⭐ ☕ COFFEE BREAK COMPLETED

Reward: Gold brick

You've probably done a lot of work so far in LEGO City. You deserve a break. Why not take one inside the office building (POI 3)? Just climb the drainpipe and break inside.

⭐ ❀ DISGUISE BOOTH

Reward: Gold brick, "Horace Cone" character token

The disguise booth is on the east side of Kings Court, right next to the train station.

⭐ 🔘 DISTRICT CONQUERED

Reward: Gold brick

Get yourself to the top of the playground rooftops (POI 1), using the "Points of Interest" section for guidance. Once there, wall-jump to the highest point of the roof. Raise a flag up here and claim this Jenny's Diner as your own!

DRILL THRILL COMPLETED

Reward: Gold brick

Look for the gold doors of the theater by the south entrance into Kings Court. There's shaky ground here, which you can drill to create a water spout to ride up to the theater awning.

Climb the ladder to get onto the roof. Fix the fuse box behind the sign, then hurry up and get drilling!

FLOWERS WATERED

Reward: Gold brick

Find this flower bed inside the office building (POI 3) on the west end of this area.

FREE RUN

Rewards: Gold brick, "Street Skater" character token

Make your way onto the rooftops near the playground (POI 1). If you have trouble, check out the "Points of Interest" section for help. Once on the roof, look for this special wall and wall-jump onto the higher section of roof, where the free run token is located.

With the token collected, the free run challenge appears on the other side of the Jenny's Diner roof.

GANG ARRESTED

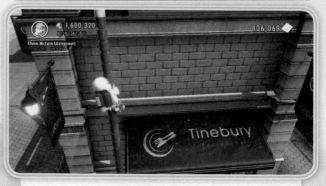

Reward: Gold brick

Over by the playground (POI 1), on the south end, is a fenced-in restaurant called Tinebury. It has a drainpipe that's perfect for climbing.

Make your way up until you reach this section. Use an astronaut to boost up and reach the ledge and roof above.

The scan spot is up even higher. Chop through a door and climb a ladder, then leap over to the highest roof's handhold. Climb to the scan spot, then bust up that gang!

INTRODUCTION

POLICE ACADEMY

CHARACTERS AND VEHICLES

WALKTHROUGH

LEGO CITY TOUR

CHECKLISTS

⭐ ①🐷 PIG RETURNED 1

Reward: Gold brick

Use the "Points of Interest" section to help reach the end of the office building rooftops (POI 3). There's a pig eagerly awaiting rescue near the crash mat. Don't disappoint it! The cannon is all the way down to the southeast.

⭐ ②🐷 PIG RETURNED 2

Reward: Gold brick

The second pig is on the roof of City Hall (POI 4). To get there, check out the "Points of Interest" section. The pig is on the roof's west end.

⭐ 🟦 RED BRICK

Reward: Invincibility

You'll need Rex Fury for this one. Follow the instructions to reach the rooftops on the playground (POI 1), as shown in the "Points of Interest" section. When you get toward the Jenny's Diner sign, don't run across it. Instead, climb this drainpipe onto another part of the roof.

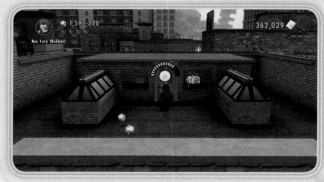

With Rex Fury, grab the orange handle on the door and tear it off with your mighty strength. The red brick is inside.

⭐ 🔘 SILVER STATUE DESTROYED

Reward: Gold brick

Get to the Rex statue on the roof of City Hall (POI 4) by following the tips in the "Points of Interest" section. The statue is right in the center of the roof and easy to find once you're up there. There's a dynamite dispenser near the theater at the south end of Kings Court.

⭐ 🔲① SUPERBUILD 1: CRASH MAT

Reward: Gold brick, "Kowalski's Shifter" vehicle token

Head to the end of the office building rooftops (POI 3), using the "Points of Interest" section if you haven't been up top yet. The superbuild is right here, just waiting to be constructed.

2 SUPERBUILD 2: FERRY

Reward: Gold brick, "Sevila" vehicle token

Head to the end of the docks (POI 2) to find this useful superbuild.

3 SUPERBUILD 3: CALL-IN POINT

Reward: Gold brick, "Bristler" vehicle token

Find this call-in superbuild along the street, at the south end of Kings Court.

TIME TRIAL

Reward: Gold brick, "Taxi Cab" vehicle token

This time trial has you racing around Kings Court and into Fresco. It begins in an alley north of the office buildings (POI 3).

TRAIN STATION

Reward: Gold brick, fast travel

The train station is on the east end of City Hall.

VEHICLE ROBBERY COMPLETED

Reward: Gold brick, "Downforce" vehicle token

There's a gated parking lot in the northeast corner of Kings Court. To steal the vehicle inside, you must blow up the gate.

Head to the garage after blowing up the gate. Climb a drainpipe to reach a skylight. Use the crowbar to break in and then take a car for an unauthorized test drive.

VEHICLE ROBBER ARRESTED

Reward: Gold brick, "Arbalest" vehicle token

Get to the end of the office building rooftops (POI 3) with the help of the "Points of Interest" section. The scan spot that kicks off this event is found on the corner of the roof.

INTRODUCTION

POLICE ACADEMY

CHARACTERS AND VEHICLES

WALKTHROUGH

LEGO CITY TOUR

CHECKLISTS

LADY LIBERTY ISLAND

POINTS OF INTEREST

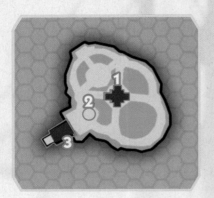

There's a transporter pad waiting for you after you get around the wall. But you won't be using it to get to the feet of Lady Liberty.

Make your way past the transporter pad and around until you spot a ladder. Ladders, as we all know, were made for climbing—so get to it! Once at the top, you can take in a scenic view of the city and get a nice close look at Lady Liberty's foot.

⭐ 1 THE STATUE OF LADY LIBERTY

This majestic statue is an enduring symbol of freedom in LEGO City. Many tourists have dreamed of standing at her feet. Well, now you can.

To get up a close-up view of Lady Liberty, start at the flagpole, which is located on the island's north side. Use an astronaut boost to get up to the climbable part of the pole.

At the pole's top, slide along a tightrope to reach the base of the Statue of Lady Liberty. Wall-hug the thin ledge on the right.

⭐ 2 INFORMATION HUT

Straight up from the docks is a helpful information hut, used by tourists who want a map showing them exactly where to find the gigantic Statue of Lady Liberty. A dynamite dispenser is conveniently located here.

⭐ 3 DOCK ROOF

Getting atop the roof of a dock covering might not seem very interesting, but it's essential in completing several of Lady Liberty Island's challenges. Start out at the flagpole, just as you would to reach the foot of Lady Liberty.

Climb the pole and slide down the tightrope. Make your way around a thin ledge to find a transporter pad. Use the pad to beam to the top of the statue.

They say Lady Liberty's light never goes out. Well, you're going to have to do something about that to continue on. Use the firefighter's extinguisher to douse the statue's flame.

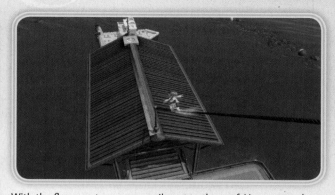

With the flame out, you can easily get to the roof. Hop across the gap and grab on to the handhold. Pull yourself up, then slide down the tightrope to reach the dock roof.

FEATS AND COLLECTIBLES

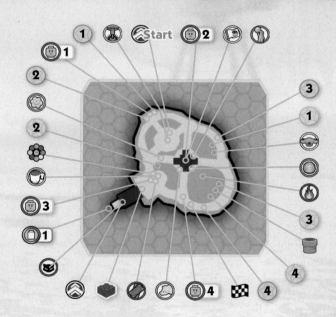

MAP LEGEND

MAP ICON(S)	FEAT/COLLECTIBLE	REWARD(S)	LOCATION/HOW TO REACH	GOT IT?
	Alien Caught	Gold brick	Up against a fence on the park's far east side.	1
	ATM Smashed	Gold brick	Next to the information hut.	2
	BBQ Fire Extinguished	Gold brick	On the south side lawn.	3
	Boulder Destroyed	Gold brick	On the side of the stairs leading up to the monument.	4
	Cat Rescued	Gold brick	Hanging out on a pole on the dock roof.	5

INTRODUCTION

POLICE ACADEMY

CHARACTERS AND VEHICLES

WALKTHROUGH

LEGO CITY TOUR

CHECKLISTS

MAP LEGEND CONTINUED

MAP ICON(S)	FEAT/COLLECTIBLE	REWARD(S)	LOCATION/HOW TO REACH	GOT IT?
1 to 4 / 1	Character Token 1	Explorer	Build the four sets of binoculars to reveal this token.	6
2	Character Token 2	Demolition Dummy	Hovering in the walkway underneath the Statue of Lady Liberty.	7
3	Character Token 3	Ellie Phillips	Break into the information hut using the robber's crowbar.	8
1 to 4 / 4	Character Token 4	Troublemaker Tim	Turn the four silver trees brown to make this token appear.	9
	Coffee Break Completed	Gold brick	Sitting on the windowsill of the information hut.	10
	Disguise Booth	Gold brick, "Security Supervisor" character token	To the left of the information hut.	11
	District Conquered	Gold brick	At the foot of Lady Liberty.	12
	Drill Thrill Completed	Gold brick	Against the flagpole on the north side of the island.	13
	Flowers Watered	Gold brick	Near the flagpole.	14
	Free Run	Gold brick, "Hockey Player" character token	On the roof of the dock.	15
	Pig Returned	Gold brick	On the side of the stairs, beneath LEGO City's monument.	16
	Red Brick	Mario Hat	Along the tightrope used to reach the dock roof.	17
	Silver Statue Destroyed	Gold brick	Between two sets of stairs leading up to Lady Liberty.	18
1	Superbuild: Ferry	Gold brick, "Cabrakan" vehicle token	At the end of the dock.	19
	Time Trial	Gold brick, "Redeemer" vehicle token	On the south walkway.	20
	Warp Pipe	Fast Travel	In the middle of the south lawn, near the BBQ fire.	21

ALIEN CAUGHT

Reward: Gold brick

Find the space crate to summon the escaped alien on the park's far east end. It's up against the fence that borders the walkway.

ATM SMASHED

Reward: Gold brick

Show that ATM machine who's boss! This one's tough to miss. It's on the south side of the information building (POI 2).

⬥ BBQ FIRE EXTINGUISHED

Reward: Gold brick

In the grass, on the south side of the Statue of Lady Liberty (POI 1), is a BBQ gone out of control. It's sitting out on the lawn, awaiting your extinguisher.

The token appears near a scenic view from the island.

◎ BOULDER DESTROYED

Reward: Gold brick

Tucked against the stairs underneath LEGO City's grand monument to freedom, this boulder can be tough to spot. It's right near the BBQ fire.

CHARACTER TOKEN 2

Reward: Demolition Dummy

Walk up the stairs underneath the Statue of Lady Liberty (POI 1) and perform a jetpack jump to collect this floating token.

🐱 CAT RESCUED

Reward: Gold brick

The cat is stuck on a pole atop the dock roof (POI 3). See the "Points of Interest" section to learn how to get on the dock roof.

CHARACTER TOKEN 3

Reward: Ellie Phillips

Snagging this token is easy. Break into the information hut with the robber and grab the token from inside.

CHARACTER TOKEN 1

CHARACTER TOKEN 4

Reward: Troublemaker Tim

Troublemaker Tim's token appears after you do a little painting. You need

to turn four silver trees brown using the robber's color gun. You can find a brown color swapper next to the stairs.

Reward: Explorer

Smash the benches to build four sets of binoculars around the perimeter of Liberty Island.

INTRODUCTION

POLICE ACADEMY

CHARACTERS AND VEHICLES

WALKTHROUGH

LEGO CITY TOUR

CHECKLISTS

The token is revealed on a golden seal on the perimeter of the island.

☕ COFFEE BREAK COMPLETED

Reward: Gold brick

A red carafe of coffee sits on one of the windowsills in the information hut (POI 2).

✿ DISGUISE BOOTH

Reward: Gold brick, "Security Supervisor" character token

Head to the information hut and look to the left. The disguise booth is just sitting there, waiting to be built.

🅿 DISTRICT CONQUERED

Reward: Gold brick

Head to the foot of the Statue of Lady Liberty (POI 1). Use the "Points of Interest" section if you need help getting there. You can raise the flag right in front of the statue.

⚙ DRILL THRILL COMPLETED

Reward: Gold brick

Find the flagpole on the north side of the island. The electrical box is at the base of the pole.

❀ FLOWERS WATERED

Reward: Gold brick

This flower bed is easy to find. It's at the bottom of the stairs, not far from the flagpole.

⌂ FREE RUN

Rewards: Gold brick, "Hockey Player" character token

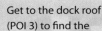

Get to the dock roof (POI 3) to find the free run token. Use the "Points of Interest" section to find out how to get onto the roof.

The challenge begins back at the flagpole.

⭐ 🐷 PIG RETURNED

Reward: Gold brick

The island's runaway pig is located on one side of the stone stairs beneath the monument. It's right across from the special boulder. Hop on that little piggy and ride him over to the cannon, which is on the east grassy area, near a space crate.

⭐ ⬡ RED BRICK

Reward: Mario Hat

You'll snag this red brick sliding down the tightrope on your way down to the dock roof (POI 1). Check the "Points of Interest" section to learn how to get to the roof.

⭐ 🏛 SILVER STATUE DESTROYED

Reward: Gold brick

Grab some dynamite from the dispenser near the information hut (POI 2), then head left. The silver statue is easy to spot, standing between two sets of stairs.

⭐ 📖1 SUPERBUILD: FERRY

Reward: Gold brick, "Cabrakan" vehicle token

Head to the end of the dock and build the ferry station. Now it'll be a little easier getting back to the mainland!

⭐ 🏁 TIME TRIAL

Reward: Gold brick, "Redeemer" vehicle token

Liberty Island has no traffic, so that should make this time trial a breeze. Find it on the south walkway.

⭐ 🟫 WARP PIPE

Reward: Fast travel

This convenient fast-travel warp pipe is sitting in the middle of the grassy area to the south, not far from the BBQ fire. Hop in to take a shortcut to downtown.

INTRODUCTION

POLICE ACADEMY

CHARACTERS AND VEHICLES

WALKTHROUGH

LEGO CITY TOUR

CHECKLISTS

LEGO CITY AIRPORT

POINTS OF INTEREST

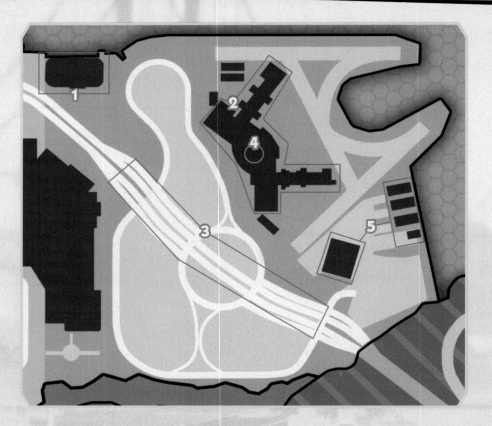

⭐ 1 FIN'S RESTAURANT

This quaint seafood joint is located west of the airport and is a favorite of locals and travelers alike. However, you can only enjoy the restaurant from the lower deck when you first arrive.

To reach the upper deck, first find this space crate near the back of the restaurant. Activating the crate teleports in an extra umbrella.

Bounce from one umbrella to the next and then onto the upper deck of Fin's.

★ ② AIRPORT ROOF

Not surprisingly, the main attraction of this area is an airport. You won't be checking any bags for a flight, though.

To start, look for this door with the special LEGO worker sticker. There's a climbable LEGO patch on the wall above, but it's a bit too high to reach.

To the right is a garage. Inside is a box you can carry. Grab it and take it back to the green LEGO pad.

Drop the box and build the pieces into a trampoline. Bounce up to the LEGO patch and then climb.

Use a wall runway on your way up to the roof. Here, you get to vault over a few beams.

This big fence stands in your way. Fortunately, you can vault over this as easily as you did one of those low beams you just hopped over. Head forward and you'll be at the center of the south roof. From here, you can get to almost everything on top of the airport.

★ ③ FREEWAY

To reach the airport, you'll likely come from the freeway. It's to the west of the airport and raised, meaning there's an underpass. You'll find some worthwhile items beneath the freeway.

★ ④ CONTROL TOWER

Once you're on the airport rooftop, there is one other sight to see—the top of the control tower. If you want to get up to where LEGO City air traffic controllers operate, start by getting on the airport roof. Head to the right, vaulting over and sliding under a few beams.

Head forward until you notice an orange pay phone. Around the corner is a set of special LEGO walls. Bounce up between them.

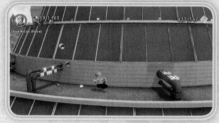

Now make your way to the left, vaulting over and sliding under more beams as you go.

Hop across a few thin poles to reach a climbable wall. Climb up to a catapult pad, and the hard work is done. Hop onto that pad.

INTRODUCTION

POLICE ACADEMY

CHARACTERS AND VEHICLES

WALKTHROUGH

LEGO CITY TOUR

CHECKLISTS

Before you know it, you find yourself at the top of the control tower. Nice!

⭐ 5 SOUTH HANGARS

South of the airport are five hangars. One of them is big and impossible to miss, but don't ignore the four smaller ones that are nearby.

Among the smaller hangars, the middle one is full of color swappers. Use the robber's crowbar to break the door and gain access to these useful stations.

FEATS AND COLLECTIBLES

MAP LEGEND

MAP ICON(S)	FEAT/COLLECTIBLE	REWARD(S)	LOCATION/HOW TO REACH	GOT IT?
? Block	? Block	"Super Wrestler" character token (after you find all ? Blocks in the city)	Underneath the freeway.	1
	Alien Caught	Gold brick	Inside a garage on the north end of the airport runway.	2
	ATM Smashed	Gold brick	In front of the airport.	3
1	BBQ Fire Extinguished 1	Gold brick	Along the north wing of the airport.	4
2	BBQ Fire Extinguished 2	Gold brick	In the far corner, past the parking lot.	5
	Boulder Destroyed	Gold brick	Underneath the freeway overpass.	6
	Cat Rescued	Gold brick	Stuck on the airport roof. You have to super jetpack hover to reach it.	7
1	Character Token 1	Air Host	Behind a locked door on the roof of the airport's north wing.	8
2	Character Token 2	Airline Attendant 2	In an office at the airport's north wing. Drill through the ceiling to get inside.	9
3	Character Token 3	Airline Pilot	Build the LCX Control Tower, then climb to the top and use the grapple point to reach this token.	10
1 to 3 / 4	Character Token 4	Cleaner	Paint the three bins red, green, and yellow.	11
5	Character Token 5	Air Hostess	Hovering in the air underneath the freeway.	12
1 to 4 / 6	Character Token 6	Pizza Delivery Boy	Paint the silver phones orange to unlock this token.	13
1 7	Character Token 7	Clown Robber Wes	Paint the flowers the correct colors to earn this token.	14
8	Character Token 8	Alexandra Greenwood	Behind a fence at the far south end of the airport.	15
	Coffee Break Completed	Gold brick	On the roof of the airport.	16
	Disguise Booth	Gold brick, "Airline Attendant 1" character token	Near the front of the airport, at the southern end.	17
	District Conquered	Gold brick	After building the LCX Control Tower, use the grapple point to reach the top.	18
	Drill Thrill Completed	Gold brick	Once on top of the airport roof, head left.	19
1	Flowers Watered 1	Gold brick	Around the back end of Fin's Restaurant.	20
2	Flowers Watered 2	Gold brick	On the roof of the airport's south wing.	21
	Free Run	Gold brick, "Skater Girl" character token	On top of the control tower.	22
	Gang Arrested	Gold brick	Atop the bus stop awning.	23
	Pig Returned	Gold brick	At the very top of a sign on the north wing of the airport roof.	24
	Red Brick	Super Fast Travel	Inside the southern hangars, behind a door with an orange handle only Rex Fury can open.	25
	Silver Statue Destroyed	Gold brick	In a plaza near Fin's Restaurant.	26
1	Superbuild 1: Stunt Ramp	Gold brick, "Pilot" character token	Next to the parking lot near Fin's Restaurant.	27

MAP LEGEND CONTINUED

MAP ICON(S)	FEAT/COLLECTIBLE	REWARD(S)	LOCATION/HOW TO REACH	GOT IT?
2	Superbuild 2: Helipad	Gold brick, "Camel" vehicle token	On the roof of the north wing, head to the right.	28
3	Superbuild 3: Loop de Loop	Gold brick	Right on the airport runway.	29
4	Superbuild 4: Call-in Point	Gold brick, "Protector" vehicle token	Along the runway.	30
5	Superbuild 5: LCX Control Tower	Gold brick	At the base of the control tower, on the airport roof.	31
6	Superbuild 6: Call-in Point	Gold brick, "M.O.V." vehicle token	West of the airport, near the far parking lot.	32
	Time Trial	Gold brick, "Vor" vehicle token	Near some planes, by the runway. Must complete Gang Arrested and superbuild the stunt ramp first.	33
	Train Station	Gold brick, Fast Travel	In front of the Rex statue.	34
	Vehicle Robbery Completed	Gold brick, "Rugged" vehicle token	In a garage on the north end of the runway.	35
	Vehicle Robber Arrested	Gold brick, "Shifter" vehicle token	On top of the large hangar at the south end of the airport.	36
	Vehicle Token	Groundhog	Superbuild the loop de loop, then drive up it.	37

⭐ ? BLOCK

Reward: "Super Wrestler" character token (after all ? Blocks in the city have been found)

The LEGO City Airport is home to one of the rare ? Blocks. Find it underneath the freeway (POI 3).

⭐ 🚗 ALIEN CAUGHT

Reward: Gold brick

There's a small hangar near the north runway of the airport. It has a boarded up door, which is no problem for your fireman. Take it down.

Once you're inside, the hangar door automatically opens, revealing a space crate inside. Activate the crate to reveal the pesky alien attempting to sneak past airport security (probably with an unchecked bottle of water). Take him down!

⭐ 💿 ATM SMASHED

Reward: Gold brick

Make sure no one can take out any cash by smashing the ATM in front of the airport.

⭐ 🔥1 BBQ FIRE EXTINGUISHED 1

Reward: Gold brick

You'll find this raging BBQ along the north wing of the airport.

⭐ 🔥2 BBQ FIRE EXTINGUISHED 2

Reward: Gold brick

This BBQ is far from the action, past the parking lots.

BOULDER DESTROYED

Reward: Gold brick

The special boulder is underneath the freeway overpass.

Wall-hug you way around the edge of the building and leap down onto the gas tanks.

From here you can jump up to some more handholds. Keep climbing to get onto the roof.

CAT RESCUED

Reward: Gold brick

A curious kitty managed to get stuck on top of the airport roof (POI 2). You better rescue it. Find this bit of shaky ground near the airport's front side. Drill it and ride the water spout up to the handhold.

Head to the right, sliding under several signs. Before you reach the end of the walkway, you'll pass a drainpipe. Climb it to reach a platform with a jetpack symbol.

Now you'll super jetpack boost twice to reach the cat in need.

Run forward and you'll see this imposing fence ahead. Not to worry, you can climb the fence and vault over the beam without even needing to jump.

After you vault over the fence, you'll see a locked door straight ahead. Break into this door and collect the character token inside.

CHARACTER TOKEN 2

Reward: Airline Attendant 2

Once you're on the roof of the airport (POI 2), head to the right, vaulting over a few beams. Stop after the last beam and drop down to a lower roof with some shaky ground.

Drill through the lower roof and you'll fall into the office below, landing near a character token. Use the nearby transporter pad to make your escape.

CHARACTER TOKEN 1

Reward: Air Host

Using the astronaut's jetpack, boost up to this handhold and pull yourself onto the thin ledge above.

3 CHARACTER TOKEN 3

Reward: Airline Pilot

This token appears after you build the LCX Control Tower. After you build the tower, you'll see a ladder you can climb. This gets you onto the control tower walkway—use your grapple gun to zip up to the top and snatch this token.

4 CHARACTER TOKEN 4

Reward: Cleaner

Paint the three silver bin doors red, green, and yellow to earn this character token. Check the maps for their locations, and find useful color swappers at the south hangars (POI 5).

Once you paint all three doors, this token appears in front of the airport.

5 CHARACTER TOKEN 5

Reward: Air Hostess

Underneath the freeway (POI 3), you'll find this token floating pretty high in the air. Too high to reach even with your jetpack. Good thing there's a special LEGO wall nearby. Bounce up and grab the token.

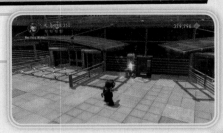 6 CHARACTER TOKEN 6

Reward: Pizza Delivery Boy

There are four silver phones around the zone. Paint them orange to get this token to appear. Check the map to see the phones' locations.

The token shows up under the freeway, near the special boulder.

7 CHARACTER TOKEN 7

Reward: Clown Robber Wes

Paint the flowers in front of Quentin's to earn this token. The token materializes on an awning above the flowers after you paint them properly. Find color swappers at the south hangars (POI 5).

8 CHARACTER TOKEN 8

Reward: Alexandra Greenwood

There's a park in the south end of the airport, bordering uptown. You'll find a tall fence here.

Follow it toward uptown and you'll find this spot where the fence ends.

Step inside and head back the other way to find this character token.

INTRODUCTION

POLICE ACADEMY

CHARACTERS AND VEHICLES

WALKTHROUGH

LEGO CITY TOUR

CHECKLISTS

 DRILL THRILL COMPLETED

Reward: Gold brick

Go to the airport roof (POI 2), using the "Points of Interest" section to assist you. Once there, head to the left and you'll see the fuse box. Use it to kick-start a frantic drill thrill challenge!

COFFEE BREAK COMPLETED

Reward: Gold brick

Get onto the roof of the airport (POI 2), using the "Points of Interest" section to assist you. If you go to the right, you'll soon find a spot for a sip of coffee.

DISGUISE BOOTH

Reward: Gold brick, "Airline Attendant 1" character token

The disguise booth is at the southern end of the airport.

DISTRICT CONQUERED

Reward: Gold brick

To conquer the LEGO City airport, you'll need to buy the LCX Control Tower superbuild. Once you build it, you can climb up the ladder onto the control tower walkway. Use your grapple gun on the grapple point to reach the top of the control tower, where you can plant your flag and claim the airport for Chase McCain!

FLOWERS WATERED 1

Reward: Gold brick

Get onto the upper deck of Fin's Restaurant (POI 1) and make your way around the side to find the flower bed.

FLOWERS WATERED 2

Reward: Gold brick

Get to the roof of the airport (POI 2). From there, head left to find the flower bed around the corner, past the drill thrill fuse box.

⬧ FREE RUN

Rewards: Gold brick, "Skater Girl" character token

The free run token is on top of the control tower (POI 4). Use the previous "Points of Interest" section to find out how to get up there.

The free run challenge starts where you first go to get onto the airport roof (POI 2).

⬧ GANG ARRESTED

Reward: Gold brick

Check out the bus stop across the street from the airport if you want a chance to uncover some gang activity. Use this flower pot to get atop the bus stop overhang.

Use the scan spot to learn that a local gang is heading over to bust up the large hangar behind the airport. This opens the large hangar, which just so happens to unlock the time trial challenge in this zone. Hurry over there and bust up those goons!

⬧ PIG RETURNED

Reward: Gold brick

Make your way onto the roof of the airport and head right, leaping over some beams as necessary. Eventually, you'll see the helipad superbuild. Perform a jetpack jump and boost up to the handholds on the back of the nearby billboard.

Climb up the handholds to reach the beam at the top. Walk across to the right to find the pig in waiting. Hop on that piggy and head for the cannon, which lies to the south, next to the freeway (POI 3).

⬧ RED BRICK

Reward: Super Fast Travel

You'll need Rex Fury to claim this red brick. With Rex, head to the hangars behind the airport. This small, red hangar has a door only Rex can bust down. Rip it open to find your prize inside.

SILVER STATUE DESTROYED

Reward: Gold brick

If you need some fun sticks, the dynamite dispenser is right in front of the airport. (So much for tightened security measures!) Take your dynamite to the Rex statue, which is out in the open in a plaza near Fin's Restaurant (POI 1).

1 SUPERBUILD 1: STUNT RAMP

Reward: Gold brick, "Pilot" character token

Get some sweet air by building a stunt ramp near Fin's Restaurant.

2 SUPERBUILD 2: HELIPAD

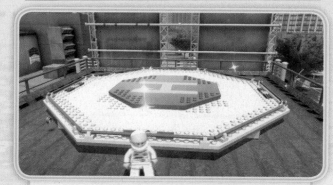

Reward: Gold brick, "Camel" vehicle token

From the roof of the airport's north wing (POI 2), head to the right to get up to this superbuild.

3 SUPERBUILD 3: LOOP DE LOOP

Reward: Gold brick

There's no better place for a loop de loop than on an airport runway. Find this superbuild on the runway, not far from the water. You won't automatically receive a vehicle token for building this superbuild, but a token appears at the crest of the loop de loop—try driving a car through!

4 SUPERBUILD 4: CALL-IN POINT

Reward: Gold brick, "Protector" vehicle token

This vehicle call-in spot is near the airport runways.

5 SUPERBUILD 5: LCX CONTROL TOWER

Reward: Gold brick

Technically, there's no working control tower on top of the LEGO City airport until you build it. Get up to the control tower (POI 4), following the tips in the "Points of Interest" section to reach the top. The superbuild is waiting for you.

INTRODUCTION

POLICE ACADEMY

CHARACTERS AND VEHICLES

WALKTHROUGH

LEGO CITY TOUR

CHECKLISTS

SUPERBUILD 6: CALL-IN POINT

Reward: Gold brick, "M.O.V." vehicle token

You'll find this superbuild west of the airport, near the far parking lot.

TIME TRIAL

Reward: Gold brick, "Vor" vehicle token

Ready for a race around the airport runways? The time trial for this area is smack-dab on a runway, close to the southern wing of the airport.

NOTE

To unlock this time trial, you must first construct this zone's stunt ramp superbuild and complete the Gang Arrested challenge, which opens up the large hangar.

TRAIN STATION

Reward: Gold brick, fast travel

This station is located in the plaza near the silver Rex statue.

VEHICLE ROBBERY COMPLETED

Reward: Gold brick, "Rugged" vehicle token

Begin this challenge by breaking into this locked garage, located on the north side of the runway.

 VEHICLE ROBBER ARRESTED

Reward: Gold brick, "Shifter" vehicle token

What better place to spy on car thieves than on the roof of a giant hangar? Head to the south hangers (POI 5) and go to the south side of the largest one. Jetpack jump and boost up onto the ledge.

Climb a drainpipe and use your grapple gun to pull yourself on top of the large hangar. The scan spot is at the roof's far end.

VEHICLE TOKEN

Reward: Groundhog

Superbuild the loop de loop on the runway, then drive a car up it to snatch this token.

PAGODA

POINTS OF INTEREST

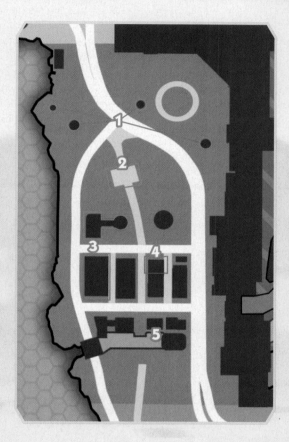

INTRODUCTION

POLICE ACADEMY

CHARACTERS AND VEHICLES

WALKTHROUGH

LEGO CITY TOUR

CHECKLISTS

⭐ ② PLAZA OF TRANQUILITY

LEGO City stressing you out? Practice some meditation in this quiet spot in northern Pagoda.

⭐ ③ CHAN'S, THE TV STORE, AND BEYOND

The rich and important love to show up to parties in one of Chan's limos. You won't be driving a limo today. Instead, you'll be using Chan's building to reach the rooftops of many of Pagoda's shops and apartments.

⭐ ① PAGODAS

Pagoda is clearly named for all of the pagodas in Pagoda. The most interesting of these are several small red pagodas in the northern section of this area.

At Chan's Limo, go to the sign by the showroom. There are handholds here, which you can leap up to reach the roof.

Ascend to the roof and then race across to this scaffolding. There's a handhold here you can use to climb up.

Head right and use the special wall to bounce up to the higher scaffolding above.

After swinging on a flagpole, you'll land on a tightrope that takes you down onto the roof of a cute little TV store.

Climb the ladder, and you're faced with a choice. Heading left will lead to the eastern rooftops. But if you go right, you'll explore a short metal balcony that leads to a transporter pad.

Using the transporter gets you up higher on these roofs. There's no wrong choice in going left or right—you'll need to take both paths eventually to find everything in Pagoda.

⭐ 4 RED BUILDING

Standing out amid the many high-rises in Pagoda is a red building with a view of Festival Square. There's no easy way up onto this building. In fact, the first thing you need to do is get yourself in a chopper. The closest place to get one is on the roof of Ellie's pad in Bright Lights Plaza.

> **NOTE**
>
> You must first visit Ellie's apartment during Story mode before you can access her apartment during normal city exploration.

Once in a chopper, fly toward the red building. The building next to it has a crash pad. Leap out of the chopper onto the crash pad. Then use a jetpack symbol to fly to the next building. Take a flying leap with a catapult pad to land on a building with a tightrope that connects to the red building's roof. Walk the tightrope to finish your journey!

⭐ 5 HANK'S

Hank's is a good place to go if you need car repairs or want to steal a car (in the name of the law, of course). Hank loves birds and you'll find one of

LEGO City's more notable pigeon coups on the roof of his garage.

Your journey starts outside Aidan's record shop, where you'll find this pipe to climb. This gets you onto the second level of some of the stores in Pagoda.

Move forward until you spot this grapple point. Use your grapple gun to get onto the roof.

Cross the tightrope to reach the roof of Hank's garage.

PAGODA

INTRODUCTION

POLICE ACADEMY

CHARACTERS AND VEHICLES

WALKTHROUGH

LEGO CITY TOUR

CHECKLISTS

FEATS AND COLLECTIBLES

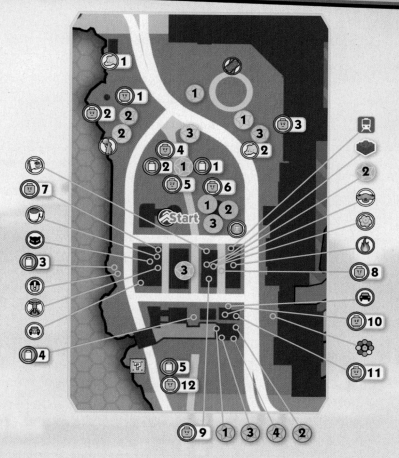

MAP LEGEND

MAP ICON(S)	FEAT/COLLECTIBLE	REWARD(S)	LOCATION/HOW TO REACH	GOT IT?
?	? Block	"Super Wrestler" character token (after you find all ? Blocks in the city)	On a walkway along the ocean.	1
	Alien Caught	Gold brick	On the second level of the southern shops.	2
	ATM Smashed	Gold brick	In front of the bank on the north end of Pagoda.	3
	BBQ Fire Extinguished	Gold brick	Between two of the shops in southern Pagoda.	4
	Boulder Destroyed	Gold brick	On the lawn near the big pagoda.	5
	Cat Rescued	Gold brick	Stuck on a billboard atop the upper rooftops near the TV store.	6
1	Character Token 1	Chan Chuang	Build the Bob-omb and throw it at the locked cage.	7
1 to 3, 2	Character Token 2	Shui Xue	Ring the bells at the three red pagodas.	8
3	Character Token 3	Miles Rebar	On a ledge above the stores on the east end of Pagoda.	9
4	Character Token 4	Li	Atop the north Arch of Tranquility.	10
5	Character Token 5	Fu	On top of the south Arch of Tranquility.	11

MAP LEGEND CONTINUED

MAP ICON(S)	FEAT/COLLECTIBLE	REWARD(S)	LOCATION/HOW TO REACH	GOT IT?
1 to 3 6	Character Token 6	Oliver Duffy	Fill the three empty fountains with water.	12
7	Character Token 7	Quentin Spencer	To the left once you're on the TV store rooftop.	13
1 to 3 8	Character Token 8	Feng	Paint the lampposts around the big pagoda yellow.	14
1 to 3 9	Character Token 9	News Reader	Build the four bonsai trees to unlock this token.	15
10	Character Token 10	Clutch	Inside the pigeon coop on the roof of Hank's garage.	16
1 to 4 11	Character Token 11	Chao Hui	Paint the silver lanterns red.	17
12	Character Token 12	Punk Rocker	Super build and then ride the Frightful Freefall.	18
	Coffee Break Completed	Gold brick	Hidden behind a fenced area on the rooftop above the TV store.	19
	Disguise Booth	Gold brick, "Hai Chen" character token	Near the big dragon statues on the east side of Pagoda.	20
	District Conquered	Gold brick	On top of the red building.	21
	Drill Thrill Completed	Gold brick	On the upper rooftop above the TV store.	22
	Flowers Watered	Gold brick	On one of the rooftops used during the free run challenge.	23
	Free Run	Gold brick, "Disguised Natalia" character token	The challenge is unlocked by playing Chapter 5 of Story mode. It begins in front of Chan's Limos.	24
	Gang Arrested	Gold brick	At the top of the pillar next to the vehicle call-in superbuild.	25
1	Pig Returned 1	Gold brick	Hanging out on top of the far northwest building.	26
2	Pig Returned 2	Gold brick	Summoned after ringing the three bells in the red pagodas.	27
	Red Brick	Super Axe Smash	Sitting on the roof of the red building.	28
	Silver Statue Destroyed	Gold brick	Along the waterfront.	29
1	Superbuild 1: Arches of Tranquility 1	Gold brick	At the north end of the Plaza of Tranquility.	30
2	Superbuild 2: Arches of Tranquility 2	Gold brick	At the south end of the Plaza of Tranquility.	31
3	Superbuild 3: Call-in Point	Gold brick, "Indulga" vehicle token	Next to the freeway at the south end of Pagoda.	32
4	Superbuild 4: Stunt Ramp	Gold brick, "Lagney" character token	On the north side of the canal.	33
5	Superbuild 5: Frightful Freefall	Gold brick	Near Festival Square, on a lawn that's part of the carnival.	34
	Train Station	Gold brick, Fast Travel	In front of the southern shops.	35
	Vehicle Robbery Completed	Gold brick, "Chan's Drakonas" vehicle token	At Hank's garage.	36
	Vehicle Robber Arrested	Gold brick, "Tigerella" vehicle token	In the far corner of the upper rooftop above the TV store.	37

? BLOCK

Reward: "Super Wrestler" character token (after you find all ? Blocks in the city)

Just south of the canal are some steps leading down into a small walkway along the ocean.

Here's where you'll find one of the five ? Blocks hidden throughout LEGO City.

ALIEN CAUGHT

Reward: Gold brick

Start making your way toward the roof of Hank's (POI 5), using the "Points of Interest" section to help you. When you reach the grapple point, stop. Turn around to discover an alien-summoning space crate up here, in clear view.

ATM SMASHED

Reward: Gold brick

This ATM stands in front of the bank in the north end of Pagoda. Time to make a withdrawal...with your fists!

BBQ FIRE EXTINGUISHED

Reward: Gold brick

Find this open flame in a walkway between some of the stores in the southern half of Pagoda.

BOULDER DESTROYED

Reward: Gold brick

Look for the big pagoda not too far from Chan's Limos (POI 3). In the corner of the lawn is where you'll find the special boulder.

CAT RESCUED

Reward: Gold brick

Get onto the building rooftops using Chan's Limos (POI 3). See the previous "Points of Interest" section for help getting to this point. Take the transporter pad to the right to find the cat up on a billboard, waiting for a savior.

CHARACTER TOKEN 1

Reward: Chan Chuang

The character token is locked behind this seemingly indestructible cage. Well, one thing can destroy it. A Bob-omb! You can build your very own Bob-omb by smashing the baskets of fireworks in front of this pillar.

INTRODUCTION

POLICE ACADEMY

CHARACTERS AND VEHICLES

WALKTHROUGH

LEGO CITY TOUR

CHECKLISTS

Once built, the Bob-omb will follow you wherever you go. But it's easier to just pick the little guy up.

Run over and throw the Bob-omb at the cage before its timer runs out, and you'll blast free the token!

⭐ Ⓜ2 CHARACTER TOKEN 2

Reward: Shui Xue

Find the gongs and ring the bells at the three small pagodas in the northern part of this area. One gong is hidden under some boulders.

One is buried underground and you'll need to scan for it.

And one of the bells is painted silver; you must paint it gold for the gong to appear.

The token appears in this fireworks hut.

⭐ Ⓜ3 CHARACTER TOKEN 3

Reward: Miles Rebar

For this token, you must find the shaky ground along the buildings at the north end of Pagoda. Drill it and ride the water spout up.

Go left and make your way along some thin ledges.

Eventually you'll reach the end of the ledge and have to leap to a handhold. From there, leap onto the special wall and then wall-jump up to the far ledge.

The token is at the end of the ledge. Woohoo!

⭐ Ⓜ4 CHARACTER TOKEN 4

Reward: Li

Build the Arches of Tranquility to complete the Plaza of Tranquility (POI 2). There are handholds on the side of the arch you can use to get up top.

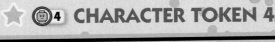

Li's token is on the north arch.

The character token is just past some air conditioners.

5 CHARACTER TOKEN 5

Reward: Fu

Collect Fu the same way you got Li, by building the Arches of Tranquility. Only, Fu is on the top of the south arch.

8 CHARACTER TOKEN 8

Reward: Feng

There are three silver lampposts around the big pagoda; paint them yellow. You can find a yellow color swapper inside the garage of the nearby Chan's Limo (POI 3).

The token appears on a walkway on the second level of the shops. You cross it on your way to Hank's rooftop (POI 5).

6 CHARACTER TOKEN 6

Reward: Oliver Duffy

Fill the three empty fountains with water from the fireman's hose.

The token appears on a rocky platform on the big pond at the center of Pagoda.

9 CHARACTER TOKEN 9

Reward: News Reader

Smash four special brown crates around Pagoda and build four bonsai trees from their bricks to reveal a hidden character token.

7 CHARACTER TOKEN 7

Reward: Quentin Spencer

Make your way from Chan's Limos rooftop to the TV store rooftop (POI 3) with the help of the "Points of Interest" section. Instead of climbing the ladder from the TV store rooftop, though, head left, along a narrow ledge.

The token appears near the space crate used for the Alien Caught challenge.

CHARACTER TOKEN 10

Reward: Clutch

Use the "Points of Interest" section to help you reach the roof of Hank's garage (POI 5). Chop your way into the pigeon coup up there, where you can snatch the token.

11 CHARACTER TOKEN 11

Reward: Chao Hui

Paint the four silver lanterns red to reveal this token. There's a red color swapper just up the road, in the small building with the colorful neon signs.

Once completed, a character token appears in a tranquil spot behind the noodle restaurant.

12 CHARACTER TOKEN 12

Reward: Punk Rocker

Super build the Frightful Freefall ride at the south end of Pagoda. Remember, Chase McCain has no fear. Ride the Frightful Freefall and you'll collect the token on your way up.

COFFEE BREAK COMPLETED

Reward: Gold brick

Get to the TV shop roof via Chan's Limos (POI 3) with the help of the "Points of Interest" section. Head left up the ramp and look for this fenced area. Go behind the fence to discover a hidden coffee oasis.

DISGUISE BOOTH

Reward: Gold brick, "Hai Chen" character token

The disguise booth is by the impressive dragon statues on the east side of Pagoda.

DISTRICT CONQUERED

Reward: Gold brick

Make your way onto the roof of the red building. Use the instructions in the "Points of Interest" section to get you there. Astronaut boost up to the top section, then raise a flag for all of Pagoda to see!

DRILL THRILL COMPLETED

Reward: Gold brick

Make your way to the TV store roof (POI 3) using the "Points of Interest" section to get you there. Take the transporter pad to reach the upper rooftops, then fix the fuse box and start drilling!

FREE RUN

Rewards: Gold brick, "Disguised Natalia" character token

This free run challenge is unlocked during Story mode, so there's no free run token to find. Simply head for the challenge marker, located outside Chan's Limo (POI 3).

FLOWERS WATERED

Reward: Gold brick

Follow the directions in the "Points of Interest" section to get onto the TV store roof (POI 3). Head left,

go up the ramp, and then vault over the beam. You'll soon reach a gap to the next roof. Don't worry, you can make this jump. Leap to the next building.

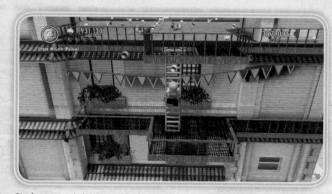

Circle around the metal balcony and climb a ladder. Run forward and scale the wall ahead.

The flower bed is on this open roof, on the right. Give it a drink!

GANG ARRESTED

Reward: Gold brick

The scan spot is on top of a pillar that seems impossible to reach. Well, it is possible, but you have to start at this pillar, which is a little to the south. Astronaut boost onto the lip of the pillar and again to reach the top.

Activate the jetpack symbol and then fly over to the far pillar with the scan spot. Scan for criminal behavior after you land, then hurry over and bust up the thugs at the Plaza of Tranquility (POI 2)!

INTRODUCTION

POLICE ACADEMY

CHARACTERS AND VEHICLES

WALKTHROUGH

LEGO CITY TOUR

CHECKLISTS

1 PIG RETURNED 1

Reward: Gold brick

It's anyone's guess how this pig got up on this building, but there's no mystery how you can get there. It starts across the street, at this shaky ground. Drill here to reveal the pieces to a catapult pad.

Build the pad and then launch yourself across the street and onto the roof with the pig. Hop on and ride south, down to the cannon at the bottom of Pagoda.

2 PIG RETURNED 2

Reward: Gold brick

This pig is summoned when you bang the three gongs to complete the pagoda bell challenge. After the pig arrives, simply hop on and ride down to the south cannon. Yeehaw!

RED BRICK

Reward: Super Axe Smash

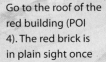

Go to the roof of the red building (POI 4). The red brick is in plain sight once you're there. See the "Points of Interest" section for details on how to get atop the red building.

SILVER STATUE DESTROYED

Reward: Gold brick

Find a dynamite dispenser on the side of the building that has one of Pagoda's lost pigs trapped on its roof. Take some dynamite a short distance south until you spot the Rex statue by the water. Time for a sweet explosion!

1 SUPERBUILD 1: ARCHES OF TRANQUILITY 1

Reward: Gold brick

The Plaza of Tranquility isn't quite complete until you build its two arches. Here's where you need to construct the first one.

2 SUPERBUILD 2: ARCHES OF TRANQUILITY 2

Reward: Gold brick

And here's where you'll construct the second arch to complete the most tranquil spot in all of LEGO City.

3 SUPERBUILD 3: CALL-IN POINT

Reward: Gold brick, "Indulga" vehicle token

This superbuild is next to the freeway at the southwest end of Pagoda.

⭐ 📇4 SUPERBUILD 4: STUNT RAMP

Reward: Gold brick, "Lagney" character token

This is on the north side of the canal, between two buildings.

⭐ 📇5 SUPERBUILD 5: FRIGHTFUL FREEFALL

Reward: Gold brick

Part of Pagoda melds right into Festival Square, which is why there's a carnival ride that needs to be built. This is over the canal, at the far south end of Pagoda.

⭐ 🚇 TRAIN STATION

Reward: Gold brick, fast travel

The train station is in front of the southern shops.

⭐ 🚗 VEHICLE ROBBERY COMPLETED

Reward: Gold brick, "Chan's Drakonas" vehicle token

Go to Hank's garage (POI 5) on the street level to find this door for the robber to break into.

⭐ 🚓 VEHICLE ROBBER ARRESTED

Reward: Gold brick, "Tigerella" vehicle token

Follow the "Points of Interest" section to reach the roof of the TV store (POI 3). Take the transporter pad to the upper rooftop, then climb a wall with a blue and white LEGO patch.

Head right to find the scan spot on the corner of the roof. Prepare to begin a high-speed chase!

INTRODUCTION

POLICE ACADEMY

CHARACTERS AND VEHICLES

WALKTHROUGH

LEGO CITY TOUR

CHECKLISTS

PARADISE SANDS

POINTS OF INTEREST

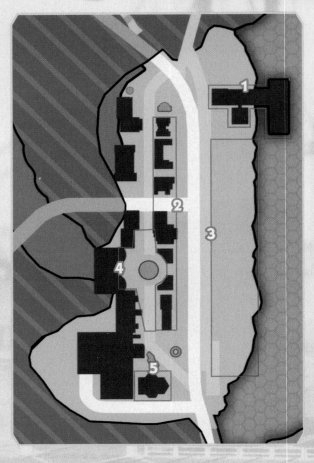

☆ 2 HOTEL ROOFS

Though the Honey Hotel is the largest and nicest place to stay in Paradise Sands, there are several other hotels, more appealing to college kids on spring break. These hotels are noted for their neon trim. You'll find lots of interesting things on these rooftops, and right now, we'll take you all the way across each one to get you to the very last building, the Herbert Hotel.

To get onto the roof of these hotels, start by heading toward the roof of the Honey Hotel. Climb the Honey Hotel, ride the mechanical bee up, and take an elevator to reach a high patio pool. Use a chicken symbol to glide way over to the distant hotels.

After you land, you'll see some vines on the side of the building that are perfect for climbing.

This fountain has sprung a leak. Ride the water spout up onto the roof.

☆ 1 BOARDWALK

It's not just fun and games at the boardwalk. Well, actually, it is mostly just fun and games. Here you'll find the gravity-defying Orion's Rockets ride and much more.

The next building has some handholds on the wall. Leap across the gap, grab on, and climb up. Make your way up and over to an air conditioner. Destroy it and build a climbable wall from its pieces.

Climb up and then slide down a tightrope to reach the next roof. Jump up the far flowers to reach a beam. Walk across a tightrope to reach the next portion of roof.

Climb a wall and cross another tightrope to reach a roof with a pool, which you actually built during Story mode.

As you did during Story mode, hop onto the ball and then onto the catapult pad to get launched over to another roof.

Oh look, another catapult pad on this roof. You know what to do!

You land on some distant handholds. Shimmy across and climb the LEGO patch on the wall.

Head through the open door to at last emerge on the roof of the Herbert Hotel. Sweet!

⭐ 3 BEACH

After a hard day of catching crooks, Chase McCain could use a little surf and sand. The beach of Paradise Sands is an excellent place to unwind. Heck, maybe you should build some sand castles here!

⭐ 4 BAZAAR

Behind the neon hotels of Paradise Sands is a lovely bazaar. There's a giant pool here as well as a BBQ and plenty of stands selling food.

⭐ 5 HONEY HOTEL

Frank Honey's family owns the plushest and most famous hotel in all of LEGO City. But no Honey can climb to the top of that hotel like Chase McCain.

To reach the top, start by finding this scaffolding around back. Climb the ladder and jump up at the end to grab on to the handholds and get to the next story of the hotel.

INTRODUCTION

POLICE ACADEMY

CHARACTERS AND VEHICLES

WALKTHROUGH

LEGO CITY TOUR

CHECKLISTS

Make your way to the right until you find this drainpipe. Climb it until you reach the giant mechanical bee. Yes, you read that right!

Ride the bee up to the next floor, leaping off to the right. There's a jetpack symbol on the railing.

Use the jetpack ring to boost over to the lowest handhold of the Honey Hotel sign. Hop up the handholds afterward to reach the roof.

You're not at the top of the world, but at least you're at the top of this hotel now!

FEATS AND COLLECTIBLES

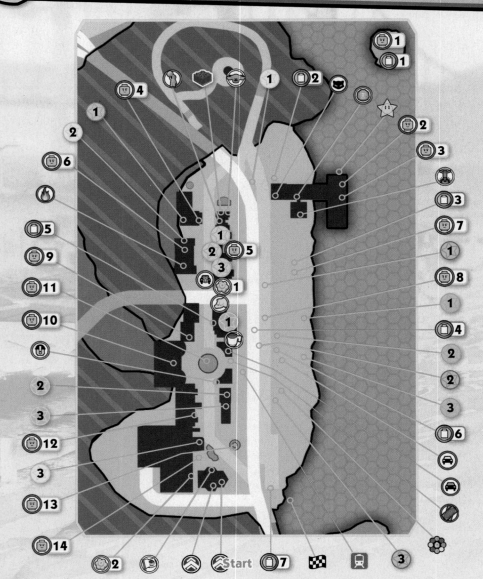

MAP LEGEND

MAP ICON(S)	FEAT/COLLECTIBLE	REWARD(S)	LOCATION/HOW TO REACH	GOT IT?
	Alien Caught	Gold brick	On the roof of the Herbert Hotel.	1
	ATM Smashed	Gold brick	At the entrance to the bazaar.	2
	BBQ Fire Extinguished	Gold brick	In the corner of a lawn just north of the bazaar.	3
	Boulder Destroyed	Gold brick	Underneath the boardwalk.	4
	Cat Rescued	Gold brick	In front of the roller coaster at the boardwalk.	5
1	Character Token 1	Captain Bluffbeard	Build Bluffbeard's Lighthouse, then break into the front door to find the token at the top.	6
2	Character Token 2	Viking	Hop on the viking ride.	7
3	Character Token 3	Crazy Scientist	Super build Orion's Rockets, then hop on and ride the roller coaster.	8
1 4	Character Token 4	Hula Dancer	Paint the four flowers the correct colors.	9
1 to 3 5	Character Token 5	Rudolph Pianola	Paint the three flamingos around the hotel pink.	10
6	Character Token 6	Doorman	On an awning in the bazaar.	11
7	Character Token 7	Surfer	Rip the door off the super sand castle after building it.	12
1 to 3 8	Character Token 8	Beach Dude	Build the three small sand castles on the beach.	13
9	Character Token 9	Rodney Baxter	On top of an awning at a hotel in the bazaar.	14
1 to 3 10	Character Token 10	Maraca Man	Build the three jukeboxes to unlock.	15
1 to 3 11	Character Token 11	Surfer Girl	Paint the three silver surfboards yellow.	16
12	Character Token 12	Becky Ballantine	On a hotel awning at the bazaar.	17
1 to 3 13	Character Token 13	Troublemaker Tom	Paint the three palm tress brown.	18
14	Character Token 14	Blubs	Hidden in a silver rock under the grotto.	19
	Coffee Break Completed	Gold Brick	In front of one of the main hotels.	20
	Disguise Booth	Gold brick, "Coastguard" character token	Near the beach in front of some stairs.	21
	District Conquered	Gold brick	Atop the Honey Hotel.	22
	Drill Thrill Completed	Gold brick	At the end of the boardwalk.	23
1	Flowers Watered 1	Gold brick	On one of the hotel rooftops.	24
2	Flowers Watered 2	Gold brick	Behind the Honey Hotel.	25
	Free Run	Gold brick, "Frank Poolside" character token	Unlocked in story mode. The challenge starts in front of the Honey Hotel.	26

INTRODUCTION

POLICE ACADEMY

CHARACTERS AND VEHICLES

WALKTHROUGH

LEGO CITY TOUR

CHECKLISTS

MAP LEGEND CONTINUED

MAP ICON(S)	FEAT/COLLECTIBLE	REWARD(S)	LOCATION/HOW TO REACH	GOT IT?
	Gang Arrested	Gold brick	In the back corner of the rooftop of one of the hotels.	27
	Pig Returned	Gold brick	Next to a crash mat. The only way to get up there is with a helicopter.	28
	Red Brick	Ring Tone: Gas	At the top of the Herbert Hotel.	29
	Silver Statue Destroyed	Gold brick	On the overhang in front of the Herbert Hotel.	30
1	Superbuild 1: Bluffbeard's Lighthouse	Gold brick	On the island northeast of the beach.	31
2	Superbuild 2: Orion's Rockets	Gold brick	In front of the roller coaster.	32
3	Superbuild 3: Super Sand Castle	Gold brick	At the north end of the beach.	33
4	Superbuild 4: Call-in Point	Gold brick, "Epona" vehicle token	Along the main street.	34
5	Superbuild 5: Paradise Pool	Gold brick, "Talos" vehicle token.	Built in Story mode.	35
6	Superbuild 6: Loop de Loop	Gold brick	In the middle of the beach.	36
7	Superbuild 7: Stunt Ramp	Gold brick, "Ice Fisherman" character token	At the south end of Paradise Sands, near the beach.	37
	Super Star	"Pop Star" character token (after you find all Super Stars in the city)	Atop the roller coaster.	38
	Time Trial	Gold brick, "Galleon" vehicle token	In the water, south of the beach.	39
	Train Station	Gold brick, Fast Travel	Near the entrance of the bazaar.	40
	Vehicle Robbery Completed	Gold brick, "Athena" vehicle token	The garage is near the entrance to the bazaar.	41
	Vehicle Robber Arrested	Gold brick, "Lusca" vehicle token	On the hotel rooftops.	42
	Vehicle Token	Sweetie	Super build the loop de loop on the beach, then drive up it.	43

ALIEN CAUGHT

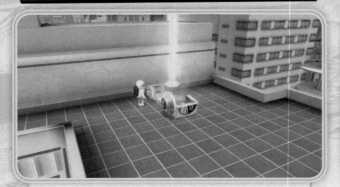

Reward: Gold brick

Make your way to the roof of the Herbert Hotel (POI 2) with the assistance of the "Points of Interest" section. Once there, inch along the thin ledge in front of the hotel sign to reach a suspicious space crate!

ATM SMASHED

Reward: Gold brick

The ATM is at the entrance to the bazaar (POI 4), in front of the giant fountain.

BBQ FIRE EXTINGUISHED

Reward: Gold brick

The BBQ blaze is located in the corner of a lawn, just north of the bazaar (POI 4).

BOULDER DESTROYED

Reward: Gold brick

The special boulder is cleverly hidden underneath the boardwalk (POI 1). Drop down onto the beach and you can run under the boardwalk to find it.

CAT RESCUED

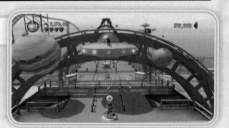

Reward: Gold brick

The cat is in front of the roller coaster entrance on the boardwalk (POI 1).

1 CHARACTER TOKEN 1

Reward: Captain Bluffbeard

Before you can get this token, you'll have to super build the lighthouse. Do so and then use the robber to break into the front door. Enter the door afterward to move to the top of the lighthouse, where you can grab the token.

2 CHARACTER TOKEN 2

Reward: Viking

Toward the back of the boardwalk is a carnival ride featuring a massive viking ship. Only, it's not working. There's a problem with the fuse box, but a good whack by the construction worker will take care of it.

Nice work! Now hop on and enjoy the ride, and you'll snatch a character token.

3 CHARACTER TOKEN 3

Reward: Crazy Scientist

First, construct the Orion's Rockets superbuild. Then jump into one of the seats and enjoy the ride. As you head around the roller coaster, you'll automatically collect this token.

4 CHARACTER TOKEN 4

Reward: Hula Dancer

Paint the four flowers the correct colors to unlock this token. You can find some helpful color swappers in a small background store near the bazaar (POI 4). Once you color all the flowers, a character token shows up on the nearby lawn.

INTRODUCTION

POLICE ACADEMY

CHARACTERS AND VEHICLES

WALKTHROUGH

LEGO CITY TOUR

CHECKLISTS

⭐ 🔵5 CHARACTER TOKEN 5

Reward: Rudolph Pianola

There are three silver flamingos around this hotel; paint them pink. One of the flamingos is hiding around back. You can find a pink color swapper right nearby. After you color all the flamingos pink, a character token appears near the hotel entrance.

⭐ 🔵6 CHARACTER TOKEN 6

Reward: Doorman

Along the bazaar (POI 4) is a hotel with a prominent awning. There's a grapple point here.

Use your grapple gun to get on top of the awning, where you'll find the token.

⭐ 🔵7 CHARACTER TOKEN 7

Reward: Surfer

You'll need to super build the Super Sand Castle to get this token. Once you build it, you can see that the castle door has a grapple point. Using your grapple gun, yank the door open to reveal the prize inside.

⭐ 🔵8 CHARACTER TOKEN 8

Reward: Beach Dude

Build the three sand castles on the beach to unlock this token. The token then appears along the surf wall.

⭐ 🔵9 CHARACTER TOKEN 9

Reward: Rodney Baxter

Look for the shaky ground in front of this hotel at the bazaar (POI 4). Drill into it and ride the water spout up.

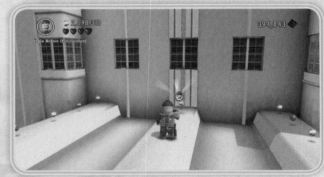

You'll find a character token up on the awning, waiting for the taking.

⭐ 🔵10 CHARACTER TOKEN 10

Reward: Maraca Man

Smash the brown crates and build the three jukeboxes to reveal this token.

The token appears on the roof of the shops in the bazaar.

⊙11 CHARACTER TOKEN 11

Reward: Surfer Girl

Along the beach are three silver surfboards. Paint them yellow to unlock this token.

The token floats over the pool at the bazaar (POI 4). Take a car and race off the ramp to collect it in style!

⊙12 CHARACTER TOKEN 12

Reward: Becky Ballentine

Give a quick look at the awnings in front of the hotels surrounding the bazaar (POI 4). You'll spot this character token on one of them. To get up to it, fill the pool in front of the awning with water using the firefighter's extinguisher.

Once full of water, the pool jets up a fountain. Ride the jet up to your prize.

⊙13 CHARACTER TOKEN 13

Reward: Troublemaker Tom

Paint the three silver palm trees brown to earn this token. Check the map to see where these special trees stand.

The token appears between these palm trees once the color puzzle is completed.

⊙14 CHARACTER TOKEN 14

Reward: Blubs

Near the Honey Hotel (POI 5), there's a little grotto with a rock formation you can walk under. Inside, you'll find a small rock. Smash it to expose a hidden character token.

☕ COFFEE BREAK COMPLETED

Reward: Gold brick

One of the easier coffee breaks you'll take in LEGO City is right in front of the main party hotel. Smash the LEGO barricade and enjoy your cup.

INTRODUCTION

POLICE ACADEMY

CHARACTERS AND VEHICLES

WALKTHROUGH

LEGO CITY TOUR

CHECKLISTS

DISGUISE BOOTH

Reward: Gold brick, "Coastguard" character token

The disguise booth is in front of some steps leading down onto the beach (POI 3).

DISTRICT CONQUERED

Reward: Gold brick

Find this flag spot at the top of the Honey Hotel (POI 5). See the "Points of Interest" section to learn how to get up here.

DRILL THRILL COMPLETED

Reward: Gold brick

A game of drill thrill is yours to enjoy near the end of the boardwalk. Fix the fuse box and have at it!

FLOWERS WATERED 1

Reward: Gold brick

As you're making your way toward the roof of the Herbert Hotel (POI 2), you'll land on this roof with some special boulders and a catapult pad. There's also a flower bed in the corner.

FLOWERS WATERED 2

Reward: Gold brick

The flower bed is behind the Honey Hotel (POI 5).

FREE RUN

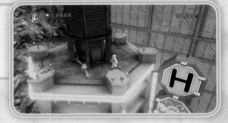

Rewards: Gold brick, "Frank Poolside" character token

Use the "Points of Interest" section to guide you to the top of the Honey Hotel (POI 5). Once you're there, the free run token is an easy grab.

The free run course begins at the bottom of the hotel.

GANG ARRESTED

Reward: Gold brick

The scan spot is on the roof of one of the first buildings you cross on your way to the Herbert Hotel (POI 2)—one that overlooks the bazaar (POI 4). The "Points of Interest" section can help you get to this spot. Listen in to hear the gang's plot and then race to break it up!

PIG RETURNED

Reward: Gold brick

The only way to reach this pick is with a helicopter. The nearest helipad is at the back entrance of Blackwell's home, in Fresco. Drop onto the crash mat atop the tall building, then hop onto the pig and ride for the cannon, which stands near the Honey Hotel.

RED BRICK

Reward: Ring Tone—Gas

Follow the "Points of Interest" section to reach the roof of the Herbert Hotel (POI 2). Once there, inch across a thin ledge in front of the hotel sign to reach the other side of the roof. Lucky you: the red brick is in plain sight!

SILVER STATUE DESTROYED

Reward: Gold brick

This statue stands on the overhang of the entrance to the Herbert Hotel. Climb the drainpipe in front of the hotel to reach the statue, then blow it sky high! Dynamite can be found on the boardwalk (POI 1) if you're in need.

 SUPERBUILD 1: BLUFFBEARD'S LIGHTHOUSE

Reward: Gold brick

There's a small island to the far northeast of Paradise Sands. Swim or take a boat out to the island and you'll find it's pretty desolate. The only thing to do here is build a lighthouse!

SUPERBUILD 2: ORION'S ROCKETS

Reward: Gold brick

The most fun to be had in LEGO City is probably riding the famed Orion roller coaster. To ride the coaster, though, you'll have to super build Orion's Rockets! Head to the boardwalk (POI 1) and build this awesome thrill ride without delay.

SUPERBUILD 3: SUPER SAND CASTLE

Reward: Gold brick

There's quite a lot of beach in Paradise Sands—the perfect place to build a giant sand castle!

SUPERBUILD 4: CALL-IN POINT

Reward: Gold brick, "Epona" vehicle token

As with most vehicle call-in superbuilds, this can be found just to the side of the main street.

SUPERBUILD 5: PARADISE POOL

Reward: Gold brick, "Talos" vehicle token

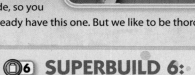

This superbuild is constructed during Story mode, so you should already have this one. But we like to be thorough!

SUPERBUILD 6: LOOP DE LOOP

Reward: Gold brick

This epic superbuild is on the beach (POI 3). Where else would you be doing loop de loops?

SUPERBUILD 7: STUNT RAMP

Reward: Gold brick, "Ice Fisherman" character token

You can find this stunt ramp superbuild at the south end of Paradise Sands, next to the beach (POI 3).

NOTE

The "Muncher" time trial challenge will not appear in Fresco until you construct this stunt ramp superbuild. This stunt ramp is vital to that race!

SUPER STAR

Reward: "Pop Star" character token (after you find all Super Stars in the city)

At the north end of Paradise Sands, there's a fork in the road. Leave the main street and drive up the path to the right toward the observatory.

Hidden along the rocky bluff is an area that overlooks the boardwalk (POI 1). There's a super chicken-glide symbol here.

Make the epic chicken-glide over to the top of Orion's Rockets.

Carefully land atop the roller coaster's narrow roof. Destroy the yellow box up here and build a Super Star from its pieces. Score!

⭐ 🏁 TIME TRIAL

Reward: Gold brick, "Galleon" vehicle token

This aquatic race against time is found just south of the beach (POI 3). You'll race through some rocky terrain, so be cautious and don't get too close to any land.

⭐ 🚉 TRAIN STATION

Reward: Gold brick, fast travel

You can build a connection to the train line in front of the entrance to the bazaar (POI 4). Head down the steps and smash the green cabinets, then build the ticket machine.

⭐ 🚗 VEHICLE ROBBERY COMPLETED

Reward: Gold brick, "Athena" vehicle token

You'll find the garage near the entrance to the bazaar.

⭐ 👮 VEHICLE ROBBER ARRESTED

Reward: Gold brick, "Lusca" vehicle token

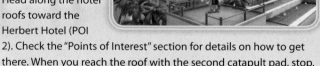

Head along the hotel roofs toward the Herbert Hotel (POI 2). Check the "Points of Interest" section for details on how to get there. When you reach the roof with the second catapult pad, stop. The scan spot is nearby, toward the back-left corner of the roof.

⭐ 🚗 VEHICLE TOKEN

Reward: Sweetie

Super build the Loop de Loop on the beach, then drive up it to collect this token.

INTRODUCTION

POLICE ACADEMY

CHARACTERS AND VEHICLES

WALKTHROUGH

LEGO CITY TOUR

CHECKLISTS

UPTOWN

POINTS OF INTEREST

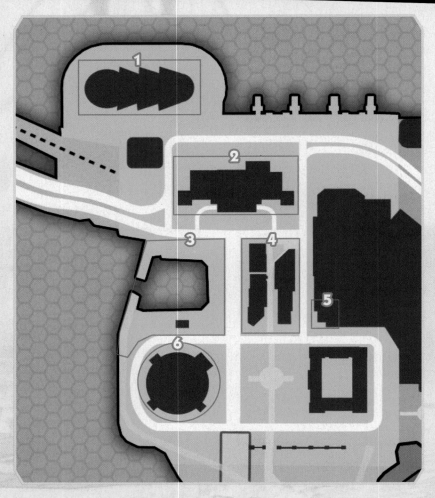

⭐ 1 ART MUSEUM

The Art Museum is home to some of the finest paintings and sculptures in the world—but you're going to be more interested in getting to the rooftop than going on a tour. The Art Museum serves as the starting point to reaching the roofs of both the Museum of Natural History (POI 2) and the library (POI 6).

Head to the side of the Art Museum, where you'll see some flower pots. If you've finished Story mode, then some vines will already be here. If not, you can use the farmer to water the plants. Climb the vine and make your way along the handholds on the ceiling and along the wall.

Once you can pull yourself up, slide under the small entryway. Every color swapper you could ever want is here. Head into the elevator.

The elevator takes you to a higher level. Even though there's a lot of space outside the museum, there's really nothing to see here. Hop on the two flowers to get onto this awning.

Head to the left across the awnings until you reach a giant fan. Leap into the gust and rise up.

Race up a long series of slopes, then climb a LEGO patch on the far wall. You'll then be enjoying the view from the top of the Art Museum!

★ ② MUSEUM OF NATURAL HISTORY

The Museum of Natural History is the most notable building in Uptown. It has an enormous and expansive rooftop and two large towers, and offers access to the library even though it's all the way across town.

To access this museum's roof, you must first reach the roof of the Art Museum (POI 1). Once there, look for this chicken symbol.

Activate the symbol and then make a long chicken-glide down to the roof of the Museum of Natural History.

★ ③ DOCKS

Though uptown is full of hustle and bustle, you can usually find a quiet moment to yourself at the docks. And then, when you want to cause a ruckus, check for a dynamite dispenser at the dock house!

★ ④ APARTMENTS

This quiet set of brownstones are located in the middle of uptown. You'll, of course, want to get onto the roof.

On the south side of the apartments is this blue and white LEGO wall. Climb it and use the handhold above to get a little higher.

There's another LEGO wall ahead. Bounce off it to reach a high flagpole, then swing to the roof.

INTRODUCTION · POLICE ACADEMY · CHARACTERS AND VEHICLES · WALKTHROUGH · LEGO CITY TOUR · CHECKLISTS

Make your way north up the rooftop and hop across some thin poles to reach this catapult pad at the end of the roof. Launch yourself

across the street, over to another set of apartments.

Walk the tightrope after you land, and keep heading left.

Hop across a few more thin poles, and before you know it, you'll reach the end of the apartment rooftops. Nice run.

⑤ TOY STORE

Across from the apartments is a sweet-looking toy store that happens to hold the most important red brick in all of LEGO City. But how to get up to the roof?

Check out the rockets. Those are actually platforms. Use the color swapper at the Art Museum to load up some green paint. Shoot the two lights below the rockets to activate them.

Grab the handhold attached to the toy block and make your way onto the moving rockets.

Jump onto a rocket platform, then ride up to the catwalk above. Now you're king of the toy store!

⑥ LIBRARY

To reach the library roof, you'll need to make your way onto the roof of the Museum of Natural History (POI 2). Once there, head toward the west tower.

Climb a drainpipe to find a transporter pad. Use it and you're teleported to the top of the tower, right onto a chicken symbol.

Activate the chicken symbol and glide over the docks and to the library. It's a long flight, so don't look down!

The lengthy chicken-glide doesn't quite get you to the roof. You land by some statues of LEGO folks reaching up to grasp knowledge.

Well, you should reach up too—and get to the handhold above you. Climb the wall and you'll step right onto a catapult pad, which will launch you to the very top of the library.

FEATS AND COLLECTIBLES

INTRODUCTION

POLICE ACADEMY

CHARACTERS AND VEHICLES

WALKTHROUGH

LEGO CITY TOUR

CHECKLISTS

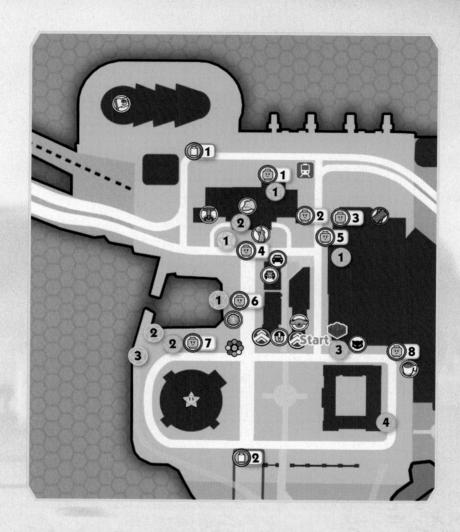

⚙ ALIEN CAUGHT

Reward: Gold brick

Head to the apartments (POI 4) and climb the wall on the south side. You can't miss this space crate. Match the color code and summon the alien invader!

⚙ ATM SMASHED

Reward: Gold brick

The ATM is neatly tucked on the side of a building on the east end of uptown. It's right near the border of the LEGO City Airport.

MAP LEGEND

MAP ICON(S)	FEAT/COLLECTIBLE	REWARD(S)	LOCATION/HOW TO REACH	GOT IT?
	Alien Caught	Gold brick	Climb the wall on the south side of the apartments.	1
	ATM Smashed	Gold brick	On the east end of uptown, near the border of the airport.	2
	Boulder Destroyed	Gold brick	Down by the docks.	3
	Cat Rescued	Gold brick	On a catwalk above the toy store.	4
1 to 2 / 1	Character Token 1	Bucky Butler	Paint the knight statues outside the museum.	5
2	Character Token 2	Mike Northeast	On a thin ledge around the back side of the Museum of Natural History's east tower.	6
3	Character Token 3	Roman Soldier	Hidden on a ledge of a building that borders the airport.	7
1 / 4	Character Token 4	Pharaoh	Paint the pharaoh statue outside the museum.	8
5	Character Token 5	Kevin Jacobs	In the back of the arcade.	9
1 to 4 / 6	Character Token 6	Janitor	Build the four bubble gum machines around uptown.	10
1 to 3 / 7	Character Token 7	Gladiator	Build the three fishing rods along the docks.	11
8	Character Token 8	Officer Park	On an awning outside the Herbert Hotel.	12
	Coffee Break Completed	Gold brick	In front of the Herbert Hotel.	13
	Disguise Booth	Gold brick, "Bus Driver" character token	Near the docks.	14
	District Conquered	Gold brick	On the roof of the Art Museum.	15
	Drill Thrill Completed	Gold brick	By the west tower of the Museum of Natural History.	16
	Free Run	Gold brick, "Cowboy" character token	At the end of the apartment rooftops.	17
	Gang Arrested	Gold brick	On the apartment roofs, at the east end.	18
	Pig Returned	Gold brick	Atop the dome of the Museum of Natural History.	19
	Red Brick	Super Color Gun	Hidden behind a wall on top of the toy store.	20
	Silver Statue Destroyed	Gold brick	In front of the Museum of Natural History.	21
1	Superbuild 1: Call-in Point	Gold brick, "Hestia" vehicle token	On the street in front of the Art Museum.	22
2	Superbuild 2: Call-in Point	Gold brick, "Hazard" vehicle token	At the south end of uptown, behind the library.	23
	Super Star	"Pop Star" character token (after you find all Super Stars in the city)	On top of the library.	24
	Train Station	Gold brick, Fast Travel	On the north side of the Museum of Natural History.	25
	Vehicle Robbery Completed	Gold brick, "Smallisimo" vehicle token	At the north end of the apartments.	26
	Vehicle Robber Arrested	Gold brick, "Flare" vehicle token	On the south end of the apartment roofs.	27

⭐ ◎ BOULDER DESTROYED

Reward: Gold brick

Down by the docks (POI 3), you'll find this little lawn. The special boulder is underneath the regular boulders.

⭐ 🐱 CAT RESCUED

Reward: Gold brick

Use the "Points of Interest" section to reach the top of the toy store (POI 5). Then go to the right to find a cat in need of rescue.

⭐ ①1 CHARACTER TOKEN 1

Reward: Bucky Butler

Paint the two knights at the Museum of Natural History (POI 2) to reveal this token.

The token appears on the museum steps.

⭐ ②2 CHARACTER TOKEN 2

Reward: Mike Northeast

Follow the "Points of Interest" section to reach the roof of the Museum of Natural History (POI 2). Once there, head to the east tower. Don't climb the wall, though. Instead, follow the thin ledge around the side of the tower.

Eventually, you'll reach a character token.

⭐ ③3 CHARACTER TOKEN 3

Reward: Roman Soldier

For this token, you'll actually start at the LEGO City Airport. Get to the second deck of Fin's Restaurant and find this flower pot. Water it and climb up onto the restaurant's roof.

Behind the billboard is a special wall. Jump onto it and then bounce on top of the roof.

Scamper up the sloped roof, heading toward a chicken symbol. Activate the symbol and then chicken-glide onto the shark billboard.

Leap up the handholds to reach the top of the billboard.

Walk along the tightrope that follows to reach the next billboard, then continue onto the next tightrope.

Once you reach the roof, head to the right to find the token.

⭐ 4 CHARACTER TOKEN 4

Reward: Pharaoh

There's a pharaoh statue in front of the Museum of Natural History (POI 2); paint it gold to reveal this token, which appears right nearby, in front of the Rex statue.

⭐ 5 CHARACTER TOKEN 5

Reward: Kevin Jacobs

Find this token in the back of the arcade.

⭐ 6 CHARACTER TOKEN 6

Reward: Janitor

Build the four bubble gum machines around the zone to reveal this token.

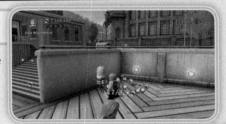

Once completed, you'll find the token in front of the docks.

⭐ 7 CHARACTER TOKEN 7

Reward: Gladiator

Go to the docks (POI 3) and smash objects, then build the three fishing poles by the water.

A token materializes at the dock house after you build all three fishing poles.

⭐ 8 CHARACTER TOKEN 8

Reward: Officer Park

This token is on the awning in front of the Herbert Hotel. Use the grapple gun to get up to it.

⭐ COFFEE BREAK COMPLETED

Reward: Gold brick

Take a load off at this coffee break station in front of the Herbert Hotel.

⭐ DISGUISE BOOTH

Reward: Gold brick, "Bus Driver" character token

The disguise booth is out in the open, near the docks (POI 3).

⭐ DISTRICT CONQUERED

Reward: Gold brick

Get to the roof of the Art Museum (POI 1) with help from the "Points of Interest" section. Once there, use an astronaut boost to get onto this flagpole. Climb the flagpole, then slide down the long tightrope. Wahoo!

You'll land right near a flag symbol. Fly your flag because uptown is all yours.

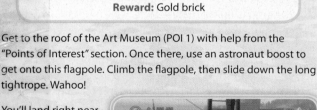

⭐ DRILL THRILL COMPLETED

Reward: Gold brick

Go to the roof of the Museum of Natural History (POI 2) and then head toward the west tower. Near the crash mat is the fuse box that starts up a drill thrill challenge.

⭐ FREE RUN

Rewards: Gold brick, "Cowboy" character token

Follow the instructions in the "Points of Interest" section to reach the end of the apartment rooftops (POI 4). Once there, climb to the top of the billboard to snatch this zone's free run token.

The free run challenge starts back at the ground floor of the apartments. Better get a move on!

INTRODUCTION

POLICE ACADEMY

CHARACTERS AND VEHICLES

WALKTHROUGH

LEGO CITY TOUR

CHECKLISTS

GANG ARRESTED

Reward: Gold brick

Head to the end of the apartment rooftops (POI 4), using the "Points of Interest" section for guidance. Once there, you'll see the scan spot at the roof's highest point. Find the gang, then make the bust!

PIG RETURNED

Reward: Gold brick

The pig awaits atop the dome of the Museum of Natural History (POI 2). Use the "Points of Interest" section to help you get to the roof. Once there, look for this handhold.

Climb up and cross a tightrope. Keep going until you reach a pig. Hop on and ride the little guy to the cannon at the docks (POI 3).

RED BRICK

Reward: Super Color Gun

Go to the roof of the toy store (POI 5). You can check the "Points of Interest" section to get there. Once on the roof, head to the left to find this transporter pad.

It will teleport you behind a wall, where you can grab the red brick. This brick gives you every color for your color gun, meaning you never have to use a color swapper again!

SILVER STATUE DESTROYED

Reward: Gold brick

Grab some dynamite from the dock house, then head to the front of the Museum of Natural History (POI 2). Get up to the Rex statue's barrel with a jetpack jump, then plant the dynamite and hop off before the statue goes boom!

SUPERBUILD 1: CALL-IN POINT

Reward: Gold brick, "Hestia" vehicle token

This superbuild is on the street in front of the Art Museum (POI 1).

SUPERBUILD 2: CALL-IN POINT

Reward: Gold brick, "Hazard" vehicle token

You can build another call-in spot at the south end of uptown, behind the library (POI 6).

SUPER STAR

Reward: "Pop Star" character token (after you find all Super Stars in the city)

With help from the "Points of Interest" section, get to the roof of the library (POI 6). Smash the yellow box and build the pieces into one of the city's five Super Stars.

TRAIN STATION

Reward: Gold brick, fast travel

The train station is on the north side of the Museum of Natural History (POI 2).

VEHICLE ROBBERY COMPLETED

Reward: Gold brick, "Smallisimo" vehicle token

The garage is on the north end of the apartments (POI 4).

VEHICLE ROBBER ARRESTED

Reward: Gold brick, "Flare" vehicle token

Start along the apartment rooftops (POI 4), following the guide in the "Points of Interest" section. Right after you use the catapult pad to reach the other set of apartments, look to your right. Jetpack jump up to the blue and white LEGO patch on the right wall.

Climb onto the roof, where you'll find this scan spot. Find the nearby car thief, then chase him down and make the arrest!

INTRODUCTION

POLICE ACADEMY

CHARACTERS AND VEHICLES

WALKTHROUGH

LEGO CITY TOUR

CHECKLISTS

CHECKLISTS AND EXTRAS

Welcome to the checklists! These final quick-reference lists can help you keep track of your progress in *LEGO City Undercover*.

 GOLD BRICK BREAKDOWN

There are 450 gold bricks for you to collect in *LEGO City Undercover*. Here's how to find them all:

GOLD BRICKS

NO.	HOW TO GET	GOT IT?	NO.	HOW TO GET	GOT IT?
1–15	Beat all 15 Special Assignments in Story mode.	1	56–61	Buy the 16 gold bricks from the gold brick terminal in the police station's basement.	5
16–30	Find all four police shield pieces in all 15 Story mode Special Assignments.	2	62–450	Complete the 388 unique feats and challenges around LEGO City (construct superbuilds, beat time trials and free runs, water flowers, douse BBQ fires, raise district flags, blast silver statues, smash special boulders, etc.). In short, complete all of the city's events and challenges!	6
31–45	Earn enough studs to receive LEGO City Hero honors in all 15 Special Assignments.	3			
46–55	Find the 10 gold bricks hidden around the police station.	4			

 RED BRICK BREAKDOWN

There are 40 red bricks for you to collect in *LEGO City Undercover*. Each one bestows a power, and some red bricks are more useful than others—but true collectors will want to find them all.

RED BRICKS

NAME	EFFECT	LOCATION	HOW TO GET	GOT IT?
Ring Tone: Belch	Changes communicator ringtone to a burp sound.	N/A	Available from game start.	1
Ring Tone: Donkey	Changes communicator ringtone to a donkey sound.	N/A	Available from game start.	2
Ring Tone: Honk	Changes communicator ringtone to a honk sound.	N/A	Available from game start.	3
Attract Bricks	Pulls loose bricks toward Chase for easier collection.	Special Assignment 14: "Breaking and Reentering"	Activate the space crate near the mansion's roof, then smash the red mailbox.	4
Attract Studs	Pulls loose studs toward Chase for easier collection.	Special Assignment 10: "Smash 'n' Grab"	Flip across the flagpoles above the vines, slide down a tightrope, fix a fuse box, and chop through a boarded door.	5
Collect Sat Nav Studs	Lets you collect the green navigational studs while driving.	Heritage Bridge	From the top of the east tower, slide down the tightrope.	6
Data Scan Upgrade: Character Challenges	Lets you use Data Scan mode to detect special challenges in LEGO City.	Auburn	Smash a small, green trash bin across the street from the disguise booth, then follow the footprints to the hidden red brick.	7
Data Scan Upgrade: City Challenges	Lets you use Data Scan mode to detect special challenges in LEGO City.	Cherry Tree Hills	Scale the police station's exterior stairs and pry open the exterior jail cell.	8
Data Scan Upgrade: Clues	Lets you use Data Scan mode to detect special clues in LEGO City.	Bluebell National Park	Use dynamite to destroy the silver crate near the Bluebell Mine.	9
Data Scan Upgrade: Red Bricks	Lets you use Data Scan mode to detect red bricks in LEGO City.	Auburn Bay Bridge	Suspended over a tightrope along the bridge tower.	10
Data Scan Upgrade: Tokens	Lets you use data scan mode to detect loose character and vehicle tokens in LEGO City.	Fort Meadows	Hidden in a pile of boulders inside the spiderweb cave.	11
Extra Hearts	Gives Chase two extra health hearts.	Special Assignment 11: "They All Scream for Ice Cream"	Astronaut jetpack jump up to the balcony above the entry door, activate the space crate, build the color swapper, and blast three switch objects around the parlor.	12
Fall Rescue	Chase will always be rescued from fatal falls and placed back on safe ground.	Fresco	Inside the greenhouse.	13
Fancy Dress	LEGO City population will all wear costumes.	Special Assignment 9: "Hot Property"	Chop through the boarded door on the fire station's right side.	14
Fast Build	Chase can build LEGO objects much faster.	Special Assignment 1: "Some Assaults"	Astronaut boost up to a higher roof, build three solar panels to power a fan, float up to the brick.	15
Instant Vehicles	Let's you call in a vehicle anywhere in the City	Bright Lights Plaza	In the hallway of Ellie's apartment.	16
Invincibility	Makes Chase immune to all combat damage.	Kings Court	Behind a door only Rex Fury can pry open, on the roof of Jenny's Diner.	17

RED BRICKS CONTINUED

NAME	EFFECT	LOCATION	HOW TO GET	GOT IT?
Larger Vehicle Boost	Vehicles with turbos can boost for longer periods of time.	Festival Square	Hidden on the far end of the mega building's roof, out of sight.	18
Mario Hat	Lets Chase wear the iconic Super Mario hat.	Lady Liberty Island	Along the tightrope used to reach the dock roof.	19
Nitrous for All	All vehicles have turbo boost.	Blackwell Bridge	On one of the other support legs under the bridge.	20
Police Siren Hat	Lets Chase wear a hat with a police siren.	Albatross Island	Break into the door at the bottom of the prison tower.	21
Ring Tone: Gas	Changes communicator ringtone to a burp sound.	Paradise Sands	At the top of the Herbert Hotel.	22
Ring Tone: Pig	Changes communicator ringtone to an oink sound.	Grand Canal	Behind a locked door on the canal walkway.	23
Studs x2	Multiplies the value of every stud Chase collects by two.	Special Assignment 2: "Trouble in Stir"	After climbing up to the second floor, pry open a cell and then smash through its left wall.	30
Studs x4	Multiplies the value of every stud by four.	Special Assignment 5: "Dirty Work"	Pry open the door near the red color swapper.	24
Studs x6	Multiplies the value of every stud Chase collects by six.	Special Assignment 12: "High Steal"	Chop through the boarded door of the small shack in the left foreground corner beyond the first gate.	25
Studs x8	Multiplies the value of every stud Chase collects by eight.	Special Assignment 13: "Disruptive Behavior"	Use Rex Fury to rip apart the super-strength crate near the security lasers, then activate the space crate and pull the lever.	26
Studs x10	Multiplies the value of every stud Chase collects by ten.	Special Assignment 15: "Fly Me to the Moon"	After ripping apart the final strength crate, blast the switch you uncover and enter the nearby dome.	27
Super Astro Crate	Chase no longer needs to input the color sequence to open space crates.	Special Assignment 6: "Astronaughty"	Fix the hangar's background fuse box, ride the lift and get some dynamite, drop and blast the silver floor hatch, beam to another room, chop through the door, and crack the safe.	28
Super Axe Smash	Chase chops down boarded doors with the fire axe much faster.	Pagoda	Sitting on the roof of the red building.	29
Super Break and Enter	Chase pries open doors and skylights with the crowbar much faster.	Special Assignment 8: "The Colossal Fossil Hustle"	Use Rex Fury to rip apart the super-strength crate in the unfinished exhibit upstairs, then bring the object down to the triceratops exhibit. Pull the two strength handles near the stairs and bring the other two objects to the triceratops to complete it.	31
Super Color Gun	Chase no longer needs to use color swappers—his color gun fires all colors.	Uptown	Hidden behind a wall on top of the toy store.	32
Super Drill Ride	Chase can move twice as fast while riding the pneumatic drill.	Crosstown Tunnel	Behind a door only Rex Fury can open, along the maintenance walkway.	33
Super Fast Travel	Chase can fast travel at any time—not just when visiting train stations, etc.	LEGO City Airport	Inside the southern hangars, behind a door with an orange handle only Rex Fury can open.	34
Super Ram	Colliding with other cars sends them flying.	Crescent Park	In a small cave along the ocean.	35
Super Ray Gun	The ray gun carried by astronauts now destroys objects with a single blast.	Apollo Island	Activate the four switches around the lil' island bunker.	36
Super Safe Crack	Chase can crack open safes without having to play the minigame.	Special Assignment 7: "Scrapyard Scrap"	Use Rex Fury to rip apart the super-strength crate, then launch off the catapult pad.	37
Super Throw	Chase will quick-throw enemies farther than normal.	Special Assignment 4: "Kung Fool"	Spin the dojo balcony crates so that their symbols match up with the disguise portraits on the lower foreground balcony.	38
Unlimited Dynamite	Chase always carries some dynamite with him.	Special Assignment 3: "Miner Altercation"	Chicken-glide from the final platform, then climb up to the brick.	39
Wonder Whistle	Chase's police whistle will make random sound effects.	Downtown	Behind a locked door on the Y building.	40

 ## ? BLOCKS

There are only five ? Blocks hidden in all of LEGO City. Find all five, and you'll unlock a secret character token—the Super Wrestler!

? BLOCKS

LOCATION	HOW TO GET	GOT IT?
Apollo Island	Behind the garages along the runway.	1
Auburn Bay Bridge	On the support beams, under the bridge.	2
Bluebell National Park	Beam up to the top of the dam, chop through the boarded door, and climb the ladder.	3
LEGO City Airport	Underneath the freeway.	4
Pagoda	On a walkway along the ocean.	5

 ## SUPER STARS

Like ? Blocks, there are just five Super Stars for you to find in all of LEGO City. Find all five Super Stars to earn another secret character token—the Pop Star!

SUPER STARS

LOCATION	HOW TO GET	GOT IT?
Bright Lights Plaza	At the very top of the luxury apartments.	1
Cherry Tree Hills	Run around the northeast rooftops until you reach the gold box at the end.	2
Fresco	At the very top of the Leaning Tower.	3
Paradise Sands	Atop the roller coaster.	4
Uptown	On top of the library.	5

INTRODUCTION

POLICE ACADEMY

CHARACTERS AND VEHICLES

WALKTHROUGH

LEGO CITY TOUR

CHECKLISTS

PRIMA OFFICIAL GAME GUIDE
WRITTEN BY:
STEVE STRATTON AND HILARY GOLDSTEIN

Prima Games
An Imprint of Random House, Inc.
3000 Lava Ridge Court, Suite 100
Roseville, CA 95661
www.primagames.com

The Prima Games logo is a registered trademark of Random House, Inc., registered in the United States and other countries. Primagames.com is a registered trademark of Random House, Inc., registered in the United States. Prima Games is an imprint of Random House, Inc.

Prima Games would like to thank
Tim Wileman, Loz Doyle, Paul Jones, Jonathan Smith, Sten Funder Lysdahi, Todd Buechele, Emiko Ohmori, Michael Northeast, Daniel Nuttall, Tim Welch, Darryl Kelley, Jack Tutton, Matthew Johns, Louise Andrew, Robert Lovegrove, Ramon Alfaro Marcilla, Lee Barber, Mike Taylor, Chris Wyatt, Masa Miyazaki, Simon Cole and everyone at TT Fusion for their help and support.

Product Manager: Jesse Anderson
Design & Layout: In Color Design
Copyedit: Carrie Andrews

ISBN: 978-0-307-89676-6
PRINTED IN THE UNITED STATES OF AMERICA
12 13 14 15 LL 10 9 8 7 6 5 4 3 2 1